Caligari's Children

Caligari's Children

The Film as Tale of Terror

S. S. PRAWER

A DA CAPO PAPERBACK

Library of Congress Cataloging in Publication Data

Prawer, Siegbert Solomon, 1925–
  Caligari's children: the film as tale of ter-
ror / S. S. Prawer.
      p.   cm.—(A Da Capo paperback)
  Reprint. Originally published: Oxford; New
York: Oxford University Press, 1980.
  Bibliography: p.
  Includes index.
  ISBN 0-306-80347-X
  1. Horror films—History and criticism. I.
Title.
[PN1995.9.H6P68   1988]
791.43'09'0916—dc19   88-32413
                                        CIP

This Da Capo Press paperback edition of
Caligari's Children is an unabridged republica-
tion of the edition published in Oxford,
England in 1980, here supplemented with
author corrections. It is reprinted by
arrangement with S. S. Prawer.

Published by Da Capo Press, Inc.
A Subsidiary of Plenum Publishing Corporation
233 Spring Street, New York, N.Y. 10013

Manufactured in the United States of America

Contents

Plates

One need not be a Chamber – to be Haunted –
One need not be a House –
The Brain has Corridors – surpassing
Material Place –

Far safer, of a Midnight Meeting
External Ghost
Than its interior Confronting –
That Cooler Host.

Far safer, through an Abbey gallop,
The Stones a'chase –
Than Unarmed, one's a'self encounter –
In lonesome Place –

Ourself behind ourself, concealed –
Should startle most –
Assassin hid in our Apartment
Be Horror's least.

The Body – borrows a Revolver –
He bolts the Door –
O'erlooking a superior spectre –
Or more –

EMILY DICKINSON

Introduction

Superstitious, perhaps; baloney—perhaps not!
The Black Cat (1934)

IN October 1826, on a visit to London, the much-travelled Prince Hermann von Pückler-Muskau visited what he called 'the English Opera'. 'The house', he reported in his anonymously published *Letters by a Dead Man* (1830),

is neither elegant nor large, but the actors are not at all bad. There was no opera, however; instead, we had terrible melodramas. First *Frankenstein*, where a human being is made by magic, without female help—a manufacture that answers very ill; and then *The Vampire*, after the well-known tale falsely attributed to Lord Byron. The principal part in both was acted by Mr Cooke, who is distinguished by a handsome person, very skilful acting, and a remarkably distinguished and noble deportment. The playing was, indeed, admirable throughout, but the pieces were so stupid and non-sensical that it was impossible to sit out the performance. The heat, the exhalations, and the audience were not the most agreeable. Besides all this, the performance lasted from seven to half past twelve—too long for the best.

The double bill which Pückler-Muskau saw at the English Opera House on that October evening was to become, over a hundred years later, the most celebrated double bill in the history of the cinema: the reissue of James Whale's *Frankenstein* along with Tod Browning's *Dracula* (both originally shown separately in 1931). And as in the English theatre of the first half of the nineteenth so in the English-speaking cinema of the first half of the twentieth century: this double bill of man-made-monster- and vampire-tales marked the emergence of personable actors specializing in grotesque and macabre creations—though the task which Thomas Potter Cooke had shouldered by himself in the 1820s was divided between two players, Bela Lugosi and Boris Karloff, in the 1930s. That is not, however, what the promoters had originally envisaged: the role of Frankenstein's monster had been offered to Bela Lugosi after his triumph as Dracula; and when Lugosi refused it, the continuity between the two offerings which was brought to the theatrical double bill by T. P. Cooke was assured by giving key parts in both the films to Dwight Frye and Edward Van Sloan. The fact that both these actors had appeared with Lugosi in a celebrated Broadway production of *Dracula* may serve to remind us that there is a strong link between tales of terror on the stage and on the screen; that the American terror-film of the early thirties was preceded, and plainly influenced, by a spate of Broadway plays in which fantasy and terror were principal ingredients.

Both the melodramas which Pückler-Muskau saw were, of course, adaptations of prose-fictions published some years before: Mary Shelley's *Frankenstein: or, The Modern Prometheus* (1818) and Dr. John Polidori's *The Vampyre* (1819). The creation of these prose-fictions goes back to an evening in the Villa Deodati near Lake Geneva, where Byron, Shelley, Mary Shelley, and Polidori had stimulated their imagination by reading a volume of ghost-stories translated from the German, and had then competed with one another in inventing spooky tales of their own which embodied— in ways whose analysis is not our present concern—their own emotional and intellectual problems. Mary Shelley, indeed, when visiting London in 1823, had seen T. P. Cooke perform in the theatrical adaptation of her novel in the same English Opera House in which Pückler-Muskau saw those two 'hideous melodramas' three years later. Her account of this experience presents further remarkable parallels with the experience she could have had, with the aid of Wells's time-machine, some one hundred and ten years later in the cinema. The list of dramatis personae included the entry '————, by Mr. T. Cooke'; the opening credits of Whale's film were to play a variation on that with the billing: 'The Monster . . .?' Frankenstein had acquired a servant, who rushes from the room when his master exclaims 'it lives'; a first sketch, it would seem, for the part assumed in the film by Dwight Frye. The laboratory in which the monster is created was reached by a staircase leading off from the stage—and the great staircase leading to Frankenstein's tower laboratory was to be one of the most impressive features of the film's studio-built sets. Last but not least, Mary Shelley's description of Cooke's performance suggests some likeness to that of Boris Karloff: 'his seeking, as it were, for support; his trying to grasp at the sounds he heard; all, indeed, he does was well imagined and executed'. Cooke, however, does not seem to have hidden his 'handsome person' and 'distinguished and noble deportment' under as striking a make-up as his cinematic successor. Mary Shelley professed herself 'much amused' by it all, and reports (as she might have reported of the film too) that 'it appeared to excite a breathless eagerness in the audience'.

These reports by Pückler-Muskau and Mary Shelley of their experiences in London theatres of the early nineteenth century are instructive on many counts. They show, first of all, that the urge to see 'the film of the book', whose satisfaction then reacts back on to the sales of 'the book of the film', is not a specifically twentieth-century phenomenon. Not content with reading *Frankenstein* in print, the nineteenth-century audience demanded, and received, several dramatic reworkings of its thrilling story. Indeed, among the most important sources of the *Dracula* and *Frankenstein* films of the early 1930s were theatrical adaptations by Hamilton Deane and Peggy Webling.

Novel, theatrical performance, and film are three very different media; and so much energy has been expended, in recent years, on working out the distinctions between them that our generation is less likely than any previous one to underestimate the part which the special possibilities and limitations of each medium plays in the shaping and reception of works of art. At the same time, however, it would be absurd to deny the continuities and links between the media. To say, for instance, as Julia Briggs does in *Night Visitors*, that the English ghost-story has been dead since 1914, without taking into account its remarkable transmigration into the cinema —think of *Thunder Rock*, *A Place of One's Own*, *The Halfway House*, *Dead of Night*, *The Queen of Spades*, *The Uninvited*, *The Haunting*, and *The Plague of the Zombies*!—is to court a charge of premature burial. The term 'ghost-story', Julia Briggs pertinently reminds us, denotes in common usage 'not only stories about ghosts, but about possession and demonic bargains, spirits other than those of the dead, including ghouls, vampires, werewolves, the "swarths" of living men and the "ghost-soul" or "Doppelgänger" '. One only has to look at this list to realize how many variations the film has played on each of its items, especially since the pioneering efforts of Paul Wegener, Stellan Rye, and Henrik Galeen in *The Student of Prague* (1913) and *The Golem* (1914). If these are indeed the subjects of the ghost-story, then that genre is alive and well and living in the cinema.

In speaking of the film as a 'tale' of terror, I want to draw attention to its links with Hoffmann, Poe, and other purveyors of literary 'tales' of this nature. The pages that follow should also show, however, that we must be ever mindful of the *dramatic* impact of films seen in the cinema; of the audience's sense, to use a formulation by Frank M. Fowler, that something 'is *happening now*, something that cannot be stopped or accelerated [by the individual viewer], something with an assertive rhythm and dynamic of its own, something that normally demands to be experienced whole, well-nigh uninterrupted, commanding undivided attention from a body of people temporarily freed from . . . distraction'.

Pückler-Muskau's and Mary Shelley's reports have served to alert us to the interaction between various media. That by no means exhausts their usefulness, however; they may also serve to illustrate three kinds of reaction which the terror-*film* was no less likely to elicit than the terror-*play*. One of these is the 'breathless eagerness' Mary Shelley noticed in the audience—the unsophisticated response of seekers after theatrical thrills on which the adaptors and exhibitors speculated, and from which they reaped handsome dividends. Mary Shelley's own response, in contrast to this, is one of amused detachment—the detachment of the intellectual observer, piquantly complicated by the fact that Mary Shelley could rightly see herself as the ultimate begetter of these thrills, and could therefore feel gratified by the power her imaginings had over the assembled multitudes. Pückler-Muskau's attitude is different again. He is clearly a connoisseur, whose varied experience enabled him to appreciate to the full the skill shown by the British actors he had paid to see, but who dismissed the plays they performed as unworthy of such a sophisticated theatre-goer as he deemed himself. The audience and its 'exhalations' were as disagreeable to him as the entertainment which had brought him into their presence; such 'stupid and nonsensical' stuff, he felt, attracted the wrong people into the theatre and pandered to a taste that lacked the refinement necessary to appreciate what is good and great.

All three of these attitudes could be observed again when the tale of terror invaded the cinema: the audience's 'breathless eagerness'; the detached amusement of intellectuals (many of whom had a hand in providing thrills for the multitude and could occasionally be seen winking over the heads of the 'hicks' they thus served); and the indignant rejection of the aristocratic connoisseur, whose appreciation of the skill involved in such entertainments only increased his scorn of their intellectual and moral content. There are, however, many other ways of responding to tales of terror on the big screen. The Surrealists' admiration of popular 'horror-movies' comes immediately to mind, with its loudly proclaimed approbation of their involuntary poetry, their unexpected visual juxtapositions, their disorientating power (*pouvoir de dépaysement*), their dream-quality, their celebration of *amour fou* and everything that is *délirant* and *convulsif*. This Surrealist response enters as an element into another attitude commonly adopted by admirers of the cinematic tale of terror: that of exalting such works as the genuine art of our time, as models of meaningful film-making much to be preferred to the more sophisticated works of a Kubrick, a Polanski, or a Fellini. Such critics, more common in France than elsewhere, will cheerfully dismiss much of the work of Ingmar Bergman while exalting Terence Fisher as a great *auteur*. Attitudes of this kind contrast with another, frequently taken up by horror-movie enthusiasts in Britain and the United States, who are aware of what is naïve and crude and banal in the films they like to see, but who find a perverse sort of delight in that very crudity and banality—a kind of appreciation to which our time has given the name 'camp'. In France too a phrase like 'un splendide film kitsch' will be taken as a commendation by experienced film-buffs. A truly unsophisticated, direct response to such movies, corresponding to the eager breathlessness of the nineteenth-century audience at a *Frankenstein* play, still occurs, but is becoming increasingly rare in these days of ubiquitous television—except, of course, with children. Many members of cinema audiences today will look to the horror-movie for violent shock-images, for titillations of sexual and aggressive instincts which have to take more indirect forms in the entertainments television companies beam into our homes.

The attitudes I have described are 'ideal types' in Max Weber's sense; actual responses will often be mixed, and may in any case vary from film to film. In some forty years of cinema-going I have to a certain extent experienced them all, and I now feel the need to look more closely at some of the works which prompted them, and at their relation to the literature that is my usual field of study. I have tried to do this, in the present book, by means of eight chapters which approach their subject—the presentation and evocation of terror in the cinema—in a manner analogous to that of the cinema itself. The first chapter takes a 'long-shot' or 'establishment-shot' view of the history of the terror-film and tries, with the help of an occasional zooming-in, to define it as a genre. The second chapter seeks to show up, in medium-shot, some of the themes, motifs, and devices that inspire in an audience the terror it delights in, while the third moves in on one representative film, Mamoulian's *Dr. Jekyll and Mr. Hyde*, to demonstrate in close-up what happens when a work of literature is transformed into a terror-film. Chapter 4 recedes again, to discuss the phenomenon of the 'uncanny' in literature as well as the film, while Chapter 5 brings another close-up: a masterpiece of the 'uncanny' in the cinema, Dreyer's *Vampyr*, which demonstrates a quite different kind of adaptation from a literary original than that examined in Chapter 3. Here the screen-play will be considered along with the film as actually shot. The sixth chapter supplements these close-ups or 'two-shots' of films derived from specific works of literature with an equally close look at a seminal film from an original script: *The Cabinet of Dr. Caligari*, which is shown to contain a wealth of examples illustrating the iconography and the rhetoric of terror. Chapter 7 pans out from this to examine how post-*Caligari* directors have used the channels of information contained on a given strip of film; and Chapter 8, alternating between closest close-up and dolly-shot, looks at a single image from a single representative motion picture and tries to describe some of the contexts in which it demands to be seen. There are also experiments in verbal montage (as when my own early recollections of films and stars of the thirties are juxtaposed with passages of more distanced analysis); 'long-shot' and 'medium-shot' chapters include glimpses of themes and examples more fully treated in later close-ups; and such questions as the significance of colour or black-and-white photography in the work of various directors inevitably crop up in more than one sequence. I hope, however, to have avoided mere repetition in this endeavour to present the appeal of terror in the cinema from varying angles and under different kinds of illumination.

A word, now, about vocabulary. The common distinction between 'film' as a work of art and 'movie' as a popular entertainment has been deliberately jettisoned, because in my experience popular entertainments often *are* works of art. In the same way I have not differentiated strictly between 'terror' and 'horror'; to mark the continuity between literary 'tales of terror' and what is popularly known as the 'horror-movie', I often replace the latter term with 'cinematic tale of terror' or 'terror-film'. This has not, however, deterred me from using the popular and familiar term in appropriate contexts, or from invoking, on some occasions, those meanings of the word 'horror' which hover around the denotation 'an emotion compounded of fear and loathing'. For the object of the other denotational pole of the word 'horror'—'a feeling of awe and imaginative fear'—I have adopted the term 'the uncanny' to which this book devotes a central chapter.

For its material *Caligari's Children* draws on its author's memories of cinema-going in many countries, refreshed and clarified by a recent reading of the books named in the Select Bibliography as well as of articles in specialist journals that range from *Midi-minuit fantastique* and *Famous Monsters of Filmland* to *Screen* and *Literature/Film Quarterly*. I hope that the authors of these works will accept a general expression of indebtedness and gratitude in lieu of specific acknowledgements that would have burdened this personal account with an excessive apparatus of footnotes. It is, however, a special pleasure to thank the librarians and staff of the Deutsche Kinemathek, Berlin, for letting me use the resources of that admirable institution and read the unpublished screen-play of *The Cabinet of Dr. Caligari*; the German Academic Exchange Service (DAAD) for a travel grant that took me to Berlin; my colleague Stephen Wall for reading an early draft of this book and suggesting improvements; Professor M. K. Joseph and the Auckland University Press for permission to quote the lines of verse on p. 204; and the Principal of Westfield College in the University of London for permission to reprint material first used, many years ago, in my inaugural lecture as Professor of German. Thanks are due also to the Stills Library National Film Archive, for help in obtaining photographs.

CHAPTER 1

The Making of a Genre

Quite a good scene, isn't it? One man crazy—and
three very sane spectators!

Frankenstein (1931)

THE Gothic terror-fictions which were so distinctive a legacy of the
eighteenth century to the nineteenth lent themselves, not only to
theatrical stage adaptation, but also to various kinds of light-and-
shadow play: E. G. Robertson's 'phantasmagorias' of the 1790s
relied a great deal on nocturnal churchyard and castle scenes, on
skeletons and ghostly apparitions that seemed to move when the
lenses and reflectors behind *lanterna magica* slides were pushed forward or backward and screens agitated. A hundred years later
similar apparitions could be seen in the pioneering fantasy-films
of the conjurer Georges Méliès: devils (usually played by Méliès
himself) were ubiquitous, bodies turned into skeletons, selenites
frightened travellers to the moon, in Bluebeard's Chamber a row
of well-dressed ladies appeared to be hanging from hooks, a living
head seemed to be blown up with a pump and finally to explode, a
seven-headed hydra writhed on the ground, and devils cavorted
with torches as Mephistopheles made off with Dr. Faustus . . . The
double exposures, jump-cuts, and other technical tricks which
Méliès played with the shots he had taken from a fixed position
corresponding to a fixed seat in the stalls of a theatre—these amused
rather than frightened their audiences, and, in the end, wearied
them sufficiently to ensure Méliès's bankruptcy. What audiences
failed to derive from Méliès's delightful fantasies were sensations of
safely terrifying shock: the kind of shock that the Lumière brothers
provided when they photographed a train pulling into a station
head-on, so that it seemed about to hurtle out of the screen on to
the spectators in the cinema; or the kind of shock provided in 1895
by Alfred Clark's *The Execution of Mary, Queen of Scots*, where interrupted camera-cranking and the substitution of a dummy gave
startled spectators the illusion that they were seeing a human head

being chopped off on the executioner's block; or that purveyed by Edwin S. Porter, when he introduced into *The Great Train Robbery* (1903) a close-up in which a bandit pointed his gun directly at the audience. Méliès's fantasy, Clark's intimate view of extreme situations, and the Lumières' as well as Porter's apparent assaults on the audience were all to become important ingredients in the cinematic tale of terror.

This genre began to define itself in the first decade of the twentieth century when the Selig Polyscope Company brought out a brief adaptation of *Dr. Jekyll and Mr. Hyde* (1908); the Danish Nordisk Company followed suit with an adaptation of the same tale (1909) and with two 'premature burial' films entitled *The Necklace of the Dead* (1910) and *Ghosts of the Vault* (1911). The Edison Company was first in the field with an adaptation of *Frankenstein* (1910), which was followed by three further adaptations of *Jekyll and Hyde*—including one produced by 'Uncle' Carl Laemmle, whose Universal Studios were to corner the market for stories of this kind in a way equalled only by Hammer Films during their period of gory glory. These early productions, together with Griffith's *The Avenging Conscience*, a cento from the works of Poe first shown in 1915, and Maurice Tourneur's *Trilby* (also 1915), which introduced the figure of the demonic hypnotist long before Krauss, Klein-Rogge, and Wegener made it their own, are the beginnings of a wave whose crest is reached in the silent German cinema, from *The Cabinet of Dr. Caligari* and Richard Oswald's terror-compendium *Uncanny Tales* (both 1919) to Galeen's *Alraune* (1928); in the grotesque creations of Lon Chaney in the U.S.A., from *The Miracle Man* (1919) to *The Unholy Three* (1930); in the films of other nations from Victor Sjöström's *The Phantom Carriage* (1920) and Carl Dreyer's *Leaves from Satan's Book* (1921) to Teinosuke Kinugasa's *A Page of Madness* of 1926 and Jean Epstein's *The Fall of the House of Usher* of 1928. On the last-named film Epstein's assistant was Luis Buñuel, whose collaboration with Dali on *An Andalusian Dog* in the same year laced surrealism with violent elements that recalled the tale of terror. The setting for all this was, of course, the First World War, its anticipatory rumbles, and the social and political upheavals that followed in its wake.

A second wave of terror-films emanated from the U.S.A. almost immediately after the coming of sound—*Dracula* (1931), *Frankenstein* (1931), and *White Zombie* (1932) were all made in Carl

Laemmle's Universal Studios, where German influences proved particularly powerful. Key figures in the dissemination of that influence were the director Paul Leni and the director/cameraman Karl Freund. The peak of this wave was reached with the masterly *King Kong* of 1933; it rolled on, with apparent vigour but slowly diminishing force, until it receded in mechanical compilations and parody towards the beginning of the Second World War. The background here is clearly the Depression in the U.S.A. and its worldwide repercussions.

The next wave comes on, against the dark sky of the Second World War and what led up to it, with a curiously muted roar. The dominant figure is the producer Val Lewton, whose modestly budgeted films, from *Cat People* (1942) to *Bedlam* (1946), tried to civilize the horror-movie into subtler evocations of terror—evocations that made the audience supply a good deal of what the screen only suggests. Arthur Lubin's remake of *The Phantom of the Opera* (1943) also toned down considerably the shocks of the original (how feeble Claude Rains's make-up looks when compared with Chaney's in the same role!); and the talkative British movies about ghostly apparitions that belong to an afterlife but set this world to rights, *Thunder Rock* (1942), for instance, or *The Halfway House* (1944), were likely to scare only the most susceptible. This cycle ended, however, with one of the universally acknowledged classics of the cinematic tale of terror: *Dead of Night*, directed by Alberto Cavalcanti, Robert Hamer, and others in 1945. In assessing the impact of Lewis Allen's *The Uninvited* (1944) and *Dead of Night*, one has to remember that before these tales of supernatural happenings ghosts appearing on the screen tended to be garrulous moralizers, as in *The Halfway House*, or were played for comedy, as in Clair's *The Ghost Goes West* (1935), or were rationally explained away, as in *The Ghost Breakers* (1940). In the history of the sound-film it was *The Uninvited* and *Dead of Night* which signalled the confluence of the ghost-story properly so called with the tale of terror.

The time had now come for a fourth wave, stirred up by the reverberations of the rockets that had terrorized England during the last days of the Second World War, and the beginning of space exploration. From the outset, from the earliest *Frankenstein* and *Jekyll and Hyde* films, the cinematic tale of terror had shaded over into science fiction; their coincidence now increased as George Pal's *Destination Moon* (1950) latched on to Fritz Lang's pioneering

Woman in the Moon (1924) and pointed forward to Christian Nyby's (and Howard Hawks's!) *The Thing from Another World* (1951) as well as to the peak of this whole sub-genre in the 1950s: Don Siegel's *The Invasion of the Body Snatchers* (1956). Siegel's title, suggested by that of Jack Finney's novel and imposed on him by the front office, bespeaks another interesting continuity—for it recalls, deliberately, the restrained exercise in terror which Val Lewton and Philip MacDonald had adapted from Robert Louis Stevenson, and which Robert Wise had directed, under the title *The Body Snatcher*, in 1945. Television now not only rivalled but fed the cinema: a process dramatically demonstrated by the small British firm Hammer Films, whose first post-war success with the public came with their 1955 production of *The Quatermass Experiment*, based on a science-fiction thriller in serial form which had kept the BBC's audience in breathless suspense for several weeks.

A great deal has been written about the science-fiction films that populated the screens in the fifties and sixties, and from this general discussion five main thematic categories have emerged:

(i) *Invasion from outer space*: Works embodying the neurosis of the Cold War, like *The Thing from Another World*, belong to this category, as do *The Invasion of the Body Snatchers* and countless films in which earthmen face the task of destroying some Bug-Eyed Monster or other undesirable alien. Soon, however, significant variants began to appear, showing different relations between earthmen and visitors from beyond. In Robert Wise's *The Day the Earth Stood Still*, made as early as 1951, the 'invader' comes, not to destroy, but to warn men against their self-destructive course. From this two developments were possible: towards a film like Nicolas Roeg's *The Man Who Fell to Earth* (1976), where the visitor from beyond is enfeebled and corrupted by the commercial civilization into which he comes; and towards one like Steven Spielberg's *Close Encounters of the Third Kind* (1977), where plainly benevolent visitors are received with an almost religious veneration and awe.

(ii) *Monsters from our own earth and seas*: An atomic test or accident rouses The Beast from 20 000 Fathoms (Eugene Lourie, 1953), Godzilla (Inoshiro Honda, 1956), or some other prehistoric giant from his slumbers, or brings about mutations (the giant ants, for instance, in Gordon Douglas's *Them*, 1954) which then go on the rampage. The hero of *Them*, the ultimate conqueror of the mutants, is an F.B.I. man haunted by fears of atomic explosion and subversion by an enemy within–a fact whose connection with American anxieties of the 1950s has not escaped film historians and commentators. Beings belonging to an earlier stage of evolution can also be discovered, and dangerously aroused, by expeditions into unknown territories, as films deriving ultimately from Conan Doyle's *The Lost World* showed frequently and impressively. King Kong had belonged to that tribe in the 1930s; in the fifties his worthiest successor was Jack Arnold's Creature from the Black Lagoon (1954). But monsters need not be discovered; they can also be *made*, like the radioactive children created by an unholy alliance of scientists and politicians in Joseph Losey's *The Damned* (1961). And if Lourie's Beast from 20 000 Fathoms still had to fall victim to the 'search it out and destroy it' philosophy of so many 'monster' films, his successors in *Gorgo*, made by the same director in 1960, were allowed to return to their own element in peace. In the seven years between these two films ecology and similar concerns had done much to throw doubt on the morality and wisdom of destroying alien modes of life that seem to threaten us.

(iii) *Atomic catastrophe and after:* Characteristic works in this category are Stanley Kramer's film of Nevil Shute's *On the Beach* (1959), which depicts a dying world after a disastrous atomic war; Franklin Shaffner's *Planet of the Apes* (1968), in which we see a group of men preserved by chance fighting for survival in a society of monkeys that have taken over the earth; and Boris Sagal's *The Omega Man* (1971), which portrays another battle for survival after a cataclysm, this time against post-atomic mutants.

(iv) *The journey to the stars:* This extension of the imaginary voyages of Jules Verne has many variants, from George Pal's *Destination Moon* to Stanley Kubrick's *2001: A Space Odyssey* (1968). Such works may include intergalactic battles, whose apogee comes in the naïve but technologically wondrous *Star Wars* (George Lucas, 1977), with its simple-minded hero fighting for good against evil much as Flash Gordon used to do in the old serials. *Star Wars* and its imitations have been seen, by several social commentators, as a reflection of the early Carter era, with its post-Watergate longings for clarity, simplicity, moral perspicuity, and a revival of the old frontier virtues.

(v) *The tyrannous future*: A multitude of films show us governments that forbid books (Truffaut's *Fahrenheit 451*, 1966) or forbid natural expressions of the human affections (Lucas's *THX 1138*, 1970) or heighten in various ways what are seen as undesirable features of our technological civilization (Godard's *Alphaville*, 1965). If the ultimate inspiration behind star-journeys, or journeys into the human interior like Richard Fleischer's *Fantastic Voyage* (1966), is Jules Verne, the inspiration behind 'tyrannous future' films are the dystopias of Aldous Huxley and George Orwell. Most frightening of all is the (near) future depicted in Joseph Sargent's *The Forbin Project* (1969), in which super-computers reveal 'ambitions' that outrun and outwit those of their makers and would-be controllers, and come to rule the world without human interference.

The anxieties which are mirrored in science-fiction films from the U.S.A. are connected, in more obvious ways than those of the horror-movies, with socio-political anxieties: fears of invasion during the Korean War and the Cuban missile crisis, fears of being 'taken over' mentally and spiritually during the McCarthy era, a compound of fear and uneasy conscience during the Vietnam War, dread of brainwashing, genetic engineering, computerized policing, and bacteriological warfare, as well as growing ecological fears connected with atomic power, aggressive defoliation techniques, various kinds of man-made pollution, the growth of populations, and the penetration of outer space by more and more man-made objects. Fairy-tales like *Star Wars* would appear on this grid as an escapist reaction against the serious or bitterly satirical symbolization of this kind of anxiety. Even *Star Wars* has plain and obvious links with the horror-movie—one remembers the galactic bar with its assorted monsters, supplied by a London firm called Uglies Limited; but entertaining films of this nature have little in common with such serious projections of the plight of man trying to cope with his own technology as Stanislav Lem's *Solaris*, memorably filmed by Andrei Tarkovsky in 1971.

It was, in fact, their venture into science fiction laced with horror which encouraged Hammer Films to believe that their public was ready for a new treatment of the old Universal favourites; a treatment which would take account of the possibilities opened up by larger screens, better colour processes, and greater permissiveness in the depiction of violence and sexual activities. *The Curse of Frankenstein*, made in 1957, proved them right: and so they started a fifth wave of terror-movies which bore with it not only Hammer's own vampire-, zombie-, and mad-scientist-films, but also films on similar themes from Italy, France, Germany, Japan, and—above all —Latin America, where there had always been a keen interest in such things; an interest sufficiently translatable into commercial terms to induce Universal to accompany their *Dracula* of 1931 with a Spanish-speaking version of the same film, shot on the same sets but employing different actors. Japan, indeed, which had evolved a marvellous cinematic tradition of cinematic ghost-stories, culminating in two crucial episodes of Mizoguchi's *Ugetsu Monogatari* (1953) and in Kobayashi's *Kwaidan* (1964), produced, with Shindo's *Onibaba* (1964), the most horrifying unmasking scene since *Mystery of the Wax Museum* (1933), and all but cornered the market in powerful monsters with Gojira (usually known as 'Godzilla' in the West) and his manifold progeny from 1955 onwards. Unlike the prototype, however, from which they derived— Lourie's *The Beast from 20 000 Fathoms*—the monsters in Japanese movies could occasionally be helpful; they could become man's allies in his fight against technological destruction and dessication. The Swedish cinema, in the meantime, through the films of Ingmar Bergman, showed the world what psychologically meaningful use could be made of the iconography the terror-film had evolved since the days of the silent German classics. There is, beyond doubt, a straight line running from Wiene's *Caligari* over Lang's *Destiny* (or *Tired Death*, 1921) and Pabst's *Secrets of a Soul* (1926) to the terror, dream, and fantasy sequences of *Sawdust and Tinsel* (1953), *The Seventh Seal* (1957), *Wild Strawberries* (1957), *The Face* (or *The Magician*, 1958), and *Hour of the Wolf* (1967). *The Hour of the Wolf* pays a self-conscious tribute to that German inspiration by means of characters who bear names like Kreisler and Lindhorst; names familiar from the tales of E. T. A. Hoffmann which had proved such a powerful influence on the early German film-makers. Even Bergman's masterpiece *Persona* (1966) can be, and has been, seen as a series of variations on the vampire and *Doppelgänger* themes of the terror-film and the literary tales that preceded it.

While Hammer were reviving the Universal monsters in their

own way, American International Pictures began a cycle whose appreciation was almost entirely tongue-in-cheek—a perfect example of 'camp' manufacture and reception of the iconography of terror. The first film in this series bore the (now notorious) title *I Was A Teenage Werewolf* (1957); it purported to show how a college student acquired bestial form through an experiment that went wrong. The absurdity of plot and acting, and the relentless pop music that filled the sound-track, gave various kinds of pleasure to young audiences and encouraged the film-makers to follow this pilot movie with *I Was A Teenage Frankenstein*, and with *Teenage Monster* and *Teenage Zombie* creations that were as awful to listen to as they were to see. Part of the profits from this *Teenage* cycle went into the financing of a more memorable series of films based, rather loosely, on the works of Edgar Allan Poe. The first of these was *The Fall of the House of Usher* (1960), directed, like most of those that were to follow, by Roger Corman, written for the screen by Richard Matheson, photographed by Floyd Crosby, imaginatively designed by Daniel Haller, and starring Vincent Price. While many of these low-budget films were meant to be taken straight, a series of deliberate spoofs were interspersed with them: *The Raven*, for instance, directed by Corman in 1963 and bringing together Boris Karloff, Peter Lorre, and Vincent Price, and *The Comedy of Terrors*, directed in the same year by Jacques Tourneur.

As I write this, early in 1978, I feel myself borne along by yet another wave of terror-films, a wave whose crest is formed by what is frequently called 'meat' or 'road accident' movies—films like *The Texas Chain Saw Massacre* (1974), which provide shock through the maximum exhibition of flesh in the process of being mangled and blood in the process of being spilt (all simulated, of course, as one must hasten to add in view of some disturbing recent developments); by sensationalist marriages of terror-film and science-fiction idioms, as in Donald Cammell's *The Demon Seed* (1977), which has Julie Christie raped by a computer; and by films of demonic possession, destructive paranormal faculties, and eerie reincarnations represented by such works as Friedkin's *The Exorcist* (1973), de Palma's *Carrie* (1976), Boorman's *The Heretic* (1977), and Skolimowski's *The Shout* (1978). Particularly characteristic of our time are suggestions, in American films of the post-Watergate era, from *The Werewolf of Washington* (1973) to *The Omen* (1976), as well as in some British films, that if we want to look for demons, monsters, and devil-worshippers, we shall be most likely to find them in the offices of those to whom the destinies of nations have been entrusted. The crest of this wave seems to have been passed, if one may judge by the uninventiveness of the imitations that are now about; but plentiful supply suggests that the demand continues.

It must not be forgotten, by those who trace the history of the terror-film in this linear way, that no development is ever as neat as the historian would have it; that, at a given period, older types and models may exist alongside more recent ones. Mexican terror-films, for instance, as Carlos Clarens and others have reminded us, managed to perpetuate the Browning–Lugosi type with all seriousness into a time in which other countries saw this merely as a subject for parody, children's amusement, or nostalgic recollection.

Three characteristic groups have been isolated in the most recent history of the terror-film: Charles Derry, in his book *Dark Dreams*, describes them as centring, respectively, on 'horror of personality', 'horror of Armageddon', and 'horror of the demonic'. In the first, the monster or monsters at the heart of the film resemble you and me rather than Frankenstein's creature, or King Kong, or Godzilla—but owing to some kink in their psychic make-up, or some pressure felt as intolerable, these beings perform the dreadful acts we read about in the newspapers when we absorb our daily ration of rapes, mutilations, and sadistic killings. The key work here is Hitchcock's *Psycho*, released in 1960; but a year later Robert Aldrich's *Whatever Happened to Baby Jane?* popularized that characteristic and particularly unpleasant variant which has become known as the 'menopausal murder story'. Ageing actresses are engaged to perform gory mayhem or be subjected to grotesque tortures not only in *Baby Jane*, but also in *Strait Jacket* (1964), *Hush, Hush, Sweet Charlotte* (1965), *Fanatic* (1965), and *Whatever Happened to Aunt Alice?* (1969). In such works the line that divides exploration from exploitation is unmistakably crossed.

The second or 'Armageddon' group dwells on large-scale rather than individual destruction, either performed or threatened: again our newspapers, ever since the dropping of the first atom bomb, have constantly fed *that* existential anxiety. Among the key works are not only the science-fiction films already discussed above, but also Hitchcock's *The Birds* (1963) and, more recently, Peter Weir's

The Last Wave (1978), an intelligent Australian film which shows civilized man seeking a better understanding of nature through contact with an aboriginal culture—but not until his own culture has upset nature's balance with apocalyptic results. As for Derry's last category, the demonic: our newspapers have not lacked, in recent times, graphic accounts of satanic rites, witchcraft, and exorcisms in a world whose religious sense has sought other outlets than the traditional modes of worshipping God. Key works in the group of films which reflect this state of affairs are Jerzy Kawalerowicz's austere black-and-white transportation of the 'Devils of Loudon' story into seventeenth-century Poland under the title *Mother Joan of the Angels* (1961) and that film's more garish and more popular successors in the English-speaking world: Ken Russell's *The Devils* (1970) and Friedkin's *The Exorcist*.

Two things deserve to be noticed here. Firstly, although Derry has correctly described dominant trends, and has given many well-chosen instances of the different ways in which the themes he isolates have been treated in recent years, the themes themselves are not new, either in the cinema or in literature. All of them, in fact, had played some part in the German cinema of the twenties: 'horror of personality' in *The Student of Prague*, a man-made Armageddon in the flood sequences of Lang's *Metropolis*, demonic possession in *Caligari*. Secondly, in two of the three cycles a key work comes from the cameras of Alfred Hitchcock, best known as a maker of suspense-thrillers not usually thought of as horror-movies. This demonstrates the fluidity of genres (what would the 'horror of personality' film be without the *film noir*, or the 'Armageddon' film without science fiction?); suggests that a genre can be power-fully affected by the work of eminent *auteurs* even if these are not primarily working in that genre; and reminds us once again that though the horror-movie or fantastic terror-film exists to scare us in delightful ways, it does not have a monopoly of terror-sequences or terror-themes. It should also turn our thoughts, once again, towards Germany; for Hitchcock worked at the UFA studios in the twenties and learnt a good deal from the German terror-film. '*The Lodger*', Hitchcock said to François Truffaut, 'is the first picture possibly affected by my period in Germany.' Lang would seem to have been a particularly powerful influence. It may be regarded as a kind of homage that a film made by Hitchcock for Gainsborough Pictures in 1926 starred Bernhard Goetzke, who had portrayed

Death in Lang's *Destiny* or *Tired Death* (a film the young Hitchcock particularly admired), and that two films he made for Gaumont British in the early thirties prominently featured Lang's latest terror-star, Peter Lorre, the psychopathic murderer of *M*—a work that had managed to transplant the Romantic fantasies of the early German cinema, and its central *Doppelgänger* image, into a realistic setting and an almost documentary story-line.

The film-makers who brought about the revival of the German cinema after the Second World War have, on the whole, trodden paths remote from those of Wiene and the early Murnau. There are continuities, however. Peter Lorre returned to Germany for a while to direct, and star in, *The Lost One* (1951), which made the psychopathic killer he had portrayed in earlier films a homicidal Nazi scientist. Fritz Lang returned to project his master criminal Mabuse into the world of electronic surveillance (*The Thousand Eyes of Dr. Mabuse*, 1960). The atmosphere of mystery and terror characteristic of the Weimar cinema has been to some degree preserved in a large number of films based on the works of Edgar Wallace; the actor Klaus Kinski has added to the cinematic repertoire a notable gallery of madmen, paranoiacs, sadistic killers, and drug addicts which recalls the Weimar period in its intensity and demonic power; Rainer Werner Fassbinder has been able to introduce Gothic-expressionistic elements into such films as *Chinese Roulette* (1976) with its monomaniac characters, its oppressive house whose obtrusive furnishings imprison the characters in geometric patterns, its sinister crippled child at the centre of the intrigue. The most talented of the younger directors, Werner Herzog, has shown an interest in unusual states of mind and soul that even led to an experiment, *Heart of Glass* (1976), in which the whole cast was filmed while under hypnosis. Herzog's *Even Dwarves Started Small* (1970) may be seen, in part, as an ironic modern variation on Tod Browning's *Freaks* (1932). For the plot of his claustrophobic *Signs of Life* (1967), Herzog went to a tale by the Romantic writer Achim von Arnim, whose evocations of terror Heine had rated above those of Hoffmann himself. *The Enigma of Kaspar Hauser* (1974) is dedicated to Lotte Eisner, the chronicler of the 'Haunted Screen' of the early German cinema and author of the standard work on Murnau; and the conjunction of Herzog and Klaus Kinski, thrillingly exhibited in *Aguirre, Wrath of God* (1972), inevitably pointed towards Murnau country—not least because Kinski had shown his mettle as a traditional horror-actor by his triumphant assumption of the part of Renfield in Jesus Franco's *Count Dracula* of 1970. Writing in *Écran* in 1975, Herzog characteristically said of his *Aguirre*: 'This film, I think, is not really a narrative of actual happenings or a portrait of actual people. At any level it is a film about what lies behind landscapes, faces, situations and words.' It comes as no surprise, therefore, to find Herzog and Kinski collaborating on a version of *Nosferatu* (released in 1979) which plays a respectful game of theme and variations with Murnau's famous film of the same name, first shown in 1922.

Herzog's deep respect for the Weimar cinema, and his determination to make its traditions valid for his own contemporaries, are shared by Hans-Jürgen Syberberg, whose trilogy of films on the lives of Karl May, Ludwig II of Bavaria, and Hitler (completed in 1978) introduces images from *Caligari* and other German movies of the same period; and by H. W. Geissendörfer, whose *Jonathan: Vampires Do Not Die* (1970) pays tribute to Murnau along with Bram Stoker. Despite its technical accomplishment and its memorable political overtones and implications, however, Geissendörfer's film had so little success at its first release that the exhibitors refused to handle it further unless scenes of explicit sex and violence were spliced in—an inverted form of censorship which has been becoming more and more common since nude shots of Brigitte Bardot were inserted into Godard's *Contempt* (*Le Mépris*, 1963) at the behest of investors anxious to secure better returns.

A host of other German directors of the most recent past have tried their hand at the evocation of Murnauesque terrors: Niklaus Schilling, for instance, whose *Shades of Night*, first shown in the early seventies, to be followed by *Expulsion from Paradise* (1977) and *Rhinegold* (1978), suggested the sinister, demonic aspects of the German landscape with considerable flair; while Johannes Schaaf, whose *Dream City*, also released in the early seventies, successfully adapted to the modern screen motifs from Alfred Kubin's uncanny novel *The Other Side* (1909). *The Tenderness of Wolves* (1973), made by Uli Lommel with the co-operation of the ubiquitous Rainer Werner Fassbinder, is often spoken of as a 'vampire'-film; it turns out, however, to be a study of a homosexual murderer, well played by Kurt Raab; its graphic presentation of killings and mutilations— Raab is even shown licking blood off a table—deliberately distances it from Fritz Lang's *M*, which had dealt with a related theme in

1931. Lang had only suggested the actual murders through shots of abandoned balloons, sweets, empty stair-wells, and so on, and had explained the philosophy behind his procedures in words very pertinent to the theme of this book:

If I could show what is most horrible for *me*, it may not be horrible for somebody else. *Everybody* in the audience—even the one who doesn't *dare* allow himself to understand what really happened to that poor child—has a horrible feeling that runs cold over his back. But everybody has a *different* feeling, because everybody imagines the most horrible thing that could happen to her. And that is something I could not have achieved by showing only one possibility—say, that he tears open the child, cuts her open. Now, in this way, I force the audience to become a collaborator of mine; by *suggesting* something I achieve a greater impression, a greater involvement, than by showing it . . . (Bogdanovich, 1967, pp. 86–7)

Lang here builds on one of the most important facts about the cinema-experience: that the spectator is never just the passive recipient of a message, but that he helps, in varying degrees, to create the experience he is enjoying. What the film-maker has to do is activate the imaginations that reach out to meet his own. Modern audiences, unfortunately, have acquired a craving for the literal and explicit which makes such artistic restraint less and less profitable in the competition for shrinking screen space.

One vitally important factor determining the state of the market for modern films is, of course, the competition and the patronage of television. In recent years the small screen has not only introduced older terror-films to a new generation of viewers, whose response is significantly conditioned by the domestic setting in which they—unlike cinema-goers—watch such works, but has also evolved its own variations. Examples are legion; they range from ghost-stories based on the tales of M. R. James or specially written by Robert Muller and others to TV movies like Dan Curtis's *The Night Stalker* (1971) and its sequel *The Night Strangler* (1972), scripted by Richard Matheson, which wittily and frighteningly revived the vampire- and rejuvenation-tales of the terror-cinema. The continuities between such works and the old 'B' movies are not only thematic; they are made under similar restraints of money, location, and shooting-time, though flexible and sophisticated technical equipment, specially adapted to the lower definition of the TV screen, is apt to disguise this. To discuss the relation between film and television is not part of this book's purpose; but it must mention, at least in passing, the effect that the rediscovery of *avant-garde* devices—'violently clashing images, unusual angles of vision, frozen frames, shooting through gauze, negative prints etc.'—by the makers of TV commercials has had on the iconography, the rhetoric, and the tempo of terror-films all over the world. 'Most of us', Pauline Kael has justly said, 'are now so conditioned by the quick cutting and free association of ideas in TV commercials that we think faster than feature-length movies can move. We understand cinematic shorthand' (Toeplitz, 1974, pp. 240, 242).

Let us now retrace our steps to look at a sequence from one of the undoubted classics of the terror-film—a seminal work of the cinema, a work that stands at a point to which many roads lead and from which many roads flow; a work, moreover, from which our culture has derived one of its most powerful, most easily recognizable, and most influential, visual images. That work is James Whale's *Frankenstein* of 1931.

By its very title this film places itself in a tradition which looks beyond the cinema: a tradition going back to an evening in the Villa Deodati in 1816 at which translations from German ghost-stories were read aloud, and to a day in 1818 when *Frankenstein: or, The Modern Prometheus* was launched on to a receptive public. That the majority of those lured into the cinema by the advertising campaign which preceded the film's release would not be aware of this provenance does not matter—though James Whale felt strongly enough about it to bring Mary Shelley, Shelley, and Byron into the rather embarrassing prologue which introduced a sequel, *The Bride of Frankenstein*, in 1935. In Whale's original *Frankenstein* enough survives of the work that has been adapted to re-evoke the literary climate of an age in which a German-sounding name in the title of a work at once brought suggestions of uncanny terrors; to suggest something of the cultural debates and heart-searchings that went on in the circle around Shelley and the Godwin family, with its passionate concern about the place of the natural sciences in the modern world, the nature of families, the acquisition of language, and the problems of moral choice; and to make probable that the central incident did indeed come to its author (as Mary Shelley assured her readers it did) in a dream. Between the elaborately structured and talkative novel—in which even the monster learns to speak learnedly and at length about Milton, Goethe, and Volney—and the straightforward story-line of the film, a large number of stage adaptations interposed themselves: Peake's version, for instance, which introduced a superstitious servant called Fritz and deprived the monster of speech (T. P. Cooke had only grunted in that part); or, a century later, the version of Peggy Webling, in which Victor Frankenstein and his friend Henry Clerval interchanged their first names, and which also brought the monster face to face with a crippled girl, confronted him amorously with Frankenstein's betrothed, and made him entranced by the sun when he first beheld it. These features were taken over, in slightly varied form, by the writers of the scenario and shooting-script, who included Robert Florey, Garret Fort, and Francis E. Faragoh. They added many new motifs, however: it was Florey, for instance, who suggested the monster's final confrontation with his maker in a wooden flour-mill, as well as the motif of the 'criminal brain' inserted, through human error and muddle, into the poor monster's skull. Despite all these additions, and despite the many omissions and simplifications necessary for the translation of the signifiers of written or printed texts into the iconic signs of the sound-film, a good deal of Mary Shelley's original conception remains: not least those associations which she sought to evoke by her allusion to the Prometheus myth in her sub-title. Whale's feelings that his film enshrined a myth—an ultimately religious myth, like that of Prometheus—is suggested by the famous answer he gave to members of his team who wanted a central scene to end in a different way. 'No', he said, 'it has to be like that; you see, it's all part of the ritual.'

The circle around Shelley took pride in the scope of man's intellect revealed in science as well as in poetry; but as Mary Shelley's novel showed, it was no stranger to worries about the ultimate effects of scientific endeavour and achievement if these outstripped social sympathies, responsibility, and imagination. Such worries had intensified in the century that elapsed between the novel and the film—a film which bears as distinct and complex a relation to the time within which it was conceived, the early thirties of our century, as did the novel to the time of Godwin, Shelley, and Erasmus Darwin. Part of a cycle of cinematic tales of terror conceived and executed in the Depression years in the U.S.A., James Whale's *Frankenstein* deals in terrors that have an underground relation to the frightening economic and social world in which they took shape: a world in which manipulations of the stock-market had recoiled on the manipulators; in which human creatures seemed to be abandoned by those who had called them into being and those who might have been thought responsible for their welfare; in which men were prevented from being men, from feeling themselves full and equal members of society, and were thereby filled with destructive rages such as those the poor monster gives way to after his taunting by the sadistic hunchback who is just a little better off than the monster himself. Like other films in this cycle, *Frankenstein* not only gave expression to such resentments but also offered escape from the burden they placed on the consciousness, through delicious thrills, through cathartic acts of violence and destruction, and through scenes of baronial high life and ethnic merry-making which have worn least well in a film that still has power to excite a modern audience.

One of the charges that have been brought against Whale's film is that it betrays its genre, and lets down the side of ever-advancing cinematic art, by failing to make use of the rich language of camera angle, camera movement, and editing which the great pioneers— Griffith, Eisenstein, Murnau—had evolved by the time James Whale came to make his celebrated movie. Even Richard Anobile, who chose this work above all others to open his Film Classics series, makes a complaint of this kind. One has only to look at the film's opening sequence, however, to convince oneself that this charge is as mistaken as similar charges brought against *The Cabinet of Dr. Caligari*. That opening sequence does three things superbly well:

(i) placing the film which is to come within not a literary but a cinematic tradition, already well established despite the comparative newness of film art;

(ii) presenting the forces which will be set clashing in the unfolding story through predominantly visual, cinematic means, without underlining by the portentous mood-music that spoils so many Hollywood films;

(iii) introducing objects, characters, and actions which are essential elements of the unfolding story but which may also be seen to have symbolic significance. Several of them, in fact, become recurrent motifs, leitmotifs, when they are recalled in later shots and sequences.

Let us look for a moment at the way all this is done. The film begins with a prologue, spoken by Edward Van Sloan in a pretence of stepping in front of a theatre curtain. This prologue links itself directly and deliberately to the original epilogue (now cut from most copies in circulation) of Tod Browning's *Dracula*, spoken by the same actor in a very similar role; and the design behind the opening credits which follow in *Frankenstein*, with its two eyes emitting beams of light, recalls the play made with Lugosi's eyes in *Dracula*, where pinpoints of light had been directed on to them by Tod Browning and his cameraman to make them shine out hypnotically. Indeed, an early poster of *Frankenstein* announces that Lugosi would play the central part and includes a visual allusion to his magnetic gaze. The 'clawing hand' motif behind these same opening credits of *Frankenstein* also refers us back to *Dracula*, and beyond that to a whole clutch of horror-movies and horror-comedies—culminating in Paul Leni's *The Cat and the Canary* (1927), a key work in the transition from the fantastic cinema of Weimar Germany to the American terror-film—in which this motif played a thrilling part. No less surely, however, does the design refer us forward—to the role which staring eyes and clawing hands will play in the early sequences of *Frankenstein* itself. Before we come to them, however, another design appears behind the titles: a revolving collage of eyes, which bears a striking and surely not accidental relation to the famous collage of eyes in the false Maria's dance sequence of Fritz Lang's *Metropolis* (1927). The shadowy demonic face that appears behind these eyes has what was known in those days as 'the German look'; it recalls advertisements for German films which concentrated on the angular features of Conrad Veidt, or the demonic apparition that materializes in Rabbi Loew's study in the conjuration scene of *The Golem: How it came into the World* (1920). This is only the first of several visual allusions, in Whale's film, to the German cinema of the macabre: the central creation-scene embodies reminiscences of a similar scene in Rotwang's laboratory in *Metropolis*, while *The Golem* is recalled, no less surely, by the impressive staircase down which Dwight Frye scuttles in Frankenstein's tower laboratory, and by the lakeside confrontation of the monster and a little girl. Like Rex Ingram in *The Magician* of 1926 (a film which Whale would seem to have studied very carefully indeed) and like Tod Browning and Robert Florey, Whale was able to draw on German traditions as well as on the American tradition of the grotesque exemplified in the films of Lon Chaney Senior.

It must be stressed, at this point, that the town and countryside constructed for James Whale in the Universal studios by Charles D. Hill and others are much less stylized than the medieval Prague Hans Poelzig had built for Wegener and Galeen in 1920. Jack C. Ellis (1979, p. 100) has described Poelzig's sets admirably: 'The abstractly fashioned medieval town, with its sharply angled roofs and tilted chimney-pots, looks like twisted gingerbread; there isn't a straight line visible. A gigantic gate dwarfs the human beings. Irregular arches and inverted V's predominate. The camera frequently shoots through the archways, imposing their strange shapes on the frame itself . . .' Nevertheless, Whale's film demonstrates that he is quite consciously working in an established and developing genre that includes the Scandinavian and German along with the American cinema, and that he is playing a significant game of theme and variation. The iconography of his own film, in its turn, influenced the developing genre indelibly, and has been a source of inspiration and allusion for a multitude of film-makers—though no one has ever paid to it as moving and as meaningful a tribute as Victor Erice, who in *The Spirit of the Beehive* (1973) confronted a little girl growing up in Franco's Spain with Whale's *Frankenstein*, showed what a central part Karloff's monster assumed in her fantasies and dreams, and demonstrated how it helped her to interpret and to come to terms with her own world.

Let us follow Whale's seminal film a little further. He boldly dispenses with the 'establishing shot' which had, by his time, become part of Hollywood's *découpage classique*, and opens on a close-up: a close-up of hands about a rope running diagonally downwards, sloping towards screen right—and a rope, as we shall afterwards see, becomes a sinister leitmotif in the film as Frankenstein's hunchbacked assistant cuts a corpse from the gallows, and as the monster, goaded into fury by this same assistant, is subdued with the help of a rope that he will later use to kill his tormentor. This opening close-up is the beginning of a long tracking-shot of various dark-clad groups, all looking downwards so that we cannot see their eyes: an old man comforting an old woman, a younger woman and her boy, a middle-aged man standing by himself, while behind and to the right of him appear the shadow of a cross and a priest holding a flag with the keys of St. Peter. Then the shadow of the cross becomes larger, bolder, more visible in the foreground, as the camera moves in on a priest holding a sacramental bell. The two priests we have seen so far have faced towards screen left; they are succeeded by the single figure of a dark-haired, dark-clad man looking downwards, also towards screen left, into what we by now surmise to be a grave—and he, in his turn, is succeeded by a startling image of Death himself, dramatically tilted towards screen right, cowled and resting his hands on the hilt of a sword formed in the shape of a cross, with hollow eyes looking upwards towards screen left but photographed in such a way that he seems also to be turning his hollow eye-sockets towards us, into the auditorium. Behind this figure bare wintry twigs appear, and some shadowy spikes point upwards. We soon realize that we are here in the presence, not of some supernatural apparition, as in Lang's *Tired Death*, or a fevered vision, as in the 'Deadly Sins' sequence of *Metropolis*, but of a churchyard statue, a sepulchral monument. And our first glimpse of that sculptured effigy is immediately succeeded by the face of the actor Dwight Frye; in closest close-up with enormous eyes staring in the same direction as the figure of Death, while one hand claws at iron spikes that frame his face as they point menacingly upwards, photographed at an angle which makes them tilt, like the effigy of Death, towards screen right.

Huge, staring eyes (the first eyes we have seen in this sequence) and a clawing hand: the design behind the opening titles seems to have come to life in the person of an actor whose presence—like that of Edward Van Sloan—links James Whale's *Frankenstein* with Tod Browning's *Dracula*. And in the shot which succeeds this close-up there looms on to the screen another face behind that of Dwight Frye, another hand, clawing Frye's humped shoulder: the tense, drawn, handsome features of Colin Clive's Frankenstein, also framed by spikes, with wintry branches in the background—a face which is then allowed, for one rapid shot, to occupy the screen by itself, before we have another view of the tilted effigy of Death, with more spikes, and with a stone sarcophagus behind which we can just make out Frankenstein's crouching figure. After this, a long-shot shows mourners and priests departing away from the camera and towards screen left, leaving the grave-digger to light his pipe (his spurting match is the first of many significant flashes of fire in this film), to complete his work, and then also to depart, in the same direction. Only Frankenstein and his dark-clad assistant now remain, to start digging in such a way that dirt is literally flung into the face of (the sculptured) Death—the first of several grotesque symbolic touches which were to become one of the hallmarks of James Whale's directorial style.

This splendid sequence introduces, with only the briefest touch of mood-music and with only one line of spoken dialogue (Frankenstein's whispered injunction to his assistant to keep down), some more of the leitmotifs of the film which has now been set in motion: the motif, so often repeated afterwards, of the hidden watcher, biding his time; the motif of one being impelling another—a more deformed being than himself—by force of his will, as later on Frankenstein will seek to impel his monster; the motif of several characters so linked that they seem to be part of a single one, as later on Frankenstein's ego will be flanked by the superego represented by his teacher and friend Dr. Waldmann and by the fragments of his id incarnated in his assistant and his monster. Above all, with the greatest economy, and with purely cinematic successions of close-up, medium-shot, and long-shot, Whale has established from the outset one of the conflicts which will be at the heart of his film and many of its successors: that between (on one side) men and women who want to follow their ordinary pursuits and at last bury their dead with fitting sorrow and dignity, within the forms prescribed by the Church, and (on the other side) the resurrection men, who have aims and purposes that go counter to such wishes. And through the dramatically angled figure of Death, together with the similarly angled shadow of the cross, Whale has also suggested the symbolic, metaphysical implications of his theme— implications discursively stated, in deliberately simple terms, in the prologue spoken by Van Sloan: 'We are about to unfold the story of Frankenstein, a man of science who sought to create a man after his own image without reckoning upon God. It is one of the strangest tales ever told. It deals with the two great mysteries of creation: Life and Death.'

Whale's first *Frankenstein* film has its detractors—but there is one thing on which there is almost universal agreement: the scenes in which the monster appears must be reckoned among the classics of the cinema. Here much of the credit must again go to Whale; but he shares it, as every director must, with his cameraman

(Arthur Edeson), with the special effects department which set up the impressive laboratory-scene, with the make-up designer Jack Pierce, and—above all—with Boris Karloff. From the moment its hand twitches into life while face and body are yet hidden beneath their shroud, Karloff's monster is unforgettable: nothing can ever quite efface the thrill of watching the successive views Whale's mobile camera allows us of the lumbering figure first announced by the sound of its heavy footsteps: a medium-shot view from behind is followed by one of head and shoulders as the monster turns around; only then are we given our first look at those infinitely sad features in two close-ups that fill the screen as no others will in the course of the whole film. A hundred imitations and parodies cannot dull the impact of the images created by Whale, Edeson, Pierce, and Karloff when we see the monster raise his misshapen hands towards the light from which he received life, to have that light immediately shut out by his creator and to be confronted with another kind of light, the flaming torch wielded by Dwight Frye's malevolently hunched figure, the fire in which the monster will ultimately find his death, in mocking inversion of the Prometheus myth of Mary Shelley's sub-title; when we see Karloff's monster discover his own humanity by comparing his hands with those of the little girl who befriends him by the lake, and when we watch him being taught the delights of *play* by this little girl—how can one ever forget the radiant happiness that illuminates and beautifies his charnel-house features at this point? No later debasements, in countless sequels, parodies, and exploitational variations—not even Mel Brooks's charmingly conceived comedy *Young Franken-stein* (1974)—can ever dispel the magic of that classic, wordless performance.

Karloff's performance was not without its precedents, however. If his make-up in *Frankenstein* occasionally reminds us of Cesare's in *Caligari*, his whole demeanour recalls even more forcibly the animated clay-figure that Paul Wegener had portrayed in the *Golem* films of 1914 and 1920. Here is a contemporary reaction to the first *Golem*:

What makes the film worth discussing is only Wegener's embodiment of the Golem—the affecting portrayal of a creature struggling out of mere existence towards some sentient connection with the world, struggling to become a man . . . In lyrical passages Wegener demonstrates possibilities of the film which transcend those of the theatre: a mere creature, he stands on the dream-breathing earth and slowly lifts his arms in astonishment, in half-conscious joy, in agitation—an image never to be forgotten. This creature of inadequacy is surrounded by an atmosphere of sadness: a melancholy sense of doomed efforts to reach the unattainable, as if the animal kingdom had sent a representative to mirror the human environment in its soul; as if, on an enchanted midnight, the gates of a felt beauty, a soul-suffused landscape, had been opened before the animal—but there it stands, in perplexity and anguish, unable to grasp what is before it; and the hour goes by. (*Die Schaubühne*, xi, 1915, 225–7)

What Arnold Zweig here says of Wegener's Golem in 1915 he could have applied verbatim, sixteen years later, to Frankenstein's monster as Boris Karloff played it.

These few remarks on *Frankenstein*—a film that affords only the briefest glimpses of acts of violence and none at all of severed limbs or streams of blood—have, I hope, served to suggest some of the delights offered by the cinematic tales of terror that have come to be known as 'fantastic horror-movies'. Such works enable us to watch gifted directors, with their team of writers, cameramen, make-up experts, and many others, create, within the limits imposed by the need of the film to show a profit at the box-office, what has been well called a 'ciné-vérité of the spirit'. To do so they employed a distinctive film-rhetoric of the macabre which has included, at various times, slanted camera angles, filterings and blurrings, distortions through wide-angled lenses, low-key lighting, double exposures, accelerated or slowed-down or arrested motion, infrared film, sudden intrusions of film negatives, the use of colours and colour-contrasts to convey moods, the shifts of scale exemplified in *King Kong, Dr. Cyclops* (1940), and *The Incredible Shrinking Man* (1957), and all the other devices pioneered by masters of the macabre from Murnau, Dreyer, and Whale to Buñuel, Polanski, and de Palma. There were those among them, like Fritz Lang and Jacques Tourneur, who liked to work through suggestions that allowed the audience to piece out what they had only half-seen with their own horrendous imaginings; others, on the contrary, like Mario Bava, whose visual imagination is at least the equal of that shown by Tourneur and the rest of the Lewton directors, deliberately shocked their audiences by showing cruel activities and denuded or mutilated states of the body over which earlier film-makers, forced by censorship or restrained by their own moral sensibilities, had drawn a kindly veil. Sounds, too, had played their part from earliest times, for films were never 'silent'—pianists, orchestras, and organists had supplied a wide range of musical effects to supplement and underline what was being shown on the screen even before the films had sound-tracks, and *benshis*, *spielers*, and other narrators had interpreted the story and supplied vocally produced sound-effects for various ethnic groups. From the 1930s onwards all this and more could be controlled by the director and his sound-engineers; doors now grated on their hinges, winds howled, thunder erupted, pipe-organs played, actors spoke, or grunted, or screamed . . . Rouben Mamoulian supplied the sound-track of *Dr. Jekyll and Mr. Hyde* (1932) with amplified and accelerated heartbeats, reversed gongs, and light-frequencies photographed directly on to the sound-track; Eisenstein's *Alexander Nevsky* (1938), which works with terror as well as grandeur, records the Teuton trumpets so near to the microphone as to achieve an almost physically distressing feedback; the unseen ghost of Thorold Dickinson's *The Queen of Spades* (1948) announces its presence through the rustlings of silk and the tappings of a cane; Bernard Herrmann's violins shriek their way through the climaxes of Hitchcock's *Psycho*; Jack Clayton's *The Innocents* (1961) is pervaded by insistent whisperings; and the visual fascination of Robert Altmann's *Images* (1972) is matched by the aural fascination of Stomu Yamash-ta's accompanying percussions. The coming of sound also brought quite new possibilities of visual and verbal counterpoint: as when, in Alexandre Astruc's *The Pit and the Pendulum* (1962), the screen shows us the events imagined and chronicled by Poe from the point of view of the torturers of the Inquisition, while on the sound-track we hear a reading of Poe's original story which adopts, of course, the point of view of the tortured victim. And not least, the coming of sound also meant the coming of silence—of meaningful silences like that which supervenes so eerily and suddenly after the voice-over beginning of the first dream-sequence in Bergman's *Wild Strawberries*. This sequence may be seen as a visual anthology of macabre effects: clocks without hands; deserted streets along which walks a figure that turns around to reveal only the rudiments of a face and then melts away, leaving a heap of clothes on the ground; a hearse which spills its coffin; a coffin-lid opening to reveal the dreamer's double inside it, a *Doppelgänger* whose hand then seizes that of the dreamer and tries to pull him inside the coffin. It is one of Bergman's many self-conscious tributes to the tale of terror in literature no less than in the cinema.

Such rhetoric of the macabre may also include, despite the anathema pronounced on infractions of realism by Erwin Panofsky, André Bazin, and Siegfried Kracauer, scenery pre-styled by artistic designers in the manner of theatrical flats. A striking recent example is Kurosawa's *Dodeska-den* (1970), which seeks in non-naturalistic use of colour, in painted sets, and in stylized acting an aesthetic equivalent for the life of people who have 'fled into illusion from the harsh realities of an "objective" world' (Joan Mellen). Dario Argento's *Suspiria* (1977) has used similar techniques, with striking success, in evoking a world distorted by witchcraft—though even at their most eye-rolling moments his performers give what strikes a Western observer as more naturalistic performances than Kurosawa's. In the realm of the cinematic tale of terror, however, the supreme example of this style of film-making remains Robert Wiene's pioneer work *The Cabinet of Dr. Caligari*, where the painted and actual objects surrounding the actors become, in Béla Bálazs's happy phrase, 'active and equal partners' with them: they hem them in by converging black lines, grimace and look at them with what seem like eyes, stretch up and tower over them, like that enormous stool from which the town clerk looks down on his petitioners, or twist and bend towards them like those winding paths over roof-tops and between crooked houses or lamp-standards set up at crazy angles. Perhaps the most subtly disturbing element of *Caligari* is that its final scene, which we would have supposed to be taking place in a 'real' world radically different from the 'fantasy' world of the tale told by one inmate of a mental home to another, turns out to be set in the same twisted and stylized scenery, and to show the same menacing aspect, as that of the madman's tale of *Caligari* and his somnambulist. This suggests that the narrator's view of the world may be justified; that he has truly seen aspects of the world which are not apparent to those of us who think ourselves superior to him by virtue of our unquestioned sanity. When we have left his consciousness we continue to see the world as he saw it—for as long as the film lasts; and may we not afterwards continue to see authority as menacing, 'things' as alien and constricting—or rather, may we not feel that what we have been shown on the screen is something we ourselves have darkly felt about certain aspects of our world in certain historical constellations?[1]

It was, in fact, the Germans, in the years just following the First World War, who most forcibly showed the world—with films like *Caligari*, *Dr. Mabuse the Gambler* (1922), *Waxworks* (1924), and *(Warning) Shadows* (1924)—the powerful attraction tales of terror could exert in the cinema even on the sophisticated. The early German film-makers were able to do this not only because the mood of the time favoured the evocation of uncanny fears (alongside the more obviously escapist type of entertainment which then as now formed the staple of the German film industry), but also because they had a rich heritage of demonic folklore, Gothic fiction, and black Romanticism on which to draw for their themes, and because the artistic and literary movements subsumed under the general heading of 'Expressionism' had furnished a style of acting and scene-design that proved admirably suited to the translation of these Romantic themes into terms of the silent film. Since the majority of the actors who animated the screen in those early years, and quite a few of the directors too, had passed through the more restrained and restraining school of Max Reinhardt, they found it easier to adapt themselves to the demands of the close-up and the medium-shot than did, say, Sarah Bernhardt, whose filmed histrionics look ludicrously stagey in a way even the most violent gestures of Werner Krauss and Rudolf Klein-Rogge and Brigitte Helm manage to avoid. To dismiss *Caligari* as a photographed stage play is therefore doubly ridiculous: the mere fact, pointed out by several critics, that it contains some 370 cuts—an average of one shot every twelve seconds!—should suffice to dispose of that hoary slander, despite Wiene's relatively static camera. As for the common argument that *Caligari* is 'uncinematic' because the film must manipulate and shoot 'unstylized reality'—if we accepted that we would have to begin by writing off the whole history of 'cartoon' and 'animation' films; and there is surely much good sense in the view of the designers of *Caligari* that films of this kind were 'drawings brought to life'.

Caligari is not only part of a national cinema which drew on the Gothic, Romantic, and Expressionist traditions of German literature and the visual arts to create a new style of film-making. Nor is it only what an important book by Anton Kaes has recently shown

[1] *The Cabinet of Dr. Caligari* will be discussed in greater detail in Chapter 6, below.

it to be: an essential link in the chain of transmission that made it possible for this German heritage (which incapsulated a good deal of the English literary heritage too) to be received, and used, in other cultures. *Caligari* is also, as my analysis of the opening of *Frankenstein* should have demonstrated, part of a developing international genre: the cinematic tale of fantastic terror, popularly known as the 'horror-movie'.

In regarding the terror-film or horror-movie as a genre one is not, of course, implying that there is some obligatory set of rules every work in that category must obey. The works so designated are united, rather, by what Wittgenstein called 'family resemblances'—likenesses analogous to those which bind together the members of a family: 'Some of them have the same nose, others the same eyebrows and others again the same way of walking; and these likenesses overlap' (*The Blue and Brown Books*, Oxford, 1964, p. 17). The terror-film or horror-movie is an 'institution' in the sense described by Harry Levin in *The Gates of Horn* (New York, 1963): something that evolves historically, something that aspiring writers or film-makers find ready to hand, something they can work within or try to widen or disrupt or transcend. To decide whether a work should be called a terror-film or horror-movie one adopts the kind of criterion R. C. Elliot suggested for deciding whether or not a given work is a 'satire':

One looks at a number of satires about which there is no question—which are all at the centre of the concept, so to speak—and then decides whether work x has resemblances enough to the undoubted examples of the type to be included in it. The point is: this is not a *factual* question to be settled by examining the work for the necessary and sufficient properties which would automatically entitle it to the name *satire*; this is a *decision* question: are the resemblances of this work to various kinds of satire sufficient so that we are warranted in including it in the category—or in extending the category to take it in? ('The Definition of Satire', *Yearbook of Comparative and General Literature*, xi, 1962, 23)

What one is asking about, ultimately, is 'common consensus' within a given society, a given culture. If someone sees a title like *The Clawing Hand, Frankenstein and the Monster from Hell*, or *The Plague of the Zombies*, he will mentally classify the film as a horror-movie or a *Gruselfilm*, or say to himself that it belongs to an important subdivision of *le cinéma fantastique*. If someone asks what is showing at the local cinema and receives the answer 'a horror-movie', he will at once think of certain characters, settings, situations, and images. Film-makers cannot but take such norms or expectations into account and decide—consciously or unconsciously —to fulfil them exactly, develop them further, deviate from them, or subvert them.

How such a genre develops and advances may be demonstrated by a brief look at the case of Val Lewton and his team at the RKO studios in Hollywood.

In the early forties RKO had so notoriously fallen on hard times that some wag advised Hollywood residents to make straight for their studios in the event of an air raid: for they hadn't had a hit for years. To repair their shattered fortunes the studio-bosses decided to establish a special unit for the production of inexpensive terror-films that would fit into the second, less prestigious half of a double bill and would fulfil some of the genre-expectations that *Dracula*, *Frankenstein*, and the Universal movies which followed them had so firmly established. To head this 'B' unit they chose Val Lewton, a Russian-born American, who was given a tiny budget, shooting-schedules measured in weeks rather than months, a running-time limit (no film to run longer than 75 minutes), and a series of sensational titles—*I Walked with a Zombie* is the most characteristic example—around which to construct his stories. The studio-authorities would view rushes, grumble, and occasionally interfere when they found the films insufficiently horrific or the directors too slow, but on the whole Lewton was allowed a free hand within the sufficiently tight restrictions already detailed, as long as his films made money. They usually opened at the Rialto cinema in New York which specialized in what was beginning to be called 'chillers' and co-operated with the studio in advertising these in sensational ways.

The films that resulted—*Cat People*, *I Walked with a Zombie* (1943), *The Leopard Man* (1943), all directed by Jacques Tourneur; *The Seventh Victim* (1943), *The Ghost Ship* (1943), *Isle of the Dead* (1945), *Bedlam* (1946), directed by Mark Robson; *The Curse of the Cat People* (1944) and *The Body Snatcher*, directed by Robert Wise— are particularly well fitted to demonstrate the interplay of genre, *auteurs*, and studio-policy in the commercial movie. The chief *auteur* in this case is the dynamic producer, Val Lewton himself, who prepared the final shooting-scripts (though he never took writer's credit under his own name), worked closely with his directors and film-editors, and imposed on the resulting works not only his own fastidious literary and visual tastes, but also, it would appear, some of his own phobias and 'hang-ups'. *Cat People* and *Curse of the Cat People*, for instance, play on his well-documented dislike of being physically touched, his fear of cats, and his keen remembrance of the agonies and fantasies of sensitive childhood. His cameraman, for the most part, was Nicolas Musaraca, who specialized in the low-key, many-shadowed, atmospheric lighting which was not only an understandable convention the horror-movie shared with certain *films noirs*, but also a necessity to disguise the cheapness of the set in a cramped corner of the studio. The resulting films varied in quality—those directed by Tourneur were notably better than the others—but as a group they made a decisive contribution to the genre in three distinct but related ways.

The first of these might be called 'negative self-definition'. De-Witt Bodeen, who worked with Lewton on several scripts, recalls that when he had been engaged as an RKO contract writer and assigned to Lewton, the latter ran off for his new collaborator 'some U.S. and British horror and suspense movies which were typical of what we did *not* want to do'. As against the crude shocks provided by hairy monsters and mutilated faces Lewton's team worked by suggestion, preferring the shadow of danger to its substance. For the increasingly stereotyped characters that peopled the American horror-movie, Lewton's team substituted psychologically differentiated human beings with complex emotions—*The Curse of the Cat People* has provided child psychologists (and, incidentally, the distinguished sociologist David Riesman) with usable examples. Black actors, who had been used in horror-movies only to mimic child-like fright, were given back their dignity in Lewton's films. Where the Universal movies had satisfied their audiences' limited appetite for verse with jingles like those which figure in the Wolf Man saga, films made by Lewton's team introduced unhackneyed quotations from John Donne; where the former tended more and more to underline their horrors with surging music, Lewton and his team use silences that made the sounds they did select much more telling. *I Walked with a Zombie*, their masterpiece, includes not only a long entirely silent sequence in which the camera tracks two women walking towards a voodoo ceremony, but also two important characters that never speak at all. The film shows genre-continuity—it uses the zombie lore familiar to horror-movie addicts from *White Zombie* to *The Ghost Breakers*; yet who but Lewton would have thought of reworking, playing variations on, the plot of *Jane Eyre* in a voodoo setting?

Besides thus defining their films against the conventions of the genre within which they consciously worked, Lewton and his team created an *œuvre* that is held together, not only by common themes like the struggle of a rational day-world against a deeper irrational night-world, but also by a whole series of other coherences and continuities. The same directors, cameramen, and editors are employed in film after film, imposing their respective styles; the psychiatrist Dr. Judd figures prominently in the list of characters in *Cat People* and *The Seventh Victim*; the pervasive presence of *Jane Eyre* in *I Walked with a Zombie* is recalled when the headmistress of the oppressive Highcliffe Academy which plays its part in *The Seventh Victim* is given the name 'Lowood'; the painting by Arnold Böcklin which had appeared peripherally in *I Walked with a Zombie* assumes central importance in *The Isle of the Dead*; the watching cat which is introduced into a murder-sequence of *The Body Snatcher* refers back to the pervasive feline imagery of *Cat People*.

The films made by Lewton and his team in the forties look backwards by adopting themes and characters of earlier horror-movies—much fun can be had, after all, from seeing how certain basic elements could be treated in new ways, what variations be played on familiar themes. They look inwards too, establishing a style of their own and emphasizing the interrelation of their films in unobtrusive ways. And, of course, they point forwards. The styles of lighting, shooting, and editing worked out at RKO in the Lewton years reappear, in significantly varied form, in such later movies made by Lewton directors as Jacques Tourneur's *The Night of the Demon* (1957) and Robert Wise's *The Haunting* (1963), and in the work of such different admirers of Lewton as Hitchcock and Carol Reed. Reed's *The Third Man* (1949) is full of Lewtonesque sequences —the scene in nocturnal Vienna in which the silence is startlingly broken by a clattering dustbin-lid vividly recalls a similar incident in *The Seventh Victim*. The famous shower-scene in Hitchcock's *Psycho*, where only the shadowy outline of the murderer may be discerned behind the shower-curtains, elaborates a parallel scene in *The Seventh Victim*; and the incidents involving a gift of caged birds at the opening of Hitchcock's *The Birds*, which have no equivalent in the Daphne du Maurier story on which that film is based, are so close to the opening passages of *Cat People* that they might almost be seen as a conscious act of homage.

There can be no doubt that Lewton and his team were influenced by the German cinema of terror and the uncanny; and here we must remember that many of those who had helped to make these German films were actually present in Lewton's Hollywood and were still working as directors, cameramen, designers, technicians, and actors. François Truffaut pinpointed important continuities and two-way influences in his review of Fritz Lang's *The Big Heat* in 1964:

Looking at Lang's entire work, it seems impossible not to notice how much of Hollywood appears in his German films. *Spies*, for example, or *Metropolis*, or *The Testament of Dr. Mabuse*—all those spectaculars. Conversely, Lang strives to keep a great many of his germanic effects in his American pictures —certain sets, certain lighting effects, the tasty vistas, lively camera angles, Gloria Grahame's mask-like bandage, and so on. (Braudy and Dickstein, 1978, p. 609)

When Georges Franju, writing on Lang in the *Cahiers du Cinéma* in November 1959, speaks of performances 'characterized by extreme attitudes, energetic expressions, and nervousness of gesture', he points to traits which, tempered and toned down, may be found in the American cinema of terror almost as readily as in the German— though not, for the most part, in the deliberately understated Val Lewton cycle.

Whoever seeks to trace the development of a genre in the art of film will inevitably come up against the principal difficulties that beset genre-studies in any medium:

(i) Every worthwhile work modifies the genre to some extent, brings something new to it, and therefore forces us to rethink our definitions and delimitations.

(ii) There are borderline cases, works that belong to more than one genre—the overlap between the 'fantastic terror' film and the 'science-fiction' film is particularly large.

(iii) Wide variations in quality are possible within a given genre— in aesthetic merit and imaginative power Dreyer's *Vampyr* is light-years away from *I Was a Teenage Werewolf*.

(iv) There are works which as a whole clearly do not belong to the genre in question but which embody references to that genre, or contain sequences that derive from, allude to, or influence it. The first dream-sequence in Bergman's *Wild Strawberries* and the post-autopsy-sequence in the same director's *The Face* clearly belong in that category; and so, as we shall see, do sequences in *Citizen Kane*, *Rebecca*, and *Sunset Boulevard*.

The terrain surveyed in this book is bounded on various sides by fairy-tale- and fantasy-films like LeRoy's *The Wizard of Oz* (1939) and Cocteau's *Beauty and the Beast* (1946), in which terror only plays a minor part; by science-fiction films like *Close Encounters of the Third Kind*, which aim at wonder rather than fright; by *films noirs* like *The Big Sleep* (1946) or 'violent intrusion' films like *The Desperate Hours* (1955), which deal with the terrors, dangers, and puzzles of the social world in a deliberately non-fantastic and (usually) non-allegorical way; and by documentations of horror and violence in non-fiction contexts, like Resnais's *Night and Fog* (1955) and Franju's *Blood of the Beasts* (1949). There will always be overlaps, of course: David Wolper's *The Hellstrom Chronicle* (1971), for instance, uses documentary footage for most of its length to allow the fictional scientist whose name appears in the title to scare us all with the prospect of an apocalyptic battle between men and insects in which the insects are likely to come out on top. It was awarded an Oscar in the 'Documentary' class! The main emphasis of the present book will fall on films in which terror is the principal ingredient and *raison d'être*; in which such terror is bound up with fantasy elements of various kinds, with metaphysical uncertainties, with shivers from some beyond; and which has at its centre beings that exist in the limbo between man and demon, animal and man, the terrestrial and the galactic, life and death. It will also, however, glance across from horror-movies of this kind to sequences in other films that seek to play on their audiences' delight in being terrified or in watching the causes and effects of terror mimed on the screen.

Caligari and *Frankenstein* between them have already introduced us to many of the principal protagonists of the cinematic tale of terror. These include the wise old man, who is usually a scientist with what the film requires us to believe to be a healthy respect for the occult; the monster-maker or controller, frequently a man lusting after power and revenge or one possessed by a Faustian urge for knowledge and experience, who pays too little heed to the consequences of his experimentation; his sinister, often grotesquely shaped assistant, subject to his will yet occasionally capable of disastrous or beneficent independent action; the monster, who may or may not be identical with that same assistant and who, in *Jekyll and Hyde* films, is in fact identical with his ostensible maker and controller; the heroine, who will, in some central scene in which she is wearing a night-gown or a wedding-dress or some other light-coloured garment, find herself seized or at least confronted by the dark-clad or furry monster; a faithful swain dedicated to the heroine's protection; ordinary folk going about their ordinary business, sometimes workaday, sometimes festive, who find themselves victims and (ultimately) hunters of the monster and his maker; and incidental figures—like bumbling old Baron Frankenstein and various screeching servants—who are introduced as comic relief, to deflect an amusement that might otherwise be directed at the grotesque aspects and actions of characters meant to be taken seriously. In *Frankenstein*, the heroine has another popular function, well described by Jack C. Ellis in *A History of Film* (p. 208): she represents one side of the conflict of love and faith (feeling) with science (reason), and her true affection is called upon, in the end, to heal the ravages of the scientist's soul.

In introducing these figures, *Caligari* and *Frankenstein* may also serve to illustrate another of the fascinations which the cinematic tale of terror can exert upon the right audience. Such films bring before us the work of a repertory company of actors specializing in grotesque or macabre creations: Paul Wegener, Werner Krauss, Conrad Veidt, Rudolf Klein-Rogge, Brigitte Helm; Lon Chaney Senior (a repertory company all by himself—'don't step on it', they used to say, 'it may be Lon Chaney!'); Boris Karloff, Bela Lugosi, Dwight Frye, Lionel Atwill, George Zucco; the dainty Fay Wray, archetypal victim and prey of various monsters, whose ability to scream was tested against King Kong, the hounds of Zaroff, and the terrifying mysteries of the Wax Museum; Peter Lorre and Vincent Price; Christopher Lee, Peter Cushing, Ingrid Pitt; Barbara Steele, Robert Quarry, Paul Naschy. There is also the undoubted pleasure of watching a repertory company that usually does other things— like the Bergman Company headed by Gunnar Björnstrand, Max von Sydow, and Ingrid Thulin—having a shot at fantastic terror in

The Face and *The Hour of the Wolf*; versatile actors like Charles Laughton, Fredric March, and Jean-Louis Barrault venturing into horror-movie territory as Dr. Moreau (in *The Island of Lost Souls*, 1932), as *The Hunchback of Notre Dame* (in William Dieterle's version of 1939), or as *Jekyll and Hyde* (in Mamoulian's version, 1932, and Renoir's, 1961); and Erich von Stroheim, who as a director did so much to merge extreme realism with symbolism and fantasy, embodying again and again, as an actor, the mad scientist of horror-fantasy. One must distinguish a whole gamut of appreciation here, which ranges from admiration of Edith Scob's luminous performance in Franju's *Eyes Without a Face* (1959)—a miraculous performance of eyes and body only, for the face is covered by a plain white mask throughout the film—to the rather 'camp' delight with which one greets Lugosi's 'I am Dracula, I bid you welcome' or his 'Children of the night' speech in Browning's film of 1931. But the pleasure of watching stylish acting is not an absolutely necessary ingredient of our pleasure at cinematic tales of terror: the cast of Dreyer's *Vampyr*—with the exception of the excellent Sybille Schmitz—is inexperienced in the ways of actors, yet this exercise in the 'terror of whiteness' remains unsurpassed in its genre, taking its place alongside such macabre masterpieces as Wiene's *Caligari*, Lang's *Tired Death* (also known as *Destiny*), Murnau's *Nosferatu*, Epstein's *Fall of the House of Usher*, Mamoulian's *Dr. Jekyll and Mr. Hyde*, Laughton's *Night of the Hunter*, Cavalcanti's *Dead of Night*, Roeg's *Don't Look Now*, and the 'Lady Wakasa' episode of Mizoguchi's *Ugetsu Monogatari*.

In the U.S.A. especially the employment of certain actors soon became a sort of character and genre shorthand. The appearance of a player like Karloff or Lugosi in the cast-list of a film established a strong presumption that the film either belonged or sought to allude to the 'horror' genre, and assured potential spectators that the characters depicted would have certain well-defined traits—traits belonging to the vampire, the mad scientist, the pitiful yet dangerous monster, and so on. In this, as the Russian critic A. Piotrovsky pointed out as early as 1927, 'genre' films came to resemble folk-tales and the *commedia dell'arte*, with their strictly defined character-types and limited situations, rather than the contemporary novel and the contemporary drama. At the same time each genre developed a kind of syntax within which to deploy these types: in terror-films the lone character shown from behind or from such vantage-points as a bush or a gallery is felt to be particularly menaced; the character that walks straight towards the camera and thus looms larger and larger will, as Peter Handke once said, soon be opening his eyes wide with terror, utter a scream, or have a hand clapped over his mouth—if he is not, like Caligari, the terror-maker himself (Denk, 1978, pp. 61–2, 155–6). The danger then is that this syntax will accommodate nothing but clichés; but gifted screen-writers and directors may find that it challenges them to convert it to new uses, to subvert it, or to break with it altogether. We have already met examples of this in our glance at the Val Lewton films, and will encounter many more in the course of this book.

As everyone knows from seeing comedy-thrillers in the cinema and watching *The Munsters* or *Monster Squad* on television, terror and laughter are near neighbours in our reaction to the iconography of the cinematic tale of terror. We are here in the presence of *grotesque* art, in which impulses towards horrified recoil are stirred up at the same time as impulses to laugh; these inhibit one another and what results is a characteristically complex response. The masters of this kind of grotesque film have worked out all sort of devices to prevent us from laughing at the wrong moments. They introduce figures specifically designed as comic relief, to drain off our laughter, or induce the sort of double-take which Ivan Butler has described as characteristic of James Whale's *The Old Dark House*: the hideous apparition everyone has been waiting for turns out to be a harmless-looking little old man; but almost as soon as this anti-climax has taken effect the camera focuses, for a moment, on that little old man's expression when he thinks himself unobserved and freezes laughter by making us realize, in a flash, that the real horror is, indeed, here. Nor have the masters of the macabre shown themselves averse to pushing their own effects towards the response of laughter through controlled experiments in parody. Paul Leni followed up the 'Ivan the Terrible' and 'Jack the Ripper' episodes of *Waxworks* with a classic comedy-thriller, *The Cat and the Canary*; James Whale succeeded his serious and dignified *Frankenstein* with the more tongue-in-cheek *Bride of Frankenstein*, where the grotesquely amusing element is most effectively concentrated in Ernest Thesiger's performance as Dr. Pretorius; and the Polanski who made *Repulsion* (1965) and *Rosemary's Baby* (1968) is the same director who also made the parodistic *Dance of the Vampires* (1967)—a parody in which large portions, particularly towards the end of the film, are played chillingly 'straight'.

With his usual virtuosity, Alfred Hitchcock has memorably demonstrated the improbable affinity of farce and terror at the opening of *Vertigo* (1958). The hero of the film, played by James Stewart, is discovered in that very position of peril at which cinema-audiences had laughed again and again in the films of Harold Lloyd: clinging perilously to the window-sill of a high building, while a city street is held in focus far below him. The terror we are made to share in that sequence is in no way diminished—is, if anything, intensified—by our recollection of such comedies as *Safety Last*. Within the terror-film, however, the bravest confrontation of the risible remains the central figure of Murnau's *Nosferatu*. The vampire's huge ears and claws, his long pointed nose, his rabbit teeth, his jerky movements would seem to be made for laughter; yet the power of the film's imagery is such that even modern audiences watch, for the most part, in awed and thrilled silence.

Comic and parodistic elements enter the various terror-film cycles with increased force as they near their end: one need think only of the sequence *Caligari–Waxworks* (with its parodistic 'Haroun al Rashid' episode)–*The Cat and the Canary*; or of the way in which the terrifying creations of the early thirties were made to encounter Abbott and Costello, the Dead End Kids, the Ritz Brothers, and Old Mother Riley; or of the fun poked at Universal and Hammer films in *Carry on Screaming* and *What a Carve Up* (1961), *Flesh for Frankenstein* (1973) and *Young Frankenstein*. In each case, however, such spoofs are accompanied and succeeded by seriously meant exercises in terror as a new cycle gets under way: the Universal cycle of the early and mid-thirties, the Val Lewton cycle in the forties, *The Exorcist*, *The Omen*, and *Burnt Offerings* in the seventies.

The cyclic development of the terror-genre which I have just sketched is accompanied by a more linear, temporally more straightforward development conditioned by the film-makers' desire to test out various degrees of explicitness and thresholds of acceptability. Early terror-films showed monsters, but had perforce to be very reticent in showing sexual activity and violence: the only blood I can remember seeing in the *Dracula* films from Universal is that which oozed from Renfield's finger when he had cut it accidentally, and such nuzzlings as were shown were very restrained indeed. The Val Lewton cycle tried even greater reticence, believing that no monster actually shown can be as frightening as the monster the audience will produce for itself if the right suggestions are implanted by what it actually sees on the screen. Films like *The Uninvited* and *The Haunting* operated on similar principles. From the emergence of the Hammer horrors on, however, films have tested their audience's shockability further and further: in the exhibition of straightforward and homosexual (especially Lesbian) libidinous activity, in the showing of blood and mutilations of all kinds, in the repulsiveness of the monsters created by make-up experts, in everything calculated to excite disgust and even nausea, from the green vomit of *The Exorcist* to the wriggling monsters emerging from a man's stomach by erupting through his skin in David Cronenberg's *Shivers* (1976). The fact that evil is so often allowed to triumph at the end of more recent films is as much connected with this change in the tolerance threshold as with the incidence of a darker, more pessimistic outlook on life. We have come a long way from the days in which Graham Greene could say, as he did in 1936, that 'terror on the screen has always, alas! to be tempered to the shorn lamb'.

Mass production, saturation advertising, and exploitation of tried and proven formulas have become ever more noticeable features of terror-film manufacture. When Hammer had shown the market for such things, companies all over the world jumped on to the bandwagon and made vampire-, monster-, and 'resurrection'-films; when *The Exorcist* made money, companies all over the world brought out films that linked demonic possession with heads spinning round 360° and graphically shown sores and vomiting. In the process, convention tended to be degraded to cliché, development to shameless imitation or unimaginative 'going one better', terror to physical repulsion, and genre to formula. In such a situation, imaginative and original film-making tends to become submerged by inferior exploitation-products; one may trust to time, however, to winnow the wheat from this mass of chaff.

As the history of the terror-film genre proceeds, directors frequently introduce allusions calculated to place their films within that genre—as when Eugene Lourie has the infant monster of *Gorgo* transported past a London cinema showing Hammer's 1959 version of *The Mummy*. At the same time the characters, themes, images, lighting-patterns, and atmospheric ambience characteristic of the genre appear more and more often in films that are not primarily terror-films or horror-movies—films by directors with a strong artistic purpose, like Buñuel, Bergman, and Fellini, and also films by entertainers like Norman Jewison, whose resurrection-scene in *Fiddler on the Roof* (1974) makes an amusing parodistic use of 'horror' conventions. Has any terror-film after *Nosferatu* ever employed a more startling shock-cut than that which occurs at the opening of David Lean's version of *Great Expectations* (1946) when Magwitch, the convict, suddenly looms up among the graves? Analysts of the Hollywood cinema in particular have vied with one another in pointing to the manifold uses distinguished directors have made of horror-movie imagery. Here is Eric Rhode on Hitchcock's *Rebecca* (1940):

Rebecca opens . . . with its camera edging forward through a dank, leafy garden to a shrouded country house called Manderley. In the past, such evocations of the eerie—of entombed emotions brought to light—had been the preserve of the horror movie. Hollywood studios now applied it to nearly every genre. (Rhode, 1976, p. 385)

Here is Pauline Kael, on resemblances between Orson Welles's *Citizen Kane* (1941) and Karl Freund's *Mad Love* (1935):

. . . there was the Gothic atmosphere, and the huge, dark rooms with lighted figures, and Peter Lorre, bald, with a spoiled-baby face, looking astoundingly like a miniature Orson Welles . . .

Not only is the large room with the fireplace at Xanadu similar to Lorre's domain as a mad doctor, with similar lighting and similar placement of figures, but Kane's appearance and make-up in some sequences might be a facsimile of Lorre's . . . (Kael, 1974, p. 64)

And here, lastly, is Richard Corliss on Wilder's *Sunset Boulevard* (1950)—a film which anticipated the 'menopausal murder story' of the 1960s:

Sunset Boulevard is the definitive Hollywood horror movie. Practically every-thing about this final Brackett—Wilder collaboration is ghoulish. The film is narrated by a corpse that is waiting to be fished out of a swimming pool. Most of it takes place in an old dark house that opens its doors only to the walking dead. The first time our doomed hero . . . enters the house, he is mistaken for an undertaker. Soon after, another corpse is buried—that of a pet monkey, in a white coffin. Outside the house is the swimming pool, at first filled only with rats, and 'the ghost of a tennis court.' The only musical sound in the house is that of the wind, wheezing through the broken pipes of a huge old organ.

The old man who occasionally plays it calls to mind Lon Chaney's *Phantom of the Opera*—that and other images of the Silent Era. The old man is Erich von Stroheim, playing himself as he plays the organ, with intimations of melancholia, absurdity and loss . . . Desmond-Swanson is Dracula, or perhaps the Count's older, forgotten sister, condemned to relive a former life, sucking blood from her victim . . . (Corliss, 1975, pp. 147–8)

Analyses such as these serve to show up vividly how the American cinema has used genre-conventions to transcend genre while most seeming to affirm it.

What we have just heard Rhode say of *Rebecca* reminds us that it is not only specific characters and specific images which migrate from the terror-film into other genres. Whole feeling-patterns re-emerge in different context as the history of the cinema proceeds along its rapid way. Take Robert Sklar's description, in *Movie-Made America*, of the claustrophobia characteristic of the Hollywood *film noir*, the psychological thriller of the 1940s:

The hallmark of the *film noir* is its sense of people trapped—trapped in webs of paranoia and fear, unable to tell guilt from innocence, true identity from false. Its villains are attractive and sympathetic, masking greed, misanthropy, malevolence. Its heroes and heroines are weak, confused, susceptible to false impressions. The environment is murky and close, the setting vaguely oppressive. In the end, evil is exposed, though often just barely, and the survival of good remains troubled and ambiguous. (Sklar, 1978, p. 253)

That evokes admirably an atmosphere which the *film noir* shares with many a studio-bound horror-movie. Nor is the influence all one way, from horror-movie to other kinds and genres. What *Citizen Kane* may have taken from *Mad Love* or *Son of Kong* it amply repaid with *The Haunting*, in which Robert Wise applied to the ghost-story the lessons he had learnt while cutting and editing *Kane* under Welles's direction. The house that turns out to be the most memorable character in the film is Kane's Xanadu transported into a New England setting.

The development traced in this chapter has, from the first, proceeded along international as well as national lines. We saw macabre German films influence Hollywood—where the most distinguished of its directors and actors found themselves at one time or another; in its turn Hollywood influenced film-making in England, France, Spain, and Italy; and just as an actor like Conrad Veidt played important roles in England and the U.S.A. as well as in his native Germany, so, at a later date, would Christopher Lee, Barbara Steele, and Boris Karloff turn up in Italian or Hispanic terror-films as readily as in British or American ones. With the growing sophistication of post-synchronizing and dubbing techniques the cinema is once again becoming as international in its appeal as it was before the coming of sound. It is obvious that audience reactions will differ to some degree from country to country, from region to region, just as expectations will vary. Popular films will therefore try to work at many levels, to appeal to many differing audiences, while attempting, at the same time, to establish conventions through which expectations and responses may be standardized. Recent British horror-movies have aimed, for instance, at an international target audience aged between eighteen and thirty; and in an interview with Edward Buscombe one of their most popular stars, Peter Cushing, has described their appeal by means of a telling comparison:

Well, you see, for eighteen years these pictures have been popular and the mass of people who go to these pictures, it's rather like those who buy their favourite brand of chocolates; they know that when they open the box they'll find the coconut creams and the truffles and that sort of thing, and they know when they see this kind of film they'll get what they're looking for. And so they're catered for by the scriptwriters. (Buscombe, 1976, p. 23)

That pinpoints admirably the paradoxically reassuring, familiar side of horror-movies, their 'culinary' or 'confectionary' qualities, as well as one kind of feed-back between audiences and movie-makers on which a profit-oriented industry has to rely.

There is no lack of socially conscious commentators who have spelt out for us what Peter Cushing's remarks imply: that the cinema is no mere technology which can be used by artists of varying kinds for their own purposes; that it is, rather, a means of production and distribution owned and to some extent controlled by entrepreneurs, 'movie moguls', tycoons, bankers, and—increasingly—vast multinational companies. Various mechanisms are, however, at work in competitive societies like our own to ensure that the cinema can never become a too easily manipulated money-spinner or a wholly reliable instrument of social control. True, the necessity of making a profit by means of an expensive commodity like the film will inevitably lead to questionable 'public relations' exercises, to the taking of easy options, to truckling (at times) to what is least attractive in the popular mood or the official 'line' of a given moment, to exploitation and over-exploitation of what has proved attractive in the past. If the public has signified its approval of a film called *Psycho* by flocking to the box-office in great numbers, we may be sure that a whole series of similar subjects will follow, under such titles as *Maniac, Paranoiac, Fanatic,* or *Hysteria.* This in turn will mean that the public's appetite becomes jaded—demanding either stronger and stronger doses of the same sensations, or something altogether new. To this demand the industry will sometimes respond with gimmicks that soon lose their attractiveness: 3-D effects, skeletons creaking across the auditorium, 'fear-flashers', 'horror-horns', cinema seats wired to give harmless tingling shocks . . . In the end, however, it will have to turn to creative film-makers, realizing that it cannot rely on 'safe' recipes, that it needs fresh ideas and forms which will appeal to many kinds of audiences, will attract new viewers, and are clearly beyond studio-hacks content to exploit well-tried formulas. 'Being entertained', the sociologist Herbert J. Gans has said, in a study of the accommodations that take place between directors, screen-writers, producers, financiers, and various kinds of audience,

means, on the one hand, that people want to satisfy various latent needs and predispositions, and on the other hand, that they want to be surprised with something new or different. Because people have these predispositions, their choices follow some analyzable pattern. But while there may be enough of a pattern to encourage the movie makers to inferences about future choices, there is never enough to provide reliable predictions. (Rosenberg and White, 1957, pp. 315–16)

The chapters that follow attempt to examine some of the 'latent needs and dispositions' to which terror-films, and terror-sequences in other films, appeal, and to show up some of the ways in which artists have been able to realize and communicate their visions within a system that seeks to market their products like boxes of chocolate, tubes of toothpaste, or cartons of washing-powder.

CHAPTER 2

The Fascination of Fear

There are more things in heaven and earth than are
dreamt of in your psychiatry, Mr. Garth.

Dracula's Daughter (1936)

THE fantastic terror-film responds to a need one can also observe
in any fairground: the need to be safely frightened, the need to test
and objectify and come to grips with one's terrors in a setting of
ultimate security, where one can tell oneself at any moment: 'It is
only a film; these are only actors; this isn't even my own dream,
I can get up and leave the darkened cinema to step into a more
familiar world at any moment.' Nevertheless, as in a fairground, the
thrills can get out of hand: the point at which the images become
too frightening, too disturbing, too obsessive will differ from person
to person, from culture to culture, and from period to period, but it
does undoubtedly exist for most of us. Three general distinctions
deserve to be kept in mind.

(i) There is all the difference in the world between a film like *The
Cabinet of Dr. Caligari*, which treats significant themes in fantastic
guise in a way that can be recognized as aesthetically shaped and
distanced, and a film like *The Exorcist*, whose underlying themes
are no less significant but which treats them with a heaping-up of
shock-effects and uses a deliberately nauseating naturalism of
presentation.

(ii) There is a difference, too, when it comes to making us face our
fears or shocking us out of greyness, between the *Dracula* films,
which have an efficient and finally victorious scientist-exorcist at
their centre—a figure played by the reassuringly guttural Edward
Van Sloan in the Hollywood versions of the 1930s and by nice,
reliable Peter Cushing in the English versions of the fifties and
sixties—and a film like *Rosemary's Baby*, where the sympathetic
friend with an understanding of the occult, played by Maurice

Evans, is soon disposed of, while the character who might seem predestined to become the equivalent of Van Sloan and Cushing, Ralph Bellamy's Dr. Sapirstein, actually co-operates with the satanic forces he should be fighting. The contrast with Murnau's Dracula film, *Nosferatu*, is particularly telling here: for Murnau also deflects emphasis away from the Van Helsing figure, but only in order to bring out more strongly the Wagneriàn ('Flying Dutchman') motif of the woman who lays down her life to bring salvation to the man she loves and, through him, to mankind. Murnau's world, dark and plague-ridden though it is, would seem in this respect as far removed from Polanski's as Tod Browning's.

(iii) While the macabre atmosphere of Dreyer's *Vampyr* is achieved through a concatenation of images that delight eye and mind while still touching the springs of terror, there is a type of horror-movie, much loved by the owners of drive-in cinemas and cinema-managers who arrange all-night showings, which uses the conventions of its genre to titillate the sadistic and voyeuristic tendencies of its audience through technicoloured exhibitions of bloody violence and stimulating nudities. Other genres have been used for similar purposes; but the cinematic tale of terror has lent itself with particular ease to such exploitations.

There is need for some vigilance here: not just because sick minds and hypersensitive nervous systems may find their sickness aggravated and their anxiety-dreams invaded by powerfully disturbing images, but also because excessive exposure to crudity and violence may desensitize the mind to a morally, as well as aesthetically, dangerous degree. The argument from catharsis has its limits.

Structuralist film-critics, adapting to their own purposes the procedures pioneered in other fields by Saussure, Lévi-Strauss, Piaget, and Jakobson, like to discuss the appeal of the terror- or fantasy-film in terms of binary oppositions. The teratology of the cinema can then be expounded in terms of such pairs as 'normal'—'abnormal', 'psychological monster'—'physiological monster', 'acting monster'—'suffering monster', 'monsters like ourselves'—'monsters as unlike us as possible', 'monsters born'—'monsters made', 'monsters through increase in size'—'monsters through decrease in size', 'life'—'death', 'good'—evil', 'beauty'—'ugliness', 'instinct'—'reason', 'anthropomorphism'—'bestialization', 'nature' —'science', 'human'—'mechanical', and so on. By playing varia- tions on these dualities, and combining them with such more fundamental structuralist notions as 'signifier'—'signified', and '*langue*'—'*parole*', an intricate taxonomy results which can be studied at its most tidy in Gérard Lenne's *Le Cinéma fantastique et ses mythes*. My own descriptions and classifications of the appeal the terror-film makes to its various audiences will not fall into such convenient relational patterns; I hope, however, that they will be no less useful, and no less true, for that.

The fantasy terror-film, as James Whale's remark about 'ritual' (see above, p. 22) may have served to remind us, has always shown itself an apt receptacle for what T. E. Hulme called 'spilt religion'. God himself suddenly speaks over the radio (or does he?) in William Wellman's disconcerting *The Next Voice You Hear* (1950). The Devil is ubiquitous, whether embodied by John Gottowt and Werner Krauss in successive versions of *The Student of Prague* and by Adolphe Menjou in *The Sorrows of Satan* (1926), or more recently by Burgess Meredith in *Torture Garden* (1967) and by Ralph Richardson in *Tales from the Crypt* (1972). An Immaculate Concep- tion figures in *Village of the Damned* (1960), where we can see the women of an English village fall asleep for twenty-four hours and then find themselves pregnant by some mysterious force from outer space. The Resurrection is re-enacted in vampire-movies; images of the Last Judgement (as envisaged by Stanley Spencer, for instance, in his Cookham series) are deliberately recalled in *The Mask of the Demon* (1960) and *The Plague of the Zombies* (1965). Science-fiction films have shown themselves particularly prone to religious charges of various sorts: Steven Spielberg's *Close Encounters of the Third Kind* systematically transfers theological imagery—annunciation, the calling of prophets, epiphanies, glorious descents from and ascents to heaven—to an optimistic flying-saucer story of first contact with beings from another planet. More characteristically we find, in terror-films proper, that the tremendous and fascinating mystery which once characterized revelations of the divine may adhere to unhallowed scientists and their creations. The demons of medieval Christianity—and earlier demons still—may be summoned up for the benefit, if that is the word, of people who, for the most part, lack the framework of faith within which such apparitions were once accommodated. In

Jacques Tourneur's *Night of the Demon* a monster appears whose grim visage has been inspired by a woodcut found in a seventeenth-century demonology. Age-old fears that alien forces may enter and take over our very bodies help to explain the undoubtedly disturbing effect which Friedkin's *The Exorcist* had on a number of susceptible viewers—including my teenage daughter, who had the screaming heebie-jeebies for weeks after seeing that film, but who seems now to have come to terms with the terrors it articulated for her. It is hardly surprising that well-brought-up girls should be affected by the spectacle of demons 'possessing' someone like themselves and making her urinate on the carpet, vomit over priests in sacred vestments, utter obscenities and blasphemies, waggle a disturbingly phallic tongue, and masturbate with a crucifix. Is that sort of spectacle really a rite of passage we want our youngsters to pass through? Movies like *The Omen* and *The Sentinel* (1977) cater for the same interest in Satanism, witchcraft, and possession of various kinds: they even managed to shoulder out for a time those most unspiritual body-obsessed of demons, the vampires who flashed their fangs across the world's screens under such names as Dracula, Carmilla Karnstein, Meinster, Yorga, and Barnabas Collins. The 'disaster' and 'atomic accident' movies of recent years can also boast theological prefigurations, as the term 'Armageddon-movies' serves to suggest. Charles Derry has demonstrated this imaginatively and drastically in his book *Dark Dreams*:

There seems to be a strong relationship between these films and many of the stories in the Bible; for instance, the many plagues sent out to express the wrath of God, or even more dramatically the most archetypal story in the Bible: the flood. *Take God away from the flood, and you have a true horror-of-Armageddon movie:* Suddenly, out of the sky, it begins to rain. What was previously considered a normal aspect of nature turns abnormal when the rain starts acting unlike rain and refuses to stop. The rain attacks and kills everyone; only Noah and his family manage to survive the existential test by working hard to hold tightly onto their floating house. Ultimately, a rainbow appears as congratulations and in promise that the existential horror has come to an end. The pattern is exactly that of *The Birds*, only Hitchcock *refuses us the satisfaction of the horror-releasing rainbow.* (Derry, 1977, p. 50) [My italics]

Those who take an interest in terror-films are uniquely well qualified to test for themselves Novalis's aphorism: 'Where there are no gods, demons will hold sway.'

Many of the terror-tales which film-makers have brought to their public play on fears that our privacy may be invaded by violent men, as happens in *Dracula* and, outside the horror-movie proper, in films like *Lady in a Cage* (1964), *Wait until Dark* (1967), and *In Cold Blood* (1967); or that someone may single us out as his quarry, may choose to hunt us down as animals are hunted. The archetype of such films, of which there have been many, is that made by Cooper and Schoedsack in 1932 under the title *The Most Dangerous Game* or *The Hounds of Zaroff*—a work whose extraordinary Sadean atmosphere is only feebly suggested by celebrated lines like 'First the hunt, then the revels!' or 'Kill, then love! When you have known that, you have known everything.' Some of the themes of *The Hounds of Zaroff* were taken up again in *The Island of Lost Souls*, based on H. G. Wells's *The Island of Dr. Moreau* and directed by Erle C. Kenton. Here the 'human quarry' motif was wedded to that of the 'unholy scientist'—a scientist, in this case, who compounds Frankenstein's blasphemy by trying to use the flesh of *animals* to create men. That, in its turn, leads over to one of the greatest of the fears which the terror-film, and the science-fiction film, articulate for us and help us to face: fear that other creatures may usurp the place of man or threaten to destroy what we think of as human civilization. Visitors from other planets may invade our world and take over our very bodies, as they do by means of the pods of *The Invasion of the Body Snatchers*; creatures of the animal world which we tread underfoot or exploit for our benefit may be able to rise against us as the result of some unexpected mutations (as in Gordon Douglas's *Them*, and Franklin Shaffner's *Planet of the Apes*, 1968) or unexpected survival from prehistoric days (as in *Godzilla*). In Hitchcock's *The Birds* there is no visible mutation, nor any invasion by prehistoric survivals: suddenly out of a clear sky the gull attacks, and other familiar species of feathered friends mass for their lethal swoops, besieging and ultimately invading the house rapidly transformed into a fortress. Like Fritz Lang, Hitchcock has a masterly way of suggesting the menace that lies hidden in the familiar, the ease with which what seems so comfortable and safe can become threatening and dangerous. In the work of other film-makers fear of the elements which no human ingenuity can ever wholly domesticate into our service may coalesce into fantastic creations like the gill-man in Jack Arnold's *The Creature from the Black Lagoon* or into what seems the more verisimilitudinous shape of the ingenious and lethal shark who starred in Steven Spielberg's *Jaws* (1975). Spielberg's shark is not, in fact, much less fantastic than Arnold's gill-man: no real shark could swallow men in two bites as we see this one doing! Science-fiction films make a great deal of play with 'dangers' of this kind; but their audience is not always as unequivocally on the side of the (usually colourless) humans as it is in Christian Nyby's and Howard Hawks's *The Thing from Another World*. What was still ambivalent in the 1933 version of *King Kong*, where our sympathies were with Carl Denham and his crew as well as with the giant ape, has become an almost unquestioning siding with the non-human visitor or invader, effectively played by a pop idol of the day, in Nicolas Roeg's *The Man Who Fell to Earth*.

Fantasy terror-films also appeal to fears that man's own animal nature or 'lower' instincts may suddenly and disastrously break out—a threat which is felt in proportion to the degree of repression to which such instincts are subjected in a given society. The most obvious, but by no means the only, example of this is that favourite subject of film-makers all over the world: *Dr. Jekyll and Mr. Hyde*. The plot of the *Jekyll and Hyde* films derives, of course, from Robert Louis Stevenson; but the movies invented their own variation by adapting the werewolf legend, first in *The Werewolf of London* (1934) and then in a series of works featuring Lon Chaney Junior as *The Wolf Man* (1941–9). In Chaney's Larry Talbot, it has been well said, hero and villain coalesce: as wolf, Talbot is a creature of blind destructive urges which society must hunt down and kill; as man, he suffers the tortures of the damned because he knows the evil but cannot control it. Unfortunately, Lon Chaney Junior was a dull and inexpressive actor—the best werewolf the screen has ever seen is surely that played by Oliver Reed in Terence Fisher's *Curse of the Werewolf* (1961).

Fears of man's instinctual nature play a thematically dominant part in Jack Arnold's complex and beautiful fantasy-film *The Creature from the Black Lagoon*. F. D. McConnell has given, in *The Spoken Seen*, what is by far the best account of that underrated work. He calls it a 'demonic pastoral'; relates it to legends of dragons and dragon-slayers in which 'we recognize the ultimate stakes to be the recreation of the world through control of the anti-human, instinctual chaos which the dragon incarnates and which the hero must slay in himself before meeting his apocalyptic adversary'; and shows how the plot of the film yields insights into what he calls 'the tragedy of human denial'. David, the human hero of the tale,

fights only when provoked by the insidious, the anarchic, the asocial. And his fight, although it may seem an entry into maturity, is in reality a struggle to *maintain* the innocence, the happy consciousness of a man who knows his place in the system and comfortably functions therein;

but the sexuality so vividly suggested in the famous underwater scene that shows the Creature swimming beneath the heroine in the warm waters of the lagoon is something *within* the human beings as well as outside them. The Creature, McConnell rightly insists, is neither alien invader nor mutant.

He is, as one of the scientists in the film observes, 'an evolutionary dead end', a man-fish who has, simply and absurdly, survived the eons since his race was spawned. He survives . . . because he is . . . [in] an out-of-the-way South American inlet where time has stood still . . . He is the result of no cause, neither accident nor devilish science nor the supernatural: he simply *is*, primal and eldest, and the outrage he generates is the curse only of those unlucky enough to discover his existence . . . The action of the film is the story of what happens to those who seek out and seek to capture the primal secrets which have been there all along in the innocence and bland-ness of their unharassed primacy.

McConnell goes on to relate Jack Arnold's film of 1954 to two later and better-known films.

The sexual-mythic point of *The Creature* is that to possess Kay is also, neces-sarily, to face and overcome the demonic threat of the monster. But in both *Rosemary's Baby* and *The Exorcist* (which I am tempted to call horror films of the Watergate era) the point of the horror is that the monster has already *achieved* sexual possession of the maiden whose winning is the quest of the film . . . The worst has already happened, . . . the maiden has been possessed, . . . the devil is in the driver's seat of this world and needs to be purged. How many other horror films, are named, [as *The Exorcist* is], not for their destructive monster, but for their distinctive monster-slayer? (McConnell, 1975, pp. 138, 144–6)

The historical and social implications of a film like *The Creature from the Black Lagoon* and its two sequels should be obvious to all who have read their D. H. Lawrence; McConnell speaks suggestively of 'the central evasion of energy, the central fear of the life-force itself, which underlay the witch-hunts and the HUAC purges'. This comes out particularly clearly in the sombre final part of the

'Creature' trilogy, *The Creature Walks Among Us* (1956, directed by John Sherwood), which shows 'civilized' men operating on the gill-man, dressing him up in American clothes, and reducing him to a caged, powerless freak. The horror/science-fiction framework enables the film to broach without offence momentous themes and sensitive issues of the late fifties: deculturization, torture, genocide, exploitation . . .

Fears about the rebellion of man's lower, instinctual nature, or about the possibility of failing to integrate it adequately into modern, 'civilized' living, are only part of a larger series of fears about human identity, about the 'wholeness' of the human personality. It is not surprising, therefore, that the film soon took over a motif by which German Romantic literature had sought, in the early nineteenth century, to express identity-fears and ego-dissociation: the motif of the 'double' or *Doppelgänger* which has an obvious relation to the whole film-experience and has therefore haunted the screen from the various versions of *The Student of Prague* (1913, 1926, 1935) to Tarkovsky's *Solaris*. Where but in a film could a mirror-image be visibly detached and transported, and a man be seen to confront an exact replica of himself? *The Picture of Dorian Gray*, made into an elegant American movie in 1945, is clearly an amalgam of *Doppelgänger* and Jekyll-and-Hyde motifs; an amalgam which led to the interesting variant in Terence Fisher's otherwise lack-lustre version of Stevenson's story under the title *The Two Faces of Dr. Jekyll* (1960), in which Hyde confronts us, not as the simian monster familiar from Fredric March's and Spencer Tracy's performances, or as the spider created by John Barrymore, but as a handsome and superficially attractive young man. In one egregious—though potentially promising—version (Roy Ward Baker's *Dr. Jekyll and Sister Hyde*, 1971) he even turns into a nubile young woman, merging the 'double' motif with that of the destructive siren or Lorelei.

Many of the beings at the centre of terror-films unite in unhappy synthesis divided and distinguished worlds. They may partake at once of the nature of men and that of beasts; they may belong to the dead yet move among the living; they may be sensitive, gifted men, yet feel possessed by demons of destruction. Leslie Banks, one side of his handsome face twisted by an old war wound, presented his two different profiles in *The Hounds of Zaroff* as an outer indication of such inner duality. The *Doppelgänger* theme is thus as central to the terror-film as the theme of sexual alienation; but more than that, the spectral double has a meaning for the cinema as a whole. The double, Leo Braudy has well said, means more to the cinema than just a vivid, truly cinematic way of indicating conflicts between physical and social self, civilized and atavistic nature, ego and id. It indicates, in addition, 'something of the nature of film form and the role of the actor within that form'; it expresses 'something of the inner aesthetic of films, the double exposure, the fleeting insubstantiality of the image, its potential lack of authority even at the moment of greatest assertion'. The use of the *Doppel-gänger* image thus illustrates what Braudy and many other cinema-goers feel to be one of the most fascinating aspects of cinematic art: '[the] way in which film can simultaneously embody some theme that is deeply rooted in the emotions of its audience and at the same time deliver as it were a disquisition on its own artistic nature' (Braudy, *The World in a Frame. What We See in Films*, 1977, pp. 226–35).

The Picture of Dorian Gray offers film-makers a chance to intro-duce one of their favourite shock-sequences—a sequence it shares with other fantasy-films derived from minor works of literature such as *She* (1935, 1965), *Lost Horizon* (1937), or *The Man in Half Moon Street* (1944), effectively remade by Terence Fisher in 1959 under the title *The Man Who Could Cheat Death*. This sequence exhibits the nemesis overtaking a man or woman who has artificially prolonged his or her youth: suddenly, in a moment, we see the marks of extreme old age and disease overtake this character. An episode of Roger Corman's *Tales of Terror* (1962) based on Poe's 'The Facts in the Case of M. Valdemar' even shows us a man whose death has been arrested by hypnosis grotesquely melting away in sudden syrup-like decomposition. The appeal of such sequences is complex: it is made up of our delight in sudden shocks experienced in the safety of our cinema-seat; our desire to look on, ourselves unseen, as others face extreme situations; our curiosity about the possible range of science and pseudo-science; our craving¹ for miraculous power over the great processes of life and death; and our satisfaction at seeing those who have, by means of such power, escaped what we know to be our common lot, suddenly snatched back from the scene of their triumph and made to share our own inevitable destiny.

In the process of yielding these satisfactions, *The Picture of*

Dorian Gray also introduces into the terror-film a motif that had been no less ubiquitous in the literary tale of terror: the uncanny portrait. The most striking cinematic embodiment of this theme is undoubtedly the series of 'waxworks' movies inaugurated by Maurice Tourneur in 1920 (*While Paris Sleeps*, released in 1923) and by Paul Leni in 1924. These combined characteristically ambivalent attitudes to art with inversions of the Pygmalion motif, age-old fears about the 'magic' potentials of duplicating the human form, and the secret shudders of necrophilia. Dorian Gray's portrait is painted, of course, not sculptured or moulded; and such painted portraits have featured, with particular prominence, in Roger Corman's adaptations from Poe and Lovecraft. In *The Haunted Palace* (1963) this motif allies itself, as so often elsewhere, with that of 'possession'—we are shown how the portrait of an ancestor exerts a hypnotic influence on Charles Dexter Ward and forces him to become the instrument of that ancestor's posthumous vengeance. In the end the portrait seems to take him over altogether, marrying ancient fears of the dead 'possessing' the living with more modern fears on which the terror-film constantly plays: fears about the degree to which men can be manipulated, individually or collectively, by their fellow-men. The films about hypnotists and other controllers, which have played so large a part in world-cinema since early versions of *Trilby*, *The Cabinet of Dr. Caligari*, and Lang's *Mabuse* films pioneered them, have shown unscrupulous or vengeful men gaining control—usually through paranormal powers—of their fellow-men's mind and will, making them perform criminal or immoral or degrading acts. *The Cabinet of Dr. Caligari* remains the supreme example; but it is worth remembering that the inner story of this film shows the sleep-walker Cesare finding a vestige of resistance when, sent out to kill a sleeping girl whose father and lover had offended his master, he refrains from using his dagger and abducts the girl instead—an action that appears, in the inner story, to cost him his life. This aspect of the work is often ignored by commentators who have used insufficient imagination in drawing the line 'from Caligari to Hitler' suggested by the very title of Siegfried Kracauer's famous book.

A glance at the history of the word 'vampire' will demonstrate immediately that it is not only power-mad *men* who act as a source of fear, and of course fascination, in terror-films. Originally denoting some supernatural being, one of the 'undead', who sucked the blood of the living to sustain its own existence, the term came to be used, metaphorically, of any person or institution that preyed on others. This metaphorical meaning narrowed, in the early days of the cinema, to denote a woman who set out to use her sexual charms in order to attract, and often to ruin, men. Shortened to 'vamp', the appelation could even take on an affectionate tinge; but the threat of the original meaning remained alive even in this monosyllabic contraction. That threat the terror-film has frequently strengthened and foregrounded by showing the vamp as a vampire—by giving back to the image of the sexually alluring and destructive female the supernatural dimension it had had in so many folk-tales and legends. The prototype of these vampiric vamps is the central protagonist of Robert Wiene's *Genuine* (1920), a beautiful woman brought up to drink blood; but it was left to the Japanese actress Machiko Kyo, playing the ghost-princess in Mizoguchi's *Ugetsu Monogatari*, to give the cinema its definitive interpretation of the Lamia legend. Not the least disturbing feature of this vamp/vampire constellation, as of all vampire and many other monster films, is the disorientation which results from finding aggression and destruction taking on forms that we associate with love. Where the male vampire appears, in the terror-film, akin to bat and wolf, the female vampire, the vamp, appears akin to serpent and cat. Cat-women, leopard-women, and such abound in American movies, from *Tiger Woman* in 1917 to *The Island of Lost Souls* in 1932 or *Cat People* in 1942, and the history of the Hollywood film is riddled with such titles as *Snake Woman* and *Cobra Woman*. Jacqueline Pearce, in John Gilling's *The Reptile* (1966), gives the snake-woman her most pathetic and appealing form. The mythological and religious resonances of such imputed kinship are obvious—but it is worth stressing, once again, that terror-films owe a good deal of their life and their force to resonances of this kind, felt by audiences who are, for the most part, unconscious of them.

   The Cabinet of Dr. Caligari, whose central importance for our theme this book has constant cause to suggest, plays on two further significant fears: the fear that strangers may invade our secure world and destroy us (in the inner story Caligari and his murdering somnambulist are itinerant showmen who move into the town from outside); and the related fear that the social underdog may rise against the establishment (as Caligari avenges himself on the town clerk who had treated him so disdainfully). But here again one must not over-simplify. Take the use which is made of the last-named motif in de Palma's *Carrie*, a film that marries the fears of paranormal powers played on by *The Exorcist* with those aroused by such disaster and panic movies as *The Towering Inferno* (1976), whose success at the box-office set all the studios that could possibly afford it vying with one another in the production of bigger and better cataclysms. As Griffith already knew so well when he made the Babylonian episode of *Intolerance* in 1916, the public takes an immense delight in seeing expensive sets come tumbling down. In *Carrie*, de Palma and his script-writers manipulate us into sympathy with the eponymous heroine rather than her victims, making part of us rejoice at the telekinetic or psychokinetic powers that enable Carrie to wreak such vengeance on her persecutors even though the innocent suffer along with the guilty. The crucifixion of Carrie's mother by flying knives is made especially powerful by the explicit use of nonconformist religion in the film; and here as in his later *The Fury* (1978) de Palma skilfully exploits that perverse delight in destruction which frequently has social roots and which links *Carrie*, alas, with such horrors as *The Texas Chain Saw Massacre*. Social hostilities of all kinds play an important part in movies that appeal to their audiences' delight in being terrified—in Steven Spielberg's *Duel* (1971) we even find a murderous truck, the face of whose driver is deliberately concealed from us throughout the film, assuming a distinctly proletarian personality as it pursues, and tries to destroy, an automobile that belongs no less obviously to the affluent middle class. *Carrie*, *The Fury*, and *Duel* all play variations on what we have learnt to call the 'Straw Dogs' syndrome: the baiting, injuring, and exploiting of the vulnerable and innocent, who then turn on their tormentors to wreak a terrible, violent vengeance.

The social roots of the delight in destruction may be seen particularly clearly in Merian Cooper's and Ernest B. Schoedsack's *King Kong* of 1933. *King Kong* is the greatest of the Depression-movies; it shows the giant ape, a once free spirit trapped in the modern city, smashing his destructive way through the very same New York streets which the little actress played by Fay Wray had walked, tired, hungry, and out of work, in the opening sequences. At the same time *King Kong* also exhibits clearly the way in which some of the greatest terror-films draw attention to their own nature as films (the first words we hear spoken are 'Is this the motion-picture ship?', and Fay Wray's Ann Darrow is required to mime terror in front of a camera before she ever encounters Kong) as well as the way in which mythical and fairy-tale material enters such films and lends them a subterranean, archetypal power. The famous closing lines of *King Kong* (see below, p. 179) link that work explicitly with the legend of Beauty and the Beast which Jean Cocteau was later to utilize more directly in another of the fantasy-classics of the cinema. It should not be thought that the resonance of *King Kong* ended with the Depression: Marco Ferreri's *Ciao Maschio* showed in 1978 that the sight of the dead Kong against the Manhattan skyline could have a symbolic impact whose power belied the jokey title *Bye Bye Monkey* under which Ferreri's tribute to Kong was exhibited. John Guillermin's remake of *King Kong* (1976) added technical sophistication but little else of any value— it also served to suggest, however, that the story of the giant ape transferred to the jungle of cities is still felt to be relevant to our lives and times.

The terrors that films articulate for us may be those of our every-day existence: many a man will have recognized his own marriage-problems, in fantastically heightened form, in *The Incredible Shrinking Man*, many a woman will have recognized her marriage-problems in *I Married a Monster from Outer Space* (1958), many an adolescent will have experienced a shock of recognition when seeing *Franken-stein* or *The Wolf Man*, and the adoption of a child's perspective in such works as *The Night of the Hunter* speaks volumes about the kind of truth its fantasies embody.

If the terror-movie is thus connected with our social concerns, it also, paradoxically, helps us to cope with our ordinary life by jolting us out of it, transporting us into problems which are clearly not our own and which are frequently shown, in the context of the film, to be solvable in ways that argue well for the solution of our own less dramatic troubles. This last feature, however, is becoming increasingly rare: the horror-movie of the seventies tends to be open-ended, in the way Polanski's *Dance of the Vampires* had pioneered in 1967; 'that night', the narrator had told us at the end of that influential though critically underrated film, 'fleeing from Transylvania, Professor Abronsius never guessed he was carrying away with him the very evil he had wished destroyed. Thanks to him, this evil would at last be able to spread across the world.' In the seventies the image of the child that is about to carry on the evil work whose adult perpetrators have perished became the cliché-ending of terror-films.

How deeply grounded all this was in the experience of the seventies may be gauged from Werner Herzog's remake of Murnau's *Nosferatu*. For almost the whole length of the film, Herzog faithfully follows Murnau's scenario, right up to the moment when Lucy lures the vampire-count to her bed and detains him beyond the sunrise that is bound to kill him. The Wagnerian echoes of this sacrifice are even underlined by Herzog's use of music from *Rhinegold* in an earlier sequence. But then comes a sharp deviation. The dead Nosferatu does not fade away, as in Murnau's film; his body remains solidly present, next to the dead Lucy, to be staked by Van Helsing in the approved way. The authorities, decimated by the plague until only a feeble old man remains as their executing officer, thereupon arrest Van Helsing for the 'murder' of the staked vampire. He allows himself to be led away—a feeble, senile scientist without real insight and therefore without the ability to carry through the work Lucy had begun. When he is gone, Jonathan Harker, now revealed as a fanged and red-eyed Nosferatu, has a maid sweep away the crumbs of a consecrated wafer with which Lucy had confined him to his chair, and rides off into the distance, to the sound of Gounod's *Sanctus*, joining Renfield in bringing the curse of vampirism to the rest of the earth.

The concluding words of Polanski's *Dance of the Vampires* point not only onwards in time but also outwards into our own world: and there can be no doubt that cinematic tales of terror frequently leave us with a feeling that the events we have seen on the screen may be linked—symbolically, or in ways which we do not fully understand—with more 'real' horrors, with inhumanities that we know men to be practising against their fellow-men at any hour of the night or day, with fears of more immediate dangers than those suggested in the fantastic film. It is perhaps not without significance that of the two masters of macabre acting who combined their talents in *Caligari* Werner Krauss stayed in Germany during the Second World War and played a whole congregation of uncanny Jews in Veit Harlan's notorious *Jew Süss* (1940), while Conrad Veidt went to Hollywood where the parts he was given included the sinister Nazis whom he played so well in *Escape* (1940), *All Through the Night* (1942), and—above all—*Casablanca* (also 1942). In real life, of course, as these very performances serve to show, it was Werner Krauss who sold himself to the Nazis and Conrad Veidt who shared the lot of German Jews that managed to escape the holocaust. Some of the most effective screen performances may thus be seen as projections of inner fears and loathings, or of usually invisible aspects of their personality by the actors, as well as the writers and directors, of a given film. The gentleness and good humour which Boris Karloff showed to all who ever had contact with him in real life is not unrelated to his projections of destructive monsters and fanatical scientists—projections which never lost entirely the sympathy of the audience that watched them unfold. Like Professor Moebius in *Forbidden Planet* (1956), such actors project 'monsters from the Id'; or if we prefer Jungian terms we may say that what they are projecting in such performances is their 'Shadow'.

As the very mention of Boris Karloff's name may serve to remind us, two of the fears which the cinematic tale of terror has exploited from the first have been that of the consequences of science on the one hand and the unhallowed aspirations of sorcerers and alchemists on the other. What happens, we are constantly being asked, when unregenerate man arrogates to himself the prerogatives traditionally reserved for God—either as creator of life, producing handsome, almost superhuman beings like the 'homunculus' who gave his name to Otto Rippert's serial of 1916, as well as poor inarticulate creatures like Karloff's monster, or as dispenser of death? What happens when machines we have made outstrip our powers of control, as in *2001: A Space Odyssey*, or are invaded—as in *Forbidden Planet* and *Solaris*—by forces of our subconscious of whose very existence we were unaware? *The Golem*, the *Frankenstein* films, and *Westworld* (1973), are influential examples from three different periods of film-making which show an increasing complexity of technology linked to a basically similar but more and more intractable problem of control. Here again it will not do to generalize too soon. We must keep ourselves aware of the different emotional charges with which technological marvels are presented: against the mutinous HAL 9000 in *2001* and the berserk computer in *The Demon Seed* we must hold the cuddly Robbie of *Forbidden Planet* and lovable R2D2 of *Star Wars*. Robbie and R2D2 clearly obey Isaac Asimov's three 'laws' of Robotics:

1. A robot may not injure a human being, or, through inaction, allow a human being to come to harm.

2. A robot must obey the orders given it by human beings except where such orders would conflict with the first law.

3. A robot must protect its own existence as long as such protection does not conflict with the first or second laws.

The script-writer of *2001*, Arthur C. Clarke, has explained his own distinguished and distinctive position in this history in an essay he contributed to Brian Ash's *Visual Encyclopedia of Science Fiction*.

The earliest thinking machines were almost invariably Frankenstein monsters, out to destroy their creators, and usually succeeding; [J. W.] Campbell was one of the first writers to make them not only benevolent but even noble. Isaac Asimov took matters further with his 'Three Laws of Robotics' . . . Some simple-minded readers have assumed that these laws are indeed *Laws*, like those of Nature—and not merely rules, akin to 'Please drive on the left (or right)'. I have had the First Law thrown in my teeth as a result of HAL 9000's mutiny; to which I have replied that so far, alas, the world's most sophisticated robots have been designed for the express purpose of killing people . . . (Ash, 1977, p. 181)

The scientist-figures presented to us in terror-films are, as would be expected, more complex than their androids, robots, cyborgs, computers, death-rays, and other inventions. They may be men of good will, as in *Solaris*; or ambivalent characters, so intent on pushing back the frontiers of science that they lose sight, at least for a time, of their responsibilities as citizens and human beings, as in *Frankenstein*. They may be using their scientific knowledge and skill to achieve personal ends, motivated by greed as in *Black Friday* (1940), by the urge for revenge as in *The Invisible Ray* (1936—where, as in many other films of this kind, representatives of 'black' and 'white' science confront one another), or by an *amour fou* as in *Mad Love*. They may be at the mercy of subconscious forces in themselves, as in *Forbidden Planet*; or they may be avid for personal power as the narrator of *The Cabinet of Dr. Caligari* would have us believe the director of the mental home to be. They may be conscienceless servants of whatever political authority employs them, like Rotwang in *Metropolis*, or compassionate men who use their skill to relieve the agonies of the poor, like Dr. Jekyll in

Mamoulian's film of 1932. Within the kindly Jekyll, however, lurks the evil Hyde who is liberated by the same scientific genius which makes Jekyll such a welcome presence in the poor-ward. He is thus akin to the mad doctors that infest terror-films with titles like *Horror Hospital*, appealing to fears of surgery that most of us know only too well. Pierre Brasseur's Dr. Genessier, in *Eyes Without a Face*, is probably the most memorable of these. In more recent years the menacing scientist has often appeared in the sphere of atomic and rocket research, of course; in Stanley Kubrick's *Dr. Strangelove; or How I Learned to Stop Worrying and Love the Bomb* (1963), Peter Sellers's impressive assumption of the name part deliberately recalled Rudolf Klein-Rogge's performance as Rotwang in Lang's questionable projection of the terrors of a technological future. The grotesques Kubrick shows in charge of the scientific wonders which can blow the whole world to pieces are significantly supplemented in Joseph Losey's *The Damned*, made two years before: the bureaucrat played by Alexander Knox, who seems so gentle and reasonable but who directs his project of raising radio-active children (children that are to take over the world after the inevitable all-out atomic war) with inhuman deliberation. James Leahy has said of him, with some justice, that he shows us what might happen if a general will to destruction assumed political power while maintaining a typically British appearance of reasonable respectability.

Bureaucracy and science, which enter a deadly alliance in Losey's *The Damned*, are elsewhere presented as opposing forces. Andrew Tudor has drawn a memorable line from the 'search-it-out-and-destroy-it' terror-film of the *Dracula* type, with its aristocratic villain and bourgeois saviours, via the *Frankenstein* type, with its culpable or 'mad' scientist, to the type represented by *The Quatermass Experiment* of 1955, whose central protagonist is portrayed as an admirably hard-hitting, incorruptible, terse, anti-bureaucratic superman before whom red tape falls apart. The film-makers clearly ask us to respect this 'individual scientist who stood out against the bureaucratic indecisiveness which placed the world in peril'. 'The fact', Tudor comments, drily, 'that he may have caused the peril in the first place is now presented as a justifiable risk for advancing knowledge' (*Image and Influence*, 1974, p. 210).

The alliance of science and bureaucracy inspires fear—but so, on occasions, may the creation and appreciation of art. Laird Cregar, Vincent Price, and Max von Sydow have more than once played men in whom love and understanding of music and the arts coexisted with murderous impulses. 'The heavy who loves beauty', Vincent Price once said, 'makes the most terrifying villain.' Price should know: the love and understanding of the visual arts which he has shown in his private life is well known to most of his many admirers, and enters as a factor into our appreciation of his performances in macabre films.

As might be expected, witchcraft is a frequent theme in the terror-film—one need think only of such representative examples as *I Walked with a Zombie*, *Rosemary's Baby*, and *The Shout*. What all these have in common is the introduction of witchcraft into modern times and modern lives. When the terror-film deals, as it does in Dreyer's *Day of Wrath* (1943) and Michael Reeves's *Witchfinder General* (1968), with an earlier age, an age in which belief in witches was widespread and officially sanctioned, then the real horrors presented on the screen tend to be not the wretched creatures accused of practising witchcraft, but those who persecute and torture them, who belong to a malevolent or misled establishment. The age of the Inquisition, and the age of witch-hunts in the old world as well as the new, has proved a favourite terrain for the makers of terror-films, who have often presented their material in such a way that audiences could draw parallels with abominations in their own time. Such films tend to leave open, however, as Dreyer certainly does, questions about the *reality* of witchcraft, about the possibility and actuality of those superhuman, paranormal powers which the inquisitors and the persecutors fear.

In the foregoing discussion we have had, occasionally, to glance at some of the complexities which help to determine our attitude to the characters terror-films place at their centre—help to determine, among other things, the kind of empathy we feel, how far we can associate ourselves with the aspirations and actions of such characters. Here we come up against one of the most intricate and interesting problems, one which has engaged many commentators on the cinema. We have to begin by saying that after childhood and outside the mentally ill there will never be complete *identification* with the characters on the screen. Even the least sophisticated adult will always be to some degree conscious that he is not *in* the space in which the action takes place, but is watching from the outside. Nevertheless the cinema, with its darkened auditorium, its viewing angle (usually slightly from below), its large screen (especially the enveloping curved screen of Cinerama), its ability to bring everything into what seems like closest proximity, its capability of making the camera to some extent our eyes, offers its patrons unique chances to regard what is happening on the screen as their own dream, and hence unique chances to associate themselves with the characters on the screen by means of identification and projection. By making the camera take the place of the spectator's eye, and showing the world now from Jonathan Harker's point of view, now from Van Helsing's, now from Dracula's, now from an independent observer's, the film-director annihilates the distance that is created by the invarying point of view we have in the theatre, involves him almost physically with the characters on the screen. Strangely enough, however, what would seem the most radical identification device—the 'first-person' or 'subjective' camera, used throughout Robert Montgomery's *The Lady in the Lake* (1947)—turns out to be unexpectedly alienating. It renders the central protagonist invisible (except when he looks at himself in the mirror) much more thoroughly than the bandages of *The Invisible Man*, and distracts attention away from him on to the surfaces the camera lights up.

Directors and cameramen have found many other, more effective means of guiding their audiences' response. Discussing the first version of *King Kong* in his book *Film—Real to Reel*, David Coynik has pointed to one of the simplest of these devices:

In *King Kong*, directed by Ernest Schoedsack in 1933, we look up to Kong, who is in power for the entire film. But at the ending, Kong stands upon the pinnacle of the Empire State Building. Misunderstood and mistreated for the entire film, Kong begins to get our sympathy. Airplanes strafe him, wounding Kong seriously. The camera angle changes. Now we look down at Kong; the change in camera angle shifts our feelings for him. The camera angle is unrealistic, one of the first unrealistic camera techniques in the film. What do you stand on to look down at a huge ape when he's standing on the pinnacle of the highest building in the world? Schoedsack, however, felt the high-angle-shot was important to draw out our sympathy for King Kong. (Coynik, 1976, p. 17)

Despite all his means of subtle or less subtle control, a director will usually leave open various possibilities of association or self-alignment. To go back to our key example of James Whale's

Frankenstein: we may align ourselves with the ordinary folk, like the father and his little girl, whose lives are menaced and disrupted by the activities of Frankenstein and his monster, and we may therefore sympathize with their desire to hunt the monster down and get rid of it as expeditiously as possible; we may align ourselves with Frankenstein himself and experience the power as well as the nemesis of usurping the place of a creator-god; or we may align ourselves, as children so readily do, with Karloff's pathetic monster, constantly thwarted in his aspirations to humanity and normal development—and the degree to which we do any or all these things in the course of the film will inevitably govern our total response. One can never stress enough that such responses cannot be wholly controlled even by the most gifted director: the viewer is not passive, he collaborates, brings emotional affinities or antipathies to the film, identifies, distances, projects, and—on occasions and in varying ways—imitates what the film-makers choose to show him.

Films that seek to play on our delight in being terrified often lure us into a sly complicity with 'evil' or 'mad' characters. Hitchcock especially has shown himself a master at creating this kind of half-unwilling audience-involvement with figures like Uncle Charlie in *Shadow of a Doubt* (1943) and Bruno Anthony in *Strangers on a Train* (1951). In more fantastic films than Hitchcock's thrillers we feel again and again the attraction of a Frankenstein or a Dracula, and thus come to know a little more about ourselves. There is considerable complexity, too, in our alignment with a creature like Frankenstein's monster, of whom Raymond Durgnat has said, in *Films and Feelings*: 'The Frankenstein Monster is *brutal* but *pathetic*; he's a *creature* who masters his *creator*; he is brute *material* capable of a lofty *idealism* that turning *sour* makes him a *devil*—but a *sympathetic* one.' That, of course, describes Mary Shelley's monster more accurately than James Whale's—the film monster, with its criminal brain, would hardly be capable of 'lofty idealism'; but it does suggest something of the tensions, the feeling of paradox, we are meant to experience when the creature hunted down as a murderous brute is shown to us, in *The Bride of Frankenstein*, in the unmistakable attitude of the crucifixion.

Boris Karloff and his successor, Christopher Lee, have not only played Frankenstein's nameless and—in the first and greatest of the *Frankenstein* films—wordless monster, but also the title-role in *The*

Mummy; and that reminds us of one of the deepest fears on which the fantastic terror-film plays, a fear universally attested—fear, that is, not of death but of the dead, fear that those whom we have buried underground may return, in mockery of the Resurrection or anticipation of the Last Judgement, to dispute our inheritance of an earth that was once theirs. The hand creeping round the slowly opening coffin-lid, as in *Dracula* films, or adaptations of Poe, the earth slowly heaving to disgorge the rotting dead, as in *The Mask of the Demon* and *The Plague of the Zombies*, have become clichés of the cinema of terror—though a gifted director like Brian de Palma can redeem these clichés, give them a new power to shock, as the startling last sequence of *Carrie* may serve to show. The archetype and model of all zombie-movies still remains Victor Halperin's *White Zombie* of 1932, which curiously links its voodoo theme with that of social exploitation; the dead are raised to serve as bodyguards and as cheap labour in a Haiti sugar-mill. John Gilling's *The Plague of the Zombies* transfers this to England; the evil squire raises the dead to work his tin-mines and thus enable him to live in the style to which his class has become accustomed.

Zombie-films may be ranged along a scale between the points marked by Jacques Tourneur's *I Walked with a Zombie*, produced by Val Lewton, which works mainly through suggestion, through our identification with two women who walk towards a voodoo cere- mony, and George Romero's *Night of the Living Dead* (1968), which leaves no gruesome death and no equally gruesome resurrection unrecorded by the camera. In Romero's film, the dead have no zombie-master to direct them, and they are raised, not by voodoo, but rather by an (unexplained) scientific accident, like the cloud from space which showers The Incredible Shrinking Man with the substance that makes his size diminish further and further in Jack Arnold's excellent movie of 1957. Romero has given the screw an extra turn, however, by showing, particularly in his final sequences, that the harm the living can do matches and even outstrips that of the pathetic clawing corpses to which the title of his film refers. The Sherriff and his posse, played by residents of the locality near Pittsburgh where the film was made, are more frightening in their callousness than any miraculously reanimated corpse. The re- working of these themes in Jorge Grau's *The Living Dead at the Man- chester Morgue* (1974) sharpens them even further: not least in that the accident which resurrects the dead is here the result of a new pesticide; and what we see of the authorities, who broadcast anodyne warnings about 'hysteria' and 'exaggerated fears' at the beginning and shoot and incarcerate those who could help them control the new plague at the end, is not well calculated to make us trust the conventionally living more than the undead.

Romero's (and Grau's) turn of the screw reminds us of a possibility which has been of the greatest importance in the history of the cinematic tale of terror. This has, as I have tried to show in my previous chapter, so rapidly become a genre, has so rapidly established conventions and expectations, that gifted film-makers have been able to use the conventions as a kind of grid against which to draw their own rather different picture—as something to be at once alluded to and subverted. One of the most celebrated early examples of this is Tod Browning's *Freaks* of 1932, in which we at first recoil from the deformed creatures we see on the screen only to come to love them, to come to recognize, as the film goes on, that it is they who are truly human and potentially humane beings and that the real horrors are the two strong and handsome 'normal' circus performers who are involved with their fate. Having established this, Browning modulates back: roused by the wrong done to one of their numbers, the freaks become dangerous and menacing, and take the terrible revenge shown in the melodramatic and grotesque finale.

In his book on *Horror Movies*, Alan G. Frank has demonstrated how Jack Arnold's *The Incredible Shrinking Man* also turns the conventions of the screen-monster upside down. As an unknown chemical causes the hero to shrink, household pets (notably the cat) and spiders become deadly enemies to be worsted in battles that it takes all the hero's ingenuity and courage to fight. 'Instead of normal man locked in combat with giant creatures loose in his own comfortably familiar environment, replete with the armour of modern science and technology', Frank writes, 'the incredible shrinking man [finds] himself in an alien environment, matched against giant monsters who had once been pets and insects of his everyday life' (Frank, 1974, p. 155). Historical justice compels us to add that E. B. Schoedsack's *Dr. Cyclops* anticipated several of these 'shrinkage' effects but used them much less imaginatively than Jack Arnold did in his accomplished film. Yet another variation had preceded Schoedsack's by three years: Tod Browning's *Devil Doll*, where miniature humans were used as instruments of revenge in a plot that owed a good deal to Alexandre Dumas's *The Count of Monte Cristo*; and there had, of course, been memorable miniature humans even earlier, in the 1924 version of *The Lost World*, and in one of the most effectively grotesque scenes of *The Bride of Frankenstein*.

An even clearer example of the way in which genre-expectations may be used and subverted is Peter Bogdanovich's *Targets* (1969), where we discover how a monster can be created within an ordinary American family, a murderous monster that looks like the proverbial all-American boy and walks through a marvellously evoked American urban landscape. The film stars none other than Boris Karloff, who plays an actor specializing in conventional horror-movies persuaded to promote his latest creation through a personal appearance at a drive-in cinema where it is being shown; but we soon realize that the true horror is not in those movies. It lurks, rather, among the ordinary-looking spectators who have come to watch them and who are being picked off by indiscriminate rifle shots under the cover of darkness and noise. Two types of horror are here confronted: that associated with Boris Karloff movies, and that associated with the sniper-murders of which we read in our newspapers in the 1960s. The very names of the characters underline that opposition. 'Byron Orlok' combines the aristocratic, romantic poet to whose world-picture the Dracula tales owe so much with the central protagonist of Murnau's *Nosferatu*, who is sometimes known as Count Orlok. This name, charged with historical, literary, and silent-film associations, contrasts with the deliberately non-descript, common name of the boy who indulges in random sniper-murders: 'Bobby Thomson'. The real horror is with Bobby Thomson, not with Byron Orlok.

And suddenly we realize that what Bogdanovich is here showing us in a contemporary American context had in fact been implicit in the cinematic tale of terror all along: in Wiene's *Cabinet of Dr. Caligari*, with its sinister alienist; in Galeen's *Student of Prague*, with its Biedermeier devil complete with umbrella; in Whale's *The Old Dark House*, with its harmless-looking little old man—and long before all these in the Romantic tale of terror in which a demonic or uncanny bourgeois (an advocate, a privy councillor, a professor of physics, a seller of spectacles) had so often played a baleful and destructive part. Henry James, indeed, had gone one step further and had made the uncanny inhere in good-looking and apparently normal children—a lead which the film, from Jack Clayton's *The Innocents*, which vulgarized James's *The Turn of the Screw*, to *Flesh for Frankenstein*, *The Exorcist*, and *The Omen*, has enthusiastically followed. The *ne plus ultra* of this to date is the vampire baby of *It's Alive!* (1974), which is no sooner delivered than it proceeds to empty the entire medical team of its blood, going on from there to terrorize an entire state. The gusto with which films like *The Omen* make the audience wish for a child's destruction has something deeply suspect about it—might there be a link, perhaps, between the way in which our more cruel instincts are here being directed against a child, and the disturbing use made of child 'actors' in pornographic films? Here, once again, we come very close to the barrier beyond which the 'cathartic' theory of violence in films ceases to operate.

Another way of using the conventions of the terror-film even after they have been over-exploited by hacks and cashers-in is well exemplified in Eduardo de Gregorio's *Serail*(1976). The hero of this film is himself a hack, a writer of best sellers who speaks knowledgeably of Poe and Wilkie Collins and of a 'degraded Gothic tradition' laced with pornography—a tradition which his books have consciously continued, in order to further their author's quest for fame and fortune. When he is first introduced to the lonely, decaying house on which the film centres, with its apparently demented chatelaine and its one locked room, he is properly scornful of the clichés such props represent to him, the poverty of the imagination which has lured him into the adventure played out on the screen. It soons turns out that he has indeed been lured, that what happens has indeed been staged for his benefit, that the chatelaine he had first met was in fact a professional actress—but no sooner have we realized this, along with the hero, when truly supernatural events begin to happen, events for which no rational explanation is possible. The last remaining character besides the hero is seen to fade into a wall and the house assumes a will of its own as it closes itself around him in one of the most claustrophobic sequences of the cinema. The Gothic terrors we had discounted, the terrors the hero had discounted, as outmoded and more than faintly ridiculous, reassert themselves with unexpected power.

The often noted connection between sex and cruelty—and, indeed, between love and death—is at its most obvious in the vampire-films that loom so large in the history of the cinema of terror. Here we need only look at the way the central figure is presented in successive treatments of Bram Stoker's *Dracula* to see how changing social attitudes have affected film-makers. Murnau's Nosferatu (1922) is hideous, and made progressively more so as the film proceeds—when the heroine tricks him into her room in order to detain him beyond sunrise and thus rid the world of him, she is clearly making a supreme sacrifice. Bela Lugosi's Dracula (1931) is good-looking and courteous in a 'foreign' sort of way, but he has an unctuousness that may well have sent many a spectator away with the thought that (to use Robert Bloch's formulation) the man who kisses your hand one moment is likely to bite your neck the next. Christopher Lee's Dracula (1958) on the other hand, David Peel's Meinster in *The Brides of Dracula* (1960), and Ferdy Mayne's Count von Crolock in Polanski's *Dance of the Vampires* (1967), are hand-some, dignified men, none of whom one would suspect of really being a ham actor in disguise—a part which Tod Browning, cruelly but with some justice, induced Bela Lugosi to play in *Mark of the Vampire* (1935). In recent vampire-movies Dracula has even been allowed to indulge in more conventional sex activity than neck-biting: a change which would seem to remove the chief *raison d'être* of Bram Stoker's Victorian creation. It may be connected with this that vampires can now be shown happy in their work, like Robert Quarry as Count Yorga (*Count Yorga, Vampire*, 1970; *The Return of Count Yorga*, 1971), without longing for release from their 'undead' state. *Love at First Bite* (1979) hilariously exploits this change—swinging chicks eagerly meet the vampire's advances, expecting the love-making they are used to, and then find the biting that comes instead thrillingly 'kinky'. The trend is reversed by Werner Herzog's memorable remake of *Nosferatu* (1979), which harks back deliberately to an older tradition; but Klaus Kinski's vampire in that film, for all his uncompromisingly grotesque appearance, has a pathos and a tragic dignity absent from Max Schreck's performance in Murnau's original. The secret, in the main, lies in Kinski's voice: those beautifully modulated, soft, world-weary tones emanating from his cadaverous head with its red-rimmed eyes and rodent fangs, like the elegant movements of his mandarin-clawed hands, make him a figure of pity as well as terror and stifle the laughter that certain sequences deliberately court.

If Stoker's novel has been the chief source of inspiration for the male vampires of the screen, and has incidentally yielded the most potent masculine symbol for the fear of being corrupted by outside forces (it is the *foreign* and *aristocratic* lover whose rivalry the local roughnecks have cause to fear!), the female vampire has owed a good deal to Sheridan Le Fanu's 'Carmilla'. Carl Dreyer's *Vampyr* (1932) pointed the way—Dreyer named Le Fanu as his source, and we shall see later what use he made of this. His chief vampire is an old woman, but there is a disturbing moment when one of her victims, a young woman, played by Sybille Schmitz, suddenly shows signs of dark vampiric desires as she glances towards her sister. Among the dream-like incidents which Dreyer presents, however, with the marvellous visual sense we expect of him, there are none with *overt* sexual suggestions, nor are there any orgiastic blood-lettings. Here too we have seen a drastic change. The lesbian implications of Le Fanu's tale are drastically brought out in Roy Ward Baker's *The Vampire Lovers* and Jimmy Sangster's *Lust for a Vampire* (both 1970); while in a number of films based on the life of the mass-murderess Countess Elisabeth Bathory a female vampire is shown to be keeping old age at bay by bathing in the blood of nubile young women whose 'corpses' we are shown in gory and sexually titillating shots (notably *Countess Dracula*, 1971, directed by Peter Sasdy). The link between vampiric and coital delights has been brought out more and more openly by the facial expressions and bodily contortions of the actors and actresses who have portrayed vampires and their victims in the last twenty years. The motif of the clawing hand—the archetypal image of menace in terror-films of the 'silent' as well as the 'sound' period—has thus assumed a more openly sexual meaning than the older movies dared to give it.

It should, however, be remembered that the story of Countess Bathory has inspired a terror-film of greater distinction than Sasdy's: Harry Kümel's *Daughters of Darkness* (1971), starring none other than Delphine Seyrig, with the aura of *Last Year in Marienbad* still clinging to her. This subtle and stylish film has been very well described by David Pirie in *The Vampire Cinema*, where he demonstrates how Kümel was able to make his tale, updated to the twentieth century, significant politically as well as sexually. 'The indolence and social alienation of the characters', Pirie writes, 'seem to breed the basic perversions on which the Countess is able to play so cunningly.' A more crudely allegorical political point was then made, two years later, by Alain Jessua's *Shock Treatment*, where the Bathory theme is transmuted into the story of wealthy clients of a French sanatorium who are rejuvenated by means of blood drawn from the bodies of Portuguese workers. The cliché-insult 'bloodsucking capitalists' is thus translated into the visual imagery of the terror-film.

In one of the episodes that make up Woody Allen's *Everything You Always Wanted to Know About Sex But Were Afraid to Ask* (1972), there is a hilarious spoof on horror-movies in the course of which a mad scientist (played by a veteran of the cinematic tale of terror, John Carradine) produces a gigantic female breast that goes on the rampage. Breasts have, of course, been ubiquitous, especially in more recent vampire-movies, as an attraction rather than a danger: since the 'X' certificate brings a 'sex' as well as 'horror' public into the cinemas, well-shaped bodies liberally exposed have become a staple ingredient of terror-films. Sensations of the uncanny, however, have usually been associated with another kind of exposure: that of the human brain, removed from its owner's cranium yet still functioning. This played its part in *Frankenstein*, and then exerted a baneful influence in no less than three adaptations of Curt Siodmak's novel *Donovan's Brain* (1943, 1953, 1962). We have also had variations of the Bug-Eyed Monster of science fiction which seemed to consist of nothing but outsize brains attached to trailing spinal cords (*Fiend Without a Face*, 1958); films in which it was not the brain itself, but the severed head that lived and thought on, as in *The Frozen Dead* (1966); and others, like Jack Gold's *The Medusa Touch* (1978), which showed the brain miraculously and destructively hyper-active in a skull smashed beyond repair or recovery. The uncanny wonders of telepathy and—especially—telekinesis account for much of the appeal of such movies.

Titles like *The Clutching Hand* (a Pearl White vehicle of 1915) and *The Beast With Five Fingers* (Robert Florey, 1946), remind us how important a part the human hand has played in the cinema of terror: creeping round slowly opening doors, reaching for the heroine from a panel above her bed, seizing the hero by the throat from a concealed passage—and continuing to do such things even when cut from the body. This motif, the motif of the severed but still moving hand, sophisticated film-makers like Buñuel (from *An Andalusian Dog* to *The Exterminating Angel*, 1962) and Bergman (in *The Face* (or *The Magician*)) have been particularly ready to borrow from the terror-film. There can be little doubt that in this post-Freudian age the severed hand is often consciously used as a castration symbol: in Robert Aldrich's *Hush, Hush, Sweet Charlotte* such symbolization is fairly obvious. In this respect the 'severed hand' motif is akin to that of the severed tongue—the tongue which is so graphically ripped from Christopher Lee's mouth in Terence Fisher's remake of *The Mummy*, as a punishment for loving too well. Beyond this, however, the severed hand suggests a series of fears on which Lon Chaney's many impersonations of amputees and deformed creatures had also played: fears of mutilation (which engender sympathetic empathy with the Chaney characters) allied to fear of the mutilated (which engenders the repulsion on which the opening and closing sequences of *Freaks* play with such virtuosity). One thinks, here, of the menacing use of blind men in such films as *The Dark Eyes of London* (1939) or *The Ministry of Fear* (1944) or *Tombs of the Blind Dead* (1972) and the deformed faces of Claude Rains, Lionel Atwill, and Vincent Price in *The Phantom of the Opera*, *The Mystery of the Wax Museum*, *House of Wax* (1953), and *The Abominable Dr. Phibes* (1971). The 'severed hand' motif is clearly connected with this; but it is also linked to the 'zombie' or 'living dead' motif, to the fear that when the brain has ceased to function and the heart has ceased to beat, the tissues of the body might still be able to go on performing purposive and destructive actions. This also suggests a connection between the 'severed hand' motif and those identity-fears and identity-doubts which are played on by the motif of the *Doppelgänger*: fears and doubts such as we find projected in Wiene's *The Hands of Orlac* (1924) and Freund's *Mad Love*, where a pianist is made to think that the hands grafted on to his arms to replace those mangled in a train accident are impelling him to perform actions that his mind abhors. How often, too, do we find the protagonist of terror-films 'losing face' in the most literal way! We actually see Dr. Genessier detach the face of one of his victims in *Eyes Without a Face*; and the worst of the grotesque horrors that abound in *The Hour of the Wolf* is surely the woman who can 'take off her face', as Johan says, 'together with her hat'. And what, after all, is more immediately connected with our identity, in our own view as in the view of others, than our face?

Within the face it is of course the eye which leads most directly to where we live—and the human eye has, indeed, played an especially important part in the terror-film. The photographed eye may be that of a sinister watcher, as in some frightening close-ups of Robert Siodmak's *The Spiral Staircase* (1946), which also shows the distorted way in which the watcher's mind interprets what his eye sees; or it may be the eye of a sad victim, the mirror of a tortured soul, as at the opening and close of Polanski's *Repulsion*. It hardly needs saying that the vulnerability of the eye is also played on by sequences enlisting our fear of physical injury, in films that range from *An Andalusian Dog* to *The Flesh and the Fiends* (1959).

Another of the fears which the terror-film articulates for us is connected with the spirit of place. Whole towns may be enveloped in an uncanny atmosphere—Hitchcock's *The Lodger* of 1926 is sub-titled *A Story of the London Fog*. The terror-film likes, especially, to convey the impression—common to 'Old Dark House' and 'Haunted Castle' movies, and powerfully re-evoked in Hitchcock's *Psycho*—that evil adheres to some particular building. *The Sentinel* even placed one of the entrances to hell in an urban American apartment house—an impression with which anyone who has seen steam rising from ground-level vents and gratings in Man-hattan will readily sympathize. Kuhns and Stanley, in *Exploring the Film*, have shown very well how in *The Haunting* Robert Wise made Hill House the main character in the film:

Early in the film we see the house for the first time, in the late afternoon sun: its enormous size, its strange, rising towers, its ugly walls all convey a mood of mystery. Within, we discover that no door is even but that all have been built at strange angles; an atmosphere of gloom and horror fills the great house. But we discover the house's true character at night. Robert Wise, who directed the film, began every evening in the film with impressive shots of the house's exterior: long-angle shots looking straight up at the towers or at the leering gargoyles jutting from the framework. Throughout the film there are over a hundred silent shots of the house, each one from a strong, unusual angle, each one suggesting the strange, disturbed nature of the old mansion. (Kuhns and Stanley, 1968, p. 105)

Specific rooms within a house can also become scenes of terror: H.-G. Clouzot (in *Les Diaboliques*, 1955), Hitchcock (again in *Psycho*), and Seth Holt (in *The Nanny*, 1965) play on the vulnera-bility we feel in bathrooms and shower-cabinets. The terrors of attic and cellar (places where unwanted things are stuffed away and can reappear with attendant horrors) and those of the stair-way (where transitions are made, where we—or something menacing us—can pass from one enclosed space to another) have also been thoroughly explored by a multitude of film-makers. Such works as Hitchcock's *The Birds* or Romero's *The Night of the Living Dead* play a contrasting variation on all this: an ordinary dwelling-house is converted into a fortress to keep out the irrational, to keep out the uncanny powers that are besieging it and trying to force their way in.

The most frequently tested means of harnessing the spirit of place to terror is that of suddenly transforming the familiar into the strange. This can be done in many ways—from focusing, as so many German film-makers did, on huge shadows thrown by everyday objects on to the walls of a stairwell or a room, to that sudden cracking or softening of walls, that opening of blocked-up doors, which make the urban apartments of *Repulsion* and *Rosemary's Baby* so uncanny. The part that the opening of a door or gate, the appearance of apertures where there were none before, play in mystical and fairy-tale texts may serve to suggest some of the archetypal hopes and fears on which the makers of terror-films have been able to draw. Such effects will be explored further in Chapter 4.

One film above all others has been able to show convincingly a supernatural enclave, a realm of otherworldly terror and awe inserted into our familiar world. The film which Fritz Lang called *Der müde Tod* and which in English is generally known as *Destiny* features one of the most haunting sets in the history of the cinema: a Palace of Death whose huge sombre wall and mysterious Hall of Lights has only to be seen once to be seared for ever into our memory. Except for Bernhard Goetzke's quietly impressive performance as Death, however, nothing in the rest of the work lives up to the visual terrors and delights of this grand architectural conception.

The makers of terror-films frequently use confined settings to play on their audiences' claustrophobia: on fears of being shut in whose ultimate expression is the dread of premature burial. The classic, the still unsurpassed, evocation of this is undoubtedly the scene in Dreyer's *Vampyr* in which the hero has a vision of his own body lying in a coffin; the camera lets us see him lying in his coffin but also assumes his perspective, as he lies there, unable to move or cry out. He sees and hears the coffin being closed and the lid screwed down, watches a face—that of the vampire—bending over a glass panel let into the coffin-lid, and looks up at a ceiling, a malevolent doctor smoking a cigar, a cloudy sky, bare tree-tops, a foreshortened church and church-tower, as (with an eerie gliding motion) his body is carried head foremost to its dark and narrow last dwelling. Hitchcock, with his usual flair for conveying the terrors of urban man, has reversed this in the 'prairie-stop' sequence of *North by North-West* (1959). Cary Grant's Roger Thornhill feels dreadfully vulnerable and exposed in the flat, deserted rural landscape where the bus has set him down and where he is about to be attacked by an enemy who swoops down on him in a crop-dusting aeroplane. Claustrophobia has often been depicted in the cinema; but I can think of no example of agoraphobia to hold against that in *North by North-West*—a thriller which cannot by any stretch of the imagination be called a horror-movie.

A whole book could be written about one symbol which from the days of *The Student of Prague* onwards the cinema of terror has used over and over again: the mirror. Here claustrophobic and agoraphobic motifs come together. The mirror-experience is claustrophobic when it hems us in and throws our own face back at us—singly, as in *The Student of Prague*, or multiplied many times, as in the scene of Lew Landers's *The Raven* (1935) which shows Boris Karloff shooting at his own reflection, or, outside the horror-movie, in one of the Xanadu sequences in *Citizen Kane* and the 'hall of mirrors' sequence in *The Lady from Shanghai* (1948). It is agoraphobic when, as in the episode of *Dead of Night* directed by Robert Hamer, the mirror opens out into an unfamiliar space, reflecting a room quite different from that in which it hangs, an older room in which a murder has been committed whose evil influence now radiates outwards into other, later lives. This episode is also remarkable, as Charles Barr has shown, for making the mirror assert darker energies, allow glimpses of a repressed part of the personality, a world of violence and sexuality with which the characters cannot come to terms. The mirror unites the claustrophobic with the agoraphobic when the hero of de Gregorio's *Serail*—a work centrally concerned with looking-glass experience—feels himself spied on by a two-way mirror and then finds there is, after all, nothing but wall behind it as the house closes itself around him. The mirror may be most disconcerting of all when it reflects nothing, registers an absence: the absence of a reflection, *das verlorene Spiegelbild*, an uncanny motif that runs from popular superstition via the tales of E. T. A. Hoffmann to the vampire-films of the thirties and sixties.

As has often been noted, mirrors have a relation to the cinema-experience itself; their shadow-images admit us to what Cocteau called *la zone*, the realm between dream and reality, the tangible and the evanescent.

From *Caligari* to Cavalcanti's *Dead of Night* to Roeg's *Don't Look Now* (1973) the cinematic tale of terror has played on apprehensions connected with the mystery of time as well as space. It likes to remind the viewer of the 'I have been here before' feeling, a feeling which we all know and which powerfully suggests that the future is something determined, something that in a way is already here, already in the present. The very title of René Clair's *It Happened Tomorrow* (1944) expresses this vividly. The hero of *Don't Look Now* is enabled to see his wife go to his own funeral shortly before that funeral is made necessary by his murder; the central consciousness of *Dead of Night* is that of an architect who wakes from a nightmare to find its incidents being repeated in his 'waking' life until he 'wakes up' once more and the whole circular process starts all over again—except that one subtle change in the sequence of opening scenes which unrolls again as the final credits go up suggests that this time these nightmare incidents might be taking place in the 'real', the outside, world. In *Caligari* it appears that Cesare the somnambulist can be lying peacefully in his coffin-like box while at the same time he is out committing his murders—as in many *Doppelgänger* films which play on similar apprehensions, a natural explanation is in the end supplied, but not before the spectator has empathetically shared the hero's consternation, disorientation, and apprehension. The entire action of Lang's *Tired Death* takes place between two strokes of a bell announcing midnight. Some of the most striking effects of the terror-film have to do with a reversal of natural sequence—as in that powerful scene from Mario Bava's *Black Sunday* or *Mask of the Demon*, in which the skull of the dead witch gradually reassumes its flesh, passing through the stage that shows the facial wounds left by the spiked mask which killed her, to end up with the unscarred, smooth-skinned, wide-eyed, interestingly irregular features of Barbara Steele. Chris Marker's *La Jetée* (1962) shifts between 'present', 'past', and 'future' in a way that has made French critics invoke the name of Bergson and that has been splendidly described by Basil Wright in *The Long View*:

The idea of time as a sort of collection of Chinese boxes which will not even keep to their appointed shapes but make their own rules and fit with alarming perfection into all the wrong spaces, is in itself quite frightening. But what really gets you is Marker's treatment of the visuals; for the film is made up from a collection of freeze-frames which in themselves cause a rupture in time. With one exception, every shot in the film is a still. But the stills are not posed photographs; they are fractional moments ripped from the flow of motion-pictures. Each shot is a frozen one-twenty-fourth of a second, a moment of life, of movement (which is life) suspended in time, until we seem to arrive at a glimpse of that infinity in which macrocosm and microcosm merge, light is bent, and time turns in on itself. To this is allied a soundtrack of voices, his, hers, the guttural hypodermic count-downs of the experimenters, the sounds of nature and, above all, the sound of his heartbeats—louder and faster, ever more urgent, until they seem about to burst right out of the screen as the masked faces of the 'surgeons' loom.

The frozen images are, of course, images of action, segments seized brutally and arbitrarily from a flow of motion—the girl's head turning to look at a stuffed monster in the natural history museum where she and he 'meet', the thrust of a hypodermic, or the patterns of running feet.

But then, for one tremendous moment, but only one, Marker restores to us 'real' time, time, that is, as we think we know it. On the bed, as the birds in the garden chorus for a summer sunrise, she opens her eyes, the lids flutter; and from this tiny fragment of living and loving (for it is on him that her waking glance falls) there seems to come a fanfare of glory, a revelation. (Wright, 1976, p. 279)

Marker's film reminds us, if reminder is needed, that 'place' and 'time' are connected. How often the journey to an uncanny place turns out, in the horror-movie, to be, in varying senses, a journey into the past! It reminds us of the relativity of time by exploiting the cinema's ability to move backwards in time as well as forwards, and of the relativity of motion by keeping a work composed almost entirely of still-photographs in constant movement by means of dissolves and panning-shots.

Marker's sophisticated film has behind it, almost certainly, the knowledge that Henri Bergson, in the lectures on 'Creative Evolution' which he first delivered in 1902–3, described human perception in terms of the early cinema. Our conceptual thought, Bergson believed, worked by means of a rapid series of impressions analogous to the separate frames of a film which our minds then set moving: 'We hardly do anything else', Bergson adds, 'than set going a kind of cinematograph inside us.' But terror-films very much less philosophically self-conscious than *La Jetée* may also jolt us into reflections that have been a constant theme of philosophers: reflections on the nature of time and space, on the notion that these may be only categories of our apprehension and that their laws may have no validity in whatever world exists outside our apprehending minds; and beyond that, they may connect themselves also with the uncertainty experienced by all of us at various times, as to the exact line that divides our waking life from our dreams and our hallucinations—uncertainty, too, as to the possible truth-value of what we call dream or hallucination.

That brings us to apprehensions and uncertainties which we can find projected in so much of our literature as well as our films: uncertainty as to what is concealing surface and what is genuine substance, what is mask and what is face. The fantastic terror-film plays on this in many different ways. One thinks immediately of the murderous dwarf dressed in the garb of the beloved little girl in *Don't Look Now*; of the centrality of the *disguise*-motif in the films Tod Browning and Lon Chaney made together in the 1920s; of the role masks play in *The Phantom of the Opera* and *Onibaba*; of the climactic moment in *The Mystery of the Wax Museum* in which the heroine—little Fay Wray, of course—claws at the dignified, bearded features of Lionel Atwill to find them crumbling in her hand, to find that they were a waxen mask covering the hideously scarred vestiges of a mutilated face. How delighted the dramatists of the German Baroque, with their endless quest for ways of depicting the stripping-away of the world's beautiful surface to reveal the corruption below—how delighted Andreas Gryphius, for instance, would have been by that glorious moment in an otherwise undistinguished movie! Again and again the masters of the macabre film have climaxed their work with images of this kind—images of what can happen to flesh, of the fate of being a body. Paul Morrissey's nauseating *Flesh for Frankenstein* has taken that theme to its *ne plus ultra* conclusion by showing the necessary fragility of the home-made bodies which earlier *Frankenstein* films had depicted as being so massive, so solid, and so strong.

The last category of fears to which the cinematic tale of terror appeals is really the largest of them all. This is the fear, familiar to most of us at some stages in our life, that our enlightened, scientific view of the world may not tell us all there is to know; that ancient superstitions may in fact be true, or have at least some solid basis in truth. Rose London, in her book on the 'zombie' motif, usefully reminds us of ancient hopes and fears that motif is liable to stir up: that we may rise again in body; that we may be reincarnated (as we see Peter Proud to be in 1974 and Audrey Rose in 1977); that a necromancer will reanimate our bodies for nefarious purposes; that we may be preserved dead—or in some sense 'alive'—for ever, as if we were waxworks; that a wronged person will return from the grave to avenge himself; that our bodies may be used as models or for necrophilic abuse. One does not have to be a Freudian to see most of this as the equivalent, in the social psyche, of what Freud calls 'the return of the repressed' in the individual mind (see Chapter 4, below). The doubt, for instance, projected by Leni's *Waxworks* or by Cavalcanti's unforgettable ventriloquist episode in *Dead of Night* —the doubt whether an apparently inanimate object may not be animated or capable of animation—takes us back to a very ancient fear indeed, a fear we may share even as we discount it as a dream or a paranoiac delusion. However much we tell ourselves that the character played by Dieterle in *Waxworks* is dreaming and the one played by Redgrave in *Dead of Night* is insane, we actually experience what they experience, see Jack the Ripper leave his waxworks pediment and pursue the lovers through a shifting, uncertain nightmare townscape, hear the dummy speak and get up without being visibly manipulated by the ventriloquist. In this way we feel our own fears projected as well as those of the film's protagonists. The same is true of the audience's reactions to *Solaris*, where the scientists portrayed on the screen suddenly find that their memories, the contents of their minds, confront them within and without their space-station as living, independently moving and acting, infinitely renewable entities. The link with primitive animism is not far to seek, either in the examples just cited, or in a film like Murnau's *Nosferatu*, where the vampire-count seems, in Eric Rhode's words, 'to take possession of . . . places and to rob them of their identity'. And as so often happens with films of this kind: what may look, at one level, like superstitious nonsense may turn out to have a symbolic significance that is anything but nonsensical. It may embody Jungian archetypes, Freudian id or super-ego projections, Hegelian or Marxian alienations and projections, social repressions and revolutionary impulses of many kinds; or it may simply baffle us by refusing to be fitted into any of our rational schemes at all. As someone said to Pauline Kael about Florey's *The Beast With*

Five Fingers: 'It doesn't make any sense, and that's the true terror!'

And here we ought perhaps to remind ourselves that there are distinguished terror-movies which are not 'tales' in the accepted sense at all; which make their effect through the evocations of an atmosphere, of moods and associations: through flights of steps that lead we know not where, dark and endless corridors through which shadows wander without apparent aim or goal, self-opening doors, billowing curtains, hands clutching or stretched out in supplication, veils floating on misty waters. Such a film is Jean Epstein's *The Fall of the House of Usher*—a work which does not, as Béla Bálazs has rightly said, offer us intelligible illustrations of a story, but which seems, rather, to convey, in a Surrealist-inspired manner, the impression left by a reading of one of the world's great terror-fictions. What he wanted, Epstein has himself explained, was not to make films in which *nothing* happens, but films in which *little* happens; works in which 'an absence of subject would let reality release all its weight of mystery and latent symbolism'. His *Fall of the House of Usher*, it may well be thought, is one of the few cinematic tributes to Edgar Allan Poe which really count—I for one would not give it for a wilderness of Cormans. But even if one's pleasure in Roger Corman's accomplished quickies is not unalloyed, they remain of intense symptomatic interest—not least in the way in which their progress, from adaptations of Poe and Lovecraft to *The Wild Angels* (1966), *The Trip* (1967), and beyond, has charted the path of what Eric Rhode has well called 'the impulse to relate Gothic romance to the sensations of contemporary life'.

Let us look back, in concluding this initial survey, to a source of terror already suggested in Leo Braudy's remarks on the *Doppelgänger* (see above, p. 56). Braudy, Edgar Morin, and many others have felt something potentially frightening in the cinematic image itself, and in the audience's relation to it. The image we see on the screen is a kind of spectral double, the simulacrum of landscapes and townscapes filled with human beings that seem to live, to breathe, to talk, and are yet present only through their absence. Their originals, indeed, may already be dead. The most powerful projection so far of the uncanniness of this relationship is Emidio Greco's *Morel's Invention* of 1974, a film based on a novel by Adolfo Bioy Casares. What Morel has invented is a machine for recording and projecting holograph images which are indistinguishable from real people and their actions and which endlessly repeat, in the 1970s, the events of a week-end in the 1920s. The central protagonist stumbles on to these projections, becomes emotionally evolved with the simulacra of the twenties (who, of course, cannot respond to him), and reactivates Morel's machine in order to project his own image into those already recorded. He finds, however, that the manufactured image feeds on his own physical substance, which begins, horrifyingly, to crumble away ... The symbolic import of this tale of terror for the cinema-experience itself is not easily missed. *Morel's Invention*, a tale of what Gene Youngblood calls 'expanded cinema', joins in self-reflexive intent such tales of voyeurism as Freund's *Mad Love*, Hitchcock's *Rear Window* (1954) and *Psycho*, Powell's *Peeping Tom* (1959), Reeves's *The Sorcerers* (1967), and de Palma's *Sisters* (1973)— works in which the cinema-audience is made to watch protagonists who, in their turn, are watching Grand Guignol or spying on others. The many films that show us some sinister being peering through a window without himself being seen invite similar recognitions. They reflect, parody, or play variations on the experience of spectators who have chosen to come into the cinema and now look out, from their darkened auditorium, at the terror-makers and their victim whose story unfolds before them, just as in Lang's *Metropolis* the beam of light from Rotwang's torch which picks out the terrified Maria duplicates, within the frame, the beam of light which throws this very image on to the screen for our delight. This is not the least important of the many ways in which the beings on the screen claim kinship with us. 'De te fabula narratur', the terror-maker would seem to be saying to us; 'hypocrite spectateur, mon semblable, mon frère.'

CHAPTER 3

Book into Film I: Mamoulian's
Dr. Jekyll and Mr. Hyde

I've played with dangerous knowledge.
I've walked a strange and terrible road.
Help me find my way back.

Dr. Jekyll and Mr. Hyde (1932)

MANY of the plots used by film-makers attracted to the macabre
derive from works of literature. In itself this fact cannot be used to
characterize the art of the film as 'parasitic' or 'derivative' any
more than Shakespeare can be blamed for seeking out plots in
narrative fiction, historiographical works, older plays, and existing
poems, and then altering and combining them, making them over
into new wholes. In translating from literature to the film, however,
the creative talents of the cinema have to take a longer leap. They
have to go from a medium that makes its main effects by means of
written or spoken words to one that uses words as well as music
and sound-effects as auxiliaries of a sequence of *photographs*
projected in such a way and at such a pace that men and objects
appear to move; from a medium in which each reader or hearer
supplies his own mental picture, rounding out suggestions made by
means of signs linked to their designate, for the most part, in what
Saussure has called an 'arbitrary' way, to one in which the principal signs, the photographs projected on to the screen, bear a more
'iconic', a more directly 'matching', relation to objects and actions.
(The photograph of a dog is more 'doggy' than a combination of the
letters d - o - g, or H - u - n - d, or c - h - i - e - n.) The film-maker
who adapts a literary work has to leap from a medium that
constantly envelops and pervades actions with reflections and can
indicate past, present, future, actuality, and possibility by the
simple means of tense and mood, to one whose strength lies in
images of the here and now, in which men and women reveal their
unspoken thoughts with the flicker of an eyelid, a change of facial

expression, a bodily stance. 'Like dreams,' Bill Nichols has said, in a passage marred only by confusion between 'metaphor' and 'simile', 'the film image lacks tenses; it operates by metaphor without labels for the metaphor itself (such as the word "like") and lacks the word "not" which allows us to create the boundaries of digital communication.'[1] It is obvious that the subtleties of the greatest works of fiction will not translate into this medium, and that those who go to the cinema to confirm and extend their apprehension of *War and Peace* or *Madame Bovary* or *Ulysses* will suffer a disappointment proportionate to their expectation of a literary experience. This is not to say, of course, that good films cannot be based on scenes, motifs, and suggestions contained in important works of literature, or that film-actors cannot, with the help of understanding scriptwriters, directors, and cameramen, impersonate characters created by great novelists and playwrights in ways which permanently enrich our conception of such characters. *David Copperfield*, *Great Expectations*, and *Henry V*, for instance, have provided a basis for films which can surprise and delight even the most literature-orientated film-goer. As a general rule, however, it is safe to assume that the literary works which will best survive translation into terms of the cinema will not be the major but the minor works of world literature, and that the cinema can even, in the right hands, develop into significant works of art stories taken from the undergrowth of mass publishing.

Among tales of terror, Stevenson's *Dr. Jekyll and Mr. Hyde* has exerted, from the first, a special fascination on film-makers in the English-speaking world and beyond. In 1908 the Selig Polyscope Company released its fifteen-minute version under the title *The Modern Dr. Jekyll*; in 1912 the Thanhouser Company followed suit, in a vehicle starring James Cruze, Marguerite Snow, and Florence La Badie, thus beginning the tradition that set Stevenson's character between two women; 'Uncle' Carl Laemmle brought out yet another version in 1913, as did a British concern, the Kineto-Kinemacolour Company, which lived up to its name by hand-colouring its images; and in 1914 the American Starlight Company based a short movie on the same story. All these primitive efforts

---

[1] To avoid misunderstanding it should perhaps be said that the montage principle so dear to the early Russian film-makers often operates as an equivalent of the word 'like': as when the image of a politician is immediately succeeded by that of a peacock, or the image of eagerly gossiping women by that of agitated geese.

The actor as hypnotist: Bela Lugosi in *White Zombie*, dir. Victor Halperin, 1932.

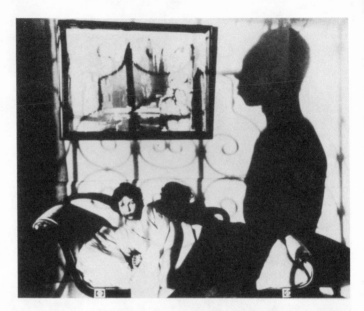

(*Above*) Patterns of fear and cultural contrasts in Val Lewton's black-and-white world. Frances Dee, Darby Jones, and Boecklin's painting *The Isle of the Dead*, in *I Walked with a Zombie*, dir. Jacques Tourneur, 1943.

(*Right*) An umbrella-carrying devil shadows young love in a nocturnal garden—juxtaposition of light and dark, large and small, architecture and vegetation, the natural and the supernatural, in *The Student of Prague*, dir. Henrik Galeen, 1926.

'These metaphysics of magicians/And necromantic books are heavenly.' Werner Krauss, with book and shadow, in *The Cabinet of Dr. Caligari*, dir. Robert Wiene, 1919.

Story-teller (Friedrich Fehér), somnambulist (Conrad Veidt), examining doctor (Rudolf Lettinger), and fairground mesmerist (Werner Krauss) in one of the stylized, claustrophobic interiors of *The Cabinet of Dr. Caligari*.

Painted shadows and Expressionist terrors: the somnambulist in quest of his victim amid leaves that clutch like hands and blades that rear like knives (*The Cabinet of Dr. Caligari*).

Flappers of the 1920s confronted by Poe's masked Death: two Americas meet in the imagined Paris of *The Phantom of the Opera*, dir. Rupert Julian, 1925.

The actor's face as living skull: Lon Chaney, his grotesque make-up set off by the handsome head of a Beethoven sculpture, in Julian's *The Phantom of the Opera*.

Demon coachman in an eerie romantic forest—the German terror-film leaves the studio in *Nosferatu. A Symphony of Terror*, dir. F. W. Murnau, 1922.

The monster at the window: geometric patterning and careful composition heighten the terror inspired by the grotesque watcher. Max Schreck as the vampire, Count Orlok, in Murnau's *Nosferatu. A Symphony of Terror*.

The monster at the door: the mingled pathos and menace of Boris Karloff's classic performance, and its affinity with Conrad Veidt's Cesare in *Caligari*, are admirably caught in this studio-shot from *Frankenstein*, dir. James Whale, 1932.

Buried alive: coffined terror in a nightmare sequence from *Vampyr*, dir. Carl Dreyer, 1932.

A study in black and grey: the grim reaper awaits the ferryman in a characteristic painterly composition from Dreyer's *Vampyr*.

were far outdistanced by John S. Robertson's version of 1920, starring John Barrymore as a dignified Jekyll and spidery Hyde whose power owed little to horrific make-up and everything to the actor's feeling for the grotesque. In the same year, in Germany, Murnau tried his hand at an adaptation of Stevenson's tale by Carl Mayer. This was entitled *The Head of Janus* (*Der Januskopf*—a reference to a piece of statuary introduced into the film for symbolic purposes); it starred Conrad Veidt and it now belongs, alas, to the many lost works of the early cinema. At least two further versions seem to have been made in 1920, both in the U.S.A., starring Hank Mann and Sheldon Lewis respectively.

This process of constantly reworking and recasting Stevenson's tale of the two faces of man has gone on right to the present day: we need only recall such significant stages in the process as Mamoulian's version of 1931–2, Victor Fleming's of 1941, Jean Renoir's of 1959 (entitled *Dr. Cordelier's Testament* and starring Jean-Louis Barrault, whose attractive, anarchistic Hyde was tantalizingly renamed 'Opale'), Terence Fisher's *The Two Faces of Dr. Jekyll* of 1960, and Jerry Lewis's modernizing parody *The Nutty Professor* of 1963, and avert our eyes from the pornographic versions that a relaxation of censorship sent into our metropolitan cinemas and cinema clubs in the 1970s, in the wake of that pioneering confluence of pornography and spoof-terror entitled *The Devil in Miss Jones*. I have seen only six of these versions (one of them, that directed by L. Henderson in 1912, by courtesy of the Nickelodeon recreated in Disneyland); and of these the most successful as a work of art was not Renoir's, even though it kept more closely to its original than many other versions while at the same time projecting a thoroughly modern, 'poet-of-action' view of Hyde, but the one directed by Rouben Mamoulian, scripted by Samuel Hoffenstein and Percy Heath, photographed by Karl Struss, and acted by Fredric March, Miriam Hopkins, Rose Hobart, Holmes Herbert, Halliwell Hobbes, and Edgar Norton. In examining a concrete instance of what happens when a work of literature is transposed into a film, I shall therefore concentrate on the Mamoulian version.

When Robert Louis Stevenson wrote his short tale in 1886, he was a sick man, suffering from continual haemorrhages and constantly running a temperature. He dreamed a great deal and took an intellectual interest in what he called, in an essay entitled

'A Chapter on Dreams', his 'Brownies': the creative impulses at work in a man's sleep, impulses that 'have not a rudiment of what we call conscience', are 'somewhat fantastic, like their stories hot and hot, full of passion and the picturesque, alive with animating incident' and 'have no prejudice against the supernatural'. Would one not think that Stevenson is here describing the early film? Can one not see here additional justification for Susanne Langer's contention that in many important respects the film is 'the dream mode' *par excellence?* May not the 'Brownies' described by Stevenson be seen as the veritable muses of the terror-film?

We have the testimony of Stevenson's wife and that of his stepson to the fact that the central incidents of *Dr. Jekyll and Mr. Hyde* came to him in a dream. One night, Mrs. Stevenson recalls, 'my husband's cries of horror caused me to rouse him, much to his indignation. "I was dreaming a fine bogey tale", he said reproachfully, following with a rapid sketch of *Jekyll and Hyde*, up to the transformation scene, where I had awakened him.' The 'Brownies' who brought him this bogey tale had, however, a whole lifetime of experience to draw on: experience which included, in Stevenson's case, a Presbyterian upbringing; childhood fascination with the case of Deacon Brodie, a respectable cabinet-maker during the day but a skilled burglar by night; the realities of Victorian respectability and its clandestine compensations; admiration for what he called, in an essay on 'Victor Hugo's Romances', the 'conjunction of the grotesque, and even of a certain bourgeois snugness, with passionate contortion and horror, that is so characteristic of Gothic art'; and finally, as Mrs. Stevenson once again attests, 'a paper . . . on subconsciousness' her husband had recently read in a French scientific journal. Freud too, we remember, had formative experiences among the questers for 'subconsciousness' who clustered around Charcot and the Salpêtrière.

The version of *Jekyll and Hyde* which Stevenson wrote down under the immediate impact of his encounter with the 'Brownies' was soon jettisoned; Lloyd Osbourne, who saw it before it was burnt, described it as 'a magnificent bit of sensationalism'. Stevenson did his rewriting, as his wife recalled, 'from another point of view—that of the allegory, which was palpable and had yet been missed, probably from haste, and from the compelling influence of the dream'. We do not know how directly the tale was told in the original version; but as we now have it, the reader stands alongside

Mr. Utterson the lawyer from the beginning, approaching Dr. Jekyll by degrees through (i) Utterson's disquiet at the strange will he has made in favour of a Mr. Hyde; (ii) Utterson's contacts with the man-about-town, Enfield, who has encountered Mr. Hyde performing one of his nocturnal *actes gratuits* of cruelty by walking over a child in full public view; and (iii) Utterson's contacts with the conventional, conservative Dr. Lanyon, who feels disturbed and threatened by the direction which his colleague Jekyll's scientific interests have been taking. In the incidents which follow, and which lead eventually to Jekyll's death, we never see more than Utterson, never learn more than *he* learns, by degrees, from Enfield, from Lanyon, from Jekyll himself, from Jekyll's servant Poole, or from the deposition of a servant-girl who witnessed another of Hyde's public *actes gratuits*: the unprovoked and random murder of Sir Danvers Carew, a Member of Parliament who had lost his way in the London streets and was unfortunate enough to ask Hyde for directions. The construction of Stevenson's tale is thus akin to that of the detective story, with Utterson in the role of detective: 'If he be Mr. Hyde', he says to himself significantly, 'I shall be Mr. Seek.' It is Utterson, too, who after Jekyll's death reads Lanyon's account of his horrified assistance at Hyde's retransformation into Jekyll, an experience which Lanyon does not long survive; and it is Utterson again over whose shoulder we read, in the final chapter, the manuscript in which Jekyll tells his own story from the beginning and thus clears up all the mysteries which still remain unsolved: all the mysteries, that is, except the mystery surrounding the exact nature of the chemicals which made the liberation of Hyde possible, and those of the human soul which made Jekyll and Hyde one person in the first place.

It is clear from all this that Utterson's consciousness is the controlling one in the whole work—a consciousness defined for us in the character sketch which (after an allegorizing dedication and motto) opens Stevenson's tale:

Mr. Utterson the lawyer was a man of a rugged countenance, that was never lighted by a smile; cold, scanty, and embarrassed in discourse; backward in sentiment; lean, long, dusty, dreary, and yet somehow lovable. At friendly meetings, and when the wine was to his taste, something eminently human beaconed from his eye; something indeed which never found its way into his talk, but which spoke not only in these silent symbols of the after-dinner face, but more often and loudly in the acts of his life. He was austere with himself; drank gin when he was alone, to mortify a taste for vintages; and though he enjoyed the theatre, had not crossed the doors of one for twenty years. But he had an approved tolerance for others; sometimes wondering, almost with envy, at the high pressure of spirits involved in their misdeeds; and in any extremity inclined to help rather than to reprove.

What is so remarkable here, in our context, is the cinematic imagination already at work before the cinema had become a reality: those 'silent symbols of the . . . face' will become one of the staples of early films, after Griffith had shown what meaningful uses could be made of close-ups. But Utterson's own imagination, too, is presented in a way that makes it (for us) recognizably cinematic:

Six o'clock struck on the bells of the church that was so conveniently near to Mr. Utterson's dwelling, and still he was digging at the problem. Hitherto, it had touched him on the intellectual side alone; but now his imagination also was engaged, or rather enslaved; and as he lay and tossed in the gross darkness of the night and the curtained room, *Mr. Enfield's tale went by before his mind in a scroll of lighted pictures.* He would be aware of the great field of lamps of a nocturnal city; then of the figure of a man walking swiftly; then of a child running from the doctor's; and then these met, and that human Juggernaut trod the child down and passed on regardless of her screams. Or else he would see a room in a rich house, where his friend lay asleep, dreaming and smiling at his dreams; and then the door of that room would be opened, the curtains of the bed plucked apart, the sleeper recalled, and, lo! there would stand by his side a figure to whom power was given, and even at that dead hour he must rise and do its bidding. The figure in these two phases haunted the lawyer all night; and if at any time he dozed over, it was but to see it glide more stealthily through sleeping houses, or move the more swiftly and still the more swiftly, even to dizziness, through wider labyrinths of lamp-lighted city, and at every street corner crush a child and leave her screaming. And still the figure had no face by which he might know it; even in his dreams it had no face, or one that baffled him and melted before his eyes; and thus it was that there sprang up and grew apace in the lawyer's mind a singularly strong, almost an inordinate, curiosity to behold the features of the real Mr. Hyde. [My italics]

No wonder that film-directors and script-writers were fascinated by Stevenson!

When it came, however, to translating Stevenson's story into terms of images and sounds that would be acceptable to, and comprehensible by, a mass audience in English-speaking countries and (possibly) beyond, Mamoulian's team felt it necessary to make a large number of changes in plot-patterning and story-content. Let us look at a few of the most instructive instances.

The film as we have it converts the limited consciousness of an implied narrator standing alongside Utterson into that of the viewer seeing the world, during a brilliant opening sequence, through Jekyll's eyes. We *are* Jekyll as the subjective camera plays the organ, dresses to go out, approaches and enters a university or academy building, greets servants, students, and colleagues, hands coat and hat to an attendant, and enters a crowded lecture-theatre which the camera surveys, still with Jekyll's eyes, until it pans round 360° to show us Jekyll himself, delivering his eagerly awaited lecture. The contents of this lecture at the beginning of the film are a reduced and Freudianized version of the theories Stevenson's Jekyll puts forward in the manuscript that Utterson reads at the very end of the tale. Thus the time structure of Stevenson's intricately composed mystery tale is deliberately simplified; what comes first in time is first revealed. Within this simplified structure, however, Mamoulian exploits to the full the cinema's capability of indicating simultaneity (through dissolves and split-screen devices still to be discussed) and of recapitulating the past (through a delirious 'flash-back' sequence which I shall examine in some detail a little later).

We begin, then, not in the consciousness of Utterson or the implied narrator, but in that of Jekyll himself, which Stevenson's tale keeps from us until the very end. After this opening sequence the camera feels free to leave Jekyll and show us, occasionally, a scene at which neither he nor his *alter ego* Hyde is present; but for the most part it stays alongside him, and at crucial moments—especially during the first transformation-scene—it readopts the limitations of his hearing and his vision, makes the camera (and us, as spectators) see once again with his eyes and the microphone hear with his ears, while rapid amplified heartbeats on the sound-track enable us to share the very rhythm of his body, the pulsing of his blood. The distancing devices Stevenson had used are therefore jettisoned; Utterson has disappeared from the story completely, along with Enfield, though some of their traits are absorbed by Lanyon, who retains his function of warner and is kept alive until the end of the film. He is a cold, conventional figure, however, presented by Mamoulian with none of the warmth Stevenson clearly radiates in Utterson's direction; we are never made to experience what he experiences with anything like the immediate sympathy, the self-identification, which the film induces in us when it transports us into what seems like the very body of Jekyll.

To make up for this reduction, Mamoulian's team brings into the foreground of the action a character who had only appeared for a moment, in Stevenson's story, as victim of an unprovoked and murderous attack. Sir Danvers Carew, an M.P. in the original tale, is transformed in Mamoulian's film into a Victorian general with a propensity for giving lavish parties for the rich and titled, with strict views on propriety and decency, and with an attractive daughter whose life he hedges around with the consequences of those views. The film thus exteriorizes, makes visible in ways the cinema demands, the element of conventional propriety which is part of Jekyll's character and essential for an understanding of all that Hyde represents, all that Hyde rebels against. The transformation from politician to army officer meaningfully underlines the element of discipline and obedience which Hyde subverts. The introduction of the general's daughter thus enables another exteriorization, one which had already become part of the genre through its use in the Robertson–Barrymore version of *Jekyll and Hyde*: that of placing the hero between two women who present different lures and dangers, different aspects of his anima. On the one side, in Mamoulian's version, is the dark upper-class virgin played by Rose Hobart, who is hedged around by proprieties and conventions and sexually attainable only through marriage—a marriage which her father keeps postponing. Against her stands the blonde lower-class girl of easy virtue, projected with great charm and warmth by Miriam Hopkins, whose combination of sensuality and poverty makes her favours easy to obtain. Jekyll, a large bland man in his fifties in Stevenson's tale (Enfield described him as 'the very pink of the proprieties'), is impersonated in the film by Fredric March, a handsome, elegant actor in his mid-thirties; his love for the general's daughter makes him long for a physical consummation that he can only reach, in the 'respectable' world he inhabits, through the marriage that keeps being postponed. His libidinous and sadistic instincts are aroused by an incident in which he rescues the blonde girl from a vicious attack—

a rescue she rewards with an open invitation to love-making. Here the audience is once again forced into complicity, as the subjective camera directs the girl's fascinations at us, makes her throw one of her garters at us—towards the camera, that is—while she takes off her clothes and slips into bed. A long dissolve which makes us, the audience, share Jekyll's fascination with the girl's gartered but otherwise bare leg swinging over the side of her bed prepares for the liberation of Hyde, who consummates what Jekyll had desired.

The externalizations so far described have the effect of playing the sexual theme of the story much more into the foreground than it is allowed to be in Stevenson. The aggression Hyde directed in the story against a child over whose body he calmly tramples, leaving her screaming on the ground ('It sounds nothing to hear, but it was hellish to see', Enfield comments; 'It wasn't like a man, it was like some damned Juggernaut'), and later against a match-seller ('Once a woman spoke to him, offering, I think, a box of lights. He smote her in the face and she fled'), he here directs against the two women who share the centre of the film with him and his *alter ego*. Even the murder of Carew is connected with sexual desire: he is killed when he comes between Hyde and Carew's daughter, whom Hyde had attacked. It would be idle to pretend that box-office considerations had nothing to do with this particular change; but this does not mean that Mamoulian and his team forfeit their artistic integrity. They do not, it should be stressed, fall into the trap of equating sexuality with sin and evil. The desire stirred in Jekyll by both the women with whom his fate involves him is presented as normal and likable, the sensuality of the lower-class girl is made charming in every sense, and there is none of the cold schematism which might have made the upper-class girl cold and forbidding by contrast. What the film's externalizing images do, however, bring out with great force is the effect repression may have on the soul, and the element of cruelty that so easily allies itself with sexual desire—even though Hyde's whip and its results on the blonde girl's body are not directly shown, and though Mamoulian does not allow the camera to linger, as later film-makers would, on the physical details of Hyde's murders.

The transformation-scenes around which the film is built—the scenes in which Jekyll turns, at first voluntarily and then involuntarily, into Hyde, and Hyde back into Jekyll—are managed by Mamoulian with great technical virtuosity, by means of special make-up which reveals successive layers when photographed through different camera filters. Hyde's appearance, however, faced the film-makers with a problem which Lessing had pin-pointed many years before, when he compared the possibilities and limitations of the pictorial and the verbal arts in his *Laocoon* of 1766. In the verbal arts, physical attractiveness or its opposite is best conveyed by a description of its effects, of the reactions of those who look at physical characteristics which in a picture or statue could confront the viewer fully and immediately. Stevenson therefore concentrated, in his tale, on the reactions of various characters to Hyde's appearance: they speak of him in terms of apes and rats, or—at the other extreme—Satan and the children of hell; they see him as much younger, shorter, and more agile than Jekyll (a set of characteristics whose allegorical force is fully brought out); but when it comes to describing Hyde's face and physique, the story turns deliberately vague and reticent:

Mr. Hyde was pale and dwarfish; he gave an impression of deformity without any nameable malformation, he had a displeasing smile, he had borne himself to the lawyer with a sort of murderous mixture of timidity and boldness, and he spoke with a husky, whispering, and somewhat broken voice—all these were points against him; but not all of these together could explain the hitherto unknown disgust, loathing and fear with which Mr. Utterson regarded him. 'There must be something else,' said the perplexed gentleman. 'There is something more, if I could find a name for it. God bless me, the man seems hardly human! Something troglodytic, shall we say? or can it be the old story of Dr. Fell? or is it the mere radiance of a foul soul that thus transpires through, and transfigures, its clay continent? The last, I think; for oh, my poor old Harry Jekyll, if ever I read Satan's signature upon a face, it is on that of your new friend.'

Stevenson makes Jekyll fill in the moral background of these evocations towards the end of the book:

I have observed that when I wore the semblance of Edward Hyde, none could come near to me at first without a visible misgiving of the flesh. This, as I take it, was because all human beings, as we meet them, are com-mingled out of good and evil: and Edward Hyde, alone, in the ranks of mankind, was pure evil.

The film could not remain vague in this way: it had to commit itself, had to show us what Hyde actually looked like. What came out was a crooked-toothed, hairy, apelike, agile creature, whom Fredric March impersonated with such success that even the

Academy of Motion Picture Arts, which in its quest of respectability usually ignored the humble horror-movie, had to award him an Oscar for his performance of the dual role. Karl Struss, the cameraman who worked on the film, was not altogether happy with the result.

When you photograph someone and change them into something else without cuts or dissolves (as with [Fredric] March from Jekyll to Hyde), you have to put red makeup on the actor's face. Then, when you put a red filter on the camera, it doesn't show the red makeup at all. The lips of course remain the same, so they are painted a neutral grey. You move the filter up or down very slowly, and as it moves, you see the makeup emerge. I worked it out for Mamoulian. I thought they made a very bad mistake; the change from Jekyll should have been largely a psychological one, with subtle changes only in the makeup. But they foolishly changed the hair and put false teeth in, and made him look like a monkey. That was terrible. (Leyda, 1977, p. 447)

Other commentators—notably W. K. Everson—have regretted that March's simian impersonation of Hyde occasionally liberates unwelcome reminiscences of that figure which so notoriously haunts the imagination of white Americans: the stereotype of the black rapist, which had been introduced to the screen with such revolting force by the white actors in black-face who impersonate rebellious blacks in Griffith's *Birth of a Nation*, and which has served, in the world outside the cinema, as an excuse for cruelties that far surpass those of Hyde.

The actors and make-up experts of the terror-film are not always, it should be remembered, thrown back upon their own resources as decisively as we have seen them to be in Mamoulian's film. We need only think of the way in which Victor Hugo, whose fictions Stevenson admired so much and whose theory of the grotesque is so readily applicable to the terror-film, makes us see his Quasimodo in the very act of disclaiming his wish to do anything of the kind:

We will not try to give the reader any idea of the tetrahedron-like nose, of that horse-shoe shaped mouth; of that small left eye overhung by a bushy red eyebrow, while the right eye was completely hidden by a monstrous wart; of those uneven, broken teeth, with sad gaps here and there like the battlements of a fortress; of that callous lip, over which one of these teeth projected like an elephant's tusk; of that forked chin; and especially of the expression pervading all this,—that mixture of malice, amazement and melancholy. Imagine, if you can, that comprehensive sight . . .

The entire man was a grimace. A large head bristling with red hair; between his shoulders an enormous hump, with a corresponding prominence in front; legs and thighs so singularly crooked that they touched only at the knees, and, seen from the front, resembled two reaping-hooks united at the handle; broad feet, huge hands; and with all this deformity, a certain awe-inspiring air of vigour, agility, and courage; strange exception to the rule which declares power, as well as beauty, to be the result of harmony,— such was the pope whom the fools had chosen to reign over them.

In their famous assumptions of the part of Quasimodo, Lon Chaney and Charles Laughton closely modelled their physical appearance on the detailed description furnished by Hugo in this and other passages of his novel; and when the recent reprint of Gaston Leroux's *The Phantom of the Opera*, in Dennis Wheatley's *Library of the Occult*, sports a cover-illustration unmistakably based on Lon Chaney's grotesque make-up, it is only repossessing what Chaney took from Leroux's romance in the first place. In the very opening chapter a scene-shifter at the Paris opera describes the 'phantom' as follows:

'He is extraordinarily thin and his dress-coat hangs on a skeleton frame. His eyes are so deep that you can hardly see the fixed pupils. You just see two big black holes, as in a dead man's skull. His skin, which is stretched across his bones likes a drumhead, is not white, but a nasty yellow. His nose is so little worth talking about that you can't see it side-face; and *the absence* of that nose is a horrible thing *to look at*. All the hair he has is three or four long dark locks on his forehead and behind his ears.'

Chaney followed out almost every suggestion in this and similar passages, torturing his face into the likeness of the living skull depicted by Leroux in such repellent detail.

Stevenson, as has been shown, offered no such help with Hyde; and when it came to Jekyll, Mamoulian, his script-writers, and his make-up experts found themselves compelled, by genre-conventions, audience-expectations, and personal tastes, to make significant changes. We have already seen that the physical impression Stevenson gives us of his large, bland doctor has little in common with that conveyed by the matinée-idol Fredric March; and this alteration chimes in perfectly with the way in which Mamoulian's team focuses on Jekyll's popular touch (in a scene with a frightened old patient in the charity hospital, and in his scenes with the girl he rescues from her attackers) and emphasizes his pioneering nature, the scientific vision that impels him along his dangerous path, in ways that recur in the *Frankenstein* films. We are also shown Jekyll playing, of all things, a pipe-organ; he is thinking of his coming marriage, no doubt, but the audience will feel reminded of the use made of organ or harmonium playing in other cinematic tales of terror—from *The Phantom of the Opera* to *The Abominable Dr. Phibes*. Such instruments are associated in many minds with religious ceremonies, and thus serve to charge the films and their demonic protagonists with energies that ultimately derive from religion.

It has frequently been observed that Fredric March's Jekyll is colourless when compared with his Hyde, and that Rose Hobart's upper-class girl is colourless when compared with Miriam Hopkins's lower-class one. Far from indicating a weakness of the film, this rather points to one of its strengths—it is part of the working-out of Mamoulian's avowed theme: the conflict between 'nature' and 'civilization'. March's forceful performance as Hyde, as Philip Johns pointed out in an article in *Screen* (xi, Jan.–Feb. 1970), accentuated this theme by distinguishing itself from previous assumptions of the same part 'in being oafish rather than merely sinister, thus presenting a dichotomy between nobility and brutishness'. March's Hyde is, among other things, a savage who cannot and will not adapt himself to the stiff conventions and stern repressions of Jekyll's Victorian society. He is one of those *Halbwesen* whose ubiquity in the horror-movie and the fantastic cinema Claudius Weil and Georg Seesslen have documented:

One of the characteristics which distinguishes the acts of beings that are part man, part beast, part alive, part dead, part human, part demon, is that their aggression takes a form which relates it to acts of tenderness and love: the kiss of the vampire, the embrace of Kong, the Frankenstein monster's murder of the little girl and his embrace of Frankenstein himself in the final scene in which he tries to hurl his creator to his death . . . (Weil and Seesslen, 1976, pp. 9–13)

Hyde's sadistic love-making tells us something of the aggression that lurks in the act of love itself. Mamoulian and his actors convey the fascination of such brutish energy as powerfully as they suggest the lure of sexual availability; and the manner in which the characters of Jekyll and his fiancée are projected strengthens our sense of that fascination and that lure.

In the essay on 'Victor Hugo's Romances' from which I have already quoted, Stevenson commends the way in which Hugo gives us the very feel of Paris, a 'Gothic profile' of Paris, in his *Hunchback of Notre Dame*. His own Gothic tale emulates this feat: its evocation of nocturnal London with its mysterious doors through which flit figures at whose life-style and business we can only guess, and its all but deserted gas-lit streets, is an important element in the attraction which it has exerted on generations of readers. When Mamoulian came to emulate this evocation of the 'spirit of place', his set-designers and lighting-experts found invaluable help in the German cinema of the 1920s. The Soho set in *Dr. Jekyll and Mr. Hyde*, with its wooden stairways, houses with jutting upper storeys, and two street lamps so placed that they leave the foreground in darkness, the middle ground illuminated by an eerie white light, and the background mysteriously receding into a misty half-light, owes an unquestionable debt to the many films in which the German film-makers of the silent period had depicted the attraction and the perils of city streets. In particular, Mamoulian's set and lighting-scheme recall the final episode in Pabst's *Pandora's Box* (1928) and some of the Soho sets in the same director's sound version of *The Threepenny Opera* (1931). The fact that even Mamoulian's 'exterior' shots are clearly produced in the studio in no way detracts from their power. On the contrary: this adds to the feeling of claustrophobia on which cinematic tales of terror so often depend for their effect, and chimes in well with the theme of repression that lies at the heart of all Jekyll-and-Hyde stories.

The concept of the city as a place of terror will be familiar to readers of Poe and Baudelaire, who have dwelt particularly on one aspect of it which neither Stevenson nor Mamoulian brings into the foreground: its jostling crowds. Later films have made up for this omission; films like Richard Fleischer's *Soylent Green* (1973), for instance, which shows us an over-populated New York of the future that can afford each of its inhabitants no more than four square yards of living-space. In such conditions the shocks that inevitably attend life in the midst of a city crowd must, necessarily, be hideously multiplied.

The exteriors in Mamoulian's *Dr. Jekyll and Mr. Hyde* are matched by a whole series of effective interior sets. These reproduce brilliantly what Irving Saposnik, in his *Robert Louis Stevenson* (New York, 1974), has called the 'central metaphor' of *Dr. Jekyll and Mr. Hyde*: Jekyll's house, with its external dualism of handsome front and sinister rear entrance, and its internal progression from the splendid but cold hall to the study and finally to the laboratory with its glass apparatus and foaming or steaming or bubbling liquids. To this we must add the poor lodging-house room which takes on an unaccustomed splendour when Hyde sets its inhabitant up as his mistress, Dr. Lanyon's book-filled and candle-lit study, the great ballroom of the Carews' opulent house, the charity ward of the hospital in which Jekyll works with a selflessness that has no equivalent in Stevenson. And passing outside again we come to the garden to which Jekyll takes his fiancée during a society rout at her father's house, and the park in which Jekyll, full of thoughts of his coming marriage and roused by an unexpected visit from the girl he had rescued from her attackers, sits down on a bench and begins to change—suddenly and involuntarily—into Hyde. Here is how Stevenson set the scene for this involuntary transformation:

It was a fine clear January day, wet underfoot where the frost had melted but cloudless overhead; and the Regent's Park was full of winter chirrupings and sweet with spring odours. I sat in the sun on a bench; the animal within me licking the chops of memory . . .

Mamoulian picks up the suggestions implicit in those 'winter chirrupings' by focusing our, and Jekyll's, attention on a single bird; and he exteriorizes the 'animal within . . . licking the chops of memory' by introducing a black cat that creeps through the bushes and stalks the bird. It is the spectacle of such natural cruelty which prepares us for Hyde's reappearance—and the scene between Hyde and his doomed mistress is full of reminiscences of this externalization of Stevenson's metaphor, when Hyde calls the girl 'my little bird', 'my little starling', 'my dove', 'my bird', as he prepares to murder her. This carefully calculated effect has been destroyed in existing copies of the film; for the cat has been snipped out by someone afraid of protests from the R.S.P.C.A. or from animal-lovers, leaving the bird apparently alive and well as Jekyll's sadistic *alter ego* liberates itself to begin a cat-and-bird game of its own.

Mamoulian has occasionally been attacked for importing into his film objects—especially works of art—for the sole purpose of making them serve a symbolic or allegorical effect. Such objects do indeed play an important part in his *Dr. Jekyll and Mr. Hyde*. There is the bust of a periwigged scientist (could it be Newton?) in the university or academy building in which Jekyll delivers his opening lecture; the decorous cupid in the garden-scene between the doctor and his fiancée and the more indecorous putto in the scene between Hyde and his mistress; the portrait of Queen Victoria, no less, beneath which Hyde changes into Jekyll before Lanyon's horrified eyes; the statuettes of the victorious warrior and the smiling woman in Jekyll's house, seen at the moment in which he is full of delight in the prospect of his coming marriage; the painting of a female nude which dominates the refurbished apartment of Hyde's mistress and the dazzling white reproduction of Canova's *Eros and Psyche* on which the camera meaningfully focuses while Hyde is murdering his mistress off-screen. It would be quite wrong, however, to condemn these symbolic objects as extraneous to the action of the film; they are part of that action, essential elements of the 'spirit of place'. The nude painting, for instance, is precisely the work of art we would expect a wealthy man to import into his mistress's boudoir, while the Canova is precisely the sort of object we might imagine her choosing for herself. The same is true of the skeleton which first appears in a two-shot with Jekyll's servant (sympathetically played by Edgar Norton) and then by itself—this is at once a symbol of Jekyll's approaching death, a prop belonging to the terror-film genre, and a natural part of the furnishings of a doctor's study. It is interesting to compare the deeply serious use Mamoulian makes of this prop and the macabre humour with which James Whale deploys it in the 'brain-stealing' sequence of his *Frankenstein* of 1931.

These local and incidental symbols take their place in a pervasive symbolic structure which shows itself in the very rhythm and movement of the film, its rapid alternation between Jekyll and Hyde scenes, between different kinds of locale, between different sets of characters. It works through household objects like a flickering candle in the foreground of one of the transformation-scenes, or the candle burning down in Lanyon's study, suggesting at once passage of time and dwindling energy as Hyde metamorphoses back into Jekyll. Mirrors, railings, window-frames shutting in and shutting out, perform similar symbolic functions. So do the different locales: the repellently cold splendour of the entrance hall in Jekyll's house, or the sensual allure of the music-hall where top-hatted girls on stocky legs recall Sternberg's *Blue Angel* (1930) as surely as the exterior sets had recalled the films of Pabst. The two women, those strangely altered reincarnations of Rebecca and

Rowena, between whom Jekyll and Hyde move, also have a clear symbolic meaning. Several of the incidents to which Mamoulian's film gives symbolic force already belonged, in his time, to the conventions of the genre: the sinister watcher at the window, seen by the audience but not by those who are being watched; the monster's 'magnetic' eyes, seen in closest close-up; the monster's attack on the innocent heroine. Others, however, became part of the genre under the impact of Mamoulian's film. Chief among these latter is the device, not used in Stevenson's tale, of showing Hyde turning back into Jekyll after his death; a device which later became a cliché not only in treatments of the Jekyll-and-Hyde story, but also in the Werewolf cycle that began in 1935 with *Werewolf of London* and gained its full momentum in the 1940s with the *Wolf Man* films starring Lon Chaney Junior.

One of the expressive devices of the film which Mamoulian uses with a virtuosity that belies his theatrical background is 'montage' or 'dynamic cutting'. He does not, however, go outside the film's *mise en scène* for the material of his shots; and he uses montage to give us some insight into his characters' state of mind rather than as a means of introducing editorial comment and distancing irony. The first transformation-scene of *Dr. Jekyll and Mr. Hyde* exemplifies his approach. As Jekyll lifts the potion to his lips, the camera, once again, becomes his eyes; the foaming potion is raised towards the camera and us, and we see Jekyll's agonized face in the mirror, his hands clutching his throat as the liquid drains down; we see him fall—in the mirror, for his eyes are now our eyes—and then the image blurs as the potion dims his consciousness. Memory images now appear, superimposed on the blur and on each other— memories of things seen, heard, and done which we share with Jekyll, for what we now see and hear are fragments of incidents shown earlier in the film. A two-shot of Jekyll and his fiancée, with Jekyll pleading: 'Marry me, I can't wait any longer', is followed by a close-up of the fiancée's father, the general, saying: 'Positively indecent'; there follows a shot of the skirt and legs of the girl Jekyll had rescued from thugs, and we hear the girl's voice saying 'Look where he kicked me'—with a comment from Lanyon: 'Your conduct is disgusting . . .' A blurred image of the general can then be heard declaring: 'It isn't done, it isn't done'; the face of Jekyll, in top hat and white tie, is superimposed on that of the general, and Jekyll now hears himself repeating with deadly hatred what he had once said in jest: 'I could strangle, strangle . . .' as the general repeats 'Indecent, indecent'. Then his face disappears, leaving Jekyll's agonized and questioning one ('Can a man dying of thirst forget water?'), to be immediately succeeded by a close-up of Lanyon, in the same kind of evening clothes as Jekyll, calling out with uncharacteristic vehemence: 'Disgusting. You're mad, mad!' Then we go back to the girl Jekyll had rescued, sitting up in bed with the bedclothes pulled closely around her body saying: 'Come back soon, won't you?' and repeating over and over again, 'Come back, come back . . .' while her gartered leg swings by the side of her bed. Then the image contracts and sharpens as, framed in darkness, the fireplace of Jekyll's laboratory shines out—bringing us back to the familiar world from that of delirium, but holding disquieting associations of hell-fire in Mamoulian's context. This shot of flames is taken from ground level, for Jekyll is lying on the floor and so (in our imaginations) are we in this subjective camera sequence; the camera then moves up to the laboratory table as we raise ourselves with Jekyll and approach the mirror in which now, for the first time, the face of Hyde appears calling out exultingly 'Free! Free at last!' As the camera moves back, its iris opens out, and we are once again looking *at* Jekyll (or rather, now, at Hyde) as well as *with* him.

As this account of the first transformation-scene will already have suggested, Mamoulian makes imaginative and unobtrusive use of the 'iris-in' and 'iris-out' effects so beloved of the directors of the silent film and hallowed in the history of the terror-movie by their prominence in *The Cabinet of Dr. Caligari*. At the very beginning of *Dr. Jekyll and Mr. Hyde* the iris draws in, leaving a brightly lit centre in an outer rim of darkness when *we* are transformed, when *we* become Dr. Jekyll as he will later become Mr. Hyde. Nor is this the only conventional transition device employed by Mamoulian in newly meaningful ways. We first see the swinging gartered leg of the girl whom Jekyll had rescued and whom Hyde is later to murder in close-up shots as Hyde is hurried, by Lanyon, from the room in which she had made—very sweetly—sexual overtures to him; these shots are then superimposed over the next scene in an extraordinarily long and lingering dissolve in order to suggest the way this sexually titillating image continues vibrating in Jekyll's mind. Even more striking is the use Mamoulian makes of the common device which allows a new shot to succeed a previous one by degrees in such a way that it appears to brush it off the screen—an action which the technical term 'diagonal wipe' likens to that of the windscreen-wiper of a car. The first time this device is used in Mamoulian's film it works the transition from the charity hospital, in which Jekyll is comforting an old woman about to undergo an operation, to an opulent drawing-room, in which Jekyll's fiancée and her father, in full evening regalia, await the arrival of their guests. The screen divides in such a way that Jekyll's fiancée, wearing a splendid ball-dress and photographed against a fluted white pillar, a painting, and an ornate chair, appears in the upper half of the frame whose lower half still reveals the old woman in her iron-framed bed against the bare wall of the charity ward. Though it must be admitted that the image of the old woman looking up at Jekyll with such trust is somewhat sentimental in a Griffith sort of way, the juxtaposition of the two images, one of which is being shouldered out, diagonally wiped away, by the other, does amount to an unobtrusive yet clear presentation of the class-structure of the society Jekyll inhabits, and the different spheres in which he moves. It also reminds us, if we need reminding, that Mamoulian made his film during the Depression: what he is showing his audience here would be felt as relevant, not only to the Victorian society into which the film transports us, but also to the very different world of America in the 1930s. The ruthless aggressiveness of the liberated Hyde may therefore hold the same kind of social overtones as that of King Kong when he smashes up the New York business district, destroying the poor along with the rich as he derails and crushes subway trains and drops unwanted girls out of skyscraper windows. Dr. Jekyll's behaviour in the charity ward when he neglects his rich friends in order to relieve the pain of the old woman and lays his hands comfortingly on her head may also be seen as socially relevant during the Depression years: is it not a somewhat sentimentalized representation, in terms of this particular film, of the impulses that resulted in the New Deal? Stevenson had said of his 'large, well-made, smooth-faced man of fifty' that he had 'every mark of capacity and kindness' along with a 'stylish cast', and that 'whilst he had always been known for charities, he was now no less distinguished for religion'; there is no equivalent in his tale, however, for the charity-ward scene with its dynamic, sympathetic, and selfless doctor neglecting his obligations to the rich in his zeal to relieve the troubles of the poor. The use of the diagonal wipe to brush the world of the poor from the screen and substitute that of the rich, with its momentary, split-screen confrontation of the old pauper and the young society beauty, may once again, like the Soho set, recall the world of Pabst, the Pabst of *The Threepenny Opera* and *The Joyless Street* (1925).

Split screen, split society, split personality—Mamoulian's transition devices are anything but arbitrary. His next use of the diagonal wipe reinforces this impression. In the upper left half appears the girl Jekyll had rescued and Hyde had set up as his mistress in her newly gorgeous room, while the new scene approaches from below in such a way that midway through the wipe Hyde's blonde, lower-class mistress shares the screen with Jekyll's darker, upper-class fiancée, again seen against a cool white fluted pillar as she sits on a sofa with Jekyll by her side. There are several more such slow diagonal wipes and all turn out to be equally meaningful, equally transcending their usefulness as a mere mark of transition from one scene to the next.

A writer needs no more than his talent, his imagination, a pen or typewriter, and a supply of paper, to give shape to his vision; a film-director, however, particularly in the days before cheap hand-held cameras and mass-produced film-stock, needs the expensive resource of a studio, with its actors, cameramen, technicians, designers, and auxiliary staff. The studio-bosses and their financial backers must be persuaded that their investment stands a reasonable chance of showing a profit, and all sorts of compromises have to be made in the process. Public expectations—which are usually genre-expectations, conditioned by previous films—have to be satisfied to some extent if the film is to succeed at the box-office; this means taking account of conventions, and gauging accurately the point at which convention can be subverted, that at which it can be used for original and meaningful effect, and that at which it becomes a cliché that can be caricatured. And even when all this has been successfully negotiated, the director working for a big studio has usually no redress if his work is re-edited, or if scenes are simply snipped out by those who think, in the studio or in censors' offices, that they are not fit to be seen by the paying public. Mamoulian's *Dr. Jekyll and Mr. Hyde* seems to have lost several sequences in this way; there was even a time, in the early forties, when the whole film seemed lost, bought up and destroyed to make room for Victor Fleming's interesting but inferior version. Fortunately, it survived even that murderous onslaught—and though we may regret that Mamoulian was not able to find a satisfactory equivalent for some of Stevenson's subtler allegorical points (Stevenson's Hyde is younger and smaller than Jekyll; he grows in the course of the story but still looks grotesquely out of place in Jekyll's large clothes), his film need not fear comparison with its original either as a moral statement or as a piece of story-telling by means of the resources of a particular medium.

A careful reading of Stevenson's story confirms that there was such a thing as a cinematic imagination before there was a cinema: his externalization of an inner conflict in the shape of Jekyll-and-Hyde, his description of Utterson's mode of dreaming and appre-hending, are cases in point. Griffith, Eisenstein, and other, lesser film-directors have often paid tribute to what they have learnt from literature in general and narrative fiction in particular and have shown in detail what devices of montage and *mise en scène* were anticipated by nineteenth-century novelists. In *The Cinematic Imagination* Edward Murray has described many of these anticipa-tions and has shown, in addition, what later novelists and drama-tists have, in their turn, learnt from the cinema; but he has also demonstrated, magisterially, how many differences result from the pictorial (as opposed to the verbal) language of the film. Mamoulian has taken account of these differences by reducing the cast of characters, simplifying the 'point of view' from which Stevenson tells his tale, and cutting out a great deal of his moral argument and explicit comment. The very fact that he chose to film a *nouvelle* rather than a novel, and a minor work of literature rather than a major one, means that less is lost—less is *felt* to be lost—in the transition to the screen than would have been the case had he elected to film, say, *The Brothers Karamazov*. Comparison between Stevenson's tale and Mamoulian's movie serves once again to confirm the impression that in the hands of a gifted director and script-writer a literary narrative is only raw material, to be reworked and reshaped into a new imaginative creation which may—like Mamoulian's *Dr. Jekyll and Mr. Hyde*—bear the same title as its literary original.

The manner in which Mamoulian and his script-writers took fire from Stevenson's image of 'the animal within . . . licking the chops of memory' alerts us to the less obvious ways in which the cinematic imagination may be stimulated by a literary narrative. Yon Barna, in his biography of Eisenstein, allows us another instructive glimpse of how his reading may affect a film-director's visual language. The catalyst here is that inspirer of many terror-films, Edgar Allan Poe.

A story by Edgar Allan Poe . . . had a powerful effect on the young Eisenstein. Poe describes how, looking out of a window, he saw a gigantic prehistoric monster dragging itself slowly to a mountain-top—only to discover that the supposed monster was a tiny insect battling its way up the window pane. It was, as Eisenstein explained on recalling the story, a composition in depth which no human eye could capture with the same objective effectiveness as the film camera. 'I suspect that my own most powerful and effective close-up compositions in depth—the skull and the pilgrims . . . from *Que Viva Mexico!*—bear the seal of . . . Poe's fantastic story.' (Barna, 1975, p. 32)

Nineteenth-century terror-fiction, which has counted so much in the history of the cinema, influenced not only its story-lines but also its montage, its *mise en scène*, and its photographic angles of vision.

There can be no doubt that with their idealizing of Jekyll (in the spirit of the New Deal) and their sexualization of Hyde, Mamoulian and his team altered Stevenson's conception in ways the author would hardly have approved. 'The harm was in Jekyll because he was a hypocrite—not because he was fond of women', Stevenson wrote to J. P. Bocock in 1887, protesting against a theatrical adaptation which played up the sexual theme. Against this we must, however, set the realization that Mamoulian's *Dr. Jekyll and Mr. Hyde* is as truly cinematic as Stevenson's story is truly literary. It uses the language of the fantasy-film to transport its audience into a social ambience at once strange to them and oddly familiar; it engages its audience's sympathies for a rebel and pioneer whose endeavours went wrong, by means of cinematic devices which transport that audience almost bodily into the hero's experience; it satisfies, vicariously, unspoken desires for destruction, desires that are socially as well as individually conditioned, by means of images and sounds that speak of human dangers and possibilities, of the close neighbourhood of love and cruelty, in ways we can respect intellectually while emotionally assenting to a sometimes overt, sometimes subliminal visual and aural symbolism; it investigates, by means of montage and *mise en scène*, what Leo Braudy has called 'the relation between scientific and sexual curiosity, between the realms of laboratory and brothel, the separation and inter-connection of mind and body'; it satisfies genre-expectations even while transcending them, showing possibilities of the cinematic tale of terror unseen by its earlier masters; and it does all this while impressing the film with a personal stamp, a style recognizably that of the same Rouben Mamoulian who also gave the world *Applause*, and *City Streets*, and *Queen Christina*. It has another, unsought distinction too: it was the first foreign film the censor banned from German screens after Hitler's accession to power in 1933. In rejecting the fantastic cinema of Weimar Germany the new rulers felt compelled to reject also the Hollywood films which had been so indelibly affected by its example.

CHAPTER 4

The Uncanny

And when he had crossed the bridge, the phantoms
came to meet him.

Nosferatu (1922)

ONE of the best, certainly one of the most knowledgeable and
useful, books ever written on the genre which is at the centre of the
present study, W. K. Everson's *Classics of the Horror Film*, contains
what I have always felt to be the astonishing contention that 'the
silent screen was unable to create any really memorable horror
films'. It depends, I suppose, on your definition of a 'horror'-film;
but if this implies the thrill of imaginative fear then we can experience more of it in a few minutes of such German silents as *The
Cabinet of Dr. Caligari*, (*Warning*) *Shadows*, and *Nosferatu* than in
the whole of Mark Robson's rather dull and pointless *Isle of the
Dead* which Everson presents to us, in his opening chapter, as a
model of the genre that is his subject. The description 'horror-film' or
'horror-movie', we should remember, has been rejected over and
over again by those who starred in, or directed, many of the films
Everson discusses, because they felt that the term 'horror' signified
a *painful* emotion composed of repugnance and fear, a shudder of
loathing, as well as terror; and it is surely true that *Isle of the Dead*
does not inspire the same sensations as the eye-slashing scene at
the opening of *An Andalusian Dog* or the gory mutilations inflicted
by the eponymous instrument of *The Texas Chain Saw Massacre*. The
emotions caused by the fantasy terror-films Everson discusses may
often be described as 'weird', 'eerie', 'ghostly', or 'uncanny' rather
than horrifying; and the term 'terror' would seem to cover a
greater range of their effects than the stronger, the more violent,
term 'horror'.

There are many reasons why it should be German works which
spring to one's mind when one thinks of such emotions; why,
indeed, so many of the early sound-films discussed in these pages
should deliberately cultivate what audiences learnt to recognize as

the 'German' look. For one thing, adjectives like 'weird', 'ghostly', 'uncanny' describe very well an aspect of the image of Germany and the Germans which has persisted in English-speaking countries, ever since Smollett chose the Harz Mountains as the setting of the most frightening—and the most memorable—incidents of *Ferdinand Count Fathom*. It was vain, after that, for the purveyors of the Gothic novel to give their heroes Italian- (or generally Latin-) sounding names like Schedoni or Ambrosio, to call their castles 'Otranto' and set their mysteries in 'Udolpho'; it was equally vain for Thackeray and others to stress the provincial *Gemütlichkeit* of the Germany they knew, or thought they knew—a host of translations of sensational novels, weird folk-tales and pseudo-folk-tales, ghostly ballads in the wake of Goethe's 'Erl-King' and Bürger's 'Lenore', made the words 'From the German' hold promise of delightful alarms. Of the seven 'horrid' novels mentioned in *Northanger Abbey*, two are actual translations from the German, and four others set their scene in Germany. 'Had my title borne *Waverley, a Romance from the German*', writes Sir Walter Scott, 'what head so obtuse as not to image forth a profligate abbot, an oppressive duke, a secret and mysterious association of Rosicrucians and Illuminati, with all their properties of black cowls, caverns, daggers, electrical machines, trap-doors and dark lanterns?' The works of 'Monk' Lewis could be characterized, by the *Monthly Review*, as 'the direful croaking of this German raven'; Maturin could announce his intention of writing a horrific novel by saying that he would 'out-Herod all the Herods of the German School'; and far into the nineteenth century the appearance of a German-sounding name in the title of a story made the right reader thrill with anticipation. *Kruitzner (The German's Tale)* . . . *Wieland, or The Transformation* . . . *The Ghost of Count Walkenried* . . . *Frankenstein: or, The Modern Prometheus* . . . *Dr. Heidegger's Experiment* . . . Edgar Allan Poe, when he first sent his *Tales of the Grotesque and Arabesque* into the world, found it necessary to assert in a preface that the terror at which he aimed was 'not of Germany, but of the soul'.

It is easy to smile at such an image of German literature and to deplore the historical accidents which made Grub Street hacks pounce on the worst German library-fodder to produce thrilling reading-matter for a public that had tired of the sweetly reasonable. But there is no smoke without a fire—and a student of German culture cannot but be struck by the prominent part which weird fantasies have played in German art, especially since the eighteenth century. In literature there have been at least two outbreaks, almost epidemics, of works whose chief *raison d'être* seemed to be the stimulation of the reader's fears: at the end of the eighteenth century, in the writings of Spiess, Cramer, Schlenkert, I. F. Arnold, and other purveyors of *Schauerromane* and *Bundesromane*; and again in the first two decades of the twentieth century, when writers like Meyrink, Panizza, Ewers, and Przybyszewski spiced horror with dashes of social comment, humour noir, and pornography. An interest in the uncanny does lead us into some bad or indifferent company. All too easily the titillation of fear allies itself with sadistic and erotic fantasies, with unhealthy nervous excitements that nourish no values, with the confirmation of social prejudice through the stereotypes that are made to carry the necessary menace. But even if our literary taste and our moral sense are fastidious enough to reject such fare, we cannot, if we are interested in German literature, escape uncanny motifs—they pervade the work of Tieck and Kleist, Eichendorff and Hoffmann, even that of Heine, for all its rationality; we find them in Gotthelf's *Black Spider*, Droste's *Jews' Beech*, Raabe's *The Plague Cart*; they are an important element in the fiction of Thomas Mann, Franz Kafka, Hugo von Hofmannsthal, and Robert Musil. Even where the uncanny is consciously resisted, it breaks through like a guilty secret: one need think only of Schiller's *The Ghostseer* which so electrified Byron, or of Goethe's 'Bride of Corinth'. We find it in German music too, most recognizably in the opera, from Weber's *Freischütz* and Marschner's *The Vampire* to Wagner's *The Flying Dutchman*; in the art of Arnold Böcklin and Alfred Kubin; and above all in the German films of the great silent years from Stellan Rye's *The Student of Prague* and Otto Rippert's *Homunculus* serial onwards. Despite their occasional absurdities and sentimentalities, these films deserve our serious attention. They have strong links with the literature of the past (their story-line, and many of their themes, derive from German Romanticism); their style is indebted to advanced movements in the art of their own day, notably Expressionism in the theatre and in painting; and when we see central motifs of a play like Dürrenmatt's *The Physicists* anticipated in *The Cabinet of Dr. Caligari* and in Fritz Lang's *Mabuse* saga, we may begin to see their relevance to present-day literature as well.

When I speak of the 'uncanny' I do not have in mind what Tzvetan Todorov calls *l'étrange* (the apparently supernatural given a natural explanation) as opposed to *le merveilleux* (the truly supernatural) and *le fantastique* (doubtful hesitation between these two opposing categories). What is in my mind, rather, is the German term *unheimlich* with its convenient semantic ambivalence: (a) the 'un-homely', that which makes you feel uneasy in the world of your normal experience, not quite safe to trust to, mysterious, weird, uncomfortably strange or unfamiliar. In this sense, *unheimlich* has frequently been used as the equivalent of a word that would seem to be its opposite, the word *heimlich*, meaning 'secret' or 'hidden'. And from here, from this dialectical tension between *heimlich* and *unheimlich*, we arrive at a second meaning which has interested several writers from Schelling to Freud: (b) the 'un-secret', that which should have remained hidden but has somehow failed to do so. 'Unheimlich'—so runs the well-known definition from Schelling's *Philosophy of Mythology*— 'nennt man alles, was in Geheimnis, im Verborgnen, in der Latenz bleiben sollte und hervorgetreten ist' ('Uncanny is a term for everything which should remain mysterious, hidden, latent and has come to light'). To be *unheimlich*, a work need not provide shocks of horror: the uncanny may be diffused over the whole as an atmosphere like the fogs that blanket London in the more macabre pages of Dickens, like the eerie light that illuminates the 'white nights' of Gogol's or Dostoevsky's St. Petersburg. To be *unheimlich*, a work need not introduce supernatural agents: the murderer Moosbrugger in Musil's *The Man without Qualities* is one of the most recognizably and explicitly uncanny figures in modern literature, yet he belongs—alas—wholly to the world we know. Nor are the grotesque and the uncanny as indissolubly linked as the late Wolfgang Kayser would have had us believe: Rabelais's *Gargantua* is grotesque without being uncanny, while Eichendorff's Lorelei and Venus figures are uncanny without being grotesque. And the true uncanny does not need—though it may, on occasions, use—melodramatic or consciously 'demonic' trappings. Few readers of the present day will find Balzac's Vautrin as *unheimlich* as those other figures in the *Comédie humaine*—Mme Cibot of *Le Cousin Pons* may stand for them all—behind whose ordinariness lurks a frightening will to destruction. Recent events have, of course, made us particularly sensitive to the evil of banality—made us shudder with intimate recognition at atrocities committed by the most colourless, the most ordinary, the most intrinsically uninteresting and undemonic of men, whose prototype in modern literature may be said to be Percy Grimm in Faulkner's *Light in August*.

The uncanny, then, is not confined to sensational, to romantic, or—indeed—to German literature. We feel it in certain portions of the Book of Job; we feel it in Shakespeare, notably in *Macbeth*; we feel it when honest Captain Delgado's stereotypes are confronted in Melville's 'Benito Cereno' by a darker truth, or when the hero of Hawthorne's 'Young Goodman Brown' has those forest visions which will prevent his ever feeling quite at home again in his family and his society; we feel it in practically all the works of Gogol, even the most apparently humorous and light-hearted, in Dostoevsky, in Leonid Andreev; we feel it in Conrad's *Heart of Darkness* as in the *Fictions* of J. L. Borges. Such works arouse feelings of uneasiness and apprehension, but an uneasiness and apprehension that seem necessary, fruitful, and true. They afford sensations of descent (reminiscent of the descent, in the Gothic novel, in de Sade, and in Poe, into vaults and underground passages): descent into the depths of the mind (and beyond) where we are faced with truths of which we have never had such knowledge; truths, certainly, of our own nature, and truths, perhaps, of something more.

Here we must draw back for a moment and remind ourselves of the uncomfortable truism which is so often forgotten: that we can only do justice to a literary phenomenon through an adequate response to its literary qualities. This means reflecting, first of all, on the difference between symbolic and discursive language. It means keeping ourselves aware of the potentialities of different genres—the ballad, for instance, with its leapings and lingerings, and what Henry James called 'the beautiful and blest *nouvelle*', the long short story which has at its centre a startling or unusual incident, have always lent themselves particularly well to evocations of the uncanny. We must look at textures of style, contrasting (say) Tieck's dreamy, almost absent-minded, para-tactic recital with Hoffmann's deliberate whipping-up of his readers' emotions through sentences crammed with insistent adjectives and cunningly constructed towards a climax. We must give due attention to narrative structures, the manipulation of tense and mood, key words, imagery, and all matters of tone. How differently the subjunctive, for instance, is used by German novelists, in whose work the uncanny plays an important part: by Thomas Mann (in whose work it reassuringly suggests ironic distance and rational appraisal), by Franz Kafka (where it is a mark of the uncertainty felt by hero and reader in face of another's confusing narrative), and by Robert Musil (where it is the sign of an open mind, an experimental mood, a sense of the potential). And how much we can learn of the world created by three American masters of uncanny effects by just looking at Newton Arvin's list of their favourite words! 'Terror', 'anxiety', 'horror', 'anguish', 'fear' (that gives you the world of Edgar Allan Poe, of course, 'three-fifths of him genius and two-fifths sheer fudge'); 'wild', 'barbarous', 'savage', 'vengeful', 'cunning', 'malignant', 'noble', 'innocent', 'grand', 'inexorable', 'inscrutable', 'unfathomable' (that's Melville); 'dusky', 'dim', 'shadowy', 'cold', 'sluggish', 'torpid', 'separate', 'estrange', 'insulate' (that's Hawthorne). Beyond that, we must remain alive to the different levels of intensity at which the uncanny may show itself; its unselfconscious appearance in fairy-tales, where ghosts and ogres represent a danger no more and no less real than wolves and robbers; its annihilation through humour in works like Wells's 'The Inexperienced Ghost' or Beerbohm's 'Enoch Soames', and its coexistence with—even heightening through—humour in the tales of E. T. A. Hoffmann; the comforting, deliberately 'old-fashioned' air it is given in even the most shuddery tales of M. R. James, where we always sense the fireside by which the antiquarian old gentleman seeks at once to harrow and to reassure; its deeply disturbing and disorientating matter-of-factness in the stories of Kafka. Here much depends on the degree of distance at which an author keeps his reader—whether he tells us, as both Hoffmann and Poe, alas, frequently tend to do, how horrible his tale is or is going to be, or whether (like Henry James or like Kafka) he presents and allows the reader to draw his own conclusions. Much depends, too, on the kind of reflecting consciousness that the author interposes between himself and his readers: 'a scientific' investigator with a bent for the occult, like Le Fanu's Dr. Hesselius, or a man of good sense and moral curiosity like Conrad's Marlow, or a frightened young girl like Mrs. Radcliffe's heroines, or a superstitious and unlettered man like Scott's Wandering Willie (who tells his story in dialect—and that also makes a difference!), or a neurotic unbalanced personality like the diarist in Maupassant's 'Le Horla', or a man who is feverish, physically sick, like Ivan Karamazov. Nor must we forget to estimate the degree of ambiguity and obliquity an author allows himself: whether we are meant to think of the happenings narrated as taking place in the real world (as in Lewis's *The Monk* or Chamisso's *Peter Schlemihl*); or whether we are to regard them as hallucinations produced by guilt and fear (as in Jonas's dream in *Martin Chuzzlewit*); or whether we are to be left in epistemological doubt, as in 'Young Goodman Brown' and possibly also in *The Turn of the Screw*; or whether (as in Büchner's *Lenz* and the episode in which William Golding's Simon confronts the Lord of the Flies) what is presented as hallucination may not be meant to afford us an insight into aspects of reality that our normal consciousness ignores at its peril. It is even profitable—as I once tried to demonstrate in another context—to work out something like a rhetoric or grammar of the uncanny; to examine the rhetorical devices—aposiopesis, anaphora, amphibology, seemingly impersonal constructions, dislocations of syntax, heaping-up of exclamations and questions, and so on—that authors have employed, at various times, in order to create a proper disposition, a feeling of and for the uncanny, in their readers.

Such observations as I have just been suggesting will help us to plot the landscape of the uncanny in literature, to see what is offered in each individual case and to distinguish between different kinds, and different levels, of appeal. We should be able to point to matters of language and structure, in order to show why we think Gogol's *Viy* a greater and deeper work than Bram Stoker's *Dracula*, although both have tapped similar areas of experience; and why the appeal of Poe and Rider Haggard should grow more threadbare after we have come to years of discretion. Yet I think that here, in this field of the uncanny, stylistic analysis cannot take us all the way. At the risk of amateurishness and eclecticism, we should look across to other disciplines in our endeavours to find out what moves us in Hoffmann and Poe with their gimcrack effects, what stirs us so deeply in Gogol with his realistic surface, or in the fantasies of a Lautréamont and an Alfred Kubin. This does not mean abdicating our duties as critics of works of art—nor must we fall into the common error of thinking incompetence in our own subject a guarantee of competence in somebody else's. But in an examination of the uncanny we cannot, I think, afford to scorn outside help; help in understanding what is behind such a judgement as that of D. H. Lawrence, who, after brilliantly exposing Poe's meretricious and mechanical style, turns on readers who think they can now discount Poe with the sentence: 'It is lurid and melodramatic, but it is true.'

Writing in 1913, after seeing a number of trick-films in which objects appeared to assume a life of their own and actions took place in reverse order or upside down, seeming to defy the laws of causality and gravity, Georg Lukács was struck by the suitability of the cinema for the presentation of meaningful fantasy—a fantasy, he stressed, that did not stand in contrast to life as actually lived but represented another aspect of it.

These are images and scenes of a world like that of E. T. A. Hoffmann or Poe, Arnim or Barbey d'Aurevilly—but the great poet who interprets and orders them, who uses the fantastic quality which merely derives from adventitious technical factors for meaningful metaphysical and stylistic purposes, has not yet appeared. What we have had so far came into being naively, simply out of the spirit of cinematic technology and technique; an Arnim or a Poe of our day, however, would here find an instrument for the fulfilment of his yearning to dramatize—an instrument as rich and intrinsically adequate as (say) the Greek stage was for Sophocles. (Kaes, 1978, pp. 116–17)

But just as we cannot adequately discuss Sophocles without some reference to the use he made of the Greek stage, so we cannot discuss the terror- or fantasy-film without looking at its use of the opportunities offered by the cinema-medium at a definite stage of its historic development. We must constantly ask ourselves, as V. F. Perkins does in his significantly titled book *Film as Film*, how imaginatively, how meaningfully, the complex sign-system, the language, of the film or of a specific genre has been used in individual instances. We must ask ourselves what difference framing-devices like those in *Caligari* and Lang's *Woman in the Window*, shifts of perspective like those in Mamoulian's *Jekyll and Hyde* (or, *a fortiori*, those in *Rashomon* and *Citizen Kane*) can make to the true and total meaning of a film; and ask, too, where we can detect signs of a personal vision, and where signs of cynical exploitation of proven effects or commercially dictated efforts to 'go one better'. What happens to the terror-genre when wise-cracking reporters are deliberately introduced as 'distancing' agents, or when Abbott and Costello 'Meet the Killer, Boris Karloff',[1] Old Mother Riley 'Meets the Vampire', and the *Carry On* gang 'Carry on Screaming'? The makers of the macabre film like to play all sorts of games with their audiences; games of allusion, as when Gloria Holden, in *Dracula's Daughter*, repeats a line spoken by Bela Lugosi in the original *Dracula* of 1931; or 'double-take' games, as when the hero-villain of Karl Freund's *Mad Love* is shown as the assiduous patron of a *Grand Guignol* show, nudging the audience into awareness that they too have come to watch Grand Guignol— a theme struck in more serious vein by Michael Powell in *Peeping Tom*, whose central protagonist photographs the agony of women he kills with the pointed stand of his camera; or film-within-film, world-within-world games: as when the vampire-count Yorga, played by Robert Quarry, watches one of the sexier Hammer vampire-films on television in *The Return of Count Yorga*. But literature is older than the film; we should therefore constantly ask ourselves what the film has in fact derived from literature, what images and devices and story-lines it has taken over and what it has done with its borrowings. Alan Spiegel, George Bluestone, and Geoffrey Wagner, in their studies of the novel and the film, have led us a good way along the right path; and David Pirie, in *A Heritage of Horror*, has shown incontrovertibly how much the films of Terence Fisher, and other recent tales of terror by British film-makers, owe to traditions going back to the English Gothic novel. No enquiry into such relationships, however, has been as illuminating as Theodore Ziolkowski's hard look, in *Disenchanted Images. A Literary Iconography*, at three uncanny images used at the beginning of Cocteau's *The Blood of a Poet*—the animated portrait; the talking statue; the magic mirror—and his patient unravelling of their literary provenance and psychological or social meaning in different contexts. Beyond that we may also, of course, enquire into what modern literature has learnt from the film and is learning from the film's successor and rival, television: an enquiry which might fruitfully begin with Dos Passos, and take in the significance of optical imagery in Proust, and Kafka's apparent emulation of scenes from grotesque American film-comedy, on its way.

As Theodore Ziolkowski has convincingly demonstrated,

[1] Karloff was the first screen-actor to have his name used in the title of a feature film.

attempts to understand the 'truth-value' of uncanny iconography, in literature and in the film, may benefit by a glance across from literary and cinematic criticism proper to such fields as anthropology, philosophy of religion, and history. I propose to confine our brief attention to the last three.

It is, in fact, the father of modern psycho-analysis to whom we owe the fullest and the best-known monograph on the uncanny. In 1919 Freud published in *Imago* the first version of his paper 'Das Unheimliche' whose centre piece is an interesting analysis of a story by E. T. A. Hoffmann. This story is 'The Sandman', which contains the episode (well known to all who frequent the opera and the ballet) of the ingenious mechanical doll with whom a highly strung young man falls in love. Freud draws parallels between events in this story and cases that have come under clinical observation and suggests that what Hoffmann has here given his readers is an enactment of the fears and fantasies of a man rendered incapable of normal love by traumatic childhood experiences —and that the tale in fact embodies, in an extreme and disguised form, tendencies present in even its most sane and 'normal' readers. His knowledge of such fears and fantasies a writer draws to some extent, in Freud's opinion, from observation of his fellow-men, but more from introspection, from following a deep tap-root into his own unconscious mind. Feelings of the uncanny arise, in this view, from our penetration into hidden areas of the author's psyche which we recognize as akin to hidden areas of our own; they are at once familiar and strange, *heimlich* and *unheimlich*. The artist who explores them is brother to both patient and analyst: he drags to light what is hidden in the individual mind, thereby purging himself of the poison of the repressed and helping others to know truths of feeling—helping others, moreover, to face their own fears in the distanced and comparatively non-committal world of art. 'Reading', Simon Lesser has said, 'is a means of dealing with our most urgent problems, even those we ordinarily shun . . . [Fiction] gives form to our most fleeting impulses and fully discloses their consequences and ramifications.' Here too the fiction-film may be seen as a continuation of literary fiction by different means. These means include the characteristic suspensions of judgement, hesitations, doubts as to whether a given phenomenon is psychological or supernatural, which characterize such works as *Cat People* and *The Other* (1972); mysterious images

like the huge wall in Lang's *Tired Death* or *Destiny* which fills the
screen so completely that we imagine its infinite extension
upwards and sideways—a wall in which a dream opens a breach
that allows us to penetrate to the cave of Death; and irruptions of
the archaic into the modern, as when in Wegener's first *Golem* film
we see the ancient clay statue come to light, and ultimately to life,
in a more recent Prague than that of its medieval maker and
controller.

Five years before Freud's paper one of his disciples, Otto Rank,
had published a study from which the master was able to draw
some of his material—an essay called 'Der Doppelgänger' ('The
Phantom Double') which examined a motif used for different purposes by writers that range from Hoffmann and Jean Paul Richter
to Stevenson and Oscar Wilde. Significantly, Rank begins his
examination with an analysis of a German film, *The Student of
Prague*; and he finds in its course yet another psychological spring
of the uncanny: regression to the primitive, the return of fears
common in primitive societies, apparently left behind in more
enlightened ages but living a shadow life even among us. Might
they not, after all, have some foundation? Might not magical
thinking, animism, belief in the power of the mind to affect the
material world directly—might not these correspond to something
in reality? The figure of the phantom double owes its perennial
fascination to doubts such as this, doubts whose causes Freud and
Rank attribute to 'a return of the repressed', *Wiederkehr des Ver-
drängten*. A *Doppelgänger* represents, in the first instance, the hidden
part of our self, whether super-ego (as in Poe's *William Wilson*) or
id (as in Hoffmann's *The Devil's Elixir* and Stevenson's *Dr. Jekyll
and Mr. Hyde*); but it also revives primitive beliefs in the independent, almost bodily, existence of our soul, mirror and puppet magic,
demons or gods that amuse themselves by taking on our shapes—
and all these combine to produce a shudder that is full of dim
memories. A study of psycho-analytic writers thus confirms a
belief to which many aestheticians now subscribe: that even the
most sophisticated writer retains (to follow Wayne Shumaker's
formulation in *Literature and the Irrational*) contact with more in-
stinctive, less intellectualized processes than our own; that he
retains control of the 'forgotten language' of presentational symbols, the language of ritual, myth, and dreams. The film-makers
too, we may now say without fear of contradiction, have often

used their mysterious, multivalent, disturbing, stimulating images as pathways to a deeper darkness than the chiaroscuro so characteristic of the cinematic tale of terror.

Freud confesses, in the course of his paper on 'Das Unheimliche', that he was not himself sensitive to feelings of the uncanny, though he did not consider this a reason for barring such well-attested phenomena from his notice. It is far different with C. G. Jung, as several passages from his autobiography—notably those dealing with his attitude to his mother—make abundantly clear. Among Jung's earliest experiences, it seems, was that of his mother's dual personality, 'one innocuous and human, the other uncanny', and of his own ambivalent feelings: 'By day she was a loving mother, but at night, in dreams, she seemed uncanny.' It is this, perhaps, which has led him to take what some of us might feel to be an inordinate interest (shared by the film-makers of many countries) in Rider Haggard's *She*, and to pay particular attention, in literature, to the figure of the nixie or mermaid, alluring and perilous beings which play a prominent part in the writings of the German Romantics. In the nixie Jung sees 'an early stage . . . of a magical feminine being that I call the anima, the woman in man'. Such images he feels to be at once uncanny and numinous, to hold at once a threat and a promise; 'It is tragic', he says in one place, 'that the demon of the inner voice should spell greatest danger and indispensable help at the same time.' Their power lies in their ability to dredge slime out of the depths, slime which contains not only unpleasant or dangerous matter, but also the germs of new life—in their ability, above all, to reach a deeper region than that of the personal unconscious. 'The anima', he declares, in *The Integration of the Personality*, 'is not always merely the feminine aspect of the individual man. It has an archetypal aspect—"the eternal feminine", *das Ewigweibliche*—which embodies an experience . . . far older than that of the individual. This anima is reflected, of course, in mythology and legend. It can be Siren or wood-nymph, Grace or Erl-King's daughter, lamia or succubus . . .' Feelings of the uncanny would seem to indicate, in Jung's view, that we are nearing that dark, transpersonal realm of the collective unconscious, that realm of mythological forms where things and persons become magical, taboo, dangerous, and yet full of the promise of enrichment and salvation. It is surely no accident that so many of the illustrations of a key work like *Man and his Symbols*, written by Jung and his pupils and published in 1964, should turn out to be stills from films of the most varied kinds. These include, on page 92, a picture of Godzilla which is adorned with the caption: 'Perhaps the monsters of modern "horror" films are distorted versions of archetypes that will no longer be repressed.'

Jung's fears of his uncanny mother find a remarkable parallel in the life of one of the greatest figures in the cinema: S. M. Eisenstein. Yon Barna quotes his account of an incident in which Eisenstein's mother terrified her young son by denying that she *was* his mother. 'As she said it, her face became set, her eyes glassy and staring. Then she came slowly towards me. There you have all the characteristic elements: a fixed, stony expression; a mask with ice-cold eyes; a face devoid of life.' These 'characteristic elements' Eisenstein later transmuted in his films. Greater historical events in which Eisenstein was caught up along with his generation also played their part, of course, in evoking that 'ocean of cruelty' which is so characteristic of his films, shaping those terrible incidents which Barna lists again and again:

In *Strike* workers are killed off like oxen in a slaughterhouse and children hurled from the rooftops; in *Potemkin* the crowd is massacred wholesale and children trampled underfoot on the steps; men and children are thrown to the flames in *Nevsky*, poisoned or stabbed to death in *Ivan the Terrible* . . . (Barna, 1975, p. 27)

—but we cannot ignore Eisenstein's own sense that his obsession with such cruelties had deep roots in his childhood; in childhood incidents which Jung would certainly have seen as the repetition of archetypal ones, and therefore apt to stir up archetypal memories when transmuted in works of cinematic art. In considering the effect of Eisenstein's work on the terror-film proper, we would do well to keep in mind David O. Selznick's advice, in a letter written late in 1926, that American directors and studio-technicians should pore over *Battleship Potemkin* 'in the same way that a group of artists might view and study a Rubens or a Raphael'.

Students of the uncanny, in film as well as in literature, have recently paid a good deal of attention to the work of Jacques Lacan, with its conjunction of neo-Freudianism, structural linguistics, and structural anthropology. Lacan's analysis of the 'disjunction' between lived experience and the sign which replaces it, his stress on the Freudian concept of *Spaltung* (a kind of psychic and social alienation easily symbolized by the *Doppelgänger*), his 'undermining of the notion of a unified and consistent subject' (R. Coward and J. Ellis), his treatment of visual images as forms of metaphor and metonymy, his demonstration of how the 'imaginary' meta-morphoses into the 'symbolic', his views on the coexistence and intersection of the Symbolic, the Imaginary, and the Real, his notion of 'suturing functions'—all these have profoundly influenced the way recent critics have looked at tales of terror and talked about them. When Paul Willemen, in an Edinburgh Festival pamphlet written in 1975, showed how Jacques Tourneur's films dramatize the barrier between the 'space' of the viewer and that of the story unfolding on the screen, how Tourneur makes the image on the screen suggest that it is 'a deceptive text to be deci-phered', a text that requires a 'secondary' reading, and how all this can be seen as 'a dramatization of the structure of phantasy itself', then we cannot but realize that present-day discourse about fantastic and uncanny films has been powerfully affected by recent conjunctions of structuralism and psycho-analysis. The leading exponent of this conjunction is, in many observer's eyes, Jacques Lacan who, in his *Four Fundamental Concepts of Psycho-analysis* (1973), revived Freud's notion of *eine andere Lokalität*, another locality, another space, another scene, between perception and consciousness; who talked, in this same collection of lectures, of 'a split between the eye and the gaze' and ventured an aphorism that will find a special resonance in the minds of those who occupy themselves with the uncanny, the fantastic, and the terrible in the cinema: 'In this matter of the visible, everything is a trap.' He has impelled his disciples to look for Freudian elements in the structure as well as the content of a literary or cinematic work. I must admit that I myself have not found Lacan's writings helpful, and that I doubt whether his influence—so strong at the time of writing—will long outlast him.

'Psychology', of course, is not simply a synonym of 'psycho-analysis'; and while no student of the uncanny in literature and the film can afford to spurn such help as psycho-analysts, from Freud and Jung to Harry Stack Sullivan, R. D. Laing, and possibly Jacques Lacan, can give him, he will also find that many earlier writers have successfully attempted to uncover the psychological springs of uncanny feelings. We need think only of Schopenhauer's celebrated analysis of the terror we feel when some apparent exception to the law of causality makes us doubt the principle of individuation; of Kierkegaard's description of our common dread 'of something unknown, something on which one dare not look, a dread of the possibilities of one's own being, a dread of oneself'; of Nietzsche's comments on the moral suppression of sex that leads to its return in 'hideous disguises' and 'uncanny vampire forms', and his constatation of a 'German soul' that has 'paths and corridors ... caves, hiding places and dungeons', that knows about 'secret ways towards chaos'. Heidegger also has some memorable pages on the way the uncanny can act as an impulsion towards authenticity of living and thinking. A judicious study of writers outside the psycho-analytic orbit, a sound dose of common sense, and training in aesthetic analysis (which includes training in exact observation and logical thinking)—these should enable us to avoid most of the perils that attend psycho-analytic ventures into literary criticism, and criticism of the film: the danger of making no distinction, like Stekel in *Dreams of the Poets* or Rank in *The Incest Theme in Poetry and Legend*, between the work of fifth-rate scribblers and that of great poets; the danger of bizarre distortions —like those of Marie Bonaparte in her book on Poe—which have the aim of reducing everything to the same infantile fantasy. Psycho-analysis tends itself to form the notions which it then 'discovers'; and nothing can be more ridiculous than a criticism of literature and the film that relies on unexamined and archaic psycho-analytic concepts. 'As an area of applied psychoanalysis', an editorial in *Screen* (xvi, summer 1976) rightly insisted,

psychoanalytic studies of film will remain tributary to psychoanalysis in two respects: any knowledge will remain dependent for its authority on a practice outside film study itself, i.e. on clinical analysis; and that knowledge will be of more value as corroboration of the theses of psychoanalytic theory than for its contribution to any understanding of the cinema.

Warnings such as these should encourage us to cultivate a degree of healthy scepticism that will help us resist a temptation to which even Jung seems on occasions to succumb: the temptation to build airy constructions which have insufficient base in observed or experienced reality. To say this is not, of course, to belittle the very real insights Jung has been able to give to sensitive critics like Maud Bodkin, Anniela Jaffé, and C. F. Keppler.

Keppler, in *The Literature of the Second Self*, used Jung's concepts of Shadow, Anima, Animus, Wise Old Man, and Chthonic Mother to illuminate the 'double' figure that confronts us so often in literature and the cinema. He showed convincingly how many different things may be meant by those who speak of doubles, *Doppelgänger*, or second selves: 'an objective second self, a case of mistaken identity'; or 'a subjective second self, a mental content mistaken for external fact'; or what he calls 'the genuine second self, always simultaneously both objective and subjective, and never explainable as a mistake'. Such 'second selves' figure in legend, literature, and film, as twin brother, pursuer, tempter, 'vision of horror', saviour, beloved, or visitor from another point in the time-sequence; they bring suffering and death, but they also bring fulfilment, for they complete the 'partial' personalities as which we must all take our place in the social world.

It is this end which is the goal of the adventure of self-meeting. If we ask why it should be sought, when the seeking is so often unpleasant and even fatal, we can only answer that there appears to be in living creatures generally the urge to do a thing which can never be justified in practical terms: to see the unseen, to sail beyond the sunset, to cross the mountains of the moon. And when the uncrossed mountains are within as well as without (for . . . one's relationship with oneself is not wholly distinguishable from one's relationship with other selves)—when this is the case there seems to be a special urgency, arising out of a sense of incompleteness, even of self-deception and self-deprivation. For to live as only half oneself is to live a kind of lie, and to live a kind of lie is to live a kind of death. (Keppler, 1972, p. 201)

The urge of which this passage so eloquently speaks is one that also helps to account for the impetus to make, and the impetus to see, the terror-films which are the subject of the present book.

From Pabst's (technically superb) *Secrets of a Soul* to Hitchcock's *Spellbound* (1945) and Wise's *The Haunting*, films have seldom benefited from an unironic use of textbook psycho-analysis; over-simplification could never be avoided. At the same time the makers of terror-films could not help being influenced, from the first, by what they had absorbed of Freud, Jung, Melanie Klein, and the rest. Writing in a German film-magazine in 1929, Henrik Galeen, who helped to script *The Golem, Nosferatu, Waxworks*, and *The Student of Prague*, spelt out why he and his colleagues felt obliged to delve, deliberately, into the unconscious when they took over motifs from fairy-tales, Romantic literature, and the subliterary *Schauerroman*:

What does the old 'fantastic' fairytale world of the Brothers Grimm and Wilhelm Hauff, of E. T. A. Hoffmann and even, perhaps, of Edgar Allan

Poe, mean to us and our children today? Let us look at it through today's spectacles. It is a stimulus to us, a stimulus of genius, but no more than that; for what we see around us today is more fantastic than anything even a Jules Verne could conceive. Today's reality has become the equivalent of yesterday's fantasy. In our films, therefore, we had to look for new problems in this field.

What can we still call 'fantastic' today? Everything that seems possible in our unconscious, although it is not to be found in our common, everyday reality. (Greve, Pehle, and Westhoff, 1976, p. 325)

It would have been surprising if film-makers in search of fantastic *frissons* had neglected the help which they felt Freudians could give them in their exploration of the personal, and Jungians in their exploration of the 'collective', unconscious.

Jung admits to having learnt a great deal from Rudolf Otto's book *The Idea of the Holy*, from which he borrowed one, at least, of his key terms, and he may therefore serve as a convenient stepping-stone to the second of the three disciplines I am calling to the aid of the critic in evaluating the phenomena of the uncanny: that of religious philosophy. In *The Idea of the Holy*, first published in 1917, Otto speaks of a feeling of the 'numinous' which he sees as the prerequisite of all religious feeling. This sense of the numinous has many constituents; but one of the most important of these is what Otto calls an apprehension of 'awe-inspiring mystery', the *mysterium tremendum* of the divine. Such religious 'dread' or 'awe' has, as an antecendent stage, 'daemonic dread . . . with its queer perversion, a sort of abortive off-shoot, the dread of ghosts. It first begins to stir in the feeling of something "uncanny" [*unheimlich* is the term Otto uses]. It is this feeling which, emerging in the mind of primeval man, forms the starting point for the entire religious development in history. "Demons" and "gods" alike spring from this root and all the products of "mythological apperception" or "fantasy" are nothing but different modes in which it has been objectified.' Otto's contention, here and elsewhere, that the numinous is an essential constituent of *all* religious experience has rightly been challenged, notably by Karl Kerenyi and Father Victor White: but no one, I think, will sever again the connection he has made between the numinous and the uncanny. It is behind Martin Buber's description, for instance, in *The Eclipse of God*, of the uncanny as a 'dark gate' through which we must pass to reach the love of God—though Buber reminds us forcibly that it is 'only a gate and not, as some theologians believe, a dwelling'. For Buber, the uncanny is something that helps to pierce the protective armour assumed by modern man in his endeavours to shut out the call of a beyond. We may remember, too, Paul Tillich's repeated assertion that the demonic belongs into the sphere of the holy, and that, wherever the demonic appears, there the question of its correlate, the divine, will also be raised. But one cannot, I think, proceed very far in the study of modern literature and film without reaching the conclusion that much of their uncanny quality is due to secularization, to a recession of a sense of the divine, to a drying-up of metaphysical aspirations, to a loss of faith.

In Poe's 'The Pit and the Pendulum' with its talk of 'demons', 'fiends', 'angels' turning to 'meaningless spectres', and so on, and in Mamoulian's *Jekyll and Hyde*, where Ivy speaks of Jekyll as 'her angel' and of Hyde as 'the devil', metaphysical imagery seems to have lost its moorings, and what is left may perhaps best be described in Sartre's phrase as 'a ghost of transcendence floating about in immanence'. But we would do well to heed the claim made by many masters of uncanny effects that they were the guardians of a metaphysical outlook in a mechanistic and positivist world—from Poe, who declared that his stories penetrated, 'however rudderless or compassless, into the vast ocean of the "light ineffable"', to Georg Heym, who saw in his own work, 'the best proof of a metaphysical land that stretches its black peninsulas far into our fleeting days'. And I think that the works so far discussed will tend to confirm the view, advanced by Mircea Eliade, of the 'real spiritual function' of the nineteenth-century novel: that it constitutes 'despite all scientific realistic or social "formulas" . . . the great repository of degraded myths'.

That the same can be said for the film, with even greater justification, should be obvious from any reflection on the motifs and themes of the terror-movie. Even if we confine our attention to Greek myths alone, we can soon recognize such myths as those of Prometheus, Hephaestus, the Sirens, the Harpies, Circe, the Medusa, Oedipus, Electra, and Procrustes determining the plot-patterns and images of such films; to say nothing of the conscious and explicit use of Greek myths announced by the very titles of *Dr. Cyclops* and *The Gorgon*. This whole subject—the existence, provenance, evolution, and decline of myth in the cinematic tale of terror—has been intelligently discussed by Gérard Lenne in

Le Cinéma fantastique et ses mythes (1970). Alas, the book was written too early to include Harry Kümel's *Malpertuis* (1973), a strange and complex tale adapted from a book by Jean Ray which takes as one of its subjects that degradation of the classical gods in the modern world which had so fascinated Heine a century before.

The conflict between a social order ostensibly based on Christian values and long-suppressed pagan cults that yet survive—a conflict which the later Heine so often made his theme—has been given frightening shape by one of the most memorable British terror-films of recent years: *The Wicker Man* (1973), written by Anthony Shaffer, directed by Robin Hardy, and acted, subtly and sympathetically, by Edward Woodward, as the representative of our established order, and Christopher Lee, as the leader of the ancient cult. The thrilling impact of this film was undoubtedly due, not only to its literate dialogue and imaginative camera-work, but also to the powerful image announced by its title: the image of a harvest-god, the Wicker Man, to whom human sacrifices are, once again, offered up.

In considering the uncanny in a religious context, we must guard against two particularly insidious dangers. One of these is the temptation to equate the uncanny too readily with the demonic, and thus treat all its manifestations as belonging, positively or negatively, into the sphere of the holy. But it needs only a glance at any anthology of ghost-stories, or at films like Lang's *Dr. Mabuse the Gambler*, to see that many *unheimlich* phenomena take us to the realm of table-tapping and mediumistic effects—and most religious thinkers will agree with Paul Tillich that such things, however inexplicable, however mysterious, belong to the sphere of nature and not to a true beyond. The second danger is that of treating the uncanny as a timeless absolute, of forgetting that it confronts us in history. Yet in fact one of the most fascinating of all the tasks that face us when we study this phenomenon is to estimate the degree to which authors and film-makers have found it possible, at various times and in various places, to assimilate their sense of the uncanny into an over-all, historically conditioned world-view. The early Gothic novel still operates with either a broadly Christian scheme, or at least an ethical scheme of right and wrong; these are both called in question in the subtler and darker novels of the nineteenth century (English readers will at once remember *Wuthering Heights*), until in the works of Kafka the un-

canny stands naked, as it were, unassimilated into any recognizable
transcendent or ethical scheme. Much of the effort of the terror-
film, in recent years, seems to have gone into attempts to reverse
this history; but even in films with less theologically bleak endings
than *Rosemary's Baby*, *The Omen*, and *Carrie*, it would seem to be
Satan rather than God who remains lord of the world.

In the detailed analysis of four representative works which
makes up the bulk of his book on *Horror Films*, R. H. W. Dillard has
pointed to their 'parabolic intensity', and to the 'metaphysical'
response these films invite:

If a viewer chooses *Frankenstein* (1931) as an example of a valid and significant esthetic expression of experience, then he has chosen an understanding of the nature of life which is light-centered, progressive, open and
ongoing—a life in which moral freedom is the natural human condition. If
he chooses *The Wolf Man* (1941), he has chosen a life which is fate-centered,
static, closed and circular—a life in which moral limitation is the natural
human condition. If he chooses *Night of the Living Dead* (1968) he has
chosen a life in which moral failure is the natural human condition. If he
chooses Fellini's *Satyricon* (1969) he has chosen a life which is life-centered,
moving, dangerous but opening out—a life in .which moral striving is the
natural human condition. (Dillard, 1976, pp. 113–14)

Not everyone will be as ready as Professor Dillard to accept
Fellini's *Satyricon* as a horror-film rather than one that makes
occasional use of the imagery characteristic of that genre—in many
ways, *The Exorcist* would have been a more appropriate film to
conclude the series; but he has seen, clearly and truly, the 'metaphysical' dimension of our response to such works, and the
historically conditioned nature of the world-view they present.

We have now turned to the third and last of the contextual
fields within which the uncanny should, indeed must, be analysed.
Is it not shaped by historical as well as by timeless and absolute
forces? Does it not sublimate—to use a term that Karl Mannheim
took over from Freud—the psychic forces of the society within which
it is produced as well as those of the individual that produced it?

From what has already been said it will have become clear that
an analysis of the uncanny in literature and the film must take
into account the historical processes generally grouped as 'secularization'; and that implies recourse to the work of sociologists
and historians like Alfred Weber and R. H. Tawney. But there is
another, related concept (a much abused one!) that will be found

indispensable: the concept of *Entfremdung* or alienation. Hegel first spoke of this, in his *Philosophy of History*, as a necessary process through which the Absolute realized its purposes—the Idea, *Geist*, must be alienated in order to become embodied in nature, man must alienate himself in order to confront himself in his own handiwork; but Feuerbach, and more forcibly Marx, soon converted Hegel's positive into a negative, deploring religious alienation (through which man projected what is best and noblest in himself into a beyond) and social alienation (which deprived man of the control of his own handiwork). A man's labour, writes Marx in 1844, 'takes on its own existence . . . it exists outside him, independently, and alien to him . . . it stands opposed to him as an autonomous power. The life which he has given to the object sets itself against him as an alien and hostile force.' In the very attempt to gain greater and greater control of natural forces man feels himself losing that control, and turning the world against himself—that is the theme which occurred to Hawthorne, for instance, when he sketched an uncanny story in one of the notebooks he kept between 1835 and 1853. 'A steam engine in a factory to be supposed to possess a malignant spirit; it catches one man's arm, and pulls it off; seizes another by the coat-tails and almost grapples him bodily, catches a girl by the hair, and scalps her; and finally draws a man and crushes him to death.' The 'possessed' machine has in fact become a favourite motif in recent films, from *2001* to the TV movie *Killdozer* (1974), in which bulldozers escape human control and go on a murderous rampage. The sinister truck of Steven Spielberg's *Duel*, which would seem to have served *Killdozer* as a model, is controlled by a human driver; but since we are never shown that driver's face we come to have the feeling that here too a machine is possessed by a destructive impulse of its own. All this is clearly related to that classic of the uncanny to which we have had to return so often: Mary Shelley's *Frankenstein*, a work that can be seen, at one of its many levels, as a symptom of a cultural neurosis, a fear of science, fear of the control of natural forces, without adequate corresponding control of the soul and psyche. It is also behind the feeling, so common in twentieth-century literature, that there is something inherently uncanny in *things*. One remembers how Törless, the hero of an early novel by Robert Musil, felt things, as well as events and people, 'as something which, through the power of some inventor, had been tied to a harmless explanatory word, and then again as something quite alien, which threatened to break loose at any moment'. It may also be relevant to recall at this point the *tropismes* of Nathalie Sarraute, described (by Sartre) as 'a proto-plasmic vision of our interior universe: roll away the stone of the commonplace and find running discharges, slobberings, mucus . . .' *Unheimlich* in fact: you start with the commonplace and find yourself suddenly confronted with something that gives you the shivers.

As for alienation in the film—we have only to close our eyes for the images to come rolling up on our interior screens. Images from the German films of Fritz Lang, for instance: the machines that enslave men in *Metropolis*, and are, at one delirious moment, seen as Moloch; the cold indifference of the empty stairwell in *M* that betokens the death of a child as surely as the abandoned balloon in the same film; or, still in *M*, the heap of lumber amidst which the terrified murderer hides, himself a reject, in a dreary attic; the printing-presses at the beginning of *The Testament of Dr. Mabuse* (1932–3), chug-chugging away while a man is hounded into madness. Nor did the American cinema need German directors to teach it the meaning of urban alienation. The very title of John Huston's *The Asphalt Jungle* (1950) indicates a constant theme of the *film noir*: the 'mean streets' through which characters invented by Chandler and Hammett must walk; the actual settings in Las Vegas and Seattle which Dan Curtis's TV terror-films, scripted by Richard Matheson, have memorably used as the scene of vampirism and fantastic rejuvenation. And what could be more alienating than the New York of Depression days, shown to us in the *King Kong* of 1933, which can find no use for Ann Darrow at the beginning, and which imprisons, and ultimately defeats, a free son of the woods seized by an *amour fou*? That the Kong we see is in fact himself only the iconic image of a man-made object, the image of an articulated machine disguised as an ape projected by another machine, the unseen cinema-projector, is one of the many delicious ironies of this imaginative movie. In his British as well as his American thrillers Alfred Hitchcock has demonstrated, from the first, a disconcerting capacity for turning objects of our ordinary world and everyday use into agents of threat and betrayal: from the bread-knife in *Blackmail* and the coffee-cup (huge in the foreground) of *Notorious* to the Statue of Liberty itself in *Saboteur*. In this as in so many other respects he has shown himself an apt pupil of Fritz Lang.

If, in one way, terror-films convey experiences of alienation, they can also, in another, provide reassurance. This point has been convincingly made by Denis Gifford when he characterized the studio-built sets and stereotyped plots in the Universal movies of the thirties:

The settings were interchangeable, the ambience unchangeable. This was the secret of the Universal universe. It gave the great films a continuity that was comforting to come back to, whatever the horror that walked abroad. Familiar faces, familiar places: a sort of security in a world of fear . . . The impossible took place in a tight false world of studio-built landscape, where every tree was carefully gnarled in expressionistic fright, every house cunningly gabled in Gothic mystery, every shadow beautifully lit into lurking terror; and where every actor was caught in the closing ring of horrors, untouched by the possibility of a normal world beyond. (Gifford, *A Pictorial History*, 1973, p. 192)

The provision of an alternative world, an imaginative widening of the horizon of common experience, is not the least of the pleasures that audiences look for in a terror-film; and having once experienced that alternative world, related to yet different from their own, they long to recapture the pleasure they felt in new variations and intensifications. The pleasure of widening experience can even be derived from being precipitated for a time, in the safety of the cinema, into the radical alienation of a world distorted by drugs or madness: the distorted drawings and flats of *Caligari*; the fish-eye lens view of Frankenheimer's *Seconds* (1966); and the ever more menacing perspectives of Polanski's *Repulsion*, which reverse the vampire-film's contention that sexuality leads to aggression by showing murderous impulses triggered off by disgust at physical, sexual contact.

An awareness of historical and social processes will illuminate at every turn the form in which the uncanny confronts us in a given period of literature or of the film. Let us go back to literature for a moment, to look at a motif which has played a significant part in the terror-film too, from *Dr. Mabuse the Gambler* to *The Devil Rides Out* (1967) and *Rosemary's Baby*: the motif, so ubiquitous in the eighteenth-century *Schauerroman*, of the secret society and its sinister emissaries. We can, we must, refer that to common paranoiac fantasies; we can, we must, see in it also a characteristic perversion of the lost faith in providence. In eighteenth-century German literature it takes the specific form it does, however, only because of the powerful part that Illuminatism, Freemasonry, and Rosicrucianism played in eighteenth-century German life, and because of widespread feelings of political and social powerlessness of which we have other historical and literary evidence. A work like Grosse's *Der Genius* (one of the most widely read of all eighteenth-century fear-jerkers, both in Germany and, under its title *Horrid Mysteries*, in England) shows highly complicated feelings towards an authority that controlled even one's private actions—the shudder of almost religious awe mingles with revolted fear. In the course of the nineteenth century the fear of higher masters is supplemented by that of invaders from below: an old theological opposition, of course, but one that now assumes a new social significance. Lord Ruthven, the aristocratic vampire, is joined in popular mythology by the demon-barber of Fleet Street, by Sweeney Todd and his pie-woman, and the menace of dark forces from the social underworld extends from Sue's *Mysteries of Paris* to the Morlocks that threaten and sustain the graceful world of the Elois in H. G. Wells's *The Time Machine*. It is not, perhaps, irrelevant to recall in this connection that the *Communist Manifesto* of 1848 begins with a recognizably uncanny image: 'Ein Gespenst geht um in Europa'—a spectre walks in Europe; the spectre of Communism. One recalls, here, the speech Val Lewton and his team gave to Boris Karloff in *The Body Snatcher*, a film adapted from a story by Robert Louis Stevenson in 1945:

I'm a small man, a humble man, and being poor, I've had to do so much that I did not want to do. But so long as the great Dr MacFarlane jumps at my whistle, that long am I a man—and if I have not that, I have nothing. Then I am only a cabman and a grave-robber.

Shades of Uriah Heep! And between these social extremes, between the threat of unseen masters above and menacing proletarians below, stands the *bon bourgeois* whom E. T. A. Hoffmann, and those followers of his who created the world of the silent German film, found perhaps the most uncanny of all: that Coppelius who seemed a solid if eccentric citizen, an *Advokat* with a firm place in society, but who turns out, if you look at him more closely, to be a demonic being that brings, wherever it appears, 'lamentation—anguish—and perdition to body and soul'.

Each age, each nation, incarnates the uncanny in a different way. It is fed by, and may be made to nourish, popular prejudices: sinister monks and nuns invade the Gothic novel in the wake of the Gordon Riots, sinister scientists appear in greater and greater numbers in the course of the nineteenth century, and the use made of grotesque Jewish figures in the consciously uncanny works of such writers as Meyrink, Ewers, Panizza, and Strobl should have given the wise food for thought.

The same might be said of the use of actors with pronounced Jewish features, or made up to simulate such features, in German films made during the Weimar Republic. There was rarely any conscious anti-Semitic intent in this. Fritz Lang was genuinely indignant when critics charged him with furthering anti-Jewish resentments by giving the wealthy, avaricious, and treacherous Alberich of *Die Nibelungen* (1923–4) what contemporaries would see as 'Jewish' traits: beard, hooked nose, thick lower lip, small stature . . . There was quite a simple explanation, Lang replied; he and his make-up artist were influenced by the grotesque character make-up used by the Habimah, the Russian-Jewish ensemble whose performances of *The Dybbuk* and other plays had excited the admiration of Berlin theatre-goers in the early twenties. But this, of course, does not explain why it was the wretched Alberich who was modelled on the Habimah players, while the make-up of the hero of the tale, Alberich's Nordic adversary Siegfried, resplendent in a blond wig that was made to shine like a halo by means of blue streaks added to the straw-coloured hair, remained quite untouched by any such influence. The film-makers were usually oblivious of what they were doing; but the subliminal influence of their work was none the less powerful for that.

When we notice, as we must, how strong a strain of the uncanny there has been in the literature of the United States, from Charles Brockden Brown to William Faulkner, and how readily the American cinema of the thirties assimilated the pioneer efforts of the German terror-films, we shall do well to remain aware of the complementary American dream of innocence and rationality (how could we appreciate a film like Robert Mulligan's *The Other* without that?); of the 'power of blackness' brought into New England life by Puritanism; and especially (for the strain is particularly strong in Southern writers) of the facts of which we are reminded in C. Vann Woodward's *The Burden of Southern*

History: 'The experience of evil and the experience of tragedy are parts of the Southern heritage that are as difficult to reconcile with the American legend of innocence and felicity as the experience of poverty and defeat are to reconcile with the legends of abundance and success.' In Europe as in America the uncanny film and the uncanny tale are part of a great historical dialogue between Enlightenment and Irrationalism or Occultism.

Sometimes the social relevance of an uncanny motif is comparatively easy to estimate: I do not think we should disagree profoundly over the significance of the kind of tale that turns up again and again, in the hey-day of the British Empire, from *The Moonstone* to *The Sign of Four*: happenings in far-away countries and more primitive societies reach terrifyingly into comfortable lives in English country houses, until all mysteries are cleared up by a rational and reassuring detective. The Lewton–Tourneur movies of the forties, *Cat People* and *I Walked with a Zombie*, use the same thematic configuration in a darker mood and with much less reassurance as they show rational, even stolid Americans threatened by dangers that originate in the Balkans and the West Indies. Psychological menace (a night-world threatening a day-world) here takes on an unmistakably socio-political dimension. It all culminates in the intricate symbolism of that famous still from *I Walked with a Zombie* which shows a white woman lying on a Biedermeier sofa in the shadow of a scrolled trellis while the shadow of a negro towers huge beside her and a framed replica of Böcklin's *The Isle of the Dead* broods over all. And does not the very nature of the terror-makers of the early American sound-film—Bela Lugosi, with his mellifluously thick Hungarian accent, Boris Karloff, with his Russian pseudonym and soft English speech, the clearly British Colin Clive and Lionel Atwill—tell us a good deal about social attitudes and expectations in the U.S.A., through the transmutation into a more popular medium of Henry James's great theme: the encounter between an aristocratic, civilized but often corrupt old world with an innocent but occasionally brash new one?

Other paranoias have of late, as many critics have noticed, dictated the story-line of American terror-movies: the film-critic of the London *Times*, reviewing de Palma's *The Fury* on 29 September 1978, noted the play made in that work, with 'sinister government agencies who abduct and imprison . . . children to conduct secret experiments on them' as well as with 'urban chases and killings'. The terror-fantasies thrown upon *European* screens in the same period are no less revealing—witness Herzog's deeply disturbing remake of *Nosferatu*, which exhibits a distrust of bourgeois values, a rejection of the scientific approach to life, and an ultimate pessimism, which go beyond anything in Murnau's original film of 1922.

In his book on *Film Propaganda* Richard Taylor has convincingly demonstrated the way in which the very fact that a vast capital outlay is involved in the making of a feature-film served the purposes of the official propagandists of Nazi Germany and Soviet Russia. These huge costs, he tells us, 'meant that the number of points at which films could be made was severely limited, and thus easier to control. The cinema was therefore a *reliable* propaganda medium: a film, unlike a theatre group, could be despatched from the centre to the periphery and the content of the performance could be determined and guaranteed in advance' (p. 31). This is undoubtedly true—but it is also salutary when looking at Hollywood products to remember, with socially conscious commentators like Felix Guattari, that they are part of a huge commercial operation designed, by their backers and producers if not by their directors, script-writers, and cameramen, to condition further a public already conditioned by family, school, factory, military barracks, and psycho-analysis; designed to programme it into consuming ever greater quantities of a certain cultural product in order to bring profit to combines of financial interests. Yet American films can also be multivalent, polysemous works of art, whose relation to the society within which, and the commercial machines by the help of which, they were created is anything but simple. They can even criticize and satirize, like Frankenheimer's *Seconds*, the kind of business corporations and interests from which their funding has come. Nothing, surely, can be more depressing in criticism of literature and the film, or more misleading, than a crude social determinism. The greater the work of art, the more complicated will be its relation to society. But this does not mean that no such relation exists, or that we should despair of analysing it.

Fritz Lang was right, we find, when he called his fantastic *Mabuse* films 'documentaries': his master of disguise, the player with human lives at the centre of his film, is a rhetorical device that enables Lang to show, in heightened form, the spirit and substance of social, professional, and business life in the Weimar

Republic, and give us a heightened, stylized view of the stock exchanges, gambling dens, psychiatrists' consulting rooms, society salons, and spiritualist seances of the time. John Baxter is also right when, in *Hollywood in the Thirties*, he looked behind the façade of the American terror-film only to find that no single aspect of its cinema reflects so accurately a country's preoccupations and psychoses as that of fantasy. But Andrew Tudor too was right when he demonstrated, in *Image and Influence*, that an appreciation of the social meaning and impact of the German terror-film required a more complicated model of reflection and response than was available to Siegfried Kracauer. What must remain beyond doubt is that even in this field of cinema, where so many external pressures are necessarily brought to bear on the team that creates a given work, artists may be able to convey a seismographic awareness of tendencies within their society and period, and that the uncanny fantasy of any generation has its roots firmly in the life of that generation. This is a truth of which students of literature have long been aware; they have even found that the terror-fantasies of one generation may—like some of the writings of Kafka—eerily anticipate the realities of the next.

Kafka, in fact, seems to me the great master of the uncanny in twentieth-century literature; and a brief glance at just one scene from *The Trial*—a book which has fascinated more than one film-maker, just as Kafka himself was fascinated by aspects of the early film—will serve to lead towards a summary and conclusion of this chapter. The central figure of *The Trial*, Josef K., has been 'arrested' by a strange authority that allows him to go about his ordinary business while his case is being investigated. In the course of his arrest two warders commit minor irregularities (in so far as one can speak of 'irregularities' at all where everything is irregular) and K. has complained about them. Now he goes through a corridor in the bank in which he works, passes a familiar door to what he thinks a lumber-room or broom-cupboard, and (hearing groans) is seized by an uncontrollable desire to open it without calling witnesses. He does so, and finds inside the two warders about to be whipped—by a formidable, executioner-like figure—for their offences against him. The warders beg K. to get them off, and he tries, in vain, to do so; the men are stripped and beaten, one of them shrieks, K. quickly pushes him back and closes the door. The shrieks stop at once. The next day he opens the door again and finds the scene absolutely as he had left it. Once again the shrieks ring out, once again he quickly shuts the door. This chapter constitutes a classic example of uncanny effects unspoilt, for once, by the lurid, the melodramatic, and the pandering to cheap stock responses into which the uncanny so often seems to tempt its devotees. It shows the strange—another order—breaking into the everyday; shows a man 'seized by', 'unable to resist', powers he had not recognized before; shows him to have set in motion, by a word uttered earlier in the novel, forces of violence over which he now has no control; takes an ancient or archetypal motif (the Bluebeard story of the grisly secret behind the door) and gives it a new application; mingles the familiar, the horrible, and the grotesquely absurd; gives objective form to fantasies (a flagellation fantasy in this case) to which few of Kafka's readers can be said to be strangers; incarnates, in the figure of the flagellant executioner, tendencies of Kafka's age that were to become dreadful reality a generation later; shows ordinary time-sequence existing side by side with another, cyclic kind of time, parodying without laughter the cyclic time of myth and religion and pointing to those unconscious regions of the mind where time has no meaning; and it does all this in a sober, undemonstrative, logical, precisely detailing manner which contrasts significantly with the anything but usual subject-matter. It exemplifies once again both the definitions of the uncanny with which we began: 'the un-homely' and the 'un-secret'; definitions at which we must now cast a backward glance.

The 'home' negatively co-present in the definition 'the un-homely' is, firstly, the conscious, the surface, the ego level of our minds; it is, secondly, this world, the world of which we are normally aware, the world in which men and things form one continuum; it is, thirdly, society, the social setting in which man may expect—so often in vain!—to find his secure place. That which is 'secret', that which usually remains hidden but is brought to light, is the unconscious mind of the individual and through and beyond this a wider region of the unconscious that we find embodied in myths, legends, and fairy-tales throughout the world; it is the realm of primitive fears, of what has been forgotten and left behind, yet returns on occasions to plague us; it is the sense of alienation, of things we have made turning against us, of historical and social forces that we are helping to shape and that yet escape our control and even our knowledge; and it may also be a sense of the 'wholly other' invading our lives, of a *deus absconditus* choosing, suddenly, to reveal himself. When Jacob experienced such a revelation he exclaimed, as the Old Testament tells us: 'How dreadful is this place! This is none other but the house of God and this is the gate of heaven.' Rudolf Otto has pointed out that the Hebrew word which the Authorized Version here translates as 'dreadful' might fittingly be rendered by the word *unheimlich*—or, as we might say in English, 'awe-ful' in its old and undegraded sense. Modern writers, on the whole, have shown themselves more aware of the demonic than of the divine; but even in Kafka— as when he speaks, in a famous parable, of the 'radiance that streams inextinguishably from the door of the law'—the uncanny may be irradiated, at any moment, by a sense of the numinous. And if we now seek an equivalent virtuoso of the uncanny in the history of the film, we shall find him, not in Orson Welles, whose imaginative transposition of *The Trial* (1962) failed to find equivalents for most of the subtleties of the original, but rather in the Danish film-director Carl Theodor Dreyer, whose *Vampyr* I shall try to consider in the chapter which follows.

CHAPTER 5

Book into Film II : Dreyer's *Vampyr*

Nurse: 'What were you dreaming about?'
Léone: 'A voice . . .'
Nurse: 'That spoke to you?'
Léone: 'That called . . . commanded . . .'

Vampyr (1932)

IT needs no *politique des auteurs* to persuade us that Carl Dreyer's films convey a vision of the world which is predominantly that of their director. In an essay written in 1939 he has himself spoken of the importance he attached to preparing his own screen-plays:

> It is [the director] who, by his selection and linking of motifs, determines the film's rhythm. The preparation of the scenario is therefore in the strictest sense the director's legitimate business; and if he doesn't fight tooth and nail against any encroachment of it, it is because he has failed to understand the real nature of the director's function.
>
> Allowing others to prepare a scenario for a director is like giving a finished drawing to a painter and asking him to put in the colours. (Dreyer, 1970, p. 12)

Accordingly, Dreyer wrote many of his own scripts, adapting them from literary works of varying merit, kept a zealous watch over all stages of shooting and *mise en scène*, and endowed his works with a slow pace and a spiritual and emotional intensity which even later re-editing (doomed attempts to make his films more commercially viable) could never wholly conceal. The few films he completed show a feeling for the human face and its nuances of expression which made it possible for him to translate his psychological interests into cinematic terms, as well as an ability to irradiate his images with symbolic power, to make the sights of this world for which he had so keen an eye—human figures, landscapes, period clothes and interiors, buildings—not only speak of themselves but also point to a world beyond. His view of life was dark and tragic; he was fascinated, above all, by fears and sufferings of all kinds, many of them socially induced; and while his Manichaean sense of evil shows itself in most of his films—nowhere more so than in *Day of Wrath*, made in his native Denmark when Nazi Germany had hemmed it in and overrun it, and speaking eloquently of witch-hunts, persecutions, cruelties, and dark desires which clearly have a relevance to more modern times than the seventeenth century in which the story is set—he also had a sense of spiritual power and the potentialities of goodness. All but submerged in the agonies of his masterpiece, *The Passion of Joan of Arc* (1928), this was to have found expression in a film of the life of Christ which he planned for many years but which remained on the drawing-board when he died in 1968.

Vampyr, first shown in 1932, seems to me one of the most power-ful projections of the uncanny in the history of the cinema. One must, however, surrender to its slow pace, and not expect from it the sort of thrills that are provided by the spurting of technicolour blood and sensational murders at the altar-rail in the very act of receiving the host which are offered by such modern horror-films as Alfred Sole's *Communion* (1977). Ivan Butler, in his useful book on *Horror in the Cinema*, has rightly called Dreyer's film 'the supreme example of horror sensed rather than seen, evil suggested rather than exposed', and has summarized his impression of its deliberately dreamlike disjointed plot as follows:

The story . . . concerns a young man, David Gray, who comes to spend a night in a lonely inn. The location is vague but has a somewhat Swiss or Austrian (or Transylvanian?) character.[1] In the middle of the night—a weird, non-dark, creeping night—a stranger slips into his room and gives him a parcel, telling him to open it should the stranger die. The following day David Gray visits a château, after a strange interlude in a white building full of flickering shadows and odd, briefly glimpsed characters, and a meet-ing with a doctor and an . . . old lady. Everything is misty, shifting, un-certain. In the château he meets the owner, who turns out to be the man who has left him the package, and also his two daughters, one of whom is suffering from a strange wasting illness. Also about the place are two servants. Shortly afterwards the owner is mysteriously shot dead. Gray opens the parcel and uncovers a book on vampires and how to destroy them. Meanwhile we have learnt that the old lady is herself a vampire and responsible, it seems—with the doctor's connivance—for the illness of the elder daughter, Léone. Odd, indefinite encounters take place between the younger girl and David Gray. Later, Léone is lured out . . . and again attacked. The young man offers his blood for transfusion. By now, however,

[1] The film was, in fact, shot in France, not far from Paris.

Léone herself is becoming infected with vampirism. As if in some way the donation of his blood somehow links him with her, he sees himself, in a dream, screwed down into a coffin and carried out to be buried alive. He awakes from this nightmare and [aids an old servant to open the old woman's coffin and drive] the customary stake through her heart. The doctor is trapped in a cage in a mill and drowned in white flour, leaving David and the younger daughter, Gisèle, to drift away in a boat [and then escape through a forest into a misty sunshine]. (Butler, 1970, pp. 55–6)

The screen-play, written by Dreyer himself in collaboration with Christen Jul, was based, according to Dreyer's own testimony, on Sheridan Le Fanu's collection *In a Glass Darkly* (1872). A vampire-story does indeed constitute the climax and conclusion of that volume; but those who know 'Carmilla' may well be forgiven for thinking that except for the idea of a female vampire rather than the male blood-sucker of *Nosferatu* and *Dracula* Dreyer took hardly anything from Le Fanu at all. This question is worth examining, however, for Dreyer did not direct our attention to his nineteenth-century source for nothing. He is inviting us to compare, inviting us to see what happens when the creative imagination of an original film-maker is stirred by a literary work into activity that results in a new—and truly cinematic—creation.

Le Fanu's tale of the beautiful vampire Carmilla, who insinuates herself into households containing young girls with whom she then enters a vampiric relationship that has strongly Lesbian overtones, and who is at last tracked down to her lair in a hidden vault, staked through the heart, and beheaded, has been aptly called by Nelson Browne 'a strange study in black and scarlet':

Blackness is everywhere—the black velvet in which Carmilla's mysterious mother is arrayed when the carriage accident occurs at the beginning of the story; the black woman within the upturned coach, gnashing her teeth in fury; the sooty black animal which paces Laura's bedroom 'with the lithe and sinister restlessness of a beast in a cage.' Against this all-pervading blackness, the crimson arterial blood spurts and congeals . . . (*Sheridan Le Fanu*, London, 1951, p. 84)

Not surprisingly, the many recent film-makers who have based their works on Le Fanu's story have seized on the possibilities offered by that 'arterial blood'—the English title of Roger Vadim's version, *Et mourir de plaisir* (1960), is *Blood and Roses*. Dreyer too has scenes in which blood plays its part; the word 'blood' recurs with remarkable frequency in the sparse dialogue of *Vampyr*; but it is noteworthy that none of the instances of black listed in the passage just quoted from Nelson Browne has found a place in his film or the screen-play on which it is based. His imagination was here stirred *e contrario*; if his source was a study in black, his would be a study in white, the 'horror of whiteness' of which Melville had spoken and which can also be found in Poe: white mists, white diffused light (reflected off gauze back into the lens), white hair, white flour, even trees painted white. This whiteness often darkened into the greyness suggested by the leading character's name; within it, shadows could move that would set it off and make it more mysterious, more uncanny.

The framework of *In a Glass Darkly* had distanced the story of Carmilla and her victims by means of a triple mediation: a narrator/editor talks to Dr. Hesselius, a German physician with an interest in the occult, in a short introductory section, and then prints, from Dr. Hesselius's papers, the first-person narrative of Laura, whom Carmilla had chosen as her victim but who was saved by the timely intervention of a group of vampire-hunters. Dreyer took over the idea of distancing mediation in his own way, as may be seen by the opening passage of his screen-play (the translation is by Oliver Stallybrass):

A man is walking down the narrow riverside path that winds its way towards the spot where a ferry crosses to the other bank. It is a summer evening, after sunset. The traveller, Nikolas,[2] is carrying a rucksack, and in his hand a pair of fishing rods. He wants to spend his holiday in solitude, which is why he has come to this remote region in search of peace.

He arrives at the old inn and finds the door closed. The inn is lying in profound silence, as if all its occupants had gone to bed. Nikolas rattles at the door, but it is well and truly locked. At this moment he sees a reaper walking along with his scythe over his shoulder. He looks at the man curiously as he walks down towards the ferry. He shouts after him:

'Hullo, you there!'

But the reaper, not hearing his cry, continues on his way. The landscape is bathed in a grey, dim twilight, every object has a tinge of unreality. Nikolas goes round to the back of the house. There he discovers a window in which a light can be seen. He comes nearer, knocks on the window pane and listens; but not a sound reaches him. Simultaneously the light goes

---

[2] Baron Nicolas de Gunzburg who (under the pseudonym Julian West) acted the part of David Gray. In the quotations that follow I have substituted 'David Gray' or 'David' for Dreyer's 'Nikolas', which I retain for this first quotation only.

out. Nikolas knocks again. Silence still. But now a window is opened quietly on the floor above, and a timid child's voice asks:

'Who's there?'

Nikolas runs his eye up the façade of the house and discovers a little girl of thirteen with a gentle, frightened face. She says to him:

'I'll come down and open the door.'

She gestures, indicating that he is to go to the front door. Then she carefully closes the window.

As Nikolas stands waiting he glances down in the direction of the ferry. The ferryman—who has a white beard—boards the ferry-boat which begins crossing the river. He goes backwards and forwards, pulling laboriously at the iron chains which run rattling and squealing round the ungreased wheels. (Dreyer, 1970, pp. 79–80)

It is easy to see what is happening in this passage. Under the impact of Le Fanu's tale Dreyer's predominantly visual imagination is stirred into transforming activity which draws on memories of things seen, things felt, things read. The transformation of Hesselius and the narrator/editor into the figure of a young man arriving, by night, at the inn of a village where he is a stranger—a village, as we learn afterwards, that is overlooked by a château or castle—has, as we shall see, a model in Le Fanu himself; it may also owe something to the traditional opposition of castle and village in the Gothic novel and to the experience of Jonathan Harker in *Dracula*; but what it recalls most forcibly to modern audiences is, surely, Kafka's *The Castle*. Whether Dreyer had in fact read Kafka I do not know—copies of his works were not as easy to come by in the early thirties as they are today; but that his imagination is Kafkaesque would be hard to deny in face of the evidence provided by *Vampyr*. The hero's arrival at the strangely forbidding inn of the village overlooked by a castle; a summons received at the moment of waking from sleep, during the inbetween state of being neither fully awake nor fully asleep; oppressive corridors and mysterious doors, at once beckoning and frightening; the ineffectuality of the hero's actions (even in the final staking of the vampire the lead is taken by a castle servant); the 'solidity of specification' with which objects and gestures are evoked while fantastic happenings are taking place in twilight; our constant feeling that the action we see unrolling has some significance beyond itself—all this and more suggests the imaginative world of Kafka superimposed upon that of Le Fanu, either by direct influence or by similar imaginative processes stirred by similar experiences. And then, at the end of the passage I have quoted, come other such superimpositions: the reaper carrying his scythe, swathed in mist, bathed in twilight (translated by Dreyer into one of the most unforgettable images in world cinema), recalls one of the popular Germanic images of death, while the ferryman no less surely recalls the classical image of Charon, who ferries souls across the Styx.

There are other superimpositions and mergings of this kind in Dreyer's film. His play with shadows leaving their bodies and walking about on their own, with a body lying on the ground while its simulacrum rises from it and contemplates it from the outside, recalls the German Romantic *Novelle* from Chamisso to Hoffmann, as mediated by the shadows and doubles and optical tricks of the early German cinema. The most justly celebrated sequence of all, the subjective camera depiction of David Gray's nightmare of lying in a coffin, unable to move but fully conscious, hearing its lid screwed down, looking up through a glass panel let into the lid while the vampire looks down on him and then seeing various overhead views pass by as the coffin is carried out for burial—well, that celebrated scene blends suggestions of appalling dreams in Le Fanu's story:

I had a dream that night that was the beginning of a very strange agony.
  I cannot call it a nightmare, for I was quite conscious of being asleep . . .
('Carmilla')

with reminiscences of Poe, nightmares whose cinematic possibilities early film-makers like Jean Epstein had already demonstrated.

It is important to notice, however, that Dreyer drew his public's attention, not specifically to 'Carmilla', but to the collection of which it is part, *In a Glass Darkly*—and the more closely we examine that collection, the more motifs will we find that Dreyer worked into his plot. The most obvious example occurs in the longest story included in the volume, entitled 'The Room in the Dragon Volant'. Here we meet an Englishman who, like Dreyer's David Gray, stays at a French country-inn and becomes involved with sinister happenings at the local château. In the course of an intricate plot involving conspiracy, robbery, and murder, the central protagonist falls into a cataleptic trance which he describes as follows:

I was, indeed, a spirit in prison; and unspeakable was my dumb and un-
moving agony.

The power of thought remained clear and active. Dull terror filled my mind. How would this end? Was it actual death?

You will understand that my faculty of observing was unimpaired. I could hear and see anything as distinctly as ever I did in my life. It was simply that my will had, as it were, lost its hold of my body.

Precipitated into another such trance the Englishman is then put into a coffin and prepared for burial:

... very distinctly came the working of a turnscrew, and the crunching home of screws in succession. Than these vulgar sounds, no doom spoken in thunder could have been more tremendous ...

The coffin-lid being screwed down, the two gentlemen arranged the room, and adjusted the coffin so that it lay perfectly straight along the boards ...

That, of course, is very close indeed to the 'burial' sequence in *Vampyr* to which this book has had to return on more than one occasion. What makes Dreyer's travelling shot so unforgettable, however, is his brilliant idea of letting a glass panel into the coffin-lid and then making the camera intermittently take David Gray's place. There is nothing in Le Fanu, or Poe for that matter, to parallel the *visual* impression of being prepared and carried out for burial which Dreyer and his great cameraman Rudolph Maté so vividly give us in their classic 'subjective camera' sequence.

Dr. Hesselius, from whose case-book the stories in *In a Glass Darkly* are said to be taken, has, as we have seen, no overt equivalent in Dreyer's film; yet the point of view of this all-important character is not altogether lost. Hesselius is a Swedenborgian who confesses his belief that

the entire natural world is but the ultimate expression of that spiritual world from which, and in which alone, it has its life. I believe that the essential man is a spirit, that the spirit is an organised substance, but as different in point of material from what we ordinarily understand by matter, as light or electricity is; that the material body is, in the most literal sense, a vesture ...

Dreyer makes us share this view when he shows—by means of photographic superimpositions which are the more impressive for being absent from the rest of the work—a wraith of David Gray leaving his body and returning to it. In 'Green Tea', the opening story of *Through a Glass Darkly*, Hesselius quotes from Swedenborg's *Arcana Caelestia*:

'If evil spirits could perceive that they were associated with man, and yet that they were spirits separate from him, and if they could flow into the things of his body, they would attempt by a thousand means to destroy him; for they hate man with a deadly hatred.'

That, we might well think, is precisely what we see in *Vampyr*. Hesselius, lastly, is presented by Le Fanu as a man particularly well able to deal with what he calls the 'intrusion of the spirit world upon the proper domain of matter' because he is a scientist with a strong belief that occult phenomena can be studied—and, to some degree, counteracted—by science. His best-known work, we are told, is entitled *Essays on Metaphysical Medicine*. Here it is pertinent to recall what Dreyer said about his own beliefs in an interview broadcast on Danish State Radio in September 1954.

The new science that followed Einstein's theory of relativity had implied that outside the three-dimensional world which we can grasp with our senses, there is a fourth dimension—the dimension of time—as well as a fifth dimension—the dimension of the psychic which proves that it is possible to live events that have not yet happened. (Sitney, 1971, p. 28)

This 'fifth dimension' Dreyer saw reflected, not only in religious teachings, but also in the findings of psychic research. A man who held such beliefs was likely to betray, in his cinematic works, attitudes that closely resemble those of Le Fanu's Dr. Hesselius.

As for the title *Through a Glass Darkly*, which Le Fanu borrowed from the King James version of the Bible and which a later Scandinavian film-maker, Ingmar Bergman, gave to one of his most disturbing films—may not the very way in which *Vampyr* is shot and recorded be seen as a following-out of suggestions contained in this biblical phrase?

We have now begun to see how very different Dreyer's use of his sources is from Mamoulian's more direct and respectful adaptation. For Dreyer, suggestions issued into contraries, blackness suggesting whiteness; or into equivalents, 'through a glass darkly' suggesting blurred sound as well as deliberately dimmed photography; or into transformations, Laura as controlling consciousness turning into a young man involved in strange events against his will and intention; or into superimpositions that combined motifs from several stories or blended Kafka, Hoffmann, Poe with Le Fanu; or they cause a jolt of the imagination, some passing or pervasive reference or motif, in 'The Familiar' or 'Mr.

Justice Harbottle', stimulating Dreyer's cinematic inventiveness to flights of its own. These processes are worth following out a little further with reference to 'Carmilla', which remains the principal source of *Vampyr*.

Laura, the narrator of Le Fanu's first-person account, begins her story as follows:

In Styria, we, though by no means magnificent people, inhabit a castle or schloss. A small income, in that part of the world, goes a long way. Eight or nine hundred a year does wonders. Scantily enough ours would have answered among wealthy people at home. My father is English, and I bear an English name, although I never saw England. But here, in this lonely and primitive place . . .

The film translates into its own visual terms the 'lonely and primitive' aspect of the scene, eschewing all studio-built sets and photographing in the French countryside—photographing in such a way that, as we have seen, Ivan Butler could gain the impression that the location was Swiss, or Austrian, or Transylvanian, despite intertitles that give the village to which David Gray comes the distinctly un-Austrian and un-Transylvanian name 'Courtempierre'. Dreyer also takes over the idea that the chief characters menaced by the vampire are the 'by no means magnificent' inhabitants of a château. In transforming the central consciousness of his tale into a young man at the periphery rather than a young woman at the centre of events Dreyer was clearly influenced by his need to distance; he was also influenced by the fascination which the face and personality of his financial backer, the young Baron Nicolas de Gunzburg, held for him. He induced him to play the part, and following out suggestions from 'The Room in the Dragon Volant' as well as from 'Carmilla', he gave the character Gunzburg played an *English* name—'David Gray' stands out in a list of dramatis personae bearing such (more or less) French names as Gisèle, Léone, Marc, and Marguerite Chopin. How significant the name 'Gray' became for the film may be seen from Dreyer's own account of the shooting, first published in *Cahiers du Cinéma* in September 1965:

Generally, you find the definitive style for a film at the end of a few days. Here we found it right away. We started to shoot the film—starting with the beginning—and, at one of our first screenings of rushes, noticed that one of the takes was gray. We asked ourselves why, until we became aware of the fact that it came from a mistaken light that had been shining on the lens.

The producer of the film, [the cameraman] Rudolf Maté and I thought about the take, in relation to the style we were looking for. Finally, we said that all we had to do was to repeat, on purpose, every day, the little accident that had happened. Henceforth, for each take, we directed a false light on the lens by projecting it through a veil, which sent the light back to the camera. (Leyda, 1977, pp. 115–16; trans. Rose Kaplin)

An accident of filming showed the director and his cameraman how to make the central protagonist's name a 'speaking' name to a degree they had not thought possible before.

The first experience that Le Fanu's Laura recounts is a childhood experience: how a female vampire visited and attacked her, how she was frightened, and how in consequence of her fright she 'yelled with all [her] might and main'. This idea of the vampire's attack on children obviously had a powerful effect on Dreyer's imagination. As we have already seen, the screen-play stipulates that the door of the inn should be opened to David Gray by a frightened child—though in the film as it was actually shot and released, the servant who opens the door is not as obviously childlike as the screen-play would lead one to imagine. The screen-play also includes a scene in which David Gray penetrates into a disused laundry-room:

Everything is covered in dust. On the copper are standing some rusty bird-cages and mousetraps. Old paraffin lamps are lying in a heap on the floor; but what astonishes David most is a collection of children's clogs standing neatly in rows. They are not quite as dusty as the other things in the old laundry room. For this reason he goes through the empty room and back to the spot where a door leads out to the staircase. There he stops, and now he hears—in the quivering stillness of the old house—hounds baying and a child weeping. Then a scream, a half-suppressed child's scream, as if a hand had closed over the mouth of the screamer.

It comes from the cellar, but just as David is about to descend he hears steps on the staircase above. Somebody is coming down. He sees only this person's hand, as it fumbles its way slowly down the handrail. (Dreyer, 1970, p. 88)

The stories of the havoc wrought by the vampire among the villagers, which permeate Le Fanu's 'Carmilla', crystallize, in Dreyer's screen-play, in this one chilling scene of the screaming child and the rows of abandoned clogs. Is not this an anticipation of images with which newsreels and documentaries were to make us all too familiar after the Second World War? In Le Fanu, the crying child is immediately comforted by nurse, nursery-maid, and housekeeper; the screaming child in Dreyer, by contrast, becomes a non-person. The sinister doctor, Marc, whose disembodied hand we saw feeling its way down the stair-rail at the end of the passage just quoted, answers David Gray's enquiry after the child whose voice he had heard with the curt statement: 'There's no child here.'

If one now looks at the film rather than its screen-play, one finds that Dreyer's transforming imagination has once again been at work. The children's clogs have disappeared (at least from all versions of the film that I have been able to see); and though the sound-track includes what sounds like barking, baying, and whimpering dogs, a child's weeping cannot be clearly distinguished on it. Instead, we have shots of a tiny skeleton, a cross between an anatomized baby and a voodoo doll. David Gray's enquiry after the weeping child is, however, retained (he, obviously, has heard a child, even if the viewer has not) and so are the doctor's negative answers: 'There is no child here', and again: 'Here there are neither children nor dogs.' This equivocal answer—for though we may not have heard a child, we have heard dogs—has been linked by Mark Nash, in an important essay published in *Screen* (xvii, autumn 1976), to a central characteristic of Dreyer's film. Again and again, Nash demonstrates, Dreyer deliberately induces doubts about the 'reality-status' of the images and sounds he has recorded and edited. Whose perspective is the film adopting at a given moment? Often it seems to be that of David Gray or another of the characters—but then Dreyer will intercut an 'objective' shot, a camera-perspective which cannot be that of the people we see on the screen. The position is particularly complicated in the great sequence of Gray's 'burial'. Here we meet David Gray[1] who sits asleep on a bench; David Gray[2], a wraith that we see leaving the sleeping body and acquiring solidity in subsequent shots; David Gray[3], the man in the coffin, glimpsed, at one point, over the shoulder of David Gray[2]; and an 'objective' or 'authorial' camera adopting, at intervals, an independent perspective. Nash usefully distinguishes two levels of uncertainty in the film: that relating to the status of what Gray sees (is it 'true'? is he imagining things?); and that relating to the status of what the viewer sees—the viewer who cannot know, at any given moment, whether the perspective suggested to him is that of an independent story-teller or that of a character in the tale. These different kinds of uncertainty, which constitute for me one of the marks of the 'uncanny', Nash justifiably links with Tzvetan Todorov's definition of *le fantastique*:

In a world which is indeed our world, the one we know, a world without devils, sylphides or vampires, there occurs an event which cannot be explained by the laws of this same familiar world. The person who experiences the event must opt for one of two possible solutions: either he is a victim of an illusion of the senses, of a product of the imagination—and the laws of the world remain what they are; or else the event has indeed taken place, it is an integral part of reality—but then this reality is controlled by laws unknown to us. . . . The fantastic occupies the duration of this uncertainty. . . . The fantastic is that hesitation experienced by a person who knows only the laws of nature, confronting an apparently supernatural event. (Todorov, *The Fantastic. A Structural Approach to a Literary Genre*, Cleveland, 1975, p. 25)

The relation of the verbal exchange between Gray and the doctor to what we actually hear on the sound-track may well be connected with the visual uncertainties which are so marked a feature of the film's style; uncertainties well described, once again, by the biblical title Le Fanu gave to the collection which culminates in 'Carmilla': *In a Glass Darkly*.

The doctor's appearance, and his link with a suffering child, seem also to have been suggested to Dreyer by 'Carmilla'. In that seminal story Laura recalls how after a frightening childhood experience 'a doctor was called in, he was pallid and elderly. How well I remember his long, saturnine face, slightly pitted with smallpox . . .' The adjectives describing the doctor suggest someone baneful and forbidding, though the role which he and other physicians play in 'Carmilla' is in fact benevolent and well intentioned. Dreyer, on the other hand, follows out the hints of the sinister in Le Fanu's adjectives and makes the doctor an accomplice and instrument of the vampire, much as Roman Polanski later did with his Dr. Sapirstein, and (indirectly) Dr. Hill, in *Rosemary's Baby*. Doctors and scientists are always apt to be regarded with suspicion in the cinematic tale of terror! Not the least effective of the means Dreyer used to impress us with the sinister nature of this character is the piecemeal way in which he brings him into view: first we see a hand groping its way down a banister, then a hat, and only then are we shown the expressive, memorable face of the non-actor whom he had chosen to embody his vampire's chief helper and instrument.

The final sentence of the opening chapter of 'Carmilla' which we have been considering is also not without relevance for Dreyer's film:

I forget all my life preceding that event, and for some time after it is obscure also; but the scenes I have just described stand out vivid as the isolated pictures of the *phantasmagoria* surrounded by darkness. [My italics]

That image, with its reference to a precursor of the cinema, describes very well the apparently 'disjointed' effect produced by *Vampyr*.

If we now read on a little in the chapter of 'Carmilla' which succeeds that from which I have just quoted, we come upon the following description of the landscape within which the events narrated take place:

Over the sward and low grounds, a thin film of mist was stealing, like smoke, marking the distances with a transparent veil; and here and there we could see the river faintly flashing in the moonlight.

Can there be any doubt that these suggestions of a 'thin film of mist . . . like smoke' creating a 'transparent veil', and of a 'faintly flashing' river, have been followed out by Dreyer's *mise en scène* and his manner of photographing scenes through a film of gauze? But once again it should be noticed that he has utterly transformed his source—for Le Fanu's narrator goes on:

No softer, sweeter scene could be imagined. The news I had just heard [of a young woman's death] made it melancholy, but nothing could disturb its character of profound serenity, and the enchanted glory and vagueness of the prospect.

Nothing could be less 'sweet' or 'profoundly serene' than the mist-swathed landscape of Dreyer's film—except at the very end; most of the time it seems 'enchanted' in a more sinister sense than Le Fanu's narrator intends, and the melancholy that Laura and her father feel has permeated Dreyer's landscape in a far more radical way than Le Fanu's.

The role which Laura plays in 'Carmilla' is played in *Vampyr* by Gisèle. Like Gisèle, Laura lives at the castle with her father, her mother being dead. Le Fanu introduces into this household two baneful figures: an imperious matron, who goes away again almost immediately, and a younger woman whom she calls her daughter, and who remains behind at the castle when the 'mother' leaves. This younger woman is in fact the vampire, Carmilla, who eventually turns out to be related to Laura on her mother's side: Carmilla and Laura's mother were both members of the Karnstein family. Dreyer's transforming imagination seizes on this relationship: in his film the place of Carmilla is taken by Léone, Gisèle's sister, while Carmilla's 'mother' becomes the old woman who is the chief of the vampires. The evil was instilled into Carmilla, in Le Fanu's story, long ago, in the seventeenth century, when the highborn and beautiful girl was turned into a vampire. Dreyer brings this process into the present, shows us the evil being instilled into Gisèle here and now. While the old woman can be dimly discerned, during a vampirizing scene in a meadow, at her nefarious work, and while her servants and minions capture and bind Gisèle, Léone herself never attacks anyone; on the contrary, it is her life we see being drained away by the vampire's attack and which David Gray vainly tries to save by means of a blood transfusion that makes him feel vicariously something of the agony of Léone. Yet in one brief close-up Dreyer manages to convey the threat as well as the pathos of the incipient vampire more effectively than any of the later more sensationalist adaptations have ever managed to do. The moment has been recreated in words by W. K. Everson:

[Léone] sits, weakened from loss of blood, tended by her innocent, bewildered sister. Suddenly, the vampire's influence begins to make itself manifest. The face awakens and in one magnificent single-frame shot, the head slowly turns from right to left, the facial expression changing from one of love and gratitude to animal cunning, then hate, and—as the lips part to reveal strong white teeth, and a tongue licking them in obscene blood lust—a final reversion to self-disgust and shame, as the sister, watching in horror, realizes what thoughts are passing through her mind. (Everson, 1974, p. 68)

Léone's expression at the end of this sequence is in fact much more ambiguous than Everson's description allows; Buzzi and Lattuada call it 'hard and menacing', and so it seems to me; but Dreyer's sequence does indeed provide a perfect cinematic counterpart of the delicate, languid, frequently exhausted, beautiful creature described by Le Fanu's Laura when she tells us that Carmilla's face, on occasions, 'underwent a change that alarmed and even terrified'. The importance of this interpretation for Dreyer may be gauged by the fact that in a film whose players are mainly amateurs (non-actors whose faces he found fascinating and whose

hidden characters the camera seems to search out) he imported the
gifted German actress Sybille Schmitz to portray Léone. Only once
more, in her long career in the cinema, would Sybille Schmitz find a
director who used her spiritual potential to the full—and that was
Frank Wisbar, who had her do battle with a personified Death in
his *Ferryman Maria* of 1936. Nineteen years later Sybille Schmitz
was to commit suicide, depressed by the lack of worthwhile parts
and the lack of directors who could bring out what was deepest in
her. It is a crowning irony that the illustrations purporting to show
Sybille Schmitz as Léone in *Vampyr*, even in such standard works
as Ivan Butler's *Horror in the Cinema*, David Pirie's *The Vampire
Cinema*, and *The Vampire Film* by A. Silver and J. Ursini, are in fact
pictures of Rena Mandel in the role of Léone's sister Gisèle.

Carmilla's 'mother', the imperious and courtly lady who
insinuates her 'daughter' into households that contain attractive
and full-blooded girls, is transformed by Dreyer's complex imagination into his chief vampire: an old woman dependent on the help
of those whom—like the village doctor—she commands. She lords it
over shadows too, wraiths that detach themselves from living men
—and here, it would seem, a spark from Le Fanu had once again
lit the tinder of Dreyer's inventiveness. The attendants on the grand
lady who proclaims herself Carmilla's mother are said to be
'strangely lean, and dark, and sullen'. What could be more lean,
dark, and if not sullen then at least silent than *shadows*—those
shadows whose cinematic possibilities the German film-makers had
so often demonstrated, especially in tales of terror like *Nosferatu* and
(*Warning*) *Shadows*—independently moving shadows and wraiths
which Dreyer integrated into the misty landscapes and dim
interiors of *Vampyr* with an unequalled visual flair?

The final scenes of the film, in which shots showing David and
Gisèle in their boat while the sun breaks through trees into the
misty landscape are intercut with scenes of the vampire's helper
drowning in whiteness, were to be accompanied by the sound of a
hymn-like song; a song whose import Mr. Stallybrass's version of
the screen-play translates as:

> Hark, an angel bears its light
>   Through the gates of heaven,
> By God's angel's beams so bright
>   All the black nocturnal shades are driven.

>   (Dreyer, 1970, p. 128)

Here once again Dreyer has taken a hint from Le Fanu, who makes his Laura and Carmilla watch a funeral procession: 'Peasants walking two and two . . . were singing a funeral hymn'—'I rose', Laura tells us, 'and joined in *the hymn they were sweetly singing* [my italics].' By transposing this hymn to the end of his screen-play, Dreyer gives it a more hopeful setting, while the fate of the doctor struggling against suffocation in the mill may bring to mind Carmilla's protest, in Le Fanu's story, against 'strangling people with hymns'. On the sound-track of the film actually produced, however, the sound of singing human voices is not heard; the 'sweet singing' of the screen-play has been replaced by the hymn-like 'release' theme of Wolfgang Zeller's admirable score.

Nelson Browne, it will be remembered, has called Le Fanu's 'Carmilla' a study in black and scarlet. The scarlet comes out clearly in Laura's vision of 'Carmilla standing, near the foot of my bed, in her white nightdress, bathed, from her chin to her feet, in one great stain of blood'. This was an effect not easily reproduced in Dreyer's grey-and-white film. Terror-movies had, of course, used colour well before 1931: early copies of *The Cabinet of Dr. Caligari* came tinted in green, brown, and blue, and there was a memorable incursion of red in the 1925 version of *The Phantom of the Opera*; and they were to use it increasingly in the 1930s. Who can ever forget the green-and-brown tint of the scarred face of Lionel Atwill revealed beneath his mask in *The Mystery of the Wax Museum*? Despite such examples as the technicoloured *Dr. Cyclops* of 1939, however, the makers of terror-films continued for the most part to use the black and white to which Universal and the 'German look' had accustomed their public. Here the Hammer films of the fifties and sixties brought a fundamental change; a change whose complex effect Alain Silver and James Ursini have attempted to describe in their book on *The Vampire Film*:

Hammer's introduction of colour to the vampire film . . . had a specific effect. On the one hand it increased the realism of the productions (some-thing Hammer was to aim for continually); vampires with blood-streaked fangs and breasts and the richly coloured tones of the sets create a mood of unsettling actuality far different from the black and white Neo-Gothic expressionism of the Universal. On the other hand, colour could suggest quite the opposite of realism, could enhance the sensual, dream-like quality of the films, as in the blue moonlight that floats through the air on the balcony of Lucy's room when she awaits Dracula's fatal embrace or the

vivid red . . . which becomes a colour motif for the title figure in many of
the films, to the point where some . . . close-ups are completely suffused
with that colour. Ultimately this use of colour is most effective in amplifying
the nightmare state of these films. While most black and white productions
do achieve visual distortions in camera angle, lighting and set construction which are suggestive of nightmare; while allegorical conflicts and
terrifying surreal events still abound, colour is uniquely able to add a layer
of ineluctable, visceral immediacy to the image. (Silver and Ursini, 1975,
p. 124)

Dreyer is not, of course, after 'visceral immediacy' of this kind; nor
could he, in his grey-and-white film, introduce such effects as
characterize Vadim's *Blood and Roses*, where in one memorable
sequence colour drains out of the film, leaving only a vivid red
blood-stain on Carmilla's white dress to shine out from the screen.
Such over-emphases are foreign to Dreyer; but he does sketch in
his screen-play, and achieve in his film, a remarkable sequence in
which Le Fanu's static image of the blood-stained nightdress is
transformed into a dynamic one and is then distanced from Léone
herself. In order to provide the old witch-vampire with a fresh
supply of the vital fluid she is drawing from Léone, the doctor has
persuaded David Gray to allow a blood transfusion from his veins
into those of Léone. David has agreed; the operation has taken
place; and he is now dozing exhausted, in a room next to Léone's,
from whose bedside strange murmurings can be heard. Then
silence supervenes.

In the silence David hears a sound: drip, drip! He leans forward and looks
down. On the floor he sees the lantern which Joseph was carrying when
the coachman arrived, apparently dead. The sound of dripping comes from
somewhere near the lantern . . . and now he sees what it is: blood running
from his wound down onto his fingers and thence to the floor, where a
regular pool has already formed. With an expression of bewilderment he
looks towards the door into the sick-room and calls:
    'Doctor! . . .'
Again the doctor answers in an ice-cold, hissing voice:
    'What is it now?'
David Gray (desperately): 'I'm losing my blood!'
Doctor: 'You're losing your blood?'
David (urgently): 'Yes!'
Doctor (slowly and emphatically): 'Nonsense! . . . It's here . . . Your
blood . . .'
David sits there for a moment—uncomprehending and irresolute—then

he leans forward and looks down. The sound of dripping has ceased, the pool of blood and the lantern have disappeared. When he lifts his hand he sees that it is completely white, and that the bandage is in order. With a weary smile he settles himself comfortably in the easy chair. He both sees and does not see the light behind the door of the sick-room moving away and disappearing. (Dreyer, 1970, pp. 112–13)

What Dreyer is showing us here, in characteristically distanced fashion—even the pool of blood disappears from the vision actually filmed!—is the vampiric draining-away from Léone of the blood that had just been given to her, experienced by the donor of that blood in a half sleeping, half wakeful vision; a much more powerful and suggestive image, in Dreyer's context, than the direct visual reproduction of Le Fanu's image of the blood-soaked nightdress could possibly have been, even in glorious Hammer colour. But if we want a description of the 'feel' of this scene and of the whole film of which it is part, then we cannot do better than Laura's account, in Le Fanu's 'Carmilla', of

dreams that seemed interminable, and were so vague that I could never recollect their scenery and persons, or any one connected portion of their action. But they left an awful impression, and a sense of exhaustion, as if I had passed through a long period of great mental exertion and danger. After all these dreams there remained on waking a remembrance of having been in a place very nearly dark . . .;

or General Spielsdorf's description of Carmilla's dawn-time excursions:

She was repeatedly seen from the windows of the schloss, in the first faint grey of the morning, walking through the trees, in an easterly direction, and looking like a person in a trance . . .;

or a characteristic exchange between Laura's father and Carmilla:

'We are in God's hands; nothing can happen without His permission, and all will end well for those who love Him. He is our faithful creator; He has made us all and will take care of us.'

'Creator! Nature!' said the young lady in answer to my gentle father. 'And this disease that invades the country is natural. Nature. All things proceed from Nature—don't they? All things in the heavens, in the earth, and under the earth, act and live as Nature ordains? I think so';

or a doctor's response, in the same chapter from which I have just quoted, to the insinuation that he might be inclined to believe in hippogriffs and dragons:

The Doctor was smiling, and made answer, shaking his head—'Never-theless, life and death are mysterious states, and we know little of the resources of either'.

That's what attracted Dreyer to 'Carmilla' and that's what he has rendered in his own terms, with a faithfulness which belies the far-reaching changes he has made in Le Fanu's story.

Two sentences from Jack Sullivan's account of the British ghost-story, *Elegant Nightmares* (Athens, Ohio, 1978, p. 75), may serve to suggest a further affinity between Dreyer and Le Fanu. 'In Le Fanu', Sullivan tells us, rightly, 'supernatural horror is peculiarly militant—it can emerge anytime it pleases. In [M.R.] James's antiquarian tales, horror is ever-present, but is not actually threatening or lethal until inadvertently invoked.' A viewing of *Vampyr* is unlikely to leave anyone without a sense of that *militant* supernatural which distinguishes Le Fanu's work from that of more comfortable purveyors of ghost-stories for the Victorian fireside.

The blood-transfusion scene suggests that Dreyer and his collaborators had consulted, not only Le Fanu, but Bram Stoker too: for transfusion-scenes—in which blood always goes from the man to the woman—play a central and overtly symbolic part in the *Dracula* novel of 1897. What we will not find in Stoker's *Dracula*, however, is anything like Dreyer's poetic use of a metaphor that was to figure in such a sinister way in continental (particularly German) ideology: the 'voice of the blood', the voice of his own blood that calls out to David Gray from Léone's veins and helps him to share Léone's experience. The hint comes from Stoker; the development is Dreyer's own. Nor was this transfusion-scene to have been the only reminiscence of the most famous vampire-story of them all: Dracula's summoning of the wolves, those 'children of the night' whose howls are music to his ears, was to have been paralleled with a similar summons by the old woman of *Vampyr*. Surviving stills would seem to suggest that Dreyer actually shot this scene; but it found no place in his complete film. Characteristic-ally, however, he does incorporate into the film his own variation on a simile that Stoker introduced into one of the wolf-summoning episodes of *Dracula*. Stoker writes: 'Close at hand came the howling of many wolves. It was almost as if the sound sprang up at the rising of his hand, just as the music of a great orchestra seems to leap up under the baton of the conductor.' In *Vampyr*, Stoker's 'as if' becomes reality; the old woman can command music that makes her attendant shadows dance, and she can stop music abruptly, in mid-cadence, when she imperiously raises her stick. In its context this obedience of unseen musicians to a gesture from the vampire's hand accompanied by a call to silence is more uncanny than the summoning of wolves could ever have been. Here as elsewhere the film profits greatly not only from Rudolph Maté's imaginative lighting and photography, but also, once again, from Zeller's score, with its sinister 'shadow polka'.

There is one presence behind Dreyer's images, however, which must not be missed on any account: the presence of the first vampire-classic of the cinema, Murnau's *Nosferatu: A Symphony of Horror* (1922). It was Murnau who had shown—in the wake of Wegener's first *Student of Prague*—how much the fantastic film could gain from using real settings: streets and interiors in Lübeck, Wismar, Lauenburg, and Dolni Kubin; Oravski Castle in the Carpathians; the waves and shores of the North Sea. It was Murnau who had shown, once and for all, how such 'real' settings could be suffused with poetic, imaginative, subjective elements; and who had also demonstrated, with shots of a Venus flytrap and of predatory polyps taken from scientific films, how fantastic nature itself can seem. It was Murnau who had shown how the cinematic frame could be transcended, how even within the closed genre of the terror-film the scene could be opened out, could point beyond itself, through an imaginative treatment of space— and who had demonstrated, in *The Last Laugh*, how the camera could be moved about in search of psychological revelation. 'The camera', Murnau had said, in words Dreyer, Astruc, and many another film-maker were to echo, 'is the director's pencil. It should have the greatest possible mobility in order to record the most fleeting harmony of atmosphere. It is important that the mechanical factor should not stand between the spectator and the film.'

In relating his uncanny figures to their surroundings Dreyer has clearly learnt from Murnau. Eric Rhode has admirably described how *Nosferatu* places its vampire-count into natural locations in such a way that he appears to be a distillation of their spirit:

When he emerges high on the edge of a horizon, or framed in a doorway, or walking the deck of a ship, he seems to take possession of these places and to rob them of their identity. Coffins and doorways become apt niches for his emaciated body, and bare fields seem to distend from his gnarled form. (Rhode, 1976, p. 183)

There is, however, a significant difference: no character in Dreyer's film is as grotesque as Max Schreck's vampire-count, or as theatrical as Alexander Granach's Renfield-figure, in *Nosferatu*. For Dreyer, the forces of evil are as natural a part of the landscape and the human beings who inhabit it as the forces of good; they need not 'take possession' of the landscape, they need not violate and distort human faces, forms, and gestures. This is particularly important to Dreyer because he was obsessed by the natural expressiveness of the face, an expressiveness which could only be diminished by grotesque make-up. 'Nothing in the world', he wrote, 'can be compared to the human face. It is a land one can never tire of exploring. There is no greater experience in a studio than to witness the expression of a sensitive face under the mysterious power of inspiration. To see it animated from inside, and turning into poetry.'

The words just quoted come from a late essay, 'Thoughts on My Craft', which Dreyer contributed to *Sight and Sound* in the winter of 1955–6. Here he expressly rejected what he called 'grey and boring naturalism'; and that rejection alerts us to the way in which the settings and figures of *Vampyr* are stylized, not through grotesque make-up, certainly, but through *mise en scène* and manner of shooting. The philosophy behind this—and it is characteristic of Dreyer that there should be a philosophy behind his practice—is once again inimitably stated in his essay.

The artist must describe inner, not outer life. The capacity to abstract is essential to all artistic creation. Abstraction allows the director to get outside the fence with which naturalism has surrounded his medium. It allows his films to be not merely visual, but spiritual. The director must share his own artistic and spiritual experiences with the audience. Abstraction will give him a chance of doing it, of replacing objective reality with his own subjective interpretation.

This means that we must find some new creative principles. I would like to stress that I am thinking merely of the image. People think in images, and images are the primary factor of a film.

The closest road at hand is the road of simplification. Every creative artist is confronted by the same task. He must be inspired by reality, then move away from it in order to give his work the form provoked by his inspiration. The director must be free to transform reality so that it becomes consistent with the inspired, simplified image left in his mind. Reality must obey the director's aesthetic sense.

To make the form more evident, more striking, simplification must

cleanse the director's inspiration of all elements that do not support his
central idea. It must transform the idea into a symbol. With symbolism we
are well on the way to abstraction, for symbolism works through suggestion.

This abstraction through simplification, so that a purified form emerges
in a kind of timeless, psychological realism, can be practised by the director
in a modest way in the actual rooms of his films. How many rooms without
souls we have seen on the screen. . . . The director can give his rooms a soul
through simplification, by removing all that is superfluous, by making a
few significant articles and objects psychological witnesses of the inmate's
personality. (MacCann, 1966, p. 315)

Dreyer completes these thoughts by looking beyond the black-and-
white photography of his best-known early works to a stylized,
almost abstract use of colour that would transcend the naturalism
which filmed images seem to invite.

Stylization, indeed, is the hall-mark of *Vampyr* too—it shows
itself in the characters' jerky movements, in their disembodied
voices, and not least in the deliberate paleness of the photography
which some commentators have linked with the anaemic condition of the vampire's victims. 'In fact', F. D. McConnell has said, 'the
whiteness of the film increases throughout the action until, in our
last sight of Gray and his lover escaping . . . it is all but impossible to
distinguish the figures at all' (*The Spoken Seen*, p. 35). These shots
of the escaping lovers are intercut with the strange drowning of
the vampire's helper in the giant hopper of a flour-mill; and here
McConnell has made an interesting suggestion about the effect
these final scenes might have on a rightly attuned spectator. 'Our
last sight of *Vampyr*', he writes in *The Spoken Seen*, 'is of the monstrous gears of the grinding machine turning slowly to a full stop.
And it is inevitable that we associate those turning gears which
have just killed the doctor with the turning gears, the sprockets, and
the wheels of the motion-picture projector itself, the machine that
has just elaborated the . . . fantasy of David Gray's strange
adventures . . . And to underscore the pun, Dreyer, for the first
time in *Vampyr*, removes the filter from his camera: we see the
gears in sharply etched, realistic chiaruscuro' (p. 36). 'Inevitable',
I fear, is not quite the right word; I for one did not make the
association before reading Professor McConnell's book. Neither
here nor elsewhere, certainly, does Dreyer point beyond his
ostensible plot to the mechanics of creating the film-experience, or
the film-illusion, as unequivocally as Bergman does at the beginning
and end of *Persona*.

Nevertheless, Professor McConnell's remarks on the effect of these closing scenes do suggest something important about Dreyer's *Vampyr*. No terror-film is better able to bring home to us certain aspects of our cinema-going experience than this seldom-seen masterpiece. Many critics and aestheticians have tried to analyse these aspects—one need only leaf through Henri Agel's useful little book on Cinema Aesthetics to find a plethora of quotations that apply to *Vampyr* with particular force. 'The cinema . . . must develop its extraordinary and poignant faculty for representing the immaterial' (Ricciotto Canudo). 'Artists of the screen must transform reality in the image of their inner vision' (Canudo again). 'Expand the richness of the real by means of the inexhaustible resources of the human imagination' (Henri Agel). 'The cinema permits us to make our dreams visible' (Jean Tedesco). 'The grand fusion of life and dream, the perceptible and the imperceptible . . . The acclimatization of the marvellous in the everyday' (Ado Kyrou). 'The realism of the unreal, visible proof that the "unreal" exists in itself, as an object' (André Fraigneau). 'The screen can show intermediary beings, beings that exist between shadow and reality' (Ramon Gomez de la Serna). 'Landscapes become states of the soul, states of the soul landscapes . . . a magic vision of the world . . . The cinema introduces the dream into our waking life . . . Objective image mirrors subjective state . . . The miraculous is miraculous because it is real; the real is real because it is miraculous' (Edgar Morin). In the hands of a master like Dreyer the cinema becomes a machine that projects the miraculous, the dream-like, and the deeper truths of the soul, into the very heart of our urban civilization.

Like the over-all greyness of the film which makes its hero's name a 'speaking' one, its ending was found through a happy accident. 'Our first idea', Dreyer told readers of the *Cahiers du Cinéma* in September 1965,

was to have the old doctor disappear in the earth, swallowed up by quicksand. But we couldn't utilize that idea as it was too dangerous for the actor. Therefore we had to find something else. One day, on the way back to Paris after a day of shooting, all the while talking about what we might do, we passed a little house that looked as if it were full of white flames. As we were unoccupied, not yet having found anything, we went into the little house and, once inside, understood that it was a little factory where they worked at reclaiming plaster. The whole interior was white, all the objects were bathed in a white dust and the workmen, too, were all white. Everything partook of that extraordinary white atmosphere. This was utilized by us as a point of departure for another stylistic element of the film. (Leyda, 1977, p. 117)

This episode shows once again how a true artist works—how a powerful, obsessive imagination seizes on the given things and the accidents of life and moulds them to its purpose.

One of the most haunting images of *Vampyr* is that of the virginal Gisèle, her strange squeaking high-pitched voice stilled, bound with her hands behind her to an iron frame. This has thematic importance, not only for this film, but for Dreyer's work as a whole. From the bird-cage in *Master of the House* (1925) to actual prisons in *The Passion of Joan of Arc* and *Day of Wrath*, the theme of mental as well as spiritual captivity is frequently suggested. Nor is this the only thematic preoccupation *Vampyr* shares with its fellows in the Dreyer canon: we might list here his constant confrontations of youth with crabbed age, the struggle to live with stifling death; supernatural forces perceived within the natural world, from *Leaves from Satan's Book* to *The Word* (1955); the theme of witchcraft, 'an exemplary site where the discourses of religion, art and the feminine intersect' (Nash, 1977, p. 19) in *Joan of Arc* and *Day of Wrath* as well as *Vampyr*; the related motifs of demonic possession and resurrection; the great theme of the failure of words, the impossibility or implausibility of purely rational and causal explanations. His non-professional actors show their amateur status rather obviously at times, and this may have been a factor in the public's cool reception of *Vampyr* when it was first exhibited; but it should by now have become obvious that Dreyer is not concerned with 'acting' in the ordinary sense. As André Bazin has so well said, he interests himself above all in

the countenance as flesh, which, when not involved in playing a role, is a man's true imprint, the most visible mark of his soul. It is then that the countenance takes on the dignity of the sign. He would have us be concerned here not with the psychology but with the physiology of existence. Hence the hieratic tempo of the acting, the slow ambiguous gestures, the obstinate recurrence of certain behavioural patterns, the unforgettable dream-like slow motion. (Bazin, 1967, p. 133)

Preconceptions about acting should no longer be allowed to obscure the drama of the soul played out in Dreyer's classic vampire-film.

From the very first moment in which the strangely shaped letters spelling out the word V A M P Y R are superimposed over the dimly discerned shape of a skull, we are transported into a mysterious world over whose presentation Dreyer retains full control. Whether he intercuts shots of David Gray arriving at the inn with others, apparently unrelated, which show a reaper and a ferryman; whether he allows a candle to travel slowly across a picture to pick out a popular representation of Death, or counterpoints that image with an arras depicting an idyllic seventeenth-century scene; whether he has a key turn slowly in its lock by itself, or a skull direct its hollow eye-sockets towards the vampire, or a skeletal hand clasp and proffer a bottle of poison; whether he accompanies his images with silence, or foregrounds the ticking of a clock, the screech of an owl, a murmured prayer, the turning of a drill in wood and the snap of a metal lock, or introduces the sound of a banjo (and who but Dreyer could have made such a sound, and its sudden cessation, so sinister?); whether he takes us into an eerily illuminated landscape or a cosily lit room in the château or the heavily shadowed shabby menace of the doctor's house; whether he instils anxiety by close-ups of his players or shows their strangely drifting, hesitant movements in medium- or long-shot; whether he introduces, suddenly and without warning, a man with a hideously deformed face who will play no further part in the action, or shows the mere shadow of the gun that will kill the owner of the château, or lights up a small stain of blood on the ground beneath a dead coachman; whether he shows an old woman doing no more than raising her stick or setting down a candle, or shows her suddenly reduced, in good vampire fashion, to her skeleton—there can never be any doubt that we have entered a world created by Dreyer, a world whose memory will remain with us for ever after we have once allowed ourselves to be drawn into it.

Through his photography and choice of location, which ensure that we discern most of the things he shows us in an eerie, uncertain, pale light; through the co-presence of mysterious gestures and actions with gestures and actions whose meaning is plain; through constant symbolic overtones, metaphysical suggestions that emanate from reaper and ferryman, skeletal hands and window-frames that throw the shadow of a cross; through the important role assigned to shadows and wraiths; through unusual camera angles; through a sound-recording technique that makes human speech seem half heard, overheard, rather than declaimed for the benefit of an audience; through haunting images and carefully selected sounds; through a deliberate, dream-like disjointedness; through an ending which, though it portends salvation, is strangely inconclusive—through these and other means Dreyer has produced what may well be called the most uncanny of all cinematic tales of terror. Its secret, as he himself said while he was making the film, lies not just in the story it tells, but in the effect his manner of telling that story may be supposed to have on sensitive spectators.

Imagine that we are sitting in an ordinary room. Suddenly we are told that there is a corpse behind the door. In an instant, the room we are sitting in is completely altered; everything in it has taken on another look; the light, the atmosphere have changed, and the objects are as we conceive them. That is the effect I want to get in my film. (Everson, 1974, p. 63)

It is to be hoped that new generations of film-goers will not become so conditioned by the rapid pace, the colour, the heaping-up of sensational incident characteristic of the cinema's more recent tales of terror as to lose altogether the capacity of responding to Dreyer's fascinating and disturbing work.

CHAPTER 6

The Iconography of the Terror-film: Wiene's *Caligari*

I must know everything . . . I must penetrate into his
innermost secrets . . . I must myself become
Caligari.

The Cabinet of Dr. Caligari (1919)

FOR all its imaginative use of sound, Dreyer's *Vampyr* has an
unmistakable connection with the silent film in general—symbolized, as it were, by its use of intertitles as well as dialogue—and with
the uncanny silent cinema of Germany in particular. This last
connection is underlined by Dreyer's importation, not only of
Sybille Schmitz, but also of Hermann Warm—an artistic designer
who had collaborated on the sets of *The Cabinet of Dr. Caligari* and
had been responsible for the idea that films could be 'drawings
brought to life'. That contention clearly appealed to Dreyer,
despite his decision to film on location rather than in the studio;
for his images are composed with an artist's care, the individual
frames again and again resemble old engravings. One need
remember only his justly famous medium-shot of the reaper at the
ferry, in which the central figure in its rural broad-brimmed hat,
seen from behind, makes a perfect composition with the blade of the
large scythe he is carrying over his shoulder, balancing the gibbet-
like structure that supports the ferryman's bell. In his next film,
Day of Wrath, made eleven years after the financial disaster that
Vampyr turned out to be, Dreyer's superb visual sense expressed
itself again and again in compositions that resembled nothing so
much as the paintings of seventeenth-century Dutch masters.

The Cabinet of Dr. Caligari was written by Carl Mayer and Hans
Janowitz, directed by Robert Wiene, designed by Hermann Warm,
Walter Reimann, and Walter Röhrig, and photographed by Willy
Hameister. We now know that its distinctive style resulted partly
from what economists call 'product differentiation'—a series of

choices explained to George A. Huaco by Erich Pommer, head of the DECLA company that made *Caligari*, in the following terms:

The German film industry made 'stylized films' to make money. Let me explain. At the end of World War I the Hollywood industry moved toward world supremacy. The Danes had a film industry. The French had a very active film industry, which suffered an eclipse at the end of the war. Germany was defeated; how could she make films that would compete with the others? It would have been impossible to try and imitate Hollywood or the French. So we tried something new: the expressionist or stylized films. This was possible because Germany had an overflow of good artists and writers, a strong literary tradition, and a great tradition of theatre. This provided a basis of good, trained actors. World War I finished the French industry; the problem for Germany was to compete with Hollywood. (Huaco, 1965, p. 36)

If that was indeed the intention, it succeeded—culturally at least, though not always financially. 'It is a matter of record', we read in Lewis Jacobs's *The Rise of the American Film*, 'that no picture, not even *The Birth of a Nation*, ever created quite as much comment, argument and speculation in one month's time as did *The Cabinet of Dr. Caligari*.' Comment was by no means all favourable; later anti-Caligarians like Panofsky, Bazin, and Andrew Tudor could look back on contemporary attacks, by such leaders of taste as Ezra Pound and Blaise Cendrars, on the 'trickiness' of the film's distortions, its decision to photograph live actors in painted settings, its failure to make use of special lenses and unusual camera angles to achieve its grotesque effects, its theatricality, and so on. Descriptively much of this is true—I cannot agree, however, with those who contend that the film lacks unity and a rhythm of its own, and I cannot subscribe to the adverse value-judgements based on the film's special mode of stylization. It is understandable that Eisenstein should have seen in it—as the *Times Literary Supplement* reminded its readers on 20 October 1978—a 'barbaric carnival' destroying the healthy infancy of film-art, a reprehensible combination of 'silent hysteria, particoloured canvases, daubed flats, painted faces, and the unnatural broken gestures and actions of monstrous chimeras'; for Eisenstein's own principles were so different from those of Wiene and his collaborators that he could not be expected to be fair. On its own terms, however, it would seem to me, the film succeeds brilliantly, justifying Paul Rotha's tribute to it, in *The Film till Now* (1949), as a significant 'attempt at the expression of a creative mind in the new medium of cinematography' which seems 'as fresh now as when first produced'.

Avant-garde film-makers, it should be remembered, have not allowed themselves to be discouraged by the dismissive remarks of highly regarded pioneers and pundits from looking to *Caligari* for inspiration. Wiene's work inevitably comes to mind when one looks, for instance, at Marcel L'Herbier's *L'Inhumaine* (1924), where written words are suspended in the air much as they are in *Caligari*, and where Claire's parlour is as obviously stylized as the sitting-room of Wiene's heroine; or at Guido Seeber's KIPHO-film of 1925, which actually culminates in a clip from *Caligari*; or Jean Epstein's *Fall of the House of Usher*, which mingles stylized settings with location-shots. 'The importance of *Caligari* for the French avantgarde film', writes S. D. Lawler in *The Cubist Cinema*, 'can hardly be overestimated'; and he quotes Jean Tedesco's account of how this German film fired the imagination of Louis Delluc and 'set off the bomb of German expressionism' in the intellectual life of the 1920s. Thirty years later we find a new American *avant-garde* again paying homage to *Caligari*. Film-makers reintroduce its characters, as Kenneth Anger brought Cesare the somnambulist into *The Inauguration of the Pleasure Dome* (1954); or they refer, unmistakably, to its structure and story-line, as did Gregory Markopoulos in his dream-movie *Swain* (1950) and Bruce Baillie in *Have You Thought of Talking to the Director?* (1962)—a quaint title which itself alludes to the plot of Wiene's film.

Even where there are no recognizable traces of direct influence or specific acknowledgements, the spirit of *Caligari* informs much of the 'visionary cinema' of the 1940s and after, from Maya Deren's *Meshes of the Afternoon* (1943) onwards—works that have been well described, by Parker Tyler, P. Adams Sitney, and Robert Sklar, as 'trance films', 'intense, private and candid explorations of the unconscious'. Wherever such explorations are made, the spirit of the early German cinema is near. It was René Schwob who best characterized that spirit when he called the German cinema of the silent period the most powerful sounding of our dark inner turmoil that has ever been made—'le plus prodigieux coup de sonde dans le trouble infini que nous portons en nous'.

The commercial cinema too has been indelibly affected by *Caligari*—not only directly, but also indirectly through the medium of *Caligari*-inspired films and scenes by Robert Florey, Paul Leni, Fritz Lang, James Young, James Whale, Charles Laughton, and many others. One remembers not only all those monster–bride confrontations and roof-top chases in the routine horror-movie, but also the masterly transformation of the stylized stage-flats of *Caligari* into the stylized architecture of films by Galeen and Lang; Karloff's Caligari-like make-up in Young's *The Bells* (1926) and his Cesare-like stance in certain scenes of Whale's *Frankenstein*; the Caligarized Paris of Florey's *Murders in the rue Morgue* (1932); the studio skies and the eerily lit, angular attic-scenes in Laughton's *The Night of the Hunter* (1955), the characterstic shadow-and-light play of the films of Karl Freund, the 'Gothic' camera-work of George Robinson, and Mario Bava's frank acknowledgements of the painted nature of some of his sets. Without knowing it the audiences of terror-films even today are again and again confronted by images that ultimately derive from the imaginations of Wiene and his gifted team.

This does not mean, however, that *Caligari* sprang fully formed into the world as though it were author of itself and knew no other kin. A great deal of earlier literature, and a great deal of earlier work in the cinema, from Méliès onwards, was involved in its gestation. Hanns Heinz Ewers, Paul Wegener, and Otto Rippert had shown the use that could be made of German Romantic motifs, and motifs from the eerier folk-ballads, in the cinema; Swedish and Danish film-makers had experimented with the creation of an uncanny atmosphere by cinematic means; Stellan Rye had anticipated the stylized decor of *Caligari* by some five years in *The House without Doors* (1914); a student had appeared as an especially vulnerable protagonist and a particular kind of marginal man in *The Student of Prague* (1913); Conrad Veidt's disconcerting eye-opening had been anticipated by Pola Negri in Lubitsch's *The Eyes of the Mummy* (1918); and Maurice Tourneur's *Trilby* had introduced a sinister hypnotist to German audiences well before *Caligari*. These cinematic experiences coalesced with some personal experiences of the script-writers—a murder in Hamburg, an unsympathetic army doctor, psychiatric treatment—and with feelings about life common in the early Weimar Republic, to produce, in the hands of Wiene and his designers, the film through which the German silent cinema first became internationally known.

The Cabinet of Dr. Caligari invites its audience to explore a *mise en scène* that sets live actors and solid furniture into stylized exterior and interior sets obviously painted on to theatrical flats and photographed by a camera which moves relatively little. Its flowing narrative does, however, make significant though sparing use of cross-cutting, flash-back, reductions and expansions of the image-field, high-angle shots, low-angle lighting, split screen, quickly flashed or long-held images, and other devices of the early film, as its tells the story baldly summarized in *The Oxford Companion to Film* as follows:

Caligari is a hypnotist whose somnambulist, Cesare, kills the hero's friend and carries off his girl. Having exposed Caligari, the hero is himself revealed as an inmate of a lunatic asylum where Caligari is director.

And the *Companion* adds:

The original outline by M A Y E R and J A N O W I T Z represented Caligari unequivocally as the insane villain: the framework, which by representing the hero as mad reverses the authors' intentions, was added by P O M M E R. (Bawden, 1976, p. 102)

Whether Pommer or another was responsible for the alteration need not concern us now. We should remember, however, that unlike *Dr. Jekyll and Mr. Hyde* and *Vampyr, Caligari* did not begin with a specific literary work that had to be adapted for the screen. Its authors conceived it, from the beginning, as a film. The difference between their conception and the finished work can now be studied with great accuracy; for the Deutsche Kinemathek in Berlin has acquired from the estate of Werner Krauss, and has kindly allowed me to see, a typescript of the original screen-play. From this it appears that a 'framework' was envisaged by the authors, but that it was a framework of a different kind. At the opening of the typescript we meet Francis, the narrator, not in a lunatic asylum, as it turns out in the film, but as a prosperous 'Dr. Francis' inhabiting a country house, where he recounts to a happy, punch-drinking group of friends the tale of Caligari and his somnambulist in which he had been involved some twenty years before. Among those who listen to him is Jane, the very Jane who also plays a central part in the Caligari story, and who is now happily married to Francis. Francis's memory has been reactivated by the sight of some gipsies travelling to a fair—but throughout his narration his present distance from the world of Caligari and his somnambulist is to be kept before us by intertitles that pointedly use the epic preterite: 'When, the next day, we went to the fair, we had no idea that in the meantime a terrible crime had been committed.' Nothing in this version leaves any room for doubt that the events recounted actually occurred—we are even shown an official plaque put up by the town of Holstenwall to mark the spot where Caligari's cabinet had once stood! Through the introduction of a sympathetic disciple as well as various other signs, including unmistakable signals in the projected intertitles, the typescript asks us to regard Caligari as a dedicated scientist whose mind has given way, as a man to be pitied, as a tragic figure. It offers little support for Kracauer's thesis of a revolutionary or anti-tyrannical tendency that those who made the actual film then perverted. The Pirandellian ambiguities introduced into the film by the altered framework, by the substitution of a narrator who may or may not be insane for one who recollects long-past unhappy events in the tranquillity of domestic happiness, seem to me a distinct improvement, a deepening of the film's import, a just reflection of historical and social uncertainties characteristic of the time just after the First World War. They take wing from one brief hint in the typescript, one passing suggestion, soon dismissed, of a less than completely reliable narrator: 'And then I felt', the typescript makes the narrator say at one point, 'as though I myself had lost my reason.'

It has become all too fashionable of late to dismiss *Caligari* as a cinematic backwater. I believe, on the contrary, that it presents a veritable anthology of figures, themes, and images which later directors have re-used, varied, expanded, and developed further, without even now exhausting their possibilities; and that it is therefore particularly well fitted to provide us with telling examples of the recurring iconography of the kind of cinema which the present book is trying to examine.

At the centre of the film is the sinister figure of Werner Krauss's Caligari, with his unforgettable shuffling walk, his obsequious showman's gestures, his leering glances through round spectacles, his weird Biedermeier costume, his gloves with their three black stripes matching the patterning of his straggling hair and the converging lines painted on to the scenery and the floors of the film-set. The significance of this figure is worth pursuing in some detail.

This *Caligari* is, first of all, a piece of scene-design: part of an over-all visual pattern which gains its meaning from a larger whole. In *The Cabinet of Dr. Caligari*, as in later films of terror, this point is driven home, unobtrusively but constantly, by the composition of the frames, the relation of the actor to the scenery and to his fellow-actors as conveyed by stance, costume, and camera angle.

Secondly, Caligari is a showman whose deliberately weird get-up and exaggerated gestures are designed to induce an audience to attend the thrilling spectacle that awaits it in his fairground tent. Here, clearly, we have a reflection, within the film, of what has brought us into the cinema to watch the film. Before and during its original showing it was, in fact, advertised, by its distributors and exhibitors in Berlin and elsewhere, with considerable show-man's flair; the advertising campaign included posters and news-paper graphics whose design resembled that of the poster which Werner Krauss's Caligari unrolls from a cross-bar stuck to a pole to advertise, within the film, the exhibition of his somnambulist. The fascination which films of this kind may exert on the individual spectators as well as the group is symbolized within *The Cabinet of Dr. Caligari* first by the crowd that attends Caligari's spectacle when Francis and Alan pay their fateful visit, and then by Jane's reactions to the solo performance Caligari maliciously arranges for her. As we have seen, many later terror-films, from *Mark of the Vampire* and *Mad Love* to *Peeping Tom*, make some of their subtlest effects by reminding their audiences of the kind of attraction that has brought them to watch what they are in fact watching. Wiene's film does this too, and in the process it jogs us into remembering that not so long ago the cinema itself, which is here self-consciously entering the realm of art, was a fairground side-show.

A French critic, C. B. Clément, writing in *Communications* in 1975, has seen a strong sexual connotation in the scene, already mentioned, in which Caligari lures the terrified and fascinated Jane into his deserted fairground booth to give her a private view of his rigid somnambulist. What we see is a malevolent old man, a demonic bourgeois, attracting a young girl by flipping open two flaps to show her something behind the scenes ('ob-scene'?)—the 'exhibitor' as 'exhibitionist'! But perhaps we had better leave that interpretation to hard-line Freudians.

Caligari is shown, thirdly, to be a multiple personality, two of whose facets are indicated by the distinct costuming and make-up which we also associate with *Jekyll and Hyde* films. As 'Caligari' he is a fairground showman, pushed around by authorities whom he has to cajole and coax, dependent on audiences whom he has to attract. The menace that comes from him in that guise is the menace of the underdog who is eager to take his revenge for social slights and oppression. As director of the mental home he is—well, dual again, for Alan sees him, and we see him for a time, as a power-obsessed maniac who belongs in a strait-jacket more surely than his patients, while the final scenes suggest that he may be an urbane and benevolent healer of sick minds. This kind of presentation of different views of the same personality, or different aspects of the same personality, through changes in the acting style and make-up and lighting of the same actor, has become a staple of the terror-film since *Jekyll and Hyde* was first made into a movie in 1908. It is no accident, of course, that Caligari is a doctor—or, more precisely, an alienist; the complex feelings he provokes were familiar to contemporaries of Charcot and Freud, 'healers' who moved among hysterics and conducted experiments with hypnotism.

Caligari is shown, fourthly, as an early victim of that favourite affliction of so many recent terror-films, culminating in *The Exorcist* and *The Heretic*: demonic possession. The original Caligari, we learn from the film, was an eighteenth-century 'mystic' (the religious associations of that term are highly significant in this context); the director of the mental home reads about him and becomes obsessed with him. For weeks before the film opened in Berlin, advertisements proclaimed in strange, jagged, hieroglyphic-like lettering: DU MUSST CALIGARI WERDEN ('You have to become Caligari'): and these letters in fact appear in the film superimposed upon the scenery to show the alienist's obsession with, and take-over by, the long-dead Caligari. 'Possession', here, comes by way of printed or written words, by means of a book and letters appearing on a wall, rather than a picture, a painted portrait, as in Corman's *The Haunted Palace* and other, similar, works. The first time we ever see Caligari, he is clutching a book! In Fritz Lang's *The Testament of Dr. Mabuse*, the director of another mental home, Dr. Baum, was to be taken over in a parallel way by the spirit of a man still alive, the super-criminal Dr. Mabuse, incarcerated as a madman and scribbling down unceasing plans for crimes and world-domination. Dr. Baum thus fulfils, in Lang's film, the functions of Caligari *and* Cesare in Robert Wiene's. In Lang, the 'taking-over', the 'possession', of Dr. Baum is shown by superimposition; in *The Exorcist*, its principal (and certainly most effective) mark is a change of voice. For many of us the real 'star' of this crude and unpleasant movie was the unseen Mercedes McCambridge, who lent the demon her voice, though no regular cinema-goer could be quite impervious to the aura around Max von Sydow, playing the title role: an aura deriving in part from his appearance as the tormented hero of many a Bergman film, and in part from his appearance as Jesus in *The Greatest Story Ever Told* (1965).

The fifth iconographic aspect of the Caligari figure for which important parallels may be found in later films of the same genre is that he is shown as a dreamer within the dream-like movie that bears his name. We see the director of the mental home in his bed, tossing in uneasy sleep, perturbed (we surmise) by dreams of persons and events that we have been seeing, and are seeing, in the film of which he is part. Such images of the dreamer within a dream, or the dreamer and his dream, will recur in many of the most successful terror-films of later times—in Cavalcanti's *Dead of Night*, for instance.

Caligari is shown, as has already been said, as a stranger who disrupts the normal lives of the inhabitants of a small town: he and his somnambulist are marked out as strangers by idiosyncrasies of costume and movement that set them to some extent apart from the rest of the cast. This is one of a cluster of themes and images which Paul Monaco, in *Cinema and Society*, has analysed in a large number of German films as 'symbols of Germany's obsession with the loss of the war of 1914–18': Monaco lists 'betrayal, the foreigner as evil-doer, guilt, racing against time, dangerous streets'. In itself, however, the image of the 'disruptive stranger' is central to the terror-film of many nations, just as it had been to a great many literary and sub-literary terror-fictions: we need think only of the part which it plays in such classics as *Dracula*, for instance, where the menace comes to England from Transylvania, or in *The Mummy*, where it comes from Egypt. This helps to explain, among other things, why so many of the most successful terror-stars of the American sound-cinema betrayed by their speech that they hailed from England or from the continent of Europe. In

Robert Florey's *Murders in the rue Morgue*, which starred Bela Lugosi, this is brought out into the open when the customers lured into Dr. Mirakle's fairground tent comment explicitly on Mirakle's foreign modes of speech: 'Did you notice his accent? I have never heard one like it.'

There is a Hoffmannesque twist, however, to this story of Caligari the 'stranger': for just as in Hoffmann's 'The Sandman' the sinister itinerant vendor of spectacles is identified with a respected local lawyer, so Caligari, as it turns out, is very much part of the little town he terrorizes in the inner story. He is, after all, the director of one of the town's most necessary institutions. Here we should perhaps remember that Caligari's outer appearance was suggested to the script-writers by a photograph of the philosopher Arthur Schopenhauer in his old age. In many a later film will we find some connection made between the terror-makers that fill the screen and small-town German life.

The Cabinet of Dr. Caligari features a number of striking images which show its eponymous hero combining qualities that were destined to play—in this particular combination—a vital role in later terror-films. On the one hand we see him as a doctor in elegant morning-dress attended by subordinate colleagues in white coats as he examines his patients; on the other we see him as an adept of curious lore, who rummages in old volumes of 'mystical' texts and is seen clutching one of them to his bosom in an extravagant gesture of delight. The combination of scientist and 'mystic' adept, exhibited as deadly and dangerous in *Caligari*, in Ulmer's *The Black Cat* (1934), and elsewhere, is, however, the very combination needed to fight the forces of evil in other films: one need think only of the Van Helsing figure in such films as *Dracula*, *The Mummy*, and their progeny.

Another aspect of Caligari may be illuminated by a passage from Heinrich Heine's *The Romantic School* in which the poet talks about attacks made by German 'supernaturalists' on the rationalists of the Enlightenment. In their hatred of the rationalists, Heine declares, these people

resemble the inmates of a madhouse who, though they are afflicted with the most diverse kinds of madness, manage to accommodate themselves with one another tolerably well, but who are filled with bitterest hatred of the man whom they regard as their common enemy: the alienist who wants to restore their reason.

Heine's perspective is clear, and the framing action of *Caligari* would seem to suggest a similar perspective to its spectators. Béla Bálazs tells us that at one time the film even appeared with the sub-title 'How a madman sees the world'. Yet a question mark continues to hang over the figure of Krauss's Caligari. He directs a madhouse—but is he not himself deluded? Is the insanity we seem to see breaking out in him simply a projection from one of his patients who externalizes in the director the madness that is 'really' in himself? Or is Francis, whatever his own state of mind, seeing truly? Who will guard the guardians? What happens when those who should cure us are themselves in need of cure? What do we do when those who should protect us are driven to persecute us? The political and social resonance of such questions is immediately apparent—as is the fact that Wiene's film, and Krauss's performance, owe a good deal of their force to their ability to raise them in our minds. They are emphasized by the very rhythm of the film, which ends (in unmutilated copies) on a long-held, puzzling close-up of Krauss's face—the longest-held close-up in the whole work.

To this disturbing portrait Krauss adds another nuance by insinuating—mainly through Caligari's shuffling walk supported by a stick—that there may also be something physically wrong with him; that he is, in some not immediately tangible way, a cripple. We are therefore free to see his lust for power and desire for revenge as in part at least an attempt to compensate for physical inferiority as well as for some real or imagined social slight. This impression, however, which many a modern viewer undoubtedly gains, may well be contrary to the film-makers' intentions. What Werner Krauss is probably attempting, with his hobbling walk, is to find a dynamic equivalent for the static distortions of the scenery—just as his hand and arm movements, when clutching a book or miming hallucination, are as deliberately exaggerated and twisted as the painted perspectives before which they are enacted. The gait and gestures of the soberly clad director of the asylum are noticeably less extravagant than those of the showman in his high hat.

Above all, however, as Noel Carroll has so convincingly shown in 'The Cabinet of Dr. Kracauer' (*Millennium Film Journal*, i (2), 1978), Krauss's movements are 'literalizations' of the metaphor that he is morally twisted—just as the sets suggest by their 'bending buildings, crooked street-lamps and cracked walls' that the world into which he enters is about to collapse on to its inhabitants, and by their many knife-like or stiletto-like shapes that this world is hostile and threatening.

Caligari owes the power that he wields to his mastery of hypnosis. He thus becomes—and this is clearly a further, most significant, aspect of the character that Wiene, Mayer, and Krauss project—the mesmerist, the controller from afar, the man who can kill without ever being seen to raise the knife himself, the man who can induce others to act or be acted upon in the way a puppet-master manipulates his marionettes. This is shown symbolically by the way Cesare awakes on Caligari's command in the fairground tent, and by the dummy which takes Cesare's place when the latter is sent out on a murderous mission. The film's intertitles make the master–slave relationship explicit:

'Cesare! Do you hear me? It is I calling you: I, Dr. Caligari, – – –your master – –Awaken for a brief while from your dark night' – – – – –;

they emphasize, too, the idea of unholy experimentation on helpless human beings:

'Now I shall be able to prove whether a somnambulist can be compelled to do things of which he knows nothing, things he would never do himself and would abhor doing if he were awake . . .'

The social, political, and moral implications of all this have been imaginatively explored in another medium by Thomas Mann's *Mario and the Magician*. There is a clear connection here with hypnotist figures favoured by non-German film-makers too—from silent American versions of *Trilby* to the Hammer *Dracula* films, directed by Terence Fisher, where the vampire-count acquires a whole bevy of minions whom he induces to act for him in the way Renfield does in the original novel. We have already seen how in zombie-movies, from Halperin's *White Zombie* of 1932 to John Gilling's *The Plague of the Zombies* in 1965, the image takes on an additional economic menace: zombies are used by their masters and controllers not just as instruments of mayhem, but also as a source of cheap labour. The symbol would, I am sure, have delighted Karl Marx.

The ultimate significance of Caligari's hypnotizing powers, and of the way in which at his very first introduction his gaze is directed outwards towards the viewer, has been perceptively glossed by Roland Barthes in his seminal essay 'On Leaving the

Cinema' (*Communications*, xix). Here Barthes has rightly drawn attention to the hypnotizing function of the cinema-screen itself, with its immobile but flickering light watched by intent spectators in the dark. Mark Nash, whose book on Carl Dreyer refers to Barthes's essay, rightly adds that

hypnosis has a privileged place in early cinema: e.g. *The Cabinet of Dr. Caligari*, the representations of the doctor with his thick spectacles and his gaze into camera, who *sees* into psychological (and supernatural) problems; Lang's *Dr. Mabuse*; the doctor in *Vampyr* where the result of the hypnosis is Gray's uncanny dream (central to vampirism) of losing his own blood. (Nash, 1977, pp. 25–6)

When Nash goes on to liken the whole experience of watching Dreyer's film—'its slowness, its controlled rhythm, its silences'—to the experience of being hypnotized, he could just as well be talking about *Caligari*, or *Tired Death* (*Destiny*), or (*Warning*) *Shadows*, or many another German film of the Weimar period.

The scene in which Caligari substitutes a dummy for the somnambulist whom he has sent out on his murderous mission suggests another aspect of this figure which was to have a long subsequent history in the terror-film. It shows him as a man who can manipulate the phenomenal world in such a way that we think we are seeing what is not, in reality, 'there'. Fritz Lang and Thea von Harbou, in *The Testament of Dr. Mabuse*, invented an aural equivalent of this visual illusion: a gramophone rigged up in such a way that when the handle of Dr. Baum's locked study door is tried at a time when he is out on nefarious business, his voice will call from inside the room: 'I do not wish to be disturbed! I have given express orders that I am not to be disturbed!' The complex delights offered by images and sounds of this nature derive in part, once again, from the cinema-experience itself. The cinema, after all, constantly shows us men and women who are not 'really' there, and lets us hear voices whose owners—if they dwell in the land of the living at all—are many miles away.

This recognition leads us to yet another important role the figure of Caligari plays in Wiene's film. One of his functions is to suggest monsters arising from the subconscious; figures who may have a socially and historically significant original outside the mind, but whose appearance and actions are shown by the framework story to be inevitably coloured by the nature of the mind that apprehends them.

Kracauer saw Caligari as a 'tyrant' figure—a view that is justified if one looks at the role he plays in controlling his somnambulist and possibly his role as director of the madhouse. In other respects, however—in his attitude to duly constituted authorities and to the Holstenwall establishment—he is, like Lang's Mabuse, a dangerously subversive force. Nor can he simply be seen as a negative figure. Even if he is taken for the murderous 'mad scientist' Francis sees in him, our reaction to him must be complex and ambiguous. He is, after all, the one character who does what his nature leads him to do, regardless of the consequences; who lives to the full, and whose fall—if fall there is—has something of tragic grandeur about it. If he has to cringe to authority, as so many of his fellow-Germans had to do, then he does so in a deliberately exaggerated, almost mocking manner and takes his revenge afterwards. He is an artist in his way, far removed from the petty criminal whom we see languishing in the city gaol: like Mabuse and Haghi he avoids the drabness, the half-measures of ordinary lives, he defies convention, rises above the mass, and thus inspires admiration and envy.

Lastly: the image of Caligari which we see on the screen is, unmistakably, the image of an actor, Werner Krauss; an actor who will later embody a whole gallery of sinister creations, from Jack the Ripper (or 'Springheeled Jack') in Paul Leni's *Waxworks* to Süss's Jewish 'co-conspirators' in Veit Harlan's revolting *Jew Süss*. Those of us who know these performances—as well as such more sympathetic creations as the troubled professor in Pabst's *Secrets of a Soul* or the ageing actor in Willi Forst's *Burgtheater* (1936)—find that the aura with which they have surrounded Krauss in our memory will, for good or ill, enter into our appreciation of his Caligari in Wiene's classic film. That aura has, in fact, radiated far beyond the Weimar cinema, as a characteristic passage from Jean Renoir's autobiography may help to attest.

It was Werner Krauss who taught me to understand the importance of actors. I greatly admired him and that is why I asked him to play the part of Count Muffat in *Nana*. My admiration dated from *Caligari*. I had also seen him in other films and in a stage production of Ibsen's *Wild Duck*. What impressed me about him was in the first place his technical skill, his knowledge of makeup and the use he made of small physical peculiarities. After a number of experiments he devised a Count Muffat who was not Werner Krauss and yet was him . . . (Leyda, 1977, p. 384)

Even though Renoir came to believe, later, that such 'skill in the physical presentation of a character is not the root of the actor's business, and that although a convincing outward appearance is certainly a help, it can never be more', his early films helped to perpetuate the kind of performance that Krauss had pioneered in *Caligari* and that penetrated the U.S.A. with successive waves of German immigrants. The same goes for Conrad Veidt, whose make-up in *Caligari* strongly influenced Jack Pierce in his horror-creations for Universal; variations on it turn up, sporadically, in other terror-cycles.

> In *Usher* I bleached my hair white and wore pure white makeup with black eyebrows—I don't think anybody had done that since Conrad Veidt—there was this whole extraordinary thing that he was ultrasensitive to light and sound, so I tried to give the impression he'd never been exposed to the light, someone who had just bleached away. Now Roger dug this entirely . . . he found it very exciting that the actor could bring [into the film] a visual creation that complemented his. (Leyda, 1977, p. 371)

The speaker here is Vincent Price, interviewed for *Films and Filming* in 1969; the version of Poe's *The Fall of the House of Usher* he is talking about is that directed by Roger Corman in 1960, which introduced to the public Price's conception of the terror-maker as Dandy, whose roots in the German cinema he here suggests.

Vincent Price's dictum has already brought before us another figure we must examine in the context of *The Cabinet of Dr. Caligari*: the somnambulist Cesare, Caligari's victim and instrument. As played by Conrad Veidt, Cesare is a 'drawing brought to life' in an even more obvious sense than his master: his black upper garment is streaked with the same white paint as that used on the scenery, and when he walks along a shadowed wall, arm upraised, it looks as though the wall had exuded him. And like his master, Cesare anticipates and comprehends a whole cluster of attributes and qualities that were to be of immense importance in the history of the terror-film. Let us examine a few of these.

In the first place, the Cesare we see on the screen in *The Cabinet of Dr. Caligari* is the first fully developed example of what was to be explored further by the two Lon Chaneys, by Boris Karloff, and by Barbara Steele: the monster whose deeds and appearance may terrify, but who is also pitiable and lovable. Wiene has stressed this side of Conrad Veidt's creation by the last glimpse he allows us of Cesare: a tall, black-clad, lonely figure gently stroking the white petals of a flower. This reminds us of an ambiguity in the figure of Cesare which matches that already analysed in the figure of Caligari: is he, in fact, simply the gentle inmate of a mental institution, transformed into a murderous monster in the mind of another inmate, or does he really have the lethal capabilities attributed to him by Francis and exhibited before our very eyes in the film in which he plays a central part? Ambiguities and tensions of this kind are, of course, the very stuff of the suspense engendered by terror-movies as well as *films noirs*.

Connected with all this is the archetypal image which we have already discussed in an earlier chapter: the confrontation of dark monster and white-clad bride. In *Caligari* this confrontation leads Cesare, for the only time, to thwart the will of his evil master: he stays his hand and abducts the girl instead of killing her. *Frankenstein, King Kong, The Mummy*, and countless other terror-films were to introduce modified versions of this confrontation, whose mythical resonances were well brought out by the last lines spoken in the 1933 *King Kong*:

Officer: 'The airplanes got it.'
Denham: 'Oh no, it was not the airplanes. . . . It was beauty killed the beast.'

Many strands lead over from this to the fairy-tale film *Beauty and the Beast*, on which Jean Cocteau, René Clément, and Christian Bérard collaborated in 1946 and which has, in its turn, greatly enriched the iconography of fantastic terror. Those disembodied arms which jut out of walls (and up from tables) holding lights have proved their fascination over and over again as other film-makers borrowed and varied them.

In its archetypal confrontation scene between Cesare and Jane *The Cabinet of Dr. Caligari* once again subtly modifies and—I believe —improves what had been envisaged in the original screen-play. The directions in the screen-play preserved in the Deutsche Kinemathek clearly insinuate that what happens when Cesare stays his hand is that a blind sexual impulse overpowers the equally blind impulse to obey his master. In the film Cesare's disobedience is not so crudely motivated: we have just a glimpse, in Jane's bedroom, of the more gentle, pathetic creature susceptible to beauty who is so unforgettably presented in the final scene which shows him caressing a flower—another scene, we should remember, which was added after the screen-play left its authors' hands. It is wholly in keeping with all this that Cesare is not required, in the film, to perform any of the common fairground strong-man tricks (like breaking an iron chain) envisaged in the screen-play.

Cesare's irruption into the peace and privacy of Jane's bedroom is preceded by another image on whose significance I have had occasion to remark in an earlier chapter: that of the watcher with evil intent who peers out from the darkness of some hiding-place at his unsuspecting victim. The menacing image of the 'watcher at the window' is common to *Caligari*, *Frankenstein*, *Vampyr*, and many, many successors. Here, once again, we cannot but be conscious of implied analogies with the cinema-goer as *voyeur*.

The figure of Cesare that we see on the screen in *The Cabinet of Dr. Caligari* is also related, through his bearing and movement, to two further familiar figures of the later terror-film. The first of these, obviously, is the zombie: the being which is neither alive nor dead, which we surmise to be in some in-between state of consciousness that is not known to ordinary living men. The second is a figure which has moved into the mainstream of terror-cinema as the zombie moved out of it: the automaton, the machine with 'human' qualities that thwarts its maker and controller at some crucial moment. In this sense Cesare is the forerunner of that multitude of robots in or out of human form, from *Metropolis* onwards, which culminates in the computers that play such a banefully 'human' part in *2001* and *The Demon Seed*. But Cesare is a tragic figure in a way the robot can never be. He is a human being robbed of an essential part of his humanity: his consciousness and his will. He is a human dreamer forced, by a malevolent agency, to lose himself in his dream.

When Cesare is out on his murderous expeditions, a dummy is substituted for him in his coffin-like box; and this substitution brings us into those regions of the uncanny which are populated by such simulacra of human beings as dolls, puppets, marionettes, and waxworks. The dummy 'stands in' for Cesare symbolically as well as physically, just as Madame Tussaud figures 'stand in' for the men they represent in Leni's *Waxworks*, the doll with the crushed head for the central figure of *Whatever Happened to Baby Jane?*, and voodoo dolls for the necromancer's victim in *White Zombie*, *The Plague of the Zombies*, and the 'Sweets to the Sweet' episode of *The House that Dripped Blood* (1970).

Cesare is also shown, in a wholly cinematic way, as a figure that acts out another's dark desires. This is suggested, not only by the fact that we know him to be sent by Caligari to execute the latter's commands ('dreaming but murderous unconsciousness', to use F. D. McConnell's formulation, at the service of 'waking but malevolent reason'); but also by the vigour with which Francis, telling his story to others, imitates the stabbing motions we saw Cesare's shadow make with a dagger in an earlier scene. It is surely significant that before Cesare murders Alan, we have been told that Alan is Francis's rival for Jane's affections! The possibilities inherent in the brilliant 'shadow' episode of *Caligari* were to be developed to the full by Arthur Robison in (*Warning*) *Shadows*. In this last-named film a *montreur d'ombres* demonstrates to a culti-vated and elegant group what dangerous potentials their character and situation hold by making their shadows act out—and thus literally 'foreshadow'—what would happen if such potentials were translated into actuality. Cesare's shadow may be seen, like those in Robison's later film, as a 'Shadow' in Jung's sense; it insinuates that Cesare, like his master, is a monster from the subconscious.

Right at the beginning of *The Cabinet of Dr. Caligari* we see Cesare taking on the function of yet another figure whose uncanny potentialities have fascinated the makers of terror-films and their audiences: the clairvoyant. Cesare's prediction that Alan will die before the next night is over terrifies us, not only by the threat this poses to the sympathetic young man, but also, more particularly, because we sense that the prophecy will come true and that Cesare is therefore exercising paranormal powers. The fear that may be engendered by such powers, not only in those whose future is seen as black, but also in the clairvoyants themselves, is powerfully communicated in the framework action of *Dead of Night*, where the future seems to be shown by a dream, and in John Farrow's *Night has a Thousand Eyes* (1948), where the character played by Edward G. Robinson tries desperately to avert a catastrophe whose advent has been communicated to him in an unsought and undesired vision.

Finally, Cesare is seen, like his master, as a 'stranger' who comes into the community from outside, with the travelling fair; and he is seen to be the actor Conrad Veidt who would later impersonate such ominous characters as Ivan the Terrible in *Waxworks*, Jekyll and Hyde in *The Head of Janus*, Orlac in *The Hands of Orlac*, the

Grand Vizier in *The Thief of Baghdad* (1940), and the Nazi officer in *Casablanca*.

An intelligent and articulate man, Veidt analysed his own performances on more than one occasion, stressing two aspects which he thought particularly significant. The first of these was the intensity with which he sank himself into whatever part he played.

For days or even weeks before filming I withdraw into myself, contemplate my navel, as it were, concentrating on a kind of infection of the soul. And soon I discover how the character I have to portray grows in me, how I am transformed into it. The intensity of the process almost frightens me. Before long I find, even before the cameras begin to turn, that in my daily life I move, talk, look and behave differently. The inner Conrad Veidt has become that other person whom I have to portray, or rather into whom my self has changed by autosuggestion. This state could best be described as one of being 'possessed'.

The metaphor of 'possession' which Veidt uses, in this interview with Paul Ickes that was first published in 1927, has an obvious connection with the kind of film in which he appeared. Two years later, in 1929, we find Veidt again commenting on his characterizations, this time in a Berlin film-magazine to whose readers he explained why he liked to portray 'evil' characters:

Characters called 'evil' are not as bad as they appear on the surface; if I enjoy playing them, it is not because their destructiveness attracts me, but rather because I want to show the remnant of humanity which is hidden in even the most evil evildoer. (Greve, Pehle, and Westhoff, 1976, pp. 293–5)

That could have been said by Karloff and Lugosi, by Cushing, Lee, and Klaus Kinski, as easily as by Conrad Veidt.

The final image we have of Veidt's Cesare in *The Cabinet of Dr. Caligari*—a black-clad, sad-visaged figure caressing a flower with beautiful, long-fingered hands—suggests that we are here in the presence of an actor who could play non-horrific roles with equal panache. This augured well for a future described by Béla Bálazs:

Not only romantic acting went out of fashion but romantic faces as well. Especially among the male stars, popularity was diverted to those who had commonplace faces. Conrad Veidt's romantic, exalted, almost expressionist head, which brought him world success in the years immediately following the first world war, no longer appealed to the public. Not only was he crowded out by ordinary commonplace faces—he himself did his best to tone down his eccentric appearance and look as commonplace as possible, in order to be able to compete with rival stars. (Bálazs, 1970, p. 78)

Veidt could never look or sound commonplace—but it is significant that after fulfilling his long-cherished ambition to play Victor Hugo's Gwymplaine in *The Man Who Laughs* (1928), he did not allow himself to be drawn into the 'grotesque horror' business. Inevitably, like so many refugee actors, he played Nazi persecutors in such Hollywood entertainments as *Escape* and *Casablanca*; but he also showed himself, in German, English, and American sound-films, a leading man whose romantic appeal was only increased by that suggestion of the sinister, of possible menace, which remained an inseparable part of his personality.

The last word on all this may be left with Veidt himself who declared, in his Hollywood years: 'No matter what roles I play, I can't get *Caligari* out of my system' (Halliwell, 1978, p. 272).

Even before introducing Veidt's Cesare, *The Cabinet of Dr. Caligari* has given us a disconcerting image of zombie-like presence and absence, of existence in a limbo between life and death, through the appearance of the heroine, Jane, walking slowly towards the camera while staring straight ahead with unseeing eyes. This happens in the very opening scene, which R. V. Adkinson, in his account of the film for the Classic Film Scripts series, has described as follows:

A cold, sombre atmosphere pervades the opening scene of the film. Francis and an older man are sitting on a bench by a high forbidding wall which curves away into shadow. The leafless branches and twigs of a tree hang down above the heads of the two men; dead leaves carpet a path in front of them, emphasizing the lifeless, still quality of the setting. On the opposite side of the path to the bench are a couple of stunted fir-trees: winter is in the air. Both the men on the bench are dressed in black; their eyes gape wildly from pale faces. The older man leans over towards his young companion to speak to him; Francis, apparently not very interested, responds by staring blankly skyward [. . .]

As he turns to speak to Francis, the eyes of the older man, beneath a pair of bushy grey eyebrows, are dilated with horror or fear.

TITLE: *'Everywhere there are spirits. . . . They are all around us. . . . They have driven me from hearth and home, from my wife and children.'*

The older man continues his monologue, while the boughs from the overhanging tree move about his face. We see that the wall behind him is painted with a bizarre leaf and line pattern.

Francis turns suddenly to look down the path past his older friend. As he turns he makes a sudden movement of surprise: the figure of a young woman, Jane, has just emerged from the shadow at the end of the path. (Adkinson, 1972, p. 41)

This description suggests how the *mise en scène* of the opening sequence slides us from a 'normal' world to the distorted one presented in the stylized settings that are yet to come. The wall and the path we see at first seem to be an actual wall, an actual garden or park, with natural branches and leaves—the painted pattern to which Adkinson refers towards the end of his description looks to me like the not unusual staining of a garden wall. The older man's opening words, in the first of the intertitles that appear in the film, act as a preparation for a different *mise en scène*: one that presents living actors and normal pieces of furniture in an unrealistic setting which yet conveys, unmistakably, the ambience of small German towns. They also announce one of the great themes of the terror-film: that of being shaken out of one's familiar world, the world of hearth and home, wife and children, by the intrusion of a 'spirit' world which is always there, always waiting, but does not always spring upon us. The words may be those of a man whom the world writes off as 'mad'; but may not such madness bring insights as well as deprivation? The old man's words have a theological, philosophical, and social resonance that cannot be simply shut off. Many a later terror-film—*The Uninvited*, *The Haunting*, *The Exorcist*, *The Sentinel*—will attempt further probings of the themes so powerfully suggested in the first intertitle of *The Cabinet of Dr. Caligari*, which might be more accurately translated as: 'Spirits exist . . . they are around us everywhere . . . They have driven me from hearth and home, from my wife and children.'

The opening scene described by R. V. Adkinson is part of the much-discussed and much-debated 'framework action' of Wiene's film—the frame which makes the tale of Caligari and Cesare appear, not an account of 'real' horrors, but the fantasies of a madman. Whether this was suggested by Pommer, or Lang, or Wiene, is now of little moment; it has become an inseparable part of the film and hence of cinema-history. Two points need to be made, however. The first of these is that even if we do take the story of Caligari and his dark doings as a madman's fantasy, we must surely feel that this fantasy has a great deal of symbolic truth; the symbolic truth of the Expressionist plays its scenery and acting-style recall, which brought out in fantastically heightened and concentrated form what men and women felt about the world-order, felt about lives in a specific time and a specific place. The 'revelation', when the frame is completed by the ending of the film, that what we have been seeing all this while may well have been a madman's fantasy, distances the story, certainly, makes us reflect on it more, but it does not lead us to write off the symbolic import of the images the director and script-writers and designers and actors have brought before us. And that leads to the second point which has to be made. The frame never closes entirely; though we go back, briefly, to the two speakers of the opening, on their park bench, the final scenes take place in the same expressionistic sets as those used in Francis's tale. The floor of the 'cell' in which we see Francis incarcerated is a stage-floor and its walls are painted cardboard; it holds nothing like the suggestions of a 'real' world conveyed by the earthy path, the autumnal or wintry leaves and branches, and the solid-looking wall, which we had been shown in the opening scene. We are, therefore, still within the world of Francis's tale when the house lights go up.

Critics have always been quick to condemn framework devices of this kind as a 'cop-out'; the general reaction to Fritz Lang's *The Woman in the Window* (1944) showed this clearly. In Lang's film the frame closes in a neater way than it does in Wiene's; in precisely the way, in fact, which he later claimed to have suggested for *Caligari* itself.

Erich Pommer offered to me *The Cabinet of Dr Caligari* . . . which I was eventually unable to do . . . It was really the work of three painters . . . who wanted to make a kind of expressionist picture; the whole story had been written, and the only contribution I made was that I said to Pommer, 'Look, if the expressionistic sets stand for the world of the insane, and you use them from the beginning, it doesn't mean anything. Why don't you, instead, make the Prologue and Epilogue of the picture normal?' So the film begins in the garden of an asylum and is told normally; then when the story is told from the viewpoint of one of the inmates, it becomes expressionistic; and at the end it becomes normal again and we see that the villain of the picture, Dr Caligari, is the doctor of the asylum. Now what else is the ending of *Caligari*—where we meet people we've seen in 'the dream'—but the ending of *Woman in the Window?* And this was unconscious —I didn't even *think* I was copying myself at the time I had the idea for *Woman in the Window*. (Bogdanovich, 1967, pp. 63–4)

Lang clearly had not seen *Caligari* for a long time when he opined that 'at the end it becomes normal again'; but even in *The Woman in the Window*, his own variant on Wiene's film, the story of the Professor's temptation and fall is not devalued by the revelation that 'it was all a dream'. What Lang shows us are possibilities latent in his hero's character, possibilities conditioned, to an important extent, by the social world in which he lives—and acting them out in a dream may help him as much as seeing them acted out may help us. Here, once again, what we see in the film reminds us of what we are doing when we watch the film: the act of waking up, mimed for us by Edward G. Robinson, corresponds to the end of the film and the going-up of the house lights. What we have seen on the screen, however, was ordered by a waking intelligence that is not ours, though it may have spoken to us in the manner of our dreams. As Susanne Langer has rightly said,

The moving picture takes over [the dream mode], and [thereby] creates a virtual present. In its relation to the images, actions, events, that constitute the story, the camera is in the place of the dreamer.

But the camera *is* not a dreamer. We are usually agents in a dream. The camera (and its complement, the sound track[1]) is not itself in the picture. It is the mind's eye and nothing more. Neither is the picture (if it is art) likely to be dream-like in its structure. It is a poetic composition, coherent, organic, governed by a definitely conceived feeling, not dictated by emotional pressures. (Langer, *Feeling and Form. A Theory of Art*, New York, 1953, p. 413)

As so often, one of the most important functions of similarity is to remind us of differences.

Caligari, as we have seen, differs from Lang's film in that its frame does not close as decisively, does not leave us back in our 'normal' world as unequivocally, as *The Woman in the Window*. In this it resembles *Dead of Night*, directed by Cavalcanti, Dearden, Hamer, and Crichton. The five stories united in that film, a veritable anthology of terror-film motifs, are linked by a sixth, a framing tale, which shows us an architect woken from a nightmare by a phone call from a prospective client whom he has never met. As he approaches the client's house he recognizes the scenery of his nightmare, and once inside the house he realizes that every one of its guests and inhabitants are part of his nightmare too. When he tells them this, they recount the stories of their own contact with the inexplicable; but everything which occurs, including the story-

[1] Should this not be 'microphone'? That, rather than the sound-track, is surely the 'complement' of the camera.

telling, is foreseen by the architect, who dreads what he knows must come: his murder of one of the guests, a sceptical psychiatrist. One way of looking at what happens at the end of the film is excellently exemplified by Ivan Butler in *Horror in the Cinema*:

The linking story is handled with a skill apt to be overshadowed by the more flamboyant episodes. The gradual encroachment of strangeness and menace upon the complete normality of the opening party indicated by the growing distortion of viewing angles, the slow fading of day to dusk . . . are still impressive today. After the killing of the Doctor, when the horror is come upon us, all reality vanishes. Dominated, ingeniously, by the innocent fancy-dressed children from the party scene, the terror of nightmare is created in a wild swirl of distorted staircases and passages, the camera swinging and twisting about as Craig himself does in his efforts to wake up.

The subtlest touch of the film, however, is a momentary shot almost at the very end. We finally leave Craig in exactly the position that we first found him—arriving at Foley's house in his car. *Dead of Night*, then, like Joyce's *Finnegans Wake*, is circular—it will go on for ever, ninety per cent dream, ten per cent awake. So, but for this one shot, it might appear. Before leaving his house, however, Craig has been speaking to Foley on the telephone. As he speaks, we see—for just a few frames—Foley himself, at his house, on the other end of the telephone. That shot tells us the truth. The film throughout has been seen from Craig's viewpoint. Even the stories, where he was not present, are seen as told to him. Now suddenly *we* see Foley. Craig has not met him. The dream has faded. He does not know what Foley and his house look like. Now, we see Foley. He really is there, waiting. This tiny shot is the most frightening in the film, for through it the dream becomes reality. This time, it is really happening. There will be no waking relief for Craig. This time, he drives to his doom. In no other medium but the film could the situation be so briefly yet devastatingly made clear. (Butler, 1970, pp. 26–7)

Dead of Night stands, unmistakably, in the tradition of the English ghost-story from which the plots of its constituent episodes directly or indirectly derive; but in its use of a disorientating framework, in its play with psychiatry and occultism, and in its climactic confrontation of ventriloquist and dummy, it betrays no less clearly its descent from Wiene's *Caligari*.

As in *Dead of Night*, so in *Caligari* the framework story is indelibly associated with one character whom the camera presents to us but whose limited vision we are also made to share. As a student, not yet fully integrated into bourgeois life, Francis is a marginal man—but he is the exact opposite of that other marginal man whose fortunes we followed in an earlier chapter, David Gray. Where David Gray drifts through the action of *Vampyr* like a sleep-walker, Francis is constantly on the move in the inner story, constantly enlisting the help of the authorities while tirelessly seeking and following out clues on his own initiative. 'I will not rest', one of the intertitles has him say, 'until I have fully fathomed the terrible things that are happening around me.' His problem is that of the seeker after truth; and what happens at the end is that his own competence is called into question, like everything else in the shifting perspectives of the film. How far has he been externalizing, projecting his own inner turmoil on to whatever world there may be outside? How far has he seen truly? What symbolic truth might his vision, whatever their experiential status, have for audiences in the world within which the film was conceived, or in that in which it is viewed by other, later audiences? These are questions which still concern us—they are raised by the film in its final form more powerfully and directly than by the more conventional frame, the recollection-in-tranquillity pattern, of the original screen-play.

In the form its director and designers actually gave it, *The Cabinet of Dr. Caligari* impressively demonstrates the cinematic possibilities opened up by an abrupt change of perspective. Having looked at certain 'events' through the eyes of a story-teller who presents himself as a participant, we are suddenly made to look at that story-teller and ask ourselves whether we have not in fact been sharing a lunatic's delusions. Later directors have played many variations on this. Herk Harvey's *Carnival of Souls* (1962), for instance, shows us a young woman surviving a car-accident and returning to a world in which people behave like stiff puppets, refusing to talk to her or even acknowledge her presence. More and more desperately she tries to make contact; and she seems, at last, to succeed when a wraith-like, corpse-like group embraces her and draws her away in a dance. Then comes the change of perspective: we see ordinary people towing a car from the bay in which our heroine sits dead at the wheel. She did not survive the accident after all; the film had been set in *la zone*, the limbo between life and death. Behind the structure of Harvey's film we perceive not only *The Cabinet of Dr. Caligari* but also a distinguished literary work: Ambrose Bierce's 'An Occurrence at Owl Creek

Bridge', itself made into an eerily impressive film by Robert Enrico in 1964.

Abrupt changes of perspective have an underground relation to the décor of *Caligari* which we can best discern through a study of Rudolf Kurz's celebrated book on Expressionism and the German film. Writing in 1926, Kurz described the settings of *Caligari* as follows:

Perpendicular lines tense towards the diagonal, houses exhibit crooked, angular outlines, planes shift in rhomboid fashion, the lines of force of normal architecture, expressed in perpendiculars and horizontals, are transmogrified into a chaos of broken forms ... A movement begins, leaves its natural course, is intercepted by another, led on, distorted again, and broken. All this is steeped in a magic play of light, unchaining brightness and blackness, building up, dividing, emphasizing, destroying.

Why the designers chose this style is given a psychological explanation.

It is a simple law of psychological aesthetics that when we feel our way into certain forms exact psychic correspondences are set up. The straight line guides our feelings differently from a crooked one; startling curves affect our souls in other ways than smoothly gliding lines; the rapid, the jagged, the suddenly ascending and descending calls forth responses that are different from those evoked by the silhouette of a modern city with its richness of transitions. (Kurz, 1926, pp. 123 and 54)

The abrupt change of perspective at the end of *Caligari*, at whatever stage it was introduced, may be seen as just as 'rapid', 'jagged', and 'suddenly ... descending' as the scenic design.

There is still one other aspect of the ending of *Caligari*, however, which deserves closer attention than it has so far received. We leave Francis, it will be remembered, strait-jacketed in a cell, while the director holds out hopes of a cure. The final 'title' reads: 'At last I understand the nature of his madness. He thinks I am that mystic Caligari— —! Now I can also see the way to cure him.' An ominous conclusion, surely—for what these words show is that the director has either not understood, or that he is wilfully misrepresenting, Francis's beliefs. Francis does not think, by any means, that the director 'is' 'that mystic Caligari'. On the contrary: the film has shown us beyond any doubt that Francis, despite his cry: 'He is Caligari ... Caligari ... Caligari!', knows the 'mystic Caligari' to have been an eighteenth-century figure, quite distinct from the sinister showman encountered many years later. What he does believe is that the director has become obsessed by this Caligari to the extent of assuming his name and repeating his crimes with the help of the same kind of instrument that the original Caligari used: a somnambulist under his hypnotic control. Francis does not believe, in other words, that the director 'is' 'that mystic Caligari'; he knows that the director is the director, but believes him to have used his position to obtain an instrument essential to the re-enactment of another's crimes. If this is a delusion then the director has failed to diagnose it correctly; if it is not a delusion, then the director is deliberately pulling wool over his colleagues' eyes. All this must be in our minds as we watch that famous long-held shot of Werner Krauss's ambiguous expression which ends the film; as must also the fact that we never, at any stage, learn the real name of the director who, in the inner story, disguises his appearance and takes on the name of Caligari. He remains as nameless as Frankenstein's monster.

The ambiguity I am trying to highlight here has been described in a different though related way by F. D. McConnell. 'We do not, of course, know', McConnell writes in *The Spoken Seen*,

what the doctor's curative treatment will be—and we need not be familiar with recent developments in behaviorist psychotherapy to fear that the remedy may be as bad as, or worse than, the disease. But more centrally, we are disturbed by the sight of Krauss's face itself, that face which the fantasy-center of the film has taught us to associate with malevolent, irrational destructiveness. We remember . . . what the explicit story of the film has taught us to forget: the potential evil and dehumanization of official authority. And it is this tension between memory and forgetfulness . . . that constitutes . . . lasting horror. (p. 33)

In the iconography of the terror-film the madhouse plays an important part. It does so partly because madness is indeed terrifying—Hitchcock's *Psycho* and Polanski's *Repulsion* are dedicated to that proposition—but it does so also because in a madhouse authority may be exercised over others in a particularly frightening or humiliating way; and because the madhouse is a closed institution in which the problems of a particular society, the wounds inflicted and the violence unleashed by that society, can be depicted in heightened, concentrated, and frequently symbolic form. From Val Lewton's *Bedlam* to Alain Jessua's *Shock Treatment*, the film has often treated the madhouse in this way. A particularly interesting use of this setting was made by Gordon Douglas and his team in *Them*; here doubt is cast, first on the existence and then on the hiding-place of the giant mutants to which the title refers because those who volunteer helpful information on these points are found in a mental home and an alcoholics' ward. And then, of course, there is Samuel Fuller's *Shock Corridor* (1963), of which Raymond Durgnat has said:

The film's tense, hard, muscular style resumes the American variation of German expressionism. Carried to Hollywood by such directors as Murnau, Leni, Lang and other exiles, expressionism was blended with its apparent antithesis, the tough deadpan, by the American *films noirs* from the late '30s to the mid-'50s. But Fuller's paroxystic situations and style reveal the tough deadpan as a kind of psychic delirium and restore an expressionistic world. (Durgnat, 1972, p. 92)

Many other closed institutions have been pressed into the service of the terror-film: an island laboratory in *The Island of Lost Souls*, a prison in *The Walking Dead* (1936), a provincial school in *Les Diaboliques*, and even a (very peculiar) dancing academy in Dario Argento's *Suspiria* (1977). The last-named film is especially important in this context because it experiments once again—less radically than *Caligari*—with stylized sets that occasionally resemble stage-flats. Above all there is the clinic or hospital—Franju's *Eyes Without a Face*, Robert Day's *Corridors of Blood* (1962), David Cronenberg's *Rabid* (1976), and countless other films have made use of a setting which played on our fear of operations as well as the terror-movie's traditional suspicion of science and scientists.

The very title of *The Cabinet of Dr. Caligari* refers us, however, to a quite different, an apparently more 'open', institution: the travelling fair or carnival, home of the earliest cinema-shows, traditional scene of thrilling entertainments, whose roller-coasters, ghost-trains, and freak-shows have proved so attractive to the makers of terror-films because they too deal in *Angstlust*, in thrills that cause delight by playing on fear. When handbills announcing the fair appear on the screen in *Caligari*:

> LATE EXTRA!
> Holstenwall Fair,
> including sideshows of all kinds,
> and marvels
> NEVER SEEN BEFORE!

cinema-goers smile with recognition—for it is precisely promises of this kind which lure us into the cinema. Paul Leni's *Waxworks*, Robert Florey's *Murders in the rue Morgue*, Erle C. Kenton's *House of Frankenstein* (1944), Hitchcock's *Strangers on a Train*, and Freddie Francis's *Torture Garden* show some of the more sinister uses to which fairground settings were put in the wake of *Caligari*. Through it all rings the fairground barker's patter: Bela Lugosi's in *Rue Morgue*:

I am Dr. Mirakle, and I am not a sideshow charlatan; if you are looking for the usual hocus-pocus, just go to the box-office and get your money back . . .

or Boris Karloff's in *House of Frankenstein*:

Believe me, my friends, this is no fake. Before your very eyes is all that remains of a vampire, one of the world's Undead. Dare I but remove the stake from where his heart once beat, he would rise from the grave in which he lies and turn into a bat, a vampire bat, and would feed hideously upon the living whose veins pulsate with warm and vibrant blood. Ladies and gentlemen, the skeleton of Count Dracula the vampire!

Who could miss the link of these and other passages with the terms in which the makers of *Rue Morgue* and *House of Frankenstein* advertised their wares! Four of the films just mentioned also play on a potent contrast first explored by Wiene: the open space occupied by the fair with its many attractions, all for sale—and the 'cabinet', the showman's booth or tent, into which spectators have to be inveigled. After the opening narration *Caligari* leads us, in fact, into a more and more enclosed space: from the patently painted and studio-built town to the fair, thence to the 'cabinet', thence to Cesare's box: and from that ultimate enclosure, reminding us of all men's ultimate enclosure in a coffin, forces are sent into the more open world outside to wreak terrifying havoc. The final scenes then lead us back into enclosure: first that of the mental home, then that of the cell and that of the strait-jacket confining Francis, whose visions we have been sharing. Our resistance to claustrophobia is thus put to a severe test in a setting where we have a greater chance of passing the test than in the 'real' world outside the cinema.

One aspect of the fair in *Caligari*, the first one we are shown, has rightly attracted the attention of several commentators: the turning roundabout. A significant scene begins with an unusual iris-in: a small circle is isolated near the right-hand corner of the screen, in which we see an organ-grinder's hand turning a barrel-organ on which a chained monkey squats. Then the iris opens out to reveal, not only the organ-grinder, but also a fairground set dominated by two roundabouts in full revolution. These may be and have been felt, not only as a synecdoche for the fair itself, but also as multivalent symbols which speak, in their context, of the innocent pleasures of childhood, the turning of the wheel of fate or history, the spin of life, the obsessive circularity of the narrator's thoughts; they have also suggested, to some observers, a simulacrum of experience—like the cinema itself. All this is deliberately associated with another 'turning' image, the organ-grinder cranking his instrument; an image whose symbolic import one of the greatest German *Lieder*, the final song of Schubert's *Winter Journey*, has indelibly impressed on the cultural consciousness of Germany and the world. It is through this symbol-charged set that Krauss's Caligari makes his way towards his 'cabinet'.

One of the merits of Kracauer's pioneering book *From Caligari to Hitler* is that it conveyed to English-speaking readers something of the readiness with which German audiences responded to symbolic suggestions. Symbols, by definition, are multivalent, unlike allegories, in which there is a one-to-one correspondence; and an 'allegorical' reading of *Caligari* is therefore bound to be inadequate or worse. 'In Germany', Fritz Lang said to Peter Bogdanovich, 'we worked with symbols'; and prompted by his interviewer, he added: 'A symbol shouldn't reinforce, it should *make* the point' (Bogdanovich, 1967, pp. 28–9).

Between the madhouse and the fair Wiene shows us the little town of Holstenwall, in which most of the characters live. This is partly, as we have already seen, the cosy familiar world into which strangers bring disaster when they break into the tiny room inhabited by Alan or the more opulent bedroom of Jane. It is also, however, through the crazy perspectives of its streets, the jagged, knife-like projections of its scenery (particularly its windows), and the insubstantiality of its theatrical flats, itself felt as threatening; and some of the menaces it contains are clearly shown in the two interiors which are not domestic. The first of these is the office of the town clerk, to which Caligari repairs for his showman's licence. We soon perceive this office to be the setting for an enjoyment of power less flamboyant but no less intense than Caligari's own. At the entrance and again on the furniture the symbol '§' has been painted several times—not, as R. V. Adkinson seems to think, a 'cabbalistic' sign, but simply the indication of a 'paragraph' in the German civil and criminal code. Under the protection of this sign the ill-tempered licensing-official lords it, on his high stool, over his subordinates and petitioners. The expressiveness and truth-value of images of this kind are in no way devalued by the film's frame. The complement of this sinister office is the even more sinister prison cell in which a criminal sits chained and immured. With its white lines all converging on to the manacled, scowling figure of Rudolf Klein-Rogge, and its one tiny, crazily angled window, high above the imprisoned man's reach, it is the other end of the chain of legal paragraphs that begins in the town clerk's little kingdom, and presents itself as a symbol of social constriction—necessary social constriction, perhaps, but none the less terrifying for that—which matches in intensity the complementary image of the madman's cell and the strait-jacket at the end of the film. Terror is not simply 'brought in by strangers', as the simplest view of the story would have it; terror is inherent in the social structure which the 'stranger' finds when he gets there and which fires in him a resentment that releases more terror. Nor, as we have already found, is the 'stranger' really a stranger: the madhouse over which he presides is as much part of Holstenwall as the town clerk's office and the prison cell.

Can all that be written off as a madman's vision? Have not these distorted perspectives, rather, succeeded in conveying the insolence of office, and the horror of being imprisoned and confined, more powerfully than naturalistic settings could have done? There are other ways, of course, of achieving such effects. The makers of *Caligari* could have followed the lead of Abel Gance in *The Madness of Dr. Tube* (1915), where distortion was achieved, not by means of painted scenery, but by a system of convex and concave mirrors. They might have tried to use distorting lenses, as Murnau did some six years after *Caligari* in a famous sequence of *The Last Laugh*. They might also have used unusual camera angles, as the Russians did in so many of their silent films, or as Pabst did, or Duvivier. Later makers of terror-films, with far more sophisticated equipment and much more money to spend than the makers of *Caligari*, have produced visual distortions of a kind that even Gance and Murnau never dreamed of; one thinks of the fly's-eye view of Kurt Neumann's *The Fly* (1958), the robot's-eye view in Michael Crichton's *Westworld*, or the special effects that made us share the tortured vision of Corman's Man with X-Ray Eyes in 1963. But the method employed in *Caligari* works excellently, and cannot be condemned simply because it was pioneered by stage-designers or because it conflicts with dogmatic notions that the cinema must photograph unstylized reality in such a way that the result has style. By what compulsion must it? *Caligari* can still excite and grip its audience today, where many a stylish photoplay causes nothing but fatigue and irritation.

The social meaning of *Caligari* has been the subject of a good deal of comment—particularly after Siegfried Kracauer's *From Caligari to Hitler* had tried to show

that during their retreat into themselves the Germans [of the period just after the First World War] were stirred to reconsider their traditional belief in authority. Down to the bulk of Social Democratic workers they refrained from revolutionary action; yet at the same time a psychological revolution seems to have prepared itself in the depths of the collective soul. The film reflects this double aspect of German life by coupling a reality in which Caligari's authority triumphs with a hallucination in which this same authority is overthrown . . . (Kracauer, 1947, p. 67)

Though one may deny, as I do, that a collective 'soul' manifests itself in film-plots in the simple way Kracauer would have us believe, and that 'reality', in *Caligari*, can be hived off neatly from 'hallucination', there can be little doubt that the uncertainties and fears the film conveys in its final form have a good deal to do with uncertainties and fears felt in the young Weimar Republic, in a Germany that had just lost a war and seen the apparent collapse of its traditional authoritarian structure. But this too must be seen in a wider context: a context sketched by David Thomson when he said of *Caligari* that it is one of the first films to exploit the resemblance between watching films and dreaming, and that it therefore asks, with particular force, 'the basic question that confronts a movie audience: are we watching reality or fantasy?' When they face us, inescapably, with this question, later terror-films can, once again, be seen as repeating, or developing further, what *Caligari* pioneered.

The literary affinities of *Caligari*, as this book has had occasion to stress more than once, are with German Romanticism in general and *Schauerromantik* in particular; and the nineteenth-century costumes worn by most of the characters serve to stress these affinities. They should not, however, be allowed to obscure the fact that it also has unmistakable affinities with literary Expressionism. Expressionist drama is recalled by the conflict of generations suggested in *Caligari*—Krauss's director is an evil father-figure for Cesare and Francis, and appears linked to older traditions, older generations, through his assumption of the personality of the original Caligari. It is recalled, too, by the film's violence and stylization of gesture, and by its deliberate employment of the grotesque. In this last respect it also resembles Expressionist fiction and poetry: the mingling of menace with the ridiculous in Krauss's performance recalls many a grotesque bourgeois in the stories of Kafka or the poems of Alfred Lichtenstein as well as the plays of Carl Sternheim. And if one now reads the description of the Angel of Death which Jakob van Hoddis, whose poem 'End of the World' is frequently said to have inaugurated German Expressionism, penned in 1914:

> Der Todesengel harrt in Himmelshallen
> Als wüster Freier dieser zarten Braut.
> Und seine wilden, dunklen Haare fallen
> Die Stirn hinab, auf der der Morgen graut.
>
> Die Augen weit, vor Mitleid glühend offen
> Wie trostlos starrend hin zu neuer Lust,
> Ein grauenvolles, nie versiegtes Hoffen,
> Ein Traum von Tagen, die er nie gewußt.
>
> (The angel of death waits in heavenly halls
> A fearsome wooer of this tender bride.
> And his wild dark hair falls
> Down his forehead, on which a grey dawn breaks.
>
> Wide open, glowing with pity, his eyes
> Stare inconsolably towards new desired delight,
> A ghastly hope that never quite dried up,
> A dream of days he never knew)—

may one not see in it an almost point-by-point anticipation of Conrad Veidt's Cesare, as he appears, not in heavenly halls, but in the white virginal expanses of Jane's room, which Francis so fervently desires to enter?

Wiene's film is also remarkable for the way in which it brings the language of twentieth-century painting into the cinema. The city-impressions of Feininger, Meidner, and Kubin, the triangular shapes of Cubism, the hysterical wavy lines and angular portraits of Munch, and even the tendril shapes of *art nouveau*, all find meaningful equivalents. As this list may serve to suggest, the designer's style is not *purely* Expressionist—and it is interesting to note in this connection that the Mayer–Janowitz typescript has none of the consciously Expressionist stylization of language that characterizes Mayer's later writings for the cinema. Nevertheless the visual style of *Caligari* has enough affinity with Expressionist painting and drawing to justify the usual label. When a later terror-film, Jack Gold's *The Medusa Touch*, imports actual paintings into its setting—Caravaggio's *Medusa*, Munch's *The Cry*, the claustrophobic shapes of Francis Bacon—these only serve to underline the film's visual and thematic banality. In *Caligari*, however, the painters' images are fully at home, harmonize perfectly with the work's theme and style: with its attempt to make the film's physical setting a hieroglyph of inner experience, its suffusion of landscapes and townscapes with feelings and states of mind.

One important set of hieroglyphs has, alas, been lost to the film as shown to English audiences. The letters that compose the original main title and intertitles exhibit the characteristic *Caligari* shapes as surely as the painted sets; the way they are formed, the directions in which they slope, how they relate to one another or vary in size, the jagged or snake-like ornamentations that accompany them, indicate and control the film's tone, mood, and atmosphere. In this too the example set by *Caligari* has been followed, as the next chapter will try to show, by other films that have among their principal ingredients the attempt to depict, evoke, and convey terror.

Within its stylized settings *Caligari* introduces a multitude of visual motifs that later terror-films were to elaborate. The huge staring eyes of Veidt's Cesare, filling the screen in the most intimate close-ups of the whole film, matched by the glare of Caligari's spectacles; the shadow of a murderer, showing his nefarious work without showing his body; the clutching, warding-off hands of a murder-victim; the arrest which brings an 'explanation' that explains nothing; the pursuit over roof-tops and along winding paths that leads to an unexpected terrifying goal—these are only some of the images that later films have drawn from the rich store of this seminal film. Commenting, in 1920, on Wiene's imaginative use of shadows on a wall to make murder visible, Kurt Tucholsky singled out an aspect of *Caligari* which is worth recalling in face of the ever greater explicitness that audiences and film-makers have demanded in recent years. 'This demonstrates again', Tucholsky writes, 'that what is guessed at is more terrible than anything that can be shown. No film can come up to our imagination.' The thoughts *Caligari* here inspires in Tucholsky were later to be restated, and put into practice, by Fritz Lang and the Val Lewton team.

A structural analysis of the plot of *Caligari* would distinguish the following stages:

(A. Opening of frame)

1. We are introduced to a story-teller, a listener, a mysterious female figure. A perspective is established: that of the story-teller.

(B. Inner story)

2. A close-knit society is penetrated by an enemy from outside.

3. By means of an innocent but lethal helper, the enemy strikes at an eminent member of the society he now menaces, and at one member of the group with which the audience, caught in the story-teller's perspective, identifies: the trio hero—beloved heroine—friend.

4. The hero alerts the authorities to the source of the danger to society, but investigators are baffled.

5. The enemy strikes at the heroine; she is saved by the incompleteness of his control over his lethal helper, and the enemy is tracked by the hero to a domain where the enemy has authority—an authority conferred on him by society.

6. With the help of subordinate members of the enemy's domain he is unmasked and rendered harmless by the hero, whose resolute action has thus saved society from a murderous onslaught.

(C. 'Closing' of frame)

7. The dramatis personae of section B are now seen in the domain in which the action of stage 6 had taken place—but under a new aspect. The enemy has *not* been defeated; he and his

helper are still alive and his power is unbroken. Our point of view can therefore no longer be unequivocally that of the story-teller 'hero'.

8. The 'hero' attacks the 'enemy' and is rendered harmless in exactly the same way the 'enemy' had been rendered harmless at stage 6, and with the aid of the same subordinates.

9. The 'enemy' speaks as a friend and is left poised to 'help' the 'hero'. It is he and not the 'hero' who preserves society from potentially destructive members. Or is it?

A glance at this structure, and at the quotation and question marks that invade it at stages 8 and 9, shows up immediately the profound disorientation the film conveys, the questions it leads us to ask about authority, about social legitimation, about the protection of society from disrupting and destructive influences, and about the shifting points of view that convert enemies into friends and friends into enemies, whose origins may well be sought in the German situation after the First World War. Like any genuine work of art, *The Cabinet of Dr. Caligari* has its roots deep in the society of its time; but its significance, its appeal, and its influence far transcend its origins.

What a structural summary like that just attempted fails to reveal is the over-all rhythm of the film: the rhythm commended by Louis Delluc in a passage Lotte Eisner used as the epigraph of her *Caligari* chapter in *The Haunted Screen*—a slow beginning, breath-taking acceleration, and the slowing-up of the long-held close-up before the word *Ende* appears on the screen in that angular *Caligari*-script which the original audiences came to know so well. All credit for this must go to Robert Wiene; for as Fritz Lang once said, the peculiar rhythm that every worthwhile film may be felt to have is the distinctive contribution of its director.

The influence of *Caligari* on later film-makers has often been indirect rather than direct, mediated rather than unmediated. In Japan, for instance, it would have come for the most part by way of Kinugasa's *A Page of Madness* rather than by way of Wiene's original. It is also incontestable that important elements of later terror-movies in Germany and abroad derived from early Scan-dinavian films, from early Hollywood movies, from *Nosferatu*, *Mabuse*, and *Metropolis*, rather than *Caligari*; that the complete control over *all* elements of our visual experience sought by

Wiene's studio-bound film (in which even light and shade were painted on to the scenery!) has been consciously abandoned by most later film-makers; that sixty years of further development have added themes, images, and technical devices, as well as an explicitness in the treatment of sex and violence that would have been inconceivable to Wiene and his collaborators. It is also incontestable that the use of theatrical flats imposed limitations on .camera angles and camera mobility that most film-makers came to find excessively irksome. Acting-styles have changed too: we shall not find in this early German film anything like the amused self-parody, the tongue-in-cheek attitude, tnat Vincent Price, for instance, brings to his flamboyant roles in *The Abominable Dr. Phibes*, *Dr. Phibes Rises Again* (1972), and *Theatre of Blood* (1973). Nevertheless, if we look closely enough we shall discover that the majority of the themes, images, and devices which distinguish the cinematic tale of terror may be detected, in rudimentary or developed form, in *The Cabinet of Dr. Caligari*; and that far from being irrelevant to the subsequent history of the motion picture, this masterly document of the Germans' search for ever new ways of articulating and presenting the fantastic is a work no student of the terror-film, and no lover of the cinema, can afford to pass by.

CHAPTER 7

Beyond *Caligari*

To a new world of gods and monsters!
The Bride of Frankenstein (1935)

THE first veritable tale of terror I ever saw in the cinema was not *Caligari*, but Victor Halperin's *White Zombie*. The time was 1939, I was fourteen years old, and the film, made in 1932, was being revived at the Alexandra, a much-loved flea-pit in Coventry, along with—I think—Roy William Neill's *The Black Room*. The experience began with the delicious thrill of passing the cinema and seeing the posters, which promised voodoo ceremonies, walking dead, and fratricide, presided over by 'Bela (Dracula) Lugosi' and 'Boris (Frankenstein) Karloff'. *Dracula* and *Frankenstein*! I had been given hair-raising accounts of that famous double billing, in which figured human brains in glass jars being dropped on the ground, a man-made monster on the loose, and three undead ladies in white kept from a desired feast of blood by an imperiously gesturing Transylvanian gentleman in full evening clothes. Hoping to circumvent the 'H' certificate which was designed to keep out everyone under sixteen, I set out for the Alexandra with a beating heart, to test and prove myself. I was not turned away and I was certainly not disappointed. Of *The Black Room* I remember very little—I am not even sure, at this distance in time, whether it was this or some other Karloff vehicle; but *White Zombie* will remain for ever unforgotten. I can still hear the eerie music and see the zombies (first presented in long-shot) make their slow way down a hill; a close-up of Lugosi's eyes superimposed over a medium-shot of his figure and face, with its strange little forked beard; a zombie with huge staring eyes carrying the apparently lifeless heroine; the carving of waxen voodoo dolls and their slow, death-bringing melting in the fire; Lugosi's expressive hands, clasped in an exertion of will, contrasting with the weirdly rigid hands of his zombie coachman; shadows of revellers among whom the hero suddenly seems to see his lost love; a poisoned rose in a bridal bouquet; zombies turning a huge wheel in a sugar-mill. The story-line is unclear, but many individual images remain, including stone steps, pillars, and candles, the sardonic smile on Lugosi's face as he whittles away at a voodoo doll and talks to his immobilized victim ('Well, well, we understand one another better now'), high-key lighting throwing into clear relief the black-and-white clothing of the cast and bringing out to the full Lugosi's hypnotic gaze and the dead-eyed stare of his zombies. The whole added up to an encounter with deep-seated fears from which I felt I emerged with credit; I remember the experience with gratitude as a liberating and exhilarating one, and it is partly responsible for my need to write the present book which tries to explore its nature.

My experience with *White Zombie* confirms the notion of the 'expectancy set' which American writers so often advance when they try to analyse the psychological presuppositions and effects of the cinema. Here is the version which William Friedkin gave to Bill Crouch in an interview conducted after the success of *The Exorcist*.

Rational fear . . . is introduced by something called expectancy set, which is the personal feeling that something terrifying is going to happen to you. For example, you're walking down the street at night and you're convinced, not from reason of paranoia, that someone is following you. So every sound you hear, whether it's a car coming around the corner, or leaves on the street, or a twig breaking under your foot, or footsteps, contributes to your fear, and this is because you're expecting to be frightened. The cinema takes advantage of this factor. Alfred Hitchcock takes advantage of the fact that an audience comes into the theatre expecting to be scared. When they are standing in line they are afraid. So he takes them for about an hour and dangles them and lets them do it for themselves until he hits them with something—and at that point, when he hits them, he either fulfills their expectations and fantasy or he lets them down, depending on how skillful is his punch. The same is true for *The Exorcist*. People are afraid while they're standing in line. And for the first hour of the film, while there is little more than exposition and some of that very hard to follow unless you've read the book, people are working themselves into an emotional state that is inducive to becoming terrified. (Derry, 1977, pp. 123–4)

As I have already suggested, one of the chief means of 'setting' my expectancy at the right level for *White Zombie* and its accompaniment was the exhibition, outside the cinema, of posters which not only announced that the films were for Adults only ('H' for Horrific!) but also that they featured, respectively, 'Bela (Dracula)

Lugosi' and 'Boris (Frankenstein) Karloff'. Posters, and the expectations they arouse, are an essential part of the cinema-going experience.

Such billing of the stars of terror-films by inserting the titles of their previous triumphs between their first name and surname has, however, a wider significance. The aura of his previous roles clings to an actor, releases memories while we are watching the film, memories that combine with the actual images we are seeing into a complex whole. The bald-headed, club-footed executioner who carries out the behests of Richard III with such obvious relish in *The Tower of London* (1939) is played by the same Boris Karloff whom we have seen as a monster or a mad doctor in earlier movies; this makes him all the more demonic, makes us all the more ready to credit him with evil intents that match those of his master, and weaves an additional aura of terror around a king who commands the allegiance of such creatures. The director of the film, Rowland V. Lee, in fact reinforced this effect by using the 'monster' motif from the score of *The Bride of Frankenstein* as a kind of signature tune for Boris Karloff's entrances. Walter Benjamin has told us that in the age of mechanical reproduction the individual work of art loses the 'aura' that was once inseparable from its mode of existence; but the star-system, and studio casting policy, created an aura of their own around certain actors and their films to which most cinema-goers would respond. Even when he meets Abbott and Costello, or—what is worse—Old Mother Riley, the magic of Dracula still adheres to Bela Lugosi, and regular cinema-goers, who grew accustomed to his speech-patterns as well as his theatrical gestures and striking appearance, would feel cheated when (as happened in certain scenes of *The Dark Eyes of London*) an immaculate English voice was dubbed on to the sound-track to match his lip-movements. In recent years Barbara Steele and Vincent Price acquired a similar aura, as did Christopher Lee and Peter Cushing— even in Fellini's $8\frac{1}{2}$ (1963) we respond to the witches and victims huge-eyed Barbara Steele has played in Italian shockers (notably Mario Bava's *Black Sunday* or *Mask of the Demon*, and Riccardo Freda's *The Terror of Dr. Hichcock*, 1962); and even in *The Man with the Golden Gun* (1974) the presence of Christopher Lee ensures thrills that must be credited, not just to his handsomely threatening presence in this James Bond vehicle, but also to his long reign as the Hammer Studios' principal terror-star.

The tone, timbre, and resonance of an actor's voice, his habitual cadences and verbal gestures, the play of his features, the movements of his hands and body, become familiar to us and make us watch for variations as well as repetitions. The aura of his previous performances enters, as we have seen, into our conception of his personality—and so, very often, does what we know or surmise of his off-screen life and personality. M. K. Joseph, the New Zealand scholar and poet, has suggested this syndrome very well in his amusing poem 'The Rosy Cats of Doctor Paracelsus':

> Doctor Pretorius (played by Ernest Thesiger)
> was a paracelsian who kept his homunculi
> imprisoned in glass belljars; when they knocked
> with tiny fists upon the glass it rang
> like toy telephones: this in *The Bride of Frankenstein*
> in which the Bride (the Monster's of course: Frankenstein's
> bride was played by Valerie Hobson who later
> married a British Cabinet minister named
> John Profumo, which is strange but not relevant)
> was played by Elsa Lanchester who in 'real'
> i.e. offscreen life was married to Charles Laughton
> who was Quasimodo in the second *Hunchback*
> *of Notre Dame* and Doctor Moreau in *The Island*
> *of Lost Souls* in which the Leader
> of the Beast Men was Bela Lugosi who
> (need I say it?) played the title-role in the original
> *Dracula* in which Renfield the madman
> who ate flies was Dwight Frye who acted
> the malignant hunchback who in *Frankenstein* the first
> selected the wrong brain for the poor Monster
> (doomed from the start) who was played
> by Boris Karloff who was played by
> a very gentle Englishman named
> William Henry Pratt.
>> Ash in the crucible revives
>> Roses and monsters hover in the mind.
>>> (M. K. Joseph, *Inscriptions on a Paper Dart. Selected
>>> Poems 1945–1972*, Auckland University
>>> Press, 1974, p. 64)

The gentleness of the 'real' Karloff, a member of the Pratt family distinguished in the diplomatic and academic life of Great Britain, makes his performances more rather than less terrifying; it makes us reflect on the mysterious, the submerged, part of the personality that is released in his films, brought out by the microphysiognomic scrutiny of the camera. Carl Dreyer cast his *Vampyr*, it would seem, on something like this principle: Gisèle, the suffering, virginal heroine who remains so puzzlingly, hauntingly, impassive when imprisoned with her hands tied behind her back to an iron frame, was played by a model much used by photographers specializing in nude studies, while a particularly kindly friend of Dreyer's played Marc, the vampire's evil accomplice and all-too-willing instrument.

One of the many things we can learn from *Vampyr*—particularly from its use of Sybille Schmitz—is that it is wrong to associate only specialized 'horror-stars' with terror in the cinema. On the contrary: one of the most interesting spectacles the screen affords is a little-known actor's moment of glory in a terror-film (Charles Gray's in *The Devil Rides Out*, or Niall Maginnis's in *The Night of the Demon*), and beyond that the sudden revelation of aspects of a well-known actor's personality latent in earlier performances but fully brought out only by that actor's appearance in a terror-film. David Thomson suggests this very well in his *Biographical Dictionary of the Cinema* when he calls the appearance of Bette Davis and Joan Crawford in Robert Aldrich's *Whatever Happened to Baby Jane?* 'an extraordinary extension of the sado-masochistic strain in their film work'. Bette Davis's incursions into Grand Guignol confirmed in a new way what E. Arnot Robertson had felt in her work in the early thirties: 'She gives the curious feeling', Miss Robertson had said in 1935, 'of being charged with a power that can find no ordinary outlet.' As for the spectacle of Davis tormenting Crawford—this gained added spice from the knowledge many cinema-goers shared with Robert Aldrich: that these two sacred monsters of the screen disliked one another in private life. But even without this extra piquancy terror-films have done for many other actors and actresses what *Baby Jane*, *Hush, Hush, Sweet Charlotte*, and *The Nanny* did for the older Bette Davis. Cases that spring immediately to mind are those of Ray Milland, Tallulah Bankhead, Susannah York, and Kim Novak, to name four very different personalities into whose ambiguities we seem to gain unexpected insights in Roger Corman's *The Man with X-Ray Eyes*, Sylvio Narizzano's *Fanatic*,

Robert Altman's *Images*, and the TV movie *The Devil's Triangle* (1975) respectively—though in the case of the delectable but inexpressive Miss Novak we should have been well prepared by Hitchcock's suggestion of her more sinister uses in *Vertigo*. The mystery and the wistful, decadent, elegant attractiveness of Delphine Seyrig, brought out in classic films by Resnais, Truffaut, and Buñuel, deepens, in Harry Kümel's *Daughters of Darkness*, into a more complex, varied, and extended study of melancholy perversion, of longing for the pleasures of life and for the peace of death at the same time. And no one who has ever seen Polanski's *Repulsion* will underestimate how much the horror of that film owes to the contrast between the cool blonde beauty of Catherine Deneuve and the bloody deeds of the disturbed and disturbing character she plays with such an effective economy of means.

Even when an actor has come, at a certain stage in his career, to specialize in 'horror' roles, different directors can bring out different facets of his personality and different techniques of projecting them. One need think only of Vincent Price's performances for Roger Corman (neurasthenia and a dandified sadism that are clearly *acted*, with occasional signals that seem to say: 'don't be frightened, it's only me!'), for Robert Fuest (Price enjoying himself, camping it up, keeping his tongue visibly in his cheek), and for Michael Reeves (what we are watching in *Witchfinder General* has the aura of real evil, and Price conveys this with subtlety and complete seriousness).

One more important distinction deserves to be noted between actors that populate the terror-film. There are some among them—Bela Lugosi is the prime example—who use their own faces as masks, varying their expression with different parts, but mostly exhibiting clearly their familiar features and bodily stance. There are others—notably Lon Chaney Senior—who try to change their faces and bodily stance from film to film, from role to role, by means of disguising make-up devices of various kinds. Chaney designed his own make-up; in later, more specializing times this became the task of make-up experts, one of whom, Jack Pierce, created a series of terror-masks that has become, for good or ill, part of our culture, and has affected the imagination of generations of men and women all over the world: Frankenstein's monster, the Werewolf, and the Mummy.

The cinema of terror does not, however, depend purely on its

fear-inspiring monsters; there are also actors and—especially—
actresses whose task it is to mime the terrors that audiences are,
vicariously, to feel. Kurt Tucholsky, an intelligent observer of the
early cinema, praised *The Cabinet of Dr. Caligari* for drawing us into
its world so powerfully that the audience seemed to hear—actually
to hear—the cries of the heroine confronted by her would-be
assassin. This was, of course, long before the days in which
technical progress had made it possible to record on the same bit
of film not only Fay Wray's distorted little face, but also her blood-
curdling screams. Here as elsewhere Griffith and his favoured
troupe of players may be seen as the great pioneers. In *The Birth of a
Nation* (1915) Mae Marsh, playing the Little Sister, had been
confronted with the problem of how to express her terror when
she and her family, having taken refuge in a basement, hear the
enemy soldiery running to and fro above them. In her *Screen
Acting* of 1921, Mae Marsh explained how she and Griffith tackled
their task.

Mr. Griffith, when we came to the cellar scene, asked me if there had been
a time in my life when I had been filled with terror. 'Yes', I said. 'What did
you do?' he enquired. 'I laughed', I answered. He saw the point immediately. 'Good', he said, 'let's try it.' It was the hysterical laugh of the little
girl in the cellar, with the drunken mob raging above, that was, I am sure,
far more effective than rolling the eyes or weeping would have been. (O'Dell,
1970, pp. 16–18)

How right she is! Her Little Sister laughing with terror worthily
matches that unforgettable scene in *Broken Blossoms* (1919) in
which Griffith's finest actress, Lillian Gish, mimes a heroine who,
threatened with a vicious beating, shuts herself into a closet and
spins round and round in a frenzy of fear. To such imaginative
moments the sound-film had little to add except sound itself.
Griffith is always being given credit for his use of parallel editing,
fast cutting, close-up, and so on—it is good to remind ourselves
sometimes that he was also one of the greatest directors of acting
the cinema has ever seen.

Later film-makers have been able, at favoured moments, to
profit by the aura with which Griffith endowed his actresses for
purposes of their own. Nowhere has this been done more effectively
than in Charles Laughton's classic terror-film *The Night of the
Hunter*, in which the character played by Lillian Gish offers
protection from, and ultimately helps to rout, the evil embodied

in the perverted preacher played by Robert Mitchum. 'By having the silent-star Gish defeat the 1940s and 1950s star Mitchum'. Leo Braudy has perceptively said in *The World in a Frame*, '[the film] seems to reject the world in which Mitchum's personality took shape and to return instead to an Eden of aesthetic innocence.' That Griffith was fully aware, and made his audience aware, that any 'Eden' he presented in his films was menaced by a multitude of serpents, should need no further demonstration—there is hardly a reel of his mature work which does not attest this.

But however distinguished Griffith's performers may have been, their performances could not have come across so vividly had it not been for Billy Bitzer's superb photography and Griffith's own sense of camera angle and timing. Here too, in the conveying of experienced terror, director and film-editor count for a great deal: for the purposes of *Vertigo* James Stewart only has to make an anguished face and leave the rest to Hitchcock. In *How to Read a Film* James Monaco has described how this director used a carefully controlled zoom, combined with track and models, to convey that terror of heights to which the film's title alludes.

Hitchcock laid the model stairwell on its side. The camera with zoom lens was mounted on a track looking 'down' the stairwell. The shot began with the camera at the far end of the track and the zoom lens set at a moderate telephoto focal length. As the camera tracked in toward the stairwell, the zoom was adjusted backwards, eventually winding up at a wide-angle setting. The track and zoom were carefully coordinated so that the size of the image appeared not to change. (As the track moved in on the center of the image, the zoom moved out to correct for the narrowing field.) The effect relayed on the screen was that the shot began with normal depth perception which then became quickly exaggerated, mimicking the psychological feeling of vertigo. (J. Monaco, 1977, p. 63)

In conveying his hero's fear of heights in this celebrated tower shot Hitchcock offers an elegant solution to a problem cinematographers had been wont to liken to that of squaring the circle: how to combine the advantages offered to film-makers by wide-angle and telephoto lenses.

The urban paranoia conveyed by Hitchcock transposes into another key the small-town paranoia conveyed by *The Cabinet of Dr. Caligari*. In the big cities in which many later terror-films were set, the social and sexual frustrations suggested by Wiene's film, its rancour and vengefulness, its cultured men possessed by evil, its varying forms of mental disturbance, could find new embodiment and expression. This process is symbolically suggested by Lang's *Metropolis*, released just eight years after *Caligari*: for here the sinister scientist Rotwang inhabits a Biedermeier enclave, a house that has an unmistakable small-town, pre-industrial ambience, between the gleaming skyscrapers of the masters (suggested, as we know, by those of Manhattan) and the underground tenements of the workers. Rotwang's laboratory, where scientific wonders like his steel robot are conceived and brought into being, is situated in a house that suggests an alchemist's rather than a scientist's dwelling-place; and indeed, the robot's assumption of Maria's face and form smacks more of magic than of science. But that, we might say, is the point. The terror-film sees continuity between magic and science, between the incantations of the past and the technological wonders of present and future, and this gives rise to those special feelings of the uncanny which may be evoked by such different works as *Metropolis*, *Frankenstein*, *2001*, and *Solaris*. Such works partake in an unmistakable fashion of the very essence of cinema: for is not the cinema itself a machine, a technological construct embodying many discoveries in chemistry and physics, which is put into the service of magic, of making the contents of the human imagination visible, projecting into a darkened room images of men, women, and objects whose 'reality' is elsewhere if it exists at all? One of the earliest theoreticians of the film, Hugo Münsterberg, formulated this insight in a way that has still not been bettered. 'The photoplay', he wrote in 1916, 'tells us the human story by overcoming the forms of the outer world, namely, space, time and causality, and by adjusting the events to the forms of the inner world, namely, attention, memory, imagination and emotion.'

There is another intermediary between the small-town paranoia of *Caligari* and the metropolitan paranoia of the American *film noir*: that group of silent films by Pabst, Grune, and others which have been collectively called the 'street' films. The streets that give these works their collective name, though more naturalistic than those that figure in *Caligari*, are clearly studio-built and stylized to yield the greatest possible symbolic resonance; Grune's *The Street* (1923) employed as its co-designer one of the greatest painters and portraitists of German Expressionism, Ludwig Meidner. Such works introduce us, in a variety of ways and with differing social emphases, to stuffy bourgeois characters drawn out of their domesticity by the lures and dangers of the nocturnal street outside. Lang's *The Woman in the Window* and *Scarlet Street*, made in the U.S.A. in the mid-forties, show the transition especially clearly. These two works are essentially German 'street' films transported to an American ambience; but Lang's *The Big Heat* (1953), with its lone investigator hero and its gangster and politician villains, is unmistakably one of the masterpieces of the American *film noir*. In *The Big Heat*, the obsessions of the German terror-film have been, not abandoned, but transformed: in the unforgettable image of Gloria Grahame, for instance, one side of her face scalded and scarred while the other retains all its doll-like prettiness—as striking a visual variation on the 'dual personality' theme as any we are likely to find.

From this kind of *film noir*, merging German and American traditions, new ways of development lead outwards—not least, once again, into science fiction, where Caligaresque distortions can be introduced by means that were not available to Wiene and his team. One need think only of the fish-eye lenses used by Frankenheimer in *Seconds*, where we share the drugged, terrified vision of the city business man who is given a new body and a new life, only to find the new as unsatisfactory as the old, and who is deprived of body and life together in the nightmare conclusion of the work. *Seconds*, however, with its trick photography, is only the Caligaresque end of a development which also includes, at the opposite pole, Don Siegel's *The Invasion of the Body Snatchers*. Here the real horror is that there is *no* distortion. The humanoids grown in pods from outer space look exactly like our neighbours, and can take on our neighbours' appearance and speech patterns, even our neighbours' knowledge and memory, while remaining utterly soulless and inhuman. Are we not in fact, Siegel's film asks, ironically, already living among pods? But between *Caligari* on the one hand and *Seconds* and *Body Snatchers* on the other, there is one other essential intermediary step—that taken by Rye and Wegener in *The Student of Prague*, Murnau in *Nosferatu*, and Dreyer in *Vampyr*, when they moved their cameras out of the studios into actual streets and landscapes; when they introduced such distortion as they allowed themselves, not by pre-styling the buildings and landscapes before their cameras, but by their manner of photographing them (unusual angles of vision, special lenses, gauze, filters, etc.) or their manner of editing the photographed record. Whenever we encounter driverless or monster-guided coaches hurtling along in strangely accelerated motion, doors that open by themselves, sinister rodents accompanying a monster that bears a more human shape, monsters photographed from below so that they seem to tower over us as they extend their clawing hands, sudden intrusions of film negatives, shock cuts from timid investigator to a grotesque vision of horror, then, whether we know it or not, we are back in the world of Murnau's *Nosferatu*.

Murnau's classic terror-film is remarkable, among other things, for the way in which it makes actual buildings and streets in German towns—notably Lübeck, standing in for the Bremen in which the story is ostensibly set—appear terrifying. The decaying house in which Nosferatu takes up residence, the street along which an official walks to put chalk-marks on doors behind which the plague has struck, the street, seen from an upper window, along which winds a procession of coffins each borne by two black-clad figures—these can strike as much terror as the more obviously disconcerting images of dusky Carpathian landscapes and Nosferatu's stark castle on its mountain-top. We are, however, shown idyllic enclaves in these fearful townscapes: notably the garden in which Nina plays with her cat while Jonathan tends his flowers, or the sunlit house of the Westenra family to which Jonathan comes to say good-bye before leaving for his fateful encounter with the vampire. Our memory of such idyllic islands, unblasted by Nosferatu, heightens our terror at the rest. A film like Michael Curtiz's *Mystery of the Wax Museum* neatly inverts this pattern; the sinister institution of the title is shown as an enclave of terror in the midst of the familiar, bustling, everyday Manhattan of the twentieth century —though like Nosferatu, its demented proprietor has the ability to carry this terror with him when he moves out of his domain. We cannot but ask ourselves, moreover, in the context of the film, how many more such enclaves Manhattan is likely to contain.

Many other variations of Murnau's relatively simple contrast are, of course, possible. It has often been noticed, for instance, how the grimness of Chabrol's *The Butcher* (1969) is heightened by the idyllic children's outing on to which the blood of a murdered woman suddenly drips, and, indeed, by the beautiful sunlight in which Jean Robier's photography bathes the whole film. Chabrol's strange, haunting tale of love and frustration, compulsion and desire, merges the theme of *M* with that of *Beauty and the Beast*; his persistent theme of the beast in man ever trying to break out links his delicately realistic work with the Jekyll-and-Hyde terror-film in a way that transcends genre-distinctions.

Within the terror-film it was Murnau and Lang rather than Wiene who most effectively pioneered what John Brosnan, in his indispensable book on 'special effects' in the cinema, has rightly entitled *Movie Magic*. Scenes like Mephisto's flight over the world in Murnau's *Faust* (1926), or the petrification of the dwarves in Lang's *Siegfried* (1923), are little short of miraculous in view of the relatively primitive equipment the directors and their cameramen had at their disposal. Since their day, especially after the development of complicated, computerized optical printers and highly refined 'animation' techniques, effects have become possible that were beyond the dreams of the early masters, though nowadays they quickly turn into the staple devices of television advertisers. A technically highly impressive sequence in Donald Cammell's otherwise disappointing *Demon Seed* of 1977 showed how a sophisticated computer, whose 'eyes' are radio-telescopes and radar-scanners, might perceive the world human beings have built—and also, of course, how such a computer might 'see' the human beings themselves. *2001*, *Star Wars*, and *Close Encounters of the Third Kind* are, at the time I write this, the most recent anthologies of such effects: but only the first-named uses them in a way that evokes, at times, the terror and awe characteristic of our response to films by Wiene, Murnau, and Lang—or, indeed, the Cooper–Schoedsack–O'Brien *King Kong* of 1933, which remains, for all its surface absurdity and occasionally creaky technology, an unfaded masterpiece of popular art.

Here we must once again remind ourselves, however, that some of the greatest masters of the supernatural tale have deliberately shunned 'special effects' and sophisticated camera trickery. Robin Wood, in the essay 'The Ghost Princess and the Seaweed Gatherer' included in *Personal Views*, has shown with admirable precision how Mizoguchi, the director of *Ugetsu Monogatari*, reconciled magical evocation of the supernatural with reality, with 'normal' human experience.

No film-maker in my experience—not even Tourneur or Dreyer—has treated the supernatural with such delicacy and respect, with such subtle force of suggestion and so rigorous a refusal to sensationalize or vulgarize.

Strikingly, the treatment involves the complete eschewal of all camera trickery and 'special effects': Mizoguchi refuses to tamper with the reality within the image, restricting his eerie effects to what décor and lighting can achieve and the camera record. Hence the suggestion that the Princess Wakasa's mansion exists in a world outside time is conveyed by our being shown it, unobtrusively and without comment, in three different conditions: first, derelict and decaying, the garden overgrown, the broken gate swinging on its hinges; second, magically restored and revivified by Genjuro's entry into it, the garden neat, the walls, windows and panels as new, servant-girls emerging with candle-flames; third, as ruins, a few blackened sticks and struts (over which lie the kimonos Genjuro bought for Wakasa) rising out of apparently uncultivated grass. The film's other great 'supernatural' effect—the apparition of Miyagi to welcome her husband home—is even more remarkable. The camera is inside the house as Genjuro approaches, looks in at the window, opens the door and enters. The room is quite bare and unkept. He walks across it hesitantly, calling Miyagi, and the camera pans left with him, excluding the right hand part of the room. He goes out through another door, left, and we see him through windows walking round outside, back to the front entrance. The camera accordingly moves back with him; but this time, as the rest of the room comes back within the frame, we see that its décor has been miraculously restored and that Miyagi is in the middle of it, cooking over a fire, awaiting Genjuro, who sees her as he re-enters, the camera now having returned to its original position. The *frisson* this moment excites is due largely to the simple technical fact that there has been no cut, no dissolve, no editing of any kind: the impossible has happened before our eyes. (Wood, 1976, pp. 234–5)

All this, Wood rightly stresses, has nothing at all to do with rationalization: our sense of wonder at the ghost-world of *Ugetsu* is, if anything, increased by the matter-of-factness with which it is presented.

One of the features partially obscured by modern copies of *Caligari* is, as we have seen, the way Wiene's designers integrated *writing* into their graphic patterning. Such integration was characteristic of other silent films too. In the 1920 version of *The Golem* there appeared, in an impressive conjuration scene, a magic, demonic head from whose mouth the letters A E M A E T wreathed out as in smoke—an approximation, no doubt, to the Hebrew word for 'truth'. Murnau's *Nosferatu* is full of writing and printing of various kinds, including the diary of Johann Cavallus from which the story is said to derive; Jonathan Harker's letter to Nina; the strange hieroglyphics in which Nosferatu and Renfield correspond;

and the Gothic print of the book on vampires which Jonathan takes on his journey and from which Nina learns how she can rid the world of Nosferatu at the cost of her own life. When Buñuel saw Lang's *Metropolis* in 1927, he was particularly impressed by the way in which writing was integrated into the movement of the film: 'Even the titles', he said, in a review that distinguishes admirably between the work's lyrical beauty and its obnoxious fable, 'ascend and descend, twist round, dissolve into light and shade, fuse with the general movement—they also burn into images.' No one, in fact, has used lettering with greater virtuosity than Lang. In *Tired Death* or *Destiny* the intertitles change character with the setting, appearing now Gothic, now pseudo-Arabic or pseudo-Chinese; in *Metropolis* the exclamation MOLOCH! appears, in white jagged letters against a black background, like a horrified cry, while elsewhere black letters suddenly erupt against a black background; and who can forget the part a chalked letter 'M' plays in *M*, or Mabuse's distinctive scribblings in *The Testament of Dr. Mabuse*!

Murnau—especially in *The Last Laugh* (1924)—had shown that even the silent film could all but dispense with intertitles; and these became in any case unnecessary when the cinema learned to talk. In its opening credits, however, the terror-film continued the Wiene–Lang tradition of significant graphics into the sound era. In Victor Halperin's *White Zombie* jagged white letters spelling out the film's title are rapidly superimposed, one by one, on to a sombre opening sequence depicting a crossroads burial, until the complete title shines out starkly against its dark-toned, moving background. In Karl Freund's *Mad Love* we find credits written on to glass overlooking a Parisian skyline; the outline of a man—probably that of Peter Lorre, the star of the film—hovers over the glass which is then startlingly smashed by a fist. In R. W. Neill's *Frankenstein Meets The Wolf Man* (1943), the opening credits are formed from wisps of smoke emerging from test-tubes. At the opening of Hitchcock's *Psycho* the lines of print slide and split apart, in anticipation of the schizophrenia to come. In Hammer films letters burn or drip on to the screen; in Polanski's *Repulsion*, to cite a more subtle and respectable example, they seem to float, at times, out of the huge eye that so frighteningly fills the screen at the opening of the film. Occasionally, handwriting is used to indicate character: how well we can recognize Mrs. Van Hopper in the very letters of the hand-

Hyde triumphant: Neanderthal man in the clothes (and with the money and opportunities!) of the Victorian swell. Frederic March in *Dr. Jekyll and Mr. Hyde*, dir. Rouben Mamoulian, 1932.

Occult knowledge locked in the human brain: what wealth-bringing, dangerous secret is hidden behind these ancient eyes? Edith Evans as the Countess in *The Queen of Spades*, dir. Thorold Dickinson, 1948.

Age, youth, and oneiric mirror in a Swedish garden: Victor Sjöström and Bibi Andersson in *Wild Strawberries*, dir. Ingmar Bergman, 1957.

The scientist as magician: Rudolf Klein-Rogge as Rotwang, with employer and robot, in *Metropolis*, dir. Fritz Lang, 1927.

Rotwang *redivivus*: Peter Sellers and uncontrollable black hand in *Dr. Strangelove; or How I Learned to Stop Worrying and Love the Bomb*, dir. Stanley Kubrick, 1963.

Within sight of his earth-filled coffin, and against an impressively monumental set, Dracula is about to slide into an icy grave, to await resurrection in the next Hammer epic. Christopher Lee in *Dracula, Prince of Darkness*, dir. Terence Fisher, 1965.

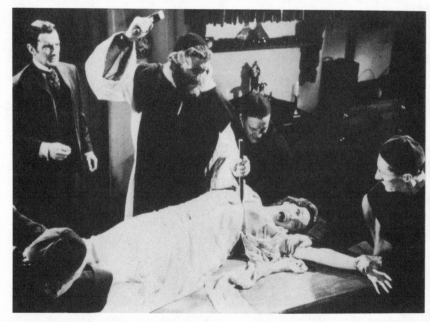

Vampire *in extremis*: Francis Matthews, Andrew Keir, Barbara Shelley, and attendant monks in *Dracula, Prince of Darkness*.

The return of the repressed: mysterious waters, phallic monster (Ricou Browning), and terrified bride in *Revenge of the Creature*, dir. Jack Arnold, 1955.

The tortured victim about to become a demonic pursuer: Barbara Steele, *Sadique* as ever, with executioner and grotesque spiked mask in *The Mask of the Demon*, dir. Mario Bava, 1960.

Diabolic killer in the guise of angelic innocence: Chloe Franks, with voodoo doll, in the 'Sweets to the Sweet' episode of *The House that Dripped Blood*, dir. Peter John Duffell, 1970.

The dizzying terrors of the stairway: Julie Harris and Richard Johnson between heaven and earth in an overhead shot from *The Haunting*, dir. Robert Wise, 1963.

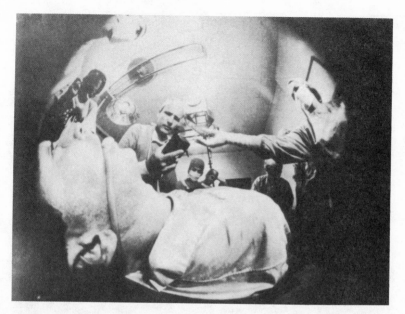

The terrors of the operating theatre: Rock Hudson, medical staff, and bright American lighting, in the fish-eye lens view of *Seconds*, dir. John Frankenheimer, 1966.

'German' chiaroscuro in an influential British thriller: *Blackmail*, dir. Alfred Hitchcock, 1929.

Can the magic writing ward off assailing demons? Katsuo Nakamura as Hoichi the Earless in *Kwaidan*, dir. Masaki Kobayashi, 1964.

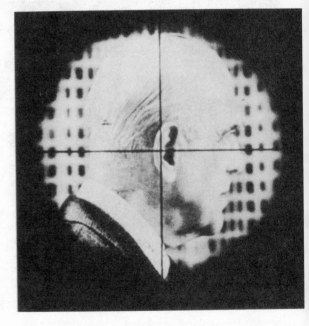

Where is the monster?
Boris Karloff and
gun-sight in *Targets*,
dir. Peter Bogdanovich,
1967.

written note which Hitchcock shows us in *Rebecca*! No sound-film, however, has ever used written symbols as unforgettably as Masaki Kobayashi in the anthology of ghost-stories which he entitled *Kwaidan*. In the episode 'Hoichi the Earless' we see Hoichi's entire body (with the fatal exception of his ears) painted over with Japanese writing as a protection from the spirits that threaten and assail him.

Wiene had also used colour, in a generalized way, through the tinting of copies of *Caligari* sent out on release. It was left to Rupert Julian, in *The Phantom of the Opera* (1925), to introduce colour at a specific moment into a black-and-white terror-film, for particular emotional effects; and it was left to Rouben Mamoulian to experiment with colour-gradations for just such effects within a film that used colour-stock throughout. Writing in *The International Photographer* in 1935, Mamoulian explained the principles he had adopted in *Becky Sharp*:

Apart from pure pictorial beauty and the entertainment value of color, there is also a definite emotional content and meaning in most colors and shades. We have lost sight of that because like all important and inevitable phenomena, it has become subconscious with us. It is not an accident that the traffic lights of a city street today are green for safety and red for danger. Colors convey to us subtly different moods, feelings and impulses. It is not an accident that we use the expressions 'To see red,' 'to feel blue,' 'to be green with envy' and 'to wear a black frown.' Is it for nothing that we believe that white is expressive of purity, black of sorrow, red of passion, green of hope, yellow of madness, and so on.

The artist should take advantage of the mental and emotional implications of color and use them on the screen to increase the power and effectiveness of a scene, situation or character. I have tried to do as much of this in *Becky Sharp* as the story allowed. To quote an example of this, I would refer to the sequence of the panic which occurs at the Duchess of Richmond's ball when the first shots of Napoleon's cannons are heard. You will see how inconspicuously, but with telling effect, this sequence builds to a climax through a series of intercut shots which progress from the coolness and sobriety of colors like grey, blue, green and pale yellow, to the exciting danger and threat of deep orange and flaming red. (Koszarski, 1976, pp. 291–2)

What Mamoulian began in the early days of Technicolour, Eisenstein developed in his unfinished film biography of the man whom Western historians know, with good reason, as Ivan the Terrible. Yon Barna has described the principles on which Eisenstein worked.

Eisenstein's basic principle was 'to dissociate the colours from the particular objects to which they were attached and make them lead on to a generalized mood or emotion, which afterwards links up once again with the object'. It is interesting, in view of its quite fortuitous application (apart from the chance stimulus of the conference, it was also sheer chance that Eisenstein managed to lay hands on a small quantity of colour negative captured among other spoils of war), that this complicated chromatic solution merged perfectly into the film's structure. But in the main body of the film already shot Eisenstein had—certainly not with future colour films in mind, but only the demand for colour in this film—used objects embodying a notion of colour: burning candles and the *oprichniki*'s costumes, embodying the colour red; the ceremonial vestments, gold; the cloaks of the *oprichniki* and of the Tsar, black. Thus the first stage of his basic principle preceded his intention of using actual colours. In the second stage, the colours came to stand for a generalized idea: red for the theme of plottings and vengeance, gold for orgies, black for death. In the third stage, through a contrapuntal construction which Eisenstein elsewhere called 'the dramaturgy of colour', the colour was again linked up with the object. Used in this way in *Ivan the Terrible*, the colours became a means of penetrating Ivan's inner world, and hence a dynamic instrument of psychological investigation. And it is precisely Ivan's psychological state, and not the *spectacle* of the dance, that is the essential feature of the sequence; and with the dynamic of the colour echoing Ivan's inner turmoil this is presented much more clearly. (Barna, 1975, p. 262)

Most films, alas, do not use colour with anything like this degree of sophistication. The terror-films of Mario Bava and Nicolas Roeg, however, have profited greatly from their directors' appreciation of the emotional effect of colour—appreciation of what D. G. Winston has called 'non-verbal thought': 'thought that does not first appear in our minds in the form of words, and is therefore inadequately expressed by them—thoughts that are more associated with color, composition and mood than with syntax and logic'. This is not to say, of course, that such effects cannot be analysed. Paul Willemen has shown, for instance, that Roger Corman not only uses often deliberately dissonant colour-schemes in his pre-credit sequences to suggest an over-all mood, but that he also makes colours thematically meaningful in more explicit ways— when, for instance, an apparently life-affirming character in *The Premature Burial* (1961) is linked with *death* by matching the mauve of her dress with that associated elsewhere in the film with the lining of a coffin. The vivid colour-scheme of *Don't Look Now—*

with its sinister incursions of red—is particularly apt because the film's central protagonist is an art-historian, a man professionally concerned with the meaning of colour-gradations.

Just as sound can make silence more meaningful, the use of colour can lend a special force and significance to black-and-white photography. The terror-film which uses this opposition and mutual enhancement to greatest effect is Michael Powell's *Peeping Tom*. That personal and many-levelled film begins with a black-and-white sequence—a 16-millimetre movie shot by the film's central character, recording a bizarre murder. The story of this photographer's murderous obsessions is then unfolded in colour; but the childhood experience which, in part, explains his obsessions is once again depicted on a black-and-white home movie, shot, this time, not by the photographer, but by his sadistic father (played, to give an extra dimension of irony to the film, by the director, Michael Powell, himself). The change from colour to black and white signals that we are watching a terror-film within a terror-film; that our experience of watching *Peeping Tom* is being paralleled, within the work, at what we are meant to regard as another level of reality, by the murderous voyeur at its centre. The women whose murder we watch in this most uncomfortable of terror-films are also made 'watchers' in a particularly agonizing way: using the point of his camera's tripod as the instrument of murder, the killer forces his victims to see their own death-throes in an ingeniously mounted mirror while he photographs them. No other work has ever made us reflect more painfully on what we are doing when we pay to watch the simulated agonies and ecstasies of the horror-movie; small wonder that when *Peeping Tom* was first released, in 1959, its reception by the critics was almost uniformly hostile.

Photographed images of actors and setting, and of print and other graphics, constitute two of the five channels of information which combine in the reel of film fed into a modern projector. The other three were, of necessity, lacking in the prints which the distributors of *Caligari* sent to exhibitors between 1919 and 1929: human speech; noises and sound-effects of various kinds; and music. Let us briefly look at the use which later terror-films have made of these.

Lon Chaney Senior once told Boris Karloff that the coming of sound had robbed him of many of his most effective make-up devices. The springs, clamps, and disks that distorted Chaney's face in *The Phantom of the Opera*, *London after Midnight*, and elsewhere would certainly have rendered articulate speech all but impossible. Nevertheless, when Chaney came to make his first sound-film, *The Unholy Three*, his voice was found to be as flexible as his face and body: he spoke, not only with his own voice, which was pleasantly resonant and could be insinuatingly soft and smooth as easily as hard and harsh, but also in the high-pitched tremolo of a sweet old lady, the throaty enunciation of a ventriloquist's dummy, and the screech of a speaking parrot. As for Karloff: the classic performance that brought him fame, though embedded in a sound-film, was a wordless one; for unlike the eloquent monster of Mary Shelley's original tale, the monster of Whale's 1931 *Frankenstein* was without speech as well as without name. In fact, Karloff showed himself anything but pleased when *The Bride of Frankenstein* compelled his monster to speak; despite the deeply moving effect of the first phrase we hear the monster articulate— 'Friend *good*'—Karloff felt, not without reason, that speech detracted from its unique dignity and pathos. He was right, in a wider sense than he intended. The words spoken in a terror-film are often the weakest elements in them. Platitudes, clichés, halting half-truths have to be brought out with conviction and received as though they were profound revelations: 'Maybe if a man is ugly he does ugly things', one character says to another in Lew Landers's *The Raven*; and in case the audience is not sufficiently impressed, his hapless interlocutor has to answer: 'You are saying something profound.' Afficionados learn to look forward with camp delight to such lines as 'You're mad—I'm going to notify the police!' or to such Transylvanian jingles as 'When the house is filled with dread/ Place the beds at head to head'. At Black Masses Latin and pseudo-Latin gibberish has to be solemnly pronounced; and the possibility of speech encouraged many producers in the thirties to introduce wisecracking reporters whose flat jokes became the bane of many an otherwise enjoyable B-category horror-movie. Script-writers found it particularly difficult to come up with convincing dialogue for supernatural characters—a fact so vividly recognized by the Hammer team that they gave their Dracula less and less to say in successive films. When he is not sinking his fangs into some luscious Hammerette, Christopher Lee is therefore reduced to standing about snarling in his later incarnations of a role he has now made as much his own as Bela Lugosi did in the Universal cycle.

As always, however, these things are more complicated than at first appears. Is there not a kind of primitive poetry in those Lugosi and Van Sloan lines we have come to know so well:

Listen to them—children of the night—what music they make . . .

or

For one who has not lived even a single lifetime, you are a wise man, Van Helsing . . .

or

To sleep . . . really to sleep . . . that must be glorious . . .

or

She was beautiful when she died . . . a hundred years ago!

And do not the wisecracks, when they are good, offer a most welcome entry into a world in which the thrill of terror and the delight of laughter coexist? Exchanges like that between Lon Chaney Junior as the Wolf Man and Lou Costello:

'You don't understand: every night, when the moon is full, I turn into a wolf!'
'You and fifty million other guys!'
(*Abbott and Costello Meet Frankenstein*, 1948)

or even that between Nydia Westman and Bob Hope:

'Do you believe people come back from the dead?'
'You mean like Republicans?'
(*The Cat and the Canary*, 1939)

may suddenly illuminate aspects of the standard horror-plots which are usually left dark and inexplicit.

Synchronized speech-recording opened up prospects which the masters of the terror-film were not slow to explore. In his *Theory of Film* Siegfried Kracauer has usefully classified the kinds of parallelism and counterpoint, of synchronism and asynchronism, which now became possible, and he has also described two of the earliest examples in which sound was enlisted in the service of terror.

Take the Elsie episode of *M*, in which Fritz Lang features the despair of a mother whose little girl does not come home from school. She looks out of the window and, at the end of her tether, shouts the name of her girl. The air is filled with her shout. Then she disappears and we see instead, still reverberating with her 'Elsie,' the empty stairwell of the house and its empty attic—images followed by Elsie's unused plate on the kitchen table, the ball she was playing with, and the balloon with which the murderer won the confidence of the child. Now the juxtaposition of the asynchronous shout 'Elsie' with the shots of the stairwell and the attic is likely to affect us in two ways: it sensitizes us to the indescribable sadness of these shots; and it causes us to relate their sadness to the despair behind that shout. In other words, the stairwell and the attic do not just serve to illustrate the state of mind of Elsie's mother; rather, they impress themselves upon us for their own sake so that, in looking at the screen, we cannot help being aware of some of their properties, innate or not; hence, what we actually experience is the interplay between them and the moods or drives responsible for the mother's outcry. The Elsie episode lures the responsive spectator deep into the dimension of psychophysical correspondences.

Another example: after having killed her assailant with a knife, the young heroine of Alfred Hitchcock's BLACKMAIL finally returns to her parents' shop and there overhears the chatter of a gossipy woman customer. The camera is just focusing on the listening girl, as the woman suddenly drops the word 'knife'. At this moment time seems to come to a stop: the word 'knife' lingers on, an ever-repeated threat, and so does the face of the girl—a drawn-out interlude filled exclusively with her close-up and the ominous word. Then the spell subsides. The woman resumes her prattle and we realize that she actually never discontinued it. (Kracauer, 1971, pp. 122–3)

Lindsay Anderson, in an essay on Hitchcock first published in 1949, has described the celebrated episode from *Blackmail* more precisely, and has placed it in the context of other sound-effects:

Two famous, and very effective, examples of the distortion of sound to convey a subjective impression of tension and near-hysteria occur as the girl sits miserably over breakfast the next morning. A garrulous neighbor is discussing the news: 'I don't hold with knives. . . . No, knives isn't right . . . now, mind you, a knife's a difficult thing. . . .' Gradually all other words are mixed together in a monotonous blur, the word 'knife' alone stabbing clearly out of the sound track over a close-up of the girl. 'Cut us a bit of bread,' says her father. The camera tilts down to a close-up of the knife; the girl's hand reaches out. Suddenly 'K N I F E !' screams the voice, the hand jerks sharply up, and the breadknife flies into the corner of the room. A similar use of distortion and sudden crescendo conveys the girl's alarm at the sudden ringing of the shop bell: Instead of dying swiftly away, the sound of the bell is held for some four seconds, swelling up to a startling intensity. (Braudy and Dickstein, 1978, p. 470)

Lang and Hitchcock had little to learn from later film-makers about ways in which sound might be related to sight in the cinema of terror.

It would certainly be wrong to deduce from the poverty of the dialogue in many terror-films that the silent, the non-talking, film was by its very nature aesthetically superior to the sound-film. 'A quite valid case', Stanley Kaufmann has said in the valuable 'Notes on Theatre-and-Film' which he contributed to *Performance* in October 1972, 'can be made to show that the silent and the sound film are aesthetically separate; but it is a different case from the one that words are intrinsically and inevitably the enemy of the sound film.' And Kaufmann goes on: 'When language is designed for film and is understood as contributory dynamics, it is as cinematic as any other film element. Bibi Andersson's account of the sex orgy in *Persona*, many of the dialogues in *My Night at Maud's* and *Claire's Knee*, Gielgud's speeches in *The Charge of the Light Brigade*, Ray Collins' farewell at the railroad station in *The Magnificent Ambersons*, these are only a few of the instances where words, understood and controlled, become film components' (J. Hurt, 1974, p. 73). In a terror-film context, one could cite Peter Lorre's speech before the kangaroo court in *M*, Ernest Thesiger's grotesque utterances in *The Old Dark House* (1932) and *The Bride of Frankenstein*, Michael Redgrave's dialogues with a ventriloquist's dummy in *Dead of Night*, the fable Boris Karloff tells in *Targets*, Vincent Price's icy instructions in *Witchfinder General*, and the crudely cheerful slogans—'Kill the brain and you kill the ghoul', 'Beat 'em or burn 'em, they go up pretty easy'—with which television broadcasters meet the emergency of *Night of the Living Dead*. Everyone has his own favourites: mine are the wrily melancholy reminiscences, observations, and pleadings of Delphine Seyrig's vampiric Countess Bathory in Kümel's *Daughters of Darkness*, including her now famous answer to the question as to how she had managed to keep her youthful good looks intact over so many years—years in which the bellboy who had served her when she last visited the hotel had turned into an aged chief porter: 'A strict diet and lots of sleep.' Ambiguous remarks of this kind constitute, as we shall see later, one of the hallmarks of the Dracula movies.

The subtler directors of terror-films—of which there have been more than most people think—have always shown themselves alive to possibilities of counterpoint opened up by dialogue and narration. Some of these we have already encountered in the course of the present study. A particularly instructive example may be taken from Leo Braudy's book on Jean Renoir. In Renoir's version of the Jekyll-and-Hyde story, *The Testament of Dr. Cordelier* (1961), Opale, the equivalent of Hyde, represents natural energies that Cordelier, the equivalent of Jekyll, has repressed: Opale is, among other things, the natural self Cordelier should have tried to understand and come to terms with. The voice-over narration of the film, Braudy points out, 'enforces a rigidly moralistic view of the relation between Cordelier and Opale' while the film itself 'invites us to see the flaws in Cordelier's moralism and the virtues in Opale's violence' (1977, pp. 188–9). Renoir's film was made for television and did not transfer well to the larger screen; it is therefore so seldom shown nowadays that few cinema-goers have had an opportunity to see his personal and distinctive variation on Stevenson's theme, which seems to me to come closer to Stevenson's own intentions than any other movie version.

Other masters of the terror-film followed the lead given by Hitchcock and Lang, and experimented with verbal sounds and rhythms, often matching them against non-verbal ones. One remembers, for instance, the splendid finale of Robert Wise's *The Body Snatcher*, where the reiterated words '[You'll] never get rid of me, never get rid of me' merge with the hoof-beats of the guilty Dr. MacFarlane's galloping horses. Once it had found a voice, the terror-film could also introduce the uncanny effect of speaking in tongues, as in the exorcism-scene of Brunello Rondi's *The Demon* (1963), or let characters speak in voices that are clearly not their own, as when the rough, deep voice of Mercedes McCambridge issues from Linda Blair's mouth in *The Exorcist*. It could also, by way of piquant paradox, *refrain* from introducing human speech where it would be expected: in the first sound-film Lang devoted to his favourite super-criminal (*The Testament of Dr. Mabuse*), Mabuse himself does not speak a single word. But beyond all this, films could now make use of voices distinctive in timbre, pitch, and speech-patterns, whose very sound reinforced the terror inspired by their possessors' appearance, actions, and sufferings: the slow, grave, dark-toned speech of Boris Karloff, with its slight but unmistakable lisp; the sinister whine of Peter Lorre; the effete, often mocking, drawl of Vincent Price; the knife-edge sharpness of Basil Rathbone's speech, which did duty as effectively for the Son of Frankenstein as for Dickens's Mr. Murdstone or—at the other end of the spectrum—for that arch-enemy of monsters and villains, Sherlock Holmes; the boom of Lionel Atwill, maddest of mad doctors and most reliable of one-armed police inspectors; the precise, cultivated tones of Peter Cushing, which could take on such a fanatic, menacing timbre when he impersonated Dr. Frankenstein and such a reassuring note of efficiency when he appeared as Dr. Van Helsing.

Even in the first of his Frankenstein films, Boris Karloff did not play a *sound*less monster: his snarls and growls were effective in a way few *words* could have been. The terror-film has exploited many other such man-emitted, non-spoken sounds in the course of its history. The most casual dip into one's memory will dredge up Carol Borland's brief animal snarl in *Mark of the Vampire*; Fay Wray's screams in *King Kong* and *Mystery of the Wax Museum*, and Elsa Lanchester's in *The Bride of Frankenstein*; Olga Baclanova's terrifying squawk in the grotesque final scene of *Freaks*; Una O'Connor's comic screechings in *The Bride of Frankenstein* and *The Invisible Man* (1933); the crowd-noises pursuing the blackmailer down the empty street in Clouzot's *The Crow* (*Le Corbeau*, 1943); the howl of the wolf blending into the cry of a new-born baby in *Curse of the Werewolf*; the gasps of Yvonne Furneaux in Polanski's *Repulsion*, first during a copulation-scene (heard but not viewed early in the film), then towards the end of the work when the character she plays sees the murderous havoc wrought during her absence by her mentally disturbed sister. The example just cited from Clouzot's film shows sound prolonging the photographed image into the characters' imagination: the crowd is heard, but only in the mind; it does not appear on the screen. Elsewhere sounds prolong the space of the image actually projected into off-screen space. In *The Hounds of Zaroff* we hear the baying and barking of the pursuing dogs at times when neither we nor their human quarry can see them. The traditional horror-movie developed a whole symphony of such recurrent non-human sounds to supple-ment speech and other man-emitted noises, ranging from the ululations of wolves and the soughing of winds to the creaking or slamming of doors, the flapping of shutters, and the crashing of coffin-lids. Later films adopted and expanded this repertoire, with the sudden screech of a cockatoo in *Mad Love*; the roaring *Tyrannosaurus* of the Cooper–Schoedsack *King Kong* (produced by combining the recording of a puma's cry with the noise of an air-compressor—Kong's own voice, we are told, was the roar of a lion lowered one octave and recorded backwards); the mixing of a dripping tap and a ticking clock to suggest a heart-beat in Jules Dassin's 1941 version of *The Tell-tale Heart*; the increasingly loud hiss of the descending scythe and the remorseless grinding of the walls that close in on the hapless hero of Astruc's *The Pit and the Pendulum*; the harsh whirring of the electrically operated surgeon's implement that approaches Rock Hudson's head in *Seconds*; the sound of a bone-saw opening up a human skull in the 1969 *Frankenstein Must Be Destroyed* (produced by sawing through a nice firm cabbage—but the audience need not know that!); the howling dogs, dripping ice, and clicking Geiger counters of *The Thing from Another World*; the electronic shrieks of the eponymous heroes of Hitchcock's *The Birds*, orchestrated by Remi Gassman and Oscar Sala.

When Rouben Mamoulian recorded his own heart-beats and amplified them on the sound-track of *Dr. Jekyll and Mr. Hyde*, he contributed to the art of the film an aural equivalent of what in the visual field is known as the close-up. We have already seen Hitchcock do something like this in *Blackmail*, when he isolated the word 'knife' from its surrounding flow of speech, recording it loud and clear while submerging the rest in mumbling imprecision. Mamoulian applied this principle to non-verbal sounds in ways that are still being explored. Robert Enrico, for instance, in *An Occurrence at Owl Creek Bridge*, suggests a change of perception, a change in the level of reality at which hero and audience move, by combining visual and aural slow motion; and Jerzy Skolimowski's *The Shout* introduces, as one of its central figures, a composer of electronic music, who in his professional capacity produces many of the sounds that accompany the action by isolating, amplifying, combining, and distorting human breathing, wasps struggling in glass jars, and the noise of a violin-bow stroking the jagged top of an open sardine-tin.

The example just cited has taken us some way towards the last of the 'channels of information' carried by modern terror-films but denied to *Caligari* when it was first released. I refer, of course, to music, for which cue-sheets and even elaborate scores were supplied with several early films, but whose actual execution had to be left, in the 'silent' era, to such musicians as the exhibitors could afford to employ, or to an occasional gramophone. A great deal of the music that came with terror-films once they had acquired a sound-track was, and is, execrable: bogeyman stuff that lays on the 'atmosphere' so thick that only the least sophisticated, or the least musical, can stand it without wincing; sentimental and banal tunes, poured over the whole film like a sticky sauce; badly played and badly recorded popular classics whining away in the background; and, occasionally, the heavy jocularity exemplified by the introduction of Mendelssohn's Wedding March when a monster is presented with its mate. Improved recording techniques encouraged more sophisticated scoring and better playing—but this often makes the run-of-the-mill horror-movie even more distressing to listen to.

Nevertheless, as this book has had occasion to show at various points, the composer's help in evoking an atmosphere of terror has not been limited to making a great deal of noise over the opening credits in order to convince the audience that this is going to be an important and thrilling work, or to the tasteless underlining and overlaying that we have all come to know and dread. Wolfgang Zeller's contribution to *Vampyr*, Max Steiner's to *King Kong*, Georges Auric's to *Dead of Night*, Walter Schumann's to *The Night of the Hunter*, Peter Maxwell Davies's to *The Devils*, Maurice Jarre's waltz at the opening of *Eyes Without a Face*, some of Elizabeth Lutyens's scores for otherwise undistinguished British horror-movies, the fastidiously chosen classical music at the climaxes of Geissendörfer's *Jonathan: Vampires Do Not Die*, the imaginatively used piano-works of Liszt in Paul Wendkos's *The Mephisto Waltz* (1971), an adagio by Albinoni in Vadim's *Blood and Roses*, and the ironic introduction of Gounod's *Sanctus* at the end of Werner Herzog's *Nosferatu*, are just a few of the more respectable musical landmarks in the history of the terror-film. Music has been effectively employed as a thematic device, linking scenes and characters and furthering the action, in Fritz Lang's *M*, where the murderer announces himself through his off-key whistling of Grieg's 'In the Hall of the Mountain King', in the hunting-horn motifs of Pichel's *The Hounds of Zaroff*, in the street-singer's song of Wise's *The Body Snatcher*, into which the clop-clop of the murderer's cab breaks, moving closer and closer until the singing abruptly stops, and in the cymbal-clash at the Albert Hall concert for which the assassin waits in Hitchcock's *The Man Who Knew Too Much* (1956); as a reflection of grotesque distortion, in the more and more sinister metamorphoses of 'You Should See Me Dance the Polka' in Victor Fleming's version of *Dr. Jekyll and Mr. Hyde* (1941); as an entry into the strange and other-worldly, when Bernard Herrmann introduces theremins or Henry Mancini autoharps, and when Stanley Kubrick makes contrasting dramatic use of Richard Strauss and György Ligeti in *2001*; as a means of heightening terror through contrast, as when a reedy okarina tune accompanies the horrifying climax of *Freaks*, or Hitchcock has a murder accompanied by hurdy-gurdy fair-ground music, or when Franju and Frankenheimer accompany the medical horrors of *Eyes Without a Face* and *Seconds* with a restrained, almost classical score. The composers of film-music have had to find sounds to suggest the activities of the Devil:

In *The Devil and Daniel Webster* [*All That Money Can Buy*, 1941], we recorded telephone wires singing at 4:00 in the morning to characterize the Devil (Mr. Scratch) and when he plays the violin at a barn dance we had a single violin playing six different variations on the same tune, each more complex than the last, and then superimposed all the tracks—so that we got solo violin music of a sort that no human violin could possibly have played. (Leyda, 1977, pp. 199–200);

and they have had to compose *against* rather than *with* the images to achieve what Jean Cocteau has called

this quite fantastic synchronization by which, at my request, Georges Auric has not kept to the rhythm of the film but cut across it, so that when film and music come together it seems as though by the grace of God. (ibid., p. 82)

With Cocteau's help Bernard Herrmann, whose experience of providing music for directors that specialize in various kinds of cinematic terror is second to none, and whose contribution to *Vertigo* must rank among the most distinguished scores ever composed for a popular film, has summed up the contribution the composer can make to terror-films as tersely and economically as could be desired.

The real reason for music is that a piece of film, by its nature, lacks a certain ability to convey emotional overtones. Many times in many films, dialogue may not give a clue to the feelings of a character. It's the music or the lighting or camera movement. When a film is well made, the music's function is to fuse a piece of film so that it has an inevitable beginning and end. When you cut a piece of film you can do it perhaps a dozen ways, but once you put music to it, that becomes the absolutely final way . . . Music essentially provides an unconscious series of anchors for the viewer. It isn't always apparent and you don't have to know, but it serves its functions. I think Cocteau said that a good film score should create the feeling that one is not aware whether the music is making the film go forward or whether the film is pushing the music forward. (Manvell and Huntley, 1975, p. 244)

There is one important distinction which Herrmann neglects to draw here, though his practice shows that he was well aware of it. This is the distinction between the 'mood technique' of Alfred Newman, which supplies separate, discrete musical mood-pieces to comment on, or more usually to underline, what we see on the screen, and the 'thematic development' technique of Max Steiner. Steiner's celebrated score for *King Kong* is an excellent example of his method.

The music is largely built upon three motifs: 'King Kong', a descending three-note figure that is the leitmotif of the title character; 'Jungle Dance', which symbolizes the natives of Skull Island; and 'Stolen Love', a plaintive melody used to suggest the 'beauty and the beast' longing of Kong for Ann. These themes are paraphrased and deployed throughout the film in numerous variations. Among other compositions are 'The Forgotten Island', 'A Boat in the Fog' and 'Sea at Night', all of which have about them a suggestion of Debussy tone poems. 'The Sailors', introduced as a march as the men plod through the jungle, is developed as exciting chase music during several episodes. 'Aboriginal Sacrifice Dance', scored for orchestra and male chorus, is played during the first native ceremony. Kong's arrival on Broadway is heralded by the 'King Kong March', which is done in the style of a theatrical overture.

Music is present through most of the film, the exceptions being during the New York and shipboard scenes prior to the arrival at the island, the fight with the Tyrannosaurus (which is so filled with curious sounds as to make music superfluous) and the battle with the airplanes.

The earnestness of Steiner is transmitted to the subconsciousness of the viewer. . . . The precise conformity of the music to the flow of the images results in a unity seldom achieved in the combining of visual and sound arts. The growing love of Ann and Jack is emphasized by waltz-like string passages in a lush romantic style, the mystery of uncharted seas by softly ominous chords with the disturbing rhythm of distant drums in the background, the frantic terror of pursuit by cyclopean giants by scherzi calculated to accelerate the beating of one's heart. Music accompanying the native ceremonies conveys the frenzy of barbaric religious passion.

It is in the delineation of the complex emotions and personality of Kong himself that the music achieves its greatest expressiveness. His savage brutality is accented by brassy, dissonant variations on the King Kong theme. The 'Stolen Love' motif subtly underlines the tragic side of his nature, portraying his loneliness and the painful bewilderment inherent in unrequited love. This theme is developed to its apogee of power and finally resolved in the finale as Kong mutely bids Ann farewell and gives himself up to the sacrifice that was, from the beginning, inevitable. It would be difficult to overestimate Steiner's share in creating a classic tragic figure . . . (Goldner and Turner, 1975, p. 191)

Even as one reads this solemn description, one smiles at the corny nature of some of the tunes and effects one remembers from *King Kong*—though they seemed less corny in their pristine freshness, no doubt, than they do now, when they have been used and re-used in dozens of later terror-films, disaster epics, adventure yarns, and even newsreels. Hollywood wastes nothing—even Fay Wray's screams were spliced into later movies! Hanns Eisler, who admired *King Kong*, thought that Steiner's famous score never began to match its visual quality, and suggested that a post-Schoenberg score, introducing 'the shocks characteristics of modern music, shocks that derived—not accidentally!—from the technification of music' would have done better. I take leave to doubt that; the throbbing, pulsating quality of Steiner's accompaniments, suggesting the very heart-beats of Kong, seem to fit that splendid work perfectly. Even the corn is part of it: much as I love Kong, I cannot bring myself to describe him, as Goldner and Turner do, as 'a classic, tragic figure' . . . Steiner's score suits *King Kong* as precisely as Franz Waxman's, with its now famous leitmotifs for the monster and its bride, suits James Whale's *The Bride of Frankenstein*.

One need only add to this that one of the greatest benefits composers have afforded the terror-film is to provide a frame for silence: the eerie silence that surrounds Karloff's famous 'little walk' in Karl Freund's *The Mummy*, or that which envelops the two women's walk towards the voodoo ceremony in the Lewton–Tourneur *I Walked with a Zombie*—a silence broken only by the gradual approach of the voodoo drums. No amount of blaring pomposity ('On horrors as a rule you need a lot of brass', said Philip Martell, and he should know) could have matched the eerie effects of that sudden absence of all musical accompaniment as well as speech.

The post-*Caligari* terror-film not only made distinctive use of new 'channels of information' added by improved technology; it also refined and reinterpreted methods of montage and *mise en scène* with which other genres, other directors and cameramen had experimented. Take the parallel editing so characteristic of Griffith: shots of a menaced heroine intercut, again and again, with shots of rescuers riding along at full tilt, and so on. Galeen and Murnau, in *Nosferatu*, played a significant variation on this. They used parallel editing for the purposes of supernatural, or para-normal, fantasy by intercutting shots of the hero menaced by the vampire in the Balkans with shots of the hero's wife sitting up in bed in her German town, in such a way that a spiritual influence is suggested, a love which is so strong that it can deflect the beloved's enemies from their dire purpose across many miles of land and sea. Yet another imaginative variation on this kind of cross-cutting occurs at the end of Dreyer's *Vampyr*. Curtis Harrington has described it as follows in an article in *Sight and Sound* first published in 1952:

The last sequence of the film is very formally constructed and gives us, I believe, insight into Dreyer's creative method, one which always tends toward formal control, especially when he is dealing with incident and out-ward movement rather than people. Here we have the escape of the young couple counterpointed with the death of the doctor in the flour mill. The sequence is cross-cut, so that at one moment we see and hear the machinery rhythmically grinding out its white death, and the next we see the young couple gliding slowly on the mist-covered lake, the image being accom-panied by a slow sustained note of music. This combination of shots is re-peated in alternation until the couple get out of the boat and go into the sunlit forest. The very final shot is a close-up of the . . . turning gears of the flour mill machinery; their movement slows, and at last stops. Fade out; we have reached the end of the adventure. The construction and the image-material here employed is perfectly cinematographic; the meaning communicated is melodramatic incident abstracted into a pattern of time, space and sound. The sum of this design towards a conclusion becomes greater than the actions of its parts; it brings to an end not only the adven-ture we have had (for it has been *our* adventure as much as the pro-tagonist's), but encloses the film perfectly in its own uniqueness as the sole cinematic work that shakes us with its revelations of the terrors that still haunt us in the deep and unknown places of the human psyche. (Huss and Ross, 1972, pp. 22–3)

Masters like Murnau and Dreyer touched nothing that they did not transform.

In this connection we should also recall the terror-film's distinctive use of what Val Lewton and his team used to term 'the bus'—a cutting technique that worked with sound as well as sight. John Brosnan, in *Horror People*, quotes some pertinent remarks by Mark Robson on the working methods adopted by Lewton and his directors:

'We took those films very seriously. We worked long and hard on them and our standards were very, very high. My contribution to *Cat People* lay in editing techniques that were quite good. We developed a sharp cutting technique we later grew to call "the bus". We first used it in the *Cat People* when we cut from a close-up of the girl running along the street in terror to a bus coming to a stop with a loud hiss of air-brakes. The sharpness of the cutting would knock people out of their seats in a theatre. We tried to do it very often. The "bus" was done again in *Bedlam* with the hands shooting out of the cell. And we did it in *The Seventh Victim* when a frightened Jean Brooks crawls along the alley wall and suddenly there is a sound of someone laughing shrilly. I recall that after a horror sequence we always tried to give the audience relief by going to something very beautiful, lyrical if possible. We tried to make the films visually interesting . . .'
(Brosnan, 1976, pp. 80–1)

Sudden shock is, of course, one of the most important elements in the evocation of terror: 'the demonic', said Kierkegaard in *The Concept of Dread*, 'is the sudden'. Makers of terror-films have always been aware of this, as Mark Robson's words serve to show; but they have been no less aware, if they knew their business, of the importance of *contrast*. When Paul Willemen discusses the way in which Roger Corman builds sequences of his Poe-films around shock-effects—sudden appearances, sudden metamorphoses, screams, objects falling, breaking, or exploding, combinations of abrupt camera movements with movements within the frame— he is, rightly, careful to explain that effects of this kind gain such power as they have from the more leisurely pace of the rest of the narrative, from the slow pans, the hypnotizing tracking-shots and dolly-shots, in which Corman and his photographer Floyd Crosbie have embedded them. Alfred Hitchcock, indeed, has shown in film after film how much more could be gained from slow, inexorable building-up of tension than from the sudden irruption of an un-expected terror.

The statement that 'suddenness' is a central ingredient in the cinematic tale of terror stands, as we see, in need of some qualification. This may be confirmed by a glance across from the Poe-movies of Roger Corman to two of the most celebrated sequences in the work of an infinitely greater film-maker. At the very beginning of the 'Odessa Steps' sequence of *Battleship Potemkin* (1925), it will be remembered, the key word 'SUDDENLY' flashes on to the screen—but the terror it introduces is due above all to Eisenstein's brilliant editing of many individual shots. Commenting on the other famous sequence, the attack of the Teutonic Knights in *Alexander Nevsky*, Eisenstein himself has analysed how he used editing to convey and evoke terror. The passage comes from *Film Form* and has been translated by Jay Leda.

This episode passes through all the shades of an experience of increasing terror, where approaching danger makes the heart contract and the breathing irregular. The structure of this 'leaping wedge' in *Alexander Nevsky* is, with variations, exactly modelled on the inner process of such an experience. This dictated all the rhythms of the sequence—cumulative, disjunctive, the speeding up and slowing down of the movement. The boiling pulsing of an excited heart dictated the rhythm of the leaping hoofs: pictorially—the *leap* of the galloping knights; compositionally—the *beat* to the bursting point of an excited heart.

To produce the success of this sequence, both the pictorial and compositional structures are fused in the welded unity of a terrifying image—the beginning of the battle that is to be a fight to the finish.

And the event, as it is unfolded on the screen according to a timetable of the running of this or that passion . . . involves the emotions of the spectator according to the same timetable, arousing in him the same tangle of passions which originally designed the compositional scheme of the work.

This is the secret of the genuinely emotional affect [*sic*] of real composition. Employing for source the structure of human emotion, it unmistakably appeals to emotion, unmistakably arouses the complex of those feelings that gave birth to the composition. (Quoted in Barna, 1975, p. 213)

What counts is not just shock, but an imaginative montage of shocks—that was one of many lessons which Eisenstein learnt from Griffith, to whose cutting-techniques he often paid warm tribute, and of whom he said: 'All that is best in the Soviet film has its origin in *Intolerance*.'

We would also do well to remember, if we want to keep this subject in perspective, that many qualified judges have seen in 'shock' the cinematic experience *par excellence*. Walter Benjamin, for instance, was not thinking specifically of horror-movies when he linked cinematic shocks with the shocks Baudelaire had seen as characteristic of the great city and when he therefore presented the film as *the* characteristic art-form of urban man in modern times. Arnold Hauser is only one of several social historians who have agreed with Benjamin about this.

Among the most 'shocking' effects in the history of the film is the eye-cutting sequence at the opening of Buñuel's *An Andalusian Dog*; and the connection of this with effects proper to the terror-film has been convincingly formulated by David Thomson. '*An Andalusian Dog*', Thomson writes in *America in the Dark*,

> may be the first film to exploit our readiness to be victims. Our feelings are exposed to whatever enters through our eyes, and we are at the mercy of every cut whereby, in about a fiftieth of a second, and too suddenly for us to avoid it, any image can be replaced. Some juxtapositions may be emphatically violent: a girl taking a shower—an intruder with a knife. But all are inherently shocking. Our knowledge that a cut can come at any time and bring any threat ensures apprehension. Some forms—the thriller and horror movie—employ that power methodically: *Jaws* is a tormenting exercise in cutting, and those teeth are the more acute because of the stylish appropriateness. But all movies must cut, and tidiness or storytelling do not smother the threat of breakdown in cutting. (Thomson, 1978, pp. 106–7)

Images in films not only refer outwards to the world and inwards to our own minds; they also have a self-intentive reference, point back again and again to the film-medium and its manipulation.

Shock-cuts and sudden zoomings-in have, by now, become such clichés that many of us respond with relief to gentler devices, like the eerie glide of the camera towards a figure approaching it in Bergman's *The Seventh Seal* and Enrico's *An Occurrence at Owl Creek Bridge*, or the magic appearance of Joan Bennett's reflection next to her portrait in Lang's *The Woman in the Window*, provoking a shudder of the uncanny rather than the violent start of terror or the recoil of horror. In recent years wide-screen projection and depth-of-field photography have done a good deal to counteract the aesthetic of shock formulated by Eisenstein and Benjamin in their different ways—but the sudden swoop, the sudden intrusion, the sudden juxtaposition, will always remain an essential ingredient of tales of terror in the cinema. 'Like the man with no eyes in *The Birds*', Hitchcock said to Peter Bogdanovich, 'zooming the camera in—the staccato jumps are almost like catching the breath. Is it? Gasp. Gasp. Yes.'

Some experiments with cinema-magic proved, in the long run, unacceptable in terror-films. Murnau's *Nosferatu* features not only one of the most justly celebrated shock-cuts in motion-picture history—the scene that shows Jonathan Harker discovering the vampire's coffin and then, abruptly, the fanged monster—but also, during Harker's approach to the castle, a memorable sequence in accelerated motion. This has found few imitators, however, chiefly because acceleration of this kind became associated, in viewers' minds, with Keystone comedy and other such farcical fare. Super-imposition-effects much loved by cinema tricksters from Méliès onwards, and brilliantly deployed to suggest supernatural appearances and disappearances in Victor Sjöström's *The Phantom Carriage* as well as in *Nosferatu*, held their own more effectively; but Lang's later dislike of his own use of this device in *The Testament of Dr. Mabuse* derived from a feeling he shared with other masters of the terror-film: that photographic superimposition had become a cliché. Slow motion, on the other hand, though now over-employed in television advertisements, excited no ridicule and has remained a popular device in films that seek to depict and evoke terror from Epstein's *The Fall of the House of Usher* to Skolimowski's *The Shout*. Slow-motion photography, Richard Arnheim has said somewhere, affects us not as the slowing-up of ordinary movement, but rather as a strangely gliding, hovering, unearthly movement of its own.

As for Richard Fleischer's attempt, in *The Boston Strangler* (1968), to show a city in fear by means of the split-screen method—'a lot of images, of many events happening simultaneously . . . the people on one side of the screen living normally, and the body on the other' (Leyda, 1977, p. 139)—this has remained, so far, an isolated and not very successful experiment. Its full potential for the terror-film has yet to be realized.

The work which most successfully exploited cinematic tricks for terror *and* laughter—with terror predominating—is James Whale's *The Invisible Man* of 1933. Paul Gilson has described this still highly effective work as a 'voyage through the impossible' and has rightly praised the way in which raindrops define the invisible man's silhouette, transforming him into a kind of prismatic spectre, fog reveals his contours and snow those of his footsteps. Objects appear enchanted: a cigarette lights itself, a pair of pyjamas slides magically into bed. When the invisible man takes off the bandages that 'serve him as a tragic mask' he becomes a headless being that still talks—just one of many terrifying images that delight us right up to the end of the film, when the fatally wounded hero's human face and form are, at last, fully revealed.

A close look at the opening sequences of Irving Pichel's *The Hounds of Zaroff*, such as was undertaken by Thierry Kuntzel in *Communications*, xxiii (1975), may serve to alert us to the way in which the popular terror-film of the thirties made some of its best effects unheralded and untrumpeted, through its *mise en scène*. From the many examples given by Kuntzel we might pick out the intermittent presence, in the background of the ship's cabin, of a pair of stuffed fish, hunter's trophies, when the thematically so important relation between hunter and hunted is first discussed by the film's protagonists. The point of this is most clearly revealed in the shipwreck sequence that follows, in which the relation between hunter and hunted is *reversed* (for the first, but by no means the last, time in the course of the film), when men are tracked and killed by predatory fish. The American title of this work, *The Most Dangerous Game*, defines the 'hunting' theme subliminally as well as overtly broached in these opening sequences much better than the British title which I have used in this book. It may also serve to remind us of the importance that *games* of various kinds have assumed in the post-*Caligari* terror-film: the game of chess has almost become a cliché since its use in Ulmer's *The Black Cat*, and the card-game, which appears prominently in *The Hounds of Zaroff*, had its greatest moment of glory and terror in Thorold Dickinson's memorable filming of Pushkin's *The Queen of Spades* in 1948.

'Supporting characters', W. K. Everson has said of Paul Leni's *The Man Who Laughs*, made in Hollywood in 1928, 'were often deliberately photographed in bizarre angles, or with low-key lighting to add suspense and elements of horror to their fairly passive characters . . . They are shown in a long sweeping tracking shot that picks them up from below, and transforms them into inhuman demons—a forerunner of many similar shots of Karloff and Lugosi in later horror films like *The Black Cat* and *The Raven*' (Everson, 1974, p. 27). This reminds us how constantly the foreshortened perspective, the unusual camera angle, the tilt-shot, the overhead crane shot, or the worm's-eye view from below have been used for evocations of terror: looming or distorted, god-like or deliberately dwarfed figures have all figured prominently in the terror-film after *Caligari*. The freeze-frame effect, brilliantly employed by Truffaut and abused by almost everyone else, has been inverted, to excellent purpose, by Chris Marker's *La Jetée*, already discussed in this book in another context: the whole of Marker's Bergsonian film may be seen as a sequence of freeze-frames, explored by a mobile camera and interrupted by that one unforgettable shot of a girl opening her eyes in which what is frozen suddenly melts, for a few seconds, into movement, only to freeze again for ever after.

The passages quoted from Everson's *Classics of the Horror Film* at the opening of the preceding paragraph rightly insists on the important part that lighting has played in evoking terror on the screen, from the low-key lighting used in the scenes in which Death appears in Bergman's *The Seventh Seal* to the deliberate over-lighting of many sequences in George Lucas's *THX 1138*. Directors and cameramen have come up with a plethora of symbolic effects: in black and white, as when Karl Freund, in *Mad Love*, lights Lorre's bald head in such a way that one side remains in complete darkness while the other is no less brightly illuminated, directly suggesting a split personality; or in colour, as when Kubrick reflects lights and tints from the instrument panel on to the space-explorer's face-shield, in *2001*, to suggest the obliteration of man's individuality by the technology he has called into being but cannot fully control. Bowman's facial features can no longer be recognized beneath the brilliant play of lights: as striking a reminder as any in the film that Kubrick's *Space Odyssey* has no epic hero who could be compared with Homer's immortal seafarer. All this belongs, of course, to the post-*Caligari* world; but it is interesting to notice how, after many successful attempts to transcend the stage-lighting effects of studio-bound films of the silent period, recent film-makers have once again looked to the theatre for lighting-effects that would adequately suggest an uncanny atmosphere. In *Suspense in the Cinema*, Gordon Gow has described the contribution made by Freddie Francis when he was lighting-cameraman on Jack Clayton's *The Innocents*.

The governess (Deborah Kerr), lured by the sensual whispers of ghosts, moves through corridors and down a staircase, and the light from her candle seems to contain itself strangely within a circle. It was for this occasion that Francis had filters made, which were subtle variations on the single-colour filters often used in black-and-white photography . . . The Francis filters have a clear area (the pool of light), but toward the outer edges there is a range of colour, merging delicately from yellow to dark red. Attached to the camera, these filters permit one clear area of light beyond which there will be underexposed areas of increasing darkness. 'It would have been a very long job to achieve this by studio lighting,' says Francis, 'because the camera had to move, and the concentrated area of light had to move with the governess.' (Gow, 1968, pp. 30–1)

Here a sophisticated filtering-device was designed and manufactured in order to reproduce the 'roving spotlight' effect known to every theatre-goer. In much the same way the held shot, the deep-focus or wide-screen composition so often exalted over the old montage principle nowadays, is at bottom, as Stanley Kaufmann has justly said, not so much a new achievement of film aesthetics as 'a realization that the film could use, when appropriate, the 2 500 year-old "deep focus" of the theater' (Hurt, 1974, p. 71).

There has, of course, been a great deal of technical progress since the days in which the Russians so eloquently proclaimed the virtues of montage. Hand-held cameras, employed by Roger Corman and others, have not only made location shooting much easier and more economical, and thus helped to end the reign of the big studios; they have also made it possible to get nearer to terror, to move in among the participants of the story, in a way barred to the early German film-makers—though Wiene's first shot of Caligari's malevolent approach to the camera, and Lang's shot of Mabuse's eyes coming closer and closer and looming larger and larger until they fill the whole screen, are still unrivalled for concentrated rancour and menace directed at the audience. New cameras and lighting-techniques have made possible an underwater photography that has given a new visual dimension to the age-old terror of the deep—notably in Jack Arnold's poetic *The Creature from the Black Lagoon* and in the cruder but commercially much more successful *Jaws*, directed by Steven Spielberg. The wonders of recent space and science-fiction thrillers have been produced by sophisticated, often computerized, optical printers; and startling levitation effects were obtained by means of magnetic fields in *The Exorcist*. The new lenses and aspect-ratios of Cinemascope and other wide-screen techniques, dismissed by Fritz Lang as fit only for snakes and funerals, have made possible—notably in *2001* and *Solaris*—a combination of agoraphobia and claustrophobia which Wiene and his team could not even dream of, as well as occasional effects, like the multiplication of the image of a screaming woman that fills the wide screen from one end to the other, which lingers in the memory long after the puerilities of the rest of Neumann's *The Fly* are happily forgotten. A technique is only as good as the mind of the man who uses it; and when it comes to quality of imagination, there are few comparisons that the makers of *Caligari* have cause to fear.

As the terror-film grew older, directors and script-writers played more and more against their audiences' patterns of expectation. Was there a tradition that horrible things happened in the dark? Right, then: Hitchcock would have his murder committed in a brightly lit bathroom and have his lethal birds swoop out of a sunny sky. Was there a tradition that the Beast from 20 000 Fathoms released into the modern world was hostile and had to be destroyed? Right, then: Inoshiro Honda would show Godzilla helping the earth defeat a technological menace from another planet while Baby Godzilla jumps up and down and claps his claws with joy. Was there a tradition that the silhouette of a dark-clad stranger and his accompanying shadow approaching a well-lit house at night meant the approach of menace and evil? Right, then: Friedkin would have his Exorcist, the *helper* against demons, photographed in exactly that way, and his publicity-men would use that photograph again and again to go with their advertising-copy. Was there a tradition that in a post-*Psycho* film Anthony Perkins would play whatever psychotic young person the script required? Right, then: Noel Black would team him, in *Pretty Poison* (1968), with the delectable Tuesday Weld, the distillation of all healthy young drum-majorettes, and show *her* to be the real psychotic menace. A similar game is played by Stephen Weeks in *Ghost Story* (1974), where he introduces his tale of supernatural killings into a P. G. Wodehouse atmosphere and makes a children's doll the instrument of murder; and by Jerzy Skolimowski, when he has the central protagonist of *The Shout* narrate his terrifying tale while keeping the score at a cricket match. In film as in the other arts, the game of arousing, disappointing, and redirecting expectations constitutes one of the principal means by which a genre is developed and altered.

If Wiene and Carl Mayer were to return to life as the heroes of terror-films so often managed to do, they would be astonished not only at the technical changes that have transformed film-making, and not only at the development and transformation of the themes and techniques they pioneered in the German cinema, but also at the sheer quantity of films aimed at the evocation of terror now being made and shown all over the world. It is often forgotten that the terror-films we regard as so characteristic of German movie-making during the silent period represent only a handful of (not very popular, and not very widely shown) works produced by an industry that ground out hundreds of entertainment films in which the uncanny, the terrible, and the horrifying played no part at all. *Caligari*, *Waxworks*, *(Warning) Shadows*, and *Nosferatu* had nothing like the vogue that Hammer films, 'meat'-movies, and dire-creature-features have among popular audiences today. But beyond even that Wiene and his team would surely be astonished at the nudities and blood-letting that have characterized more recent terror-films. Not that suggestions of all this had been lacking in earlier days: Boris Karloff often told the anecdote of how Myrna Loy came to him in 1932, during the making of *The Mask of Fu Manchu*, to complain that she was being asked to portray 'sadistic nymphomania'. Nothing, however, could have prepared cinema-audiences of the twenties and thirties for the sado-masochistic imagery of Jean Rollin, with its close-ups of vampire-bats burrowing into female pubic hair, the gruesome blood-letting that seems to form the chief *raison d'être* of many of the films of Herschell Gordon Lewis, or even the often reproduced image of Yutte Stensgaard in Jimmy Sangster's *Lust for a Vampire*, which shows that actress as Le Fanu's Carmilla

> sitting up in her coffin in a state of bloody voluptuousness: shreds of drenched and tattered clothing hang ineffectually over her right [this should, I think, read: 'left'] shoulder, blood drips from both sides of her mouth, forming a little river on her neck which runs down onto both exposed breasts.

That description comes from David Pirie's *The Vampire Cinema*, where it is followed by memorable speculations on the *raison d'être* of such images after sex had been, by and large, taken out of the context of diabolical temptation and put back into the bedroom.

Now supposing that this was not a still from a Gothic fantasy but from a psychological horror movie about a female sadist. Immediately the shot becomes an impossibility. The British censor would only pass it in a film of immense artistic prestige, the American MPAA would either give it an 'X' (which in American terms is the kiss of death for a horror movie; even *The Exorcist* got a more lenient 'R' rating) or ask that the shot be cut to facilitate a less restrictive grading. Clearly in the early 1970s the supernatural was still able to go further than the sex movie, especially in the suggestion of sadistic pleasure. (Pirie, 1977, p. 100)

The implications of Pirie's analysis will be followed out further in the Conclusion of this book; but before we come to that, we must take a closer look at another, related image from a very similar source.

CHAPTER 8

An Image and its Context

'He should be reported to the authorities!'
'We're not in Wimbledon now, Helen. I doubt if there
are any authorities to report him to.'

Dracula—Prince of Darkness (1965–6)

THE scene is a sparsely furnished room in whose background we
can make out a set of fringed shelves with what might be artist's
materials, a cupboard with a vase, a small table serving as an
altar on which two candles illuminate a statuette of Virgin and
Child, and a slatted, solid-looking door, while the foreground is
occupied by a large table. On this table, which is brightly illuminated, lies a woman dressed in a long, diaphanous night-gown;
her eyes are dilated with terror, her mouth is wide open in a
scream revealing unnaturally long and pointed eye-teeth; her
arms, from which the sleeves have fallen back and which are
therefore bare, are firmly held by two monks dressed in black, her
legs, slightly apart, are similarly held. Above and behind her
towers a burly bearded monk, wearing a white robe and cowl
with a black tabard; his left hand grasps a pointed wooden stake,
while his right, whose wrist has been reinforced with what looks
like a leather wrist-strap, holds a hammer which is poised to
come down on the stake with great force. The point of the stake is
firmly wedged below the woman's left breast; and the scene is lit
from right to left in such a way that the shadow of the stake falls
across her breasts and rib-cage and that the central group is fully
visible. Behind the table, in front of the door in the left background,
we discern another figure, a handsome youngish man whose face
and stance are clearly meant to convey a tense excitement; he
is dressed in a secular suit of sober cut, with a high collar and
cravat that suggest the Victorian period. The fringes on the shelves
in the background also give a Victorian impression.

There can be few men and women in the Western world today
who would fail to recognize the most general context of the still

photograph that depicts this scene. The woman's pointed teeth, the stake over the heart, and the hammer about to descend upon it, clearly indicates that it comes from a vampire-story and that it portrays the moment at which a female vampire is about to be 'released' from her life-in-death. It is also easy to surmise that it must be a still from, or a specially posed publicity photograph for, a film. The violent contortion of the struggling vampire, the use of monks in (to say the least) equivocal postures, the bright lighting, and (in some prints) the colour photography make it obvious that this is not an image from the Universal 'horror' cycle of the 1930s; its careful, rather stolid composition and the absence of nudity suggest that it is not the work of such neo-baroque stylists as Mario Bava and Jean Rollin. If one recognizes, in the central pair, the actress Barbara Shelley as the Vampire and the actor Andrew Keir as the Vampire-Killer, and in the secular figure at the back that hero of many a British television thriller, Francis Matthews, one will immediately guess that the film is part of the Hammer 'horror' or 'fantasy' series of the fifties and sixties; and, more particularly, that it comes from one of the works of that much lauded and equally much abused doyen of Hammer horrors, Terence Fisher. And this, indeed, would be the right guess: we are looking at a still from *Dracula—Prince of Darkness*, scripted by John Sansom, directed by Terence Fisher, designed by Bernard Robinson, photographed by Michael Reed, with music by James Bernard, made in 1965 and released in 1966, towards the end of what French critics admire as the 'golden age' of the British fantasy-film.

The powers that governed Hammer Films during this 'golden age' have never been shy of publicizing the principles that guided their movie-making and earned them the Queen's Award for Industry. The quotations which follow can all be found in John Brosnan's collection of interviews and press-clippings in *Horror People*; ample supporting material is contained in the semi-official *The House of Horror. The Story of Hammer Films*, edited by Allen Eyles, Robert Adkinson, and Nicholas Fry. 'We hate message films; we make entertainment' (Sir James Carreras). 'The best film is the one that makes the most money. Our job is to entertain and promote something that is really exploitable. Exploitation is the thing' (Michael Carreras). 'To the sceptics who peer at me super-ciliously and demand to know why I make pictures like *Dracula* and *Frankenstein*, I answer that it is my job—I do it for the money.

And to those who depict me as the exploiter of the basest human tastes and desires for the sake of profit, the answer is equally simple: I don't drive the public into the cinemas. They go because they want to go, but only when there is something they want to see. That they go to see the pictures I make apparently in their millions surely is pretty strong proof of that. There is no more simple or positive formula to motion-picture success than the oldest one in the showman's creed: Give 'em what they want and they'll keep coming back for more' (Anthony Hinds, who, under the pen-name 'John Elder', wrote many scripts for Hammer films; that for *Dracula—Prince of Darkness* is based on 'an idea' by him). 'I know the film industry must allow at least forty per cent of its total output to have thoughtful and artistic ingredients, but that is for other producers to provide, not Hammer. But for those other producers to exist, and to have the opportunity for self-expression, you've got to maintain a healthy industry. We like to think we keep the industry as a whole healthy by getting people into the cinemas; and while they're there they can see the trailers for those other types of films and hopefully they'll go and see them as well' (Michael Carreras).

In accordance with this philosophy the Hammer management turned out thrillers, science-fiction films, spin-offs of television series, fantasies about life in 'prehistoric' times, as well as the terror-films or horror-movies for which it is best known. It was all done on very modest budgets and tight time-schedules that produced some 140 films in twenty-five years. In their studios at Bray, a converted country house near Maidenhead which still served them when *Dracula—Prince of Darkness* was made, they built up a devoted team of specialists in terror-fantasy headed by directors like Terence Fisher, Roy Ward Baker, Freddie Francis, and John Gilling; script-writers Jimmy Sangster, 'John Elder', and John Sampson; the art-director Bernard Robinson, who did wonders with whatever material or landscape he found to hand; the cameramen Jack Asher and Michael Reed, the composer James Bernard, the make-up expert Roy Ashton, and other technicians lower down the hierarchy but equally essential for a smooth running of this fantasy-factory. And under the bright lights which became one of the hallmarks of the Hammer style (no half-lit cobwebbed Universal sets for them!) they gathered a company of actors who became as identified with the terror-fantasies of the fifties and sixties as Karloff, Lugosi, Fay Wray, Atwill, and Van Sloan had been with those of the thirties: Christopher Lee, Peter Cushing, Barbara Shelley, Richard Wordsworth, Michael Gough, and many others. This company included actors who went on to do other things—like the young Oliver Reed, the most successful werewolf of them all—or who, like Bette Davis and Tallulah Bankhead, were nearing the end of a successful career in films of a different type.

Terence Fisher, born in 1904, was not new to films when the Hammer organization, emboldened by the success of its science-fiction fantasy *The Quatermass Experiment*, asked him to direct yet another version of *Frankenstein*. He had come into the movie-business from life as a merchant seaman and in the rag trade, and had been making films, with modest success, since 1947; but none of his works had ever found such favour with the public at large, in Britain and abroad, or aroused such indignation among the 'quality' critics, as *The Curse of Frankenstein* which Hammer released in 1957. C. A. Lejeune, writing in the *Observer*, ranked it 'among the half dozen most repulsive films I have ever encountered'. Such indignation, however, only whetted the public's appetite and increased the film's success; Fisher was commissioned to make a new *Dracula* to go with this new *Frankenstein*, and when that too proved exceedingly popular and profitable—not least in the United States, where it was given the title *Horror of Dracula* to distinguish it from the Browning–Lugosi version of 1931—a whole series of similar remakes, of sequels and parallels followed in quick succession. Like Carreras and Hinds, Fisher has not been niggardly of comments on the spirit in which he approached his task. Here are three from Brosnan's book: 'I was just a hack director who was asked to direct their picture.' 'I look on myself, not as an intellectual film director, but as an emotional film director.' 'It is no good going into a long spiel of intellectual bullshit about why you do things, or why you don't—the only thing that can speak is what you've actually directed, and all you've directed is a visual interpretation of the written word [Fisher means the screen-play] and perhaps bugged it about a bit—given it a few more guts in one direction or a few less in another.' It would be quite wrong, however, to see anything basely cynical in this 'honest hack' attitude, just as it would be wrong to see anything cynical or tongue-in-cheek in the performances of Christopher Lee, Peter Cushing, or Barbara Shelley. A quotation from *The House of Horror* is apposite here. 'The real task of the fantasy director', Fisher is there quoted as saying, 'is to bring integrity of intention to his film-making. I always ask for a similar response from my actors, and I rarely fail to get it, especially from Peter Cushing and Christopher Lee. If my films reflect my own personal view of the world in any way, it is in their showing of the ultimate victory of good over evil, in which I do believe. It may take human beings a long time to achieve this, but I do believe that this is how events work out in the end' (p. 15). Fisher's central protagonists, therefore, never 'send up' their roles in the way Vincent Price likes to do; there is nothing tongue-in-cheek about Christopher Lee's lean and elegant Dracula, for instance, whose gentlemanly garb and appearance and deliberately played-up masculine attractiveness stand in piquant relation to the bared fangs, red eyes, and animal-like snarls which appear when Dracula's blood-lust is up. 'One must immerse oneself completely in the character,' Lee has said, 'and forget one's own personality entirely. The portrayal from start to finish must be straight, honest and sincere.' Peter Cushing and Barbara Shelley clearly share this view.

The framework, then, within which the Hammer team works, is that of a competitive society, in which articles manufactured in series and according to approved general formulas are offered in the open market to potential customers who have to be lured to buy, in order to ensure the company that offers these products, and its financial backers, a reasonable return on their investment. This means that the company will not be able to go far beyond the taste and tolerance level of its own society or other societies within which markets are sought, but that it will constantly seek to offer stronger thrills, more sensations, than before, in order to stimulate appetites jaded by its own products and those of its competitors in television as well as in films. The standards and tolerance of the British Board of Film Censors and similar institutions abroad will thus be tested constantly, as more blood and—later—more nudity become acceptable. Scenes will even be shot in two or three different versions, to take account of differing standards in Britain, the U.S.A., and Japan. This does not mean, however, that the goods offered will be made deliberately shoddy: on the contrary, Fisher and his team clearly try to do the best they can within the limits set to them by their small budgets, their restricted shooting-schedule, the tiny space in and around Bray available for their settings, the necessity of attracting a paying public, the lack of a

British film industry that encourages bold experiments, and the boundaries of their own talent, taste, and imagination.

In Jack Asher and Bernard Robinson Hammer Films found a cameraman and designer who could help them achieve a fantastic realism that contrasts with the more baroque fantasies of a Mario Bava or a Nicolas Roeg. Within his almost documentary technique Jack Asher achieved, as has recently been shown, remarkable effects through colour contrasts that would be noticed almost subliminally: as when he surrounds the pale faces and hands of sick or evil characters with particularly bright areas of colour in order to heighten their otherness (cf. Jung, Weil, and Seesslen, 1977, p. 17). Compared with Asher's sober brilliance the work of Michael Reed, who photographed *Dracula—Prince of Darkness*, seems sadly lack-lustre.

When the first Hammer *Frankenstein* and *Dracula* films hit the screens, many English critics were shocked and outraged by the overt sexuality, and the modest but nevertheless visible bloodletting, which distinguished the Hammer versions from the Universal ones; but here Hammer was so soon overtaken by continental and American film-makers that it is hard now for anyone to imagine what all the fuss was about. Terence Fisher, indeed, had an unmistakable streak of Puritanism in his make-up which led him on more than one occasion to counter moralizing attacks on his films by explaining that in portraying Dracula's sexuality more openly than Tod Browning had done he was merely conveying 'the fundamental power of evil' that had to be overcome in the last reel. He denied with equal vehemence that the blood-letting shown in his films was ever gratuitous: it was part of his theme, connected either with perverted religious ritual or with the release of vampires from the force that prevented them from finding the peace of death which they desired. His published comments on such matters reveal a morality resembling that of the Victorian society whose modes of dress and styles of decoration were so lovingly recreated by his art-director and designers; what his films show, however, will not always fit easily into the mould suggested by this copy-book maxim morality, this simple opposition of 'good' and 'evil'.

The society within which this middle-aged director and his (usually younger) team created their fantasy-films, and to which these films appealed in the first instance, was that of a Britain newly orientated towards 'youth', 'vitality', 'creativity', 'energy', 'originality', 'life', and 'excitement'; an England changing course from the era of Harold Macmillan (whose slogan 'you've never had it so good' survived his reign along with the phrase 'the wind of change') to that of Harold Wilson and Edward Heath; an England in which 'classless', 'unstuffy', 'straightforward', 'toughly professional', 'down to earth', 'sceptical', 'aware', and 'irreverent' were accepted terms of praise, in which the 'satire-industry' flourished, in which sexual activity was discussed and exhibited with a frankness never known before; the England of the Beatles and Carnaby Street boutiques; the England of miniskirts and eclectic modes of dress that drew freely on the discarded fashions of the Victorian and the Edwardians; the England of 'swinging London', which saw itself as 'the entertainment capital of the world'—but also the England of anti-nuclear demonstrations, Aldermaston marches, Vietnam protests, and Cold War consciousness as well as that of race-riots, the Kray and Richardson gangs, the Profumo and Devonshire sex-scandals, the Great Train Robbery, and the Moors Murders. It was the England of 'Free Cinema' and Woodfall films, with their nostalgia for working-class culture and Northern grittiness, but also that of the Theatre of Cruelty; the England of Dick Lester's frenzied comedies, but also that of Polanski's *Repulsion*, Watkins's *The War Game*, and Edward Bond's *Saved*. Christopher Booker, who has admirably documented these trends in *The Neophiliacs*, has spoken of the popularity of spy-stories in this period, which extended from the mid-fifties to the late sixties: stories like Ian Fleming's James Bond series 'in which no-one's identity was certain, in which self assertive lone heroes could wander at will, in any disguise, through any social milieu, and in which acts of violence and promiscuity, vaguely condoned by the fact that the heroes were always fighting for "our side" against "the enemy", could take place at any time, without any need for elaborate explanation' (Booker, 1970, p. 186). The early James Bond movies, which are now regarded as suitable entertainment for children, are to my mind potentially more harmful and degrading than any Hammer horror-fantasy—particularly through the way in which 'physical beastliness is used to get cheap laughs' (Wood and Walker, 1970), and through their persistent reduction of sexual mores to tomcat level.

It is no accident that the rise of Hammer Films accompanied the decline of Ealing Studios, with their increasingly cosy distaste for commerce, for horror, for violence, along with the emotional inhibition, the deference to age and authority, and the cult of lovable provincial eccentrics, which have been so brilliantly described by Charles Barr in his book on the Ealing style. Hammer Films released the very forces that Ealing Studios, after the exorcism of *Dead of Night* and *Kind Hearts and Coronets* (1949), sought to deny—and they were aided and abetted in this by the *Carry On* farces (1958 ff.), whose cheerful vulgarity exercised itself on themes Ealing would have considered shocking and in bad taste.

In the 1950s it was discovered, by means of various polls and public relations enquiries, that 70 per cent of those who went to horror-movies were aged between 12 and 25. This acted as a spur to manufacturers of such products to cash in on the newly affluent youth market by providing more of the same; and it also acted as a reminder, if reminder were needed, that screen-monsters had always held a special fascination for adolescents. There is, after all, as psychologists have frequently pointed out, a good deal of analogy between the fate of such monsters and the adolescent experience: an appearance felt to be awkward and ungainly, the sprouting of hair in unaccustomed places, conflicts with father/creators, experiments with 'bodies' in secluded spots, advances towards others in which aggression takes the form of love and love that of aggression . . . Films like Whale's *Frankenstein*, however, which were made without thought of a teenage market, still have a good deal more to say on various processes and stages of socialization than the dire products which indicate that they were manufactured specifically to appeal to younger audiences by such titles as *I Was a Teenage Frankenstein* ('Body of a boy!', the advertisements proclaimed, 'Mind of a monster! Soul of an unearthly thing!').

Despite their escapist tendencies British terror-films of the Hammer era are by no means devoid of political and social criticism; one need think only of Joseph Losey's *The Damned* of 1961, with its frightening presentation of an ice-cold civil servant, or of *Scream and Scream Again*, which Gordon Hessler directed for Amicus in 1969 and which Fritz Lang described as the first adult horror-film he had ever seen. In this last-named film we find humanoids invading the very centre of power and taking over, in human disguise, the British government. Such entertainments brought echoes of the Profumo scandal too, and reminded audiences, by means of their presentations of Victorian families, of the schizo-phrenogenic family-life indicted by R. D. Laing and his disciples in and out of the cinema. And it is not irrelevant to recall that despite Christopher Lee's reservations ('There is only one Dracula, and his period must never be changed') Hammer's *The Satanic Rites of Dracula*, directed by Alan Gibson in 1973, was to show us Stoker's vampire-count holed up in a modern office-block, where he assumes the name Denham and builds up a business empire. This once again takes the popular analogy of 'vampire' and 'blood-sucking capitalist' literally; but the film is so crude and clumsy that one longs for the old-fashioned Draculas who play on fears engendered by the foreign and aristocratic rather than those engendered by property speculation and financial wizardry.

Attempts to relate a given film to the society within which and for which it is produced must always remain speculative, and must always take into account the internal development of film-language and the film-industry. *Dracula—Prince of Darkness* has a place in the history of the rhetoric of terror in the cinema and more particularly in that of the neo-Gothic sub-group of the terror-film. It is part of a wide variety of films offered during the 1960s to audiences anxious to be safely terrified. The British market was dominated by Hammer, of course, which had had great success in exporting its products (and its star Christopher Lee) to other countries, and which had recently revived the werewolf legend in *Curse of the Werewolf* (1961), remade an old Lon Chaney vehicle (*The Phantom of the Opera*, 1962), brought back vampires in various guises (*The Brides of Dracula*, 1960, *Kiss of the Vampire*, 1964), emulated *Psycho* with *Paranoiac* (1963) and *Fanatic* (1965), and transferred classical mythology to a modern setting with *The Gorgon* (1964). Hammer no longer had the British horror-market to itself, however. A new firm, Amicus Productions, had started up which also specialized in terror-films and drew on much the same reserves of acting and talents as Hammer. Its main contribu-tion was a revival of the format that had been pioneered in Germany by Richard Oswald's *Uncanny Tales* of 1919 and had produced its British classic in *Dead of Night*: the multi-story format of such films as *Dr. Terror's House of Horrors* (1964). Where Oswald and his team of writers, however, had drawn their themes largely from the nineteenth-century ghost-story, Amicus consciously provided cinematic equivalents of the (largely American) horror-comics which reached their peak of popularity in the sixties and attracted a good deal of the kind of hostility that brings publicity in its wake. Other British firms and producers also jumped on to the 'horror' bandwagon: notably Independent Artists, who made the very respectable *Night of the Eagle* (or *Burn, Witch, Burn*), directed by Sidney Hayers in 1961. The most serious rivals, however, with whose work Hammer had to contend in the early sixties, were without a doubt an American director, Roger Corman, and an American company, American International Pictures or AIP. Corman's series of adaptations of Edgar Allan Poe's writings for AIP ('Poe supplies the beginning and the end, Roger supplies the rest'), began with *The Fall of the House of Usher* in 1960; it was followed in quick succession by *The Pit and the Pendulum* (1961), *The Premature Burial* (1961), *The Raven* (1963), *The Tomb of Ligeia* (1964), and, in that same year, what is generally thought the best of all Corman's films: *The Masque of the Red Death*, superbly photographed in colour by Nicolas Roeg. Roeg and the camera-man Corman usually worked with, Floyd Crosby, made the spiritual desert of his movies at least visually tolerable. Besides Poe, Corman enlisted H. P. Lovecraft (*The Haunted Palace*, 1963, has little to do with Poe's poem of that name: it is a fairly straight adaptation of Lovecraft's *The Case of Charles Dexter Ward*, tricked out with modish mutants); he anticipated Amicus by reviving the multi-story format with his Poe-anthology *Tales of Terror* (1963); and he initiated a series of films that exploited the grotesquely humorous potential of horror-movie imagery with *The Raven* (1963). Not content with these demonstrations of what could be done with tiny budgets, shooting-schedules measured in days, a gifted cameraman and art-director, and a combination of ageing stars of great talents with younger stars that often had no talent at all, Corman also gave one of his protégés, Francis Ford Coppola, the chance to make his mark with an axe-murder horror entitled *Dementia 13* in the U.S.A., but released as *The Haunted and the Hunted* in Britain. This was in 1963, the same year that saw the inauguration of Herschell Gordon Lewis's sadistic 'meat-movie' series with *Blood Feast*, followed in 1964 by *Two Thousand Maniacs*. These films were not widely seen in Britain; British audiences of the early sixties made do with the latest of William Castle's 'gimmick' films, another murderous-maniac tale entitled *Homicidal* (1961), whose special feature was a 'fright break' to warn faint-hearted members of the audience when to avert their eyes from the screen. Italy, Spain, and Japan also sent films with 'horror' ingredients: Bava's *The Mask of the Demon* (known abroad under titles like *Black Sunday* and *Revenge of the Vampire*) was held up by the British censor for many years; *Crypt of Horror* (*La Maldición de los Karnstein*, 1963) disappeared from view almost immediately, despite the presence of Christopher Lee; but Shindo's *Onibaba*, with its physical horror and overt sexuality, was widely seen. Along with all this came films in which masters of the cinema showed, in various ways discussed earlier in this book, how meaningful terror could be projected: Hitchcock with *Psycho* and *The Birds*, Losey with *The Damned*, Wise with *The Haunting*, Marker with *La Jetée*, Kobayashi with *Kwaidan*, and Polanski with *Repulsion*. Into this scene *Dr. Strangelove*, Stanley Kubrick's grim horror-comic of atomic catastrophe, inserted an image of the 'mad scientist' which parodied not only Klein-Rogge's performance in *Metropolis* but also Lionel Atwill's in *Son of Frankenstein*.

Such parodies were alien to the Hammer style of the early sixties. Hammer Films played their horrors straight. They were not, they could not be, immune to the pressures of the competition just described, pressures which inevitably impelled them towards more overt sexuality and more explicit violence on the screen. The need to differentiate their products from those offered by television companies added further impulses in the same direction. As early as 1960 Christopher Lee quipped about the 'harmlessness' of the Hammer remake of *The Mummy*, in which 'I only kill three people—and not in a ghastly way. I just break their necks' (Halliwell, 1978, p. 12). But at the time of their greatest prosperity Hammer were in fact becoming quite an old-fashioned organization, with their studio team controlled by men wholeheartedly involved in the making and distribution of films, working in what was by all accounts a cosy family atmosphere that surrounded the woman who made the sandwiches as much as the technicians, actors, directors, and studio-heads. This at a time when studio-lots were being sold off to property-developers all over Hollywood and control passed from the old studio-moguls to vast multinational companies! There is, in fact, a telling resemblance between the family atmosphere at Hammer's Bray studios and that at Ealing Studios on which all who experienced it look back with such nostalgia.

Hammer Films appealed to their young and (to a lesser but not inconsiderable extent) their middle-aged audiences through their unselfconscious updating of material that had proved its attractiveness in an earlier period of the cinema; through their reassuring use of clichés in what looked like new and bolder contexts; through their portrayal of sexual attractiveness, their consciousness of violence and animal passions always threatening to break out, their questioning of personal identity (is my sister, my brother, my closest friend a vampire, a werewolf, or a zombie?), their occasional implicit indictment of social corruption; through their attempts at simple distinction between good and evil, subverted, again and again, by the ambiguity of the tales they told and the actors they employed; and last but by no means least through their revivalism: their fascinated evocations of the dress, decoration, and manners of the Victorian period, their reintroduction of the Byronic hero, their conscious or unconscious return to the traditions of the Gothic novel and the Victorian romance.

Dracula—Prince of Darkness represents a triple revival, a threefold return.

(i) It reintroduces a character created by Bram Stoker in 1897, in a novel which itself drew on a great deal of historical and literary tradition.

(ii) Its Dracula recalls the smooth-faced, immaculately dressed count of the Universal movies rather than Stoker's martial, bewhiskered creation.

(iii) It begins with a sequence from the film *Dracula* (or *Horror of Dracula*) which Fisher had directed some seven years earlier.

The sequence that is repeated at the opening of *Dracula—Prince of Darkness* is that which had closed the earlier *Dracula* film; it shows Peter Cushing's Van Helsing tearing down the curtains to let the sunlight fall on Christopher Lee's vampire-count who is then, in a beautifully managed series of shots, seen to disintegrate and crumble into dust blown away by the wind. In the *Daily Telegraph* of 14 April 1972 Hammer's special-effects man, Les Bowie, revealed how this twice-seen sequence had been put together:

The whole sequence is filmed backwards, starting with the little pile of dust that will be left at the end. He then adds more dust and films the bigger pile. He continues take by take, all in an air of mystery with fumes blowing, first adding a few bones to the pile, then a few more bones, then a skull with fragments of cloth and hair hanging on to it, and then bones with flesh on them. Putty makes useful flesh. He then reverses the whole sequence of perhaps 20 takes, starting with the whole body and ending with the dust, and the result is a finished disintegration running for, say, one and a quarter minutes.

When fitting this sequence into *Dracula—Prince of Darkness*, Fisher and his team gave the lie to those who tell us that the cinema has no equivalent of quotation marks: they enclosed it in a cloud-wreathed frame which sets it apart from the rest of the film and signals that it comes from a different though related work.

As yet the title *Dracula—Prince of Darkness* has not appeared on the screen; but its biblical ring is anticipated by the religiose tone of the voice which tells us, as the images just described are unrolled: 'Here at last was an adversary armed with sufficient knowledge of vampirism to destroy him. . . . Thousands had been enslaved by the obscene cult of vampirism—now, the fountainhead himself perished.' The adversary, of course, is Van Helsing, the secular scholar-scientist who arms himself with the cross in his combat with what the voice-over has called the 'obscene cult' of vampirism. The dreadful mixed metaphor ('the fountainhead . . . perished') is only too typical, alas, of the linguistic texture of Hammer films.

The religious and 'cult' suggestions of these opening images and words are carried on, before the main title goes up to reinforce them, by one of those funeral sequences which had become a standard opening gambit of uncanny fantasy-movies since the days of James Whale's *Frankenstein* and Victor Halperin's *White Zombie*. At this funeral a tearful mother is seen arguing with a priest and with villagers who are about to drive a stake through the heart of a recently deceased girl suspected of vampirism—indicating at once that the villagers are far from considering the 'obscene cult' vanquished for ever. What happens then has been described by Alain Silver and James Ursini in their book *The Vampire Film*.

Figures move from foreground to background; then the camera pans with the crazed [mother] as a man positions a stake over the girl's heart and raises a hammer. Before he can strike, a shot reverberates on the sound track. At the moment of maximum anxiety caused by the men's action and the unseen report of a firearm and sustained by the unbroken continuity of image, there is a cut to a low-angle long-shot of a mounted figure. This stylised introduction of Father Sandor as he rides out of the shadows to accuse the [villagers] of 'blasphemous sacrilege . . . and superstition', identifies him instantly as a dominant figure and, the viewer anticipates from convention, the representative of reason. Sandor is unusual in that he combines the function of priest (evident from his monkish garb) with those of hunter (the gun he carries) and scientist (his contempt for the villagers' hysteria). (Silver and Ursini, 1975, pp. 83–4)

Father Sandor is, in fact, a reincarnation of Van Helsing (whose armoury had included a cross and sacred wafers, and who had also been a scientist and a hunter) pushed further in the direction of organized religion, aggressiveness, and celibacy. We feel more uneasy, however, in his presence than in that of Van Helsing: there is surely something disturbing in those low-angled shots of a monk who rides out against 'blasphemous sacrilege' and 'superstition' shooting off his gun!

The pre-credits sequences described so far are meant to be taking place in some Carpathian or Transylvanian setting, though regular cinema-goers will have no difficulty in recognizing the Bray and Black Park background familiar from many previous Hammer epics. What follows introduces Victorian England into this 'foreign' ambience: we meet two English couples travelling in a horse-drawn carriage and alighting at an inn, in the approved fashion of terror-movies. They are Charles and Diana Kent, a bright young man and his lively young wife, who are accompanied on their tour of the sights of Europe by Charles's more staid brother Alan with his wife, the prim, reserved, rather unadaptable, super-English Helen. At the inn they meet, not only the usual assortment of muttering rustics, but also Father Sandor (he *would* haunt inns!) in a rather different mood, warning them against visiting the castle near the town to which they are about to proceed. They disregard his warning, of course; are abandoned at the dusky crossroads by their coachman and met by a driverless carriage which they mount, despite Helen's misgivings, and which carries them to the castle. It is notable that all the scenes so far—the funeral sequence, the inn with its superstitious villagers and well-meant warnings, the abandonment at the crossroads, the sinister carriage in the gathering gloom, the arrival at a castle in the Carpathian Mountains—had been staple ingredients of terror-movies ever since *Nosferatu* and—especially—since Universal's first adaptation of Bram Stoker's *Dracula* in 1931. But within his wide-screen, coloured 'Techniscope' images Fisher and his team play variations on these old favourites: most of all in their substitution of an unconventional monk-figure for Van Helsing, underlined by the appearance of Peter Cushing's familiar incarnation of Van Helsing in the first pre-credits sequence.

The next scene again brings a variation on an old favourite: the travellers enter the castle and find no one to receive them, though the fire is lit, the table is laid, and they are clearly expected. They investigate the rooms, find their beds made up and their luggage laid out, and then return to the dining-room to be suddenly startled—it is once more the newly sensitized Helen who is the first to notice what there is to be noticed—by a dark figure looming in a doorway and stepping out into the light. Fisher had managed a similar scene particularly well in what will always remain his best film, the *Dracula* (or *Horror of Dracula*) he made in 1958: 'The boy standing in the hall of the house turns and looks up at the staircase, and way up above is the figure of Dracula, silhouetted at the top of the stairs. The camera is shooting up towards this figure as he descends, still in silhouette, towards us. The audience expects the worst possible horror as he comes right up to the camera, then into view comes this charming, handsome man. The shock-effect is totally successful.' (This is Fisher's own description, in *The House of Horror*, of a scene in which he takes a justifiable pride.) In *Dracula—Prince of Darkness*, however, it is not Christopher Lee's Dracula who appears to the startled visitors, but merely a dark-clad servant, Klove, who explains that his master is dead but that he extends hospitality to travellers even beyond the grave. The travellers thereupon sit down to partake of that hospitality, and over the supper-table we hear again the sort of double-edged conversation which has become familiar to cinema-goers ever since Bela Lugosi's Dracula informed Dwight Frye's Renfield with a significant pause before the last word: 'I never drink —wine'. 'My master died without issue', Klove tells the visitors, and adds, with heavy emphasis: 'in the accepted sense of the term.' Charles in his innocence offers a toast to their 'dead' host, which has an irony of which he is not conscious: 'Here's to him. May he rest in peace'—whereupon a thunderclap is heard, in the best Gothic tradition, and Fisher points his camera at Helen's glass to show that she has not joined in the toast along with the others.

The guests now retire to their rooms; and as they do so there follows what has become the best-known sequence in the film: an 'objective' travelling-shot along the corridors, which suggests an unseen presence prowling the house. Corridors and staircases, the indeterminate spaces between rooms, with shadows cast by banisters like imprisoning bars, have always—as we saw earlier—played a prominent part in the iconography of the terror-film. And so, of course, have cellars. In *Dracula—Prince of Darkness* the way leads downwards: a 'subjective' travelling-shot shows Alan lured into the cellars by Klove; he is stabbed to death, is suspended over Dracula's ashes, and then has his throat cut. This was about as far as British films had ever gone in the direction of physical horror, and the critics were duly outraged. Terence Fisher was unrepentant, however: 'Come, come,' he said to John Brosnan, 'What was horrifying about that? It was a religious ritual. I said to the actor at the time: "Play it like a religious ritual", and you never saw the throat actually being cut, all you saw was the blood falling on the ashes. And he was supposed to be dead anyway.'

What the audience does see, in this parody of religious ritual, is blood dripping on to the ashes in glorious Technicolour (the red of blood and the green of decay were Hammer's favoured hues); a blue mist forms, and a hand reconstitutes itself, groping its way out of the sarcophagus. Klove then lures Helen down into the cellar, where out of the darkness Christopher Lee's Dracula comes towards her in a black coat lined with scarlet, suave, smiling, and baring his animal-like fangs.

Alan is now dead, and Helen one of the undead, a bride of Dracula. One hardly recognizes, in the sexually alluring and threatening figure that Barbara Shelley now presents, the prim matron of the opening sequences. The scene changes to Father Sandor's monastery, where Diana and Charles find temporary refuge from the murderous Dracula and his helpers; in an effective sequence, again recalling earlier *Dracula* films, Helen appears at the monastery window to lure Diana away, while a monastic reincarnation of the zoophagous lunatic Renfield, one Brother Ludwig, whom we had earlier seen illuminating manuscripts, affords entrance to Dracula himself. As in Bram Stoker's book, Dracula makes his new female victim drink his own blood from a self-inflicted gash. He sucks and he gives suck. While Helen is staked by Father Sandor in Brother Ludwig's cell, Dracula abducts Diana with the help of the ever-faithful Klove. Father Sandor and Charles give chase, Klove is killed, Diana is snatched from the vampire's clutches, and the vampire himself disappears beneath the ice of a frozen river which is cracked open by Father Sandor's gun. Charles and Diana can now return to the safety of England, Father Sandor to the sanctity of his monastery and—an important nuance— his book-lined study; while Dracula—well, this new method of ridding the world of him, suggested by a remark in Bram Stoker's novel, leaves the door wide open for yet another 'return', yet another profitable sequel.

Terence Fisher's most eloquent apologist in England, David Pirie, has described this director's work in terms which may not reach the ecstatic heights of those used by French Hammer-enthusiasts, but which are nevertheless more favourable than those employed by most other British film-critics of comparable stature. In *A Heritage of Horror* Pirie described Fisher's 'solemn, almost pedantic style', his relatively static direction of the camera, as akin to that of the nineteenth-century story-teller, and therefore more appropriate to his subject than the fashionable zoomings of his televisual contemporaries. Pirie explains Fisher's lack of technical adventurousness, the scarcity of flashback and dream sequences in his work, and, indeed, his lack of psychological insight as virtues rather than failings: virtues akin to 'a quality of robustness', an 'English form of logic within fantasy', and the ability to create 'a powerful atmosphere augmented by an under-lying sexuality' which Pirie also finds in 'the best Gothic novelists' of the English language. One may quarrel with Pirie's positive evaluation of all this—but the description which accompanies and prompts this evaluation is surely just. He then goes on, again in a context of praise rather than blame, to describe the 'universe' created by Fisher and his Hammer team of writers, cameramen, and designers at Bray and, later, at Elstree:

The universe in which [Fisher's films] are set is strictly dualistic, divided rigidly between ultimate Good and ultimate Evil, Light and Darkness, Spirit and Matter, while visually the opposition is more often expressed in images of bourgeois splendour juxtaposed with those of madness, decay and death. The two sides fight out their battles as macrocosmic chess-games in which human pawns are lured from one side to the other, and the heroes are Renaissance scholars,[1] scientists and doctors whose weapons are items of occult knowledge and power: ritual formulae, books, crucifixes, etc. The agents of evil are vampires, werewolves, gorgons, mummies, apparitions and monsters of all kinds, but they are also prostitutes, corrupt sadistic

---

[1] Fisher and Renaissance scholars! The mind boggles at the juxtaposition.

noblemen, Fatal Women, sinister foreigners and English gentlemen. In Fisher's work evil is usually highly attractive on the surface and is never reflected by human deformity which rather reflects suffering and goodness . . . At times . . . the two opposing forces clash in one man and the result is highly ambiguous but usually ultimately destructive. . . .

Pirie then speaks of the 'vividly moralistic attitude towards sex' exhibited in films directed for Hammer by Terence Fisher, and adds:

The raw sexual attractiveness of evil was to reach its peak in the vampire movies where overt sexuality becomes synonymous with decay and death . . . In Fisher's films it is essential for the soul to come to terms with its bodily prison for the duration of its stay on earth, but there is a terrible danger that the shell of matter will begin to dominate ît. For this reason the most powerful and spiritual males in his films are celibate. . . . (Pirie, 1973, pp. 51–2)

Fisher himself, though suspicious of the analytical approach to what he himself felt to be honest hack-work, was nevertheless understandably pleased by Pirie's book. He told John Brosnan that he liked it immensely 'because it has probably taught me more about what I do instinctively and intuitively than I realized myself'. Did he recall, one wonders, that moment of truth in *A Heritage of Horror* in which Pirie said that the 'didactic' (!) power of such work ultimately derived from the way it permits the audience to enjoy virtue in principle and vice in practice?

That, surely, is the sentence which can help us most in 'placing' the still photograph with whose description this chapter began. What it purports to show is the force of Good defeating the force of Evil, the force of Light defeating the force of Darkness, the force of God defeating the force of the Devil, as peace is brought to the soul of the vampire's struggling victim. What it shows in fact is figures in the garb of sanctity performing an obscene parody of a gang-rape that ends with murder, while a secular voyeur looks on with tense interest. In his book *The Vampire Cinema* Pirie describes this scene as 'an expressive metaphor for the subjugation of the flesh'. Perhaps so; but the vehicle of the metaphor, the image before us, depicts an indulgence rather than a subjugation: a sadistic-erotic act performed, not by gang-banging louts, but by figures of sanctity and authority, forces of 'holiness' and 'order'. The grouping of male hands and struggling female figure is remarkably reminiscent of the composition of what is clearly a rape-scene in Jack Smith's *Flaming Creatures*, made just two years before *Dracula—Prince of*

Darkness. In the context of Fisher's film this impression of a misuse of power in the guise of a benevolent, even sacred, act is strengthened by what we have already seen of the arrogance of the gun-toting priest at the centre of his composition, and by the extraordinary way in which Barbara Shelley's Helen metamorphoses from sour matron to attractive and alluring bride under the influence of Dracula. The still from *Dracula—Prince of Darkness* thus leads us to ask once more the central question raised by the cinema's terror-fantasies: which is the real monster? Is it Dracula, who liberates something in Helen? Is it Helen herself, writhing on the table before us? Is it the Devil, at work in both of them? Or is it Father Sandor and the monks who are holding her down and are about to 'release' her from the burden of a diabolic, vampiric life-in-death? The image that should speak to us of the conquest of institutionalized good has a latent subversive content: it shows a roomful of males overpowering and symbolically violating a struggling, screaming female. The Victorian garb, the ostensibly Transylvanian setting, the non-realistic plot, all distance the image from the 'swinging' London in which it was first unveiled; yet it has a complex underground relation to England in the mid-sixties, whose youth culture, and new classlessness, and early women's lib, were beginning to turn sour while continuing to induce suspicion of elderly authority-figures of all kinds.

The image that occupied our attention throughout this chapter is not just a still photograph, of course, and it has a more immediate context, and more immediate accompaniments, than were suggested by our summary of the film's main action. One of the accompaniments, obviously, is sound: the music of James Bernard, the snarls and cries of Barbara Shelley's vampire, and the absence of sound, the almost tangible silence of the monks that aid Father Sandor in his grisly task. And just as we notice absence of sound as well as sound itself, so we prolong lines of sight into spaces absent from the screen at that moment: to the walls of the cell cut off by the closure of the frame; beyond these walls into the corridors and cells of the monastery which the camera built up for us in earlier sequences; and beyond these into the open country around. This additional space is, to a greater or lesser degree, co-present in our imaginations because of what Fisher and his cameraman Michael Reed had selected to show us before: the abbot's book-lined cell, the cell that gave shelter to Diana, the wind-swept plain outside from which the vampire now being staked had pleaded to be taken into the relative warmth of the monastery. Our memory supplies a good deal of this information as we watch the scene before us; it makes the enclosed space of the narrow, crowded cell the more oppressive and nudges us, too, into drawing a contrast between this scene and the previous context in which we had been shown the cell and the table that serve for the execution of the vampire. Helen is being staked, it would seem, in the very space which we had earlier seen devoted to one of the most peaceful and beautiful of artistic activities: the illumination of manuscripts. Nor can we remain unconscious of the fact that the scene which may be contemplated at length and at leisure as a still photograph is, in the film, part of a sequence of motions, not only of the persons shown within the frame, but also of the camera that determines our point of view. 'Camera movement', Godard has said, 'has moral implications': *le travelling est affaire de morale*. Reed's camera homes in on the vampire's agony, and lets us see the staked Helen; but it does not show the process of staking in nauseous detail, leaves more to the imagination than a Herschell Gordon Lewis film would.

We must not forget, when considering the implications of all this, that a 'staking'-scene was an obligatory part of a vampire-movie; in 1931 Browning's *Dracula* had turned Karl Freund's camera away while the staking was going on; Terence Fisher's, in 1958, had shown stake and mallet-blow as shadows on a wall, but had then cut to a shot of blood flowing from the staked female vampire's chest and had married that shock with another traditional one: the sight of a nubile young woman suddenly turned into a withered and toothless crone. Nor must we ever forget that the impact and meaning of such a scene depends to some degree on the narrative structure of which it forms part. In *Dracula—Prince of Darkness* that structure might now be described as follows:

1. (Reprise from the 1958 *Dracula*): a supernaturally powerful and destructive enemy is worsted by a champion a menaced social group has called in from outside.
2. A social group (continental villagers) which does not believe in the finality of the enemy's destruction tries to protect itself by the use of traditional weapons but is stopped by a figure of authority who wears the garb and symbols of professional sanctity and the professional hunter.

3. A family group from England comes—as tourist outsiders—to the society that thinks itself menaced and disregards warnings from both the sides that had been in conflict at stage 2. Under the threat of danger these two sides draw together: the hunter-priest is now seen as the protector of society.

4. Drawn into the orbit of the enemy by Dracula's one remaining servant, one of the Englishmen becomes the unwilling means of his return to life and activity, and one of the English women is enlisted in the ranks of his helpers. The remaining English couple flees from the domain of the enemy to that of the hunter-priest.

5. By means of helpers outside and inside the domain of the hunter-priest and his monks, the enemy penetrates that domain and is fought with fire and stake.

6. The enemy tries to escape to his own domain but is pursued and destroyed, along with his servant, by the hunter-priest and the remaining Englishman. Through its own energies and good sense, and the indispensable help of the hunter-priest, the remaining English couple is saved and can return to its bourgeois life and business in England; and the menace to the native social group, which has faded from the picture since its appearance in 2 and 3, has also been deflected.

This structure has several obvious social meanings: one notes, for instance, the increasing reliance of society not on some loner whose help it enlists, but on a group of specialists who keep apart when their help is not needed and whose leader behaves in a much more arrogant way than the old loner (Van Helsing) had done. One notes, too, that the staking-scene at the centre of our attention in this chapter shows us representatives of three of the four groups involved in the plot:

1. The enemy and his helpers.

2. The specialists—guided by their leader and manager—who know the ruthless means by which the enemy can be defeated, and the right time to apply them.

3. The English tourists, one of whom is forced to join group 1, while the others seek the help, and in their turn become helpers, of group 2.

The fourth group, the society of villagers menaced by the enemy, fades from the picture after its bungled attempts at self-help and its well-meant warnings. The battle against the enemy is a matter for specialists with their own separate organization, who are given some help by a sensible middle-class British couple with whom English-speaking audiences might be expected to identify.

It might also be worth remembering, when speculating on the social meanings of the variations on Stoker played in *Dracula—Prince of Darkness*, that the role played by resolute *women* in worsting the enemy is much smaller (much smaller, too, than in Murnau's *Nosferatu*) and that Dracula gains his entry into the domain of his specialist enemies (whose leader combines religious and scientific learning with the hunter's instincts) by enlisting the help of the one member of the monks' confraternity whom we see actively engaged in manuscript illumination—in the pursuit, that is, of *art*.

The appeal of Dracula himself largely remains, in Fisher's world, the traditional one described by W. Evans in his useful essay 'Monster Movies: A Sexual Theory':

[*Dracula*] is a seduction fantasy vitally concerned with the conditions and consequences of premarital indulgence in forbidden physical relations with attractive members of the opposite sex. Of all the movie monsters Dracula seems to be the most attractive to women . . . [He] embodies the chief characteristics of the standard Gothic hero; tall, dark, handsome, titled, wealthy, cultured, attentive, mannered, with an air of command, an aura of sin and secret suffering; . . . he is invariably impeccably dressed . . . (Atkins, 1975, p. 156)

In the 'reconstitution'-scene of *Dracula—Prince of Darkness* we have a glimpse of the count in a raw state in which he is not, for once, 'impeccably dressed'; for the rest, however, Fisher's film demonstrates that even in a permissive society the Byronic hero, and the seduction fantasies at the centre of which the Gothic novelists had placed him, have not lost their fascination.

For all the limitations its various contexts place on the scene of organized violence we have been looking at in such detail, the scene retains its fundamental ambiguity. It can be interpreted, it is almost certainly meant to be interpreted, as the restoration of order, the overcoming of evil, the bringing of peace to a tormented soul; but the vibrations it sets going in the mind suggest repression, excesses of religious zeal, sadistic compensations for celibacy, gang-rape, and the subjugation of youth by crabbed age. The multivalence and moral ambiguity of this image is typical of fantasy-movies, and helps to explain their appeal to so many different people, and so many different interests, in our society.

Richard Wordsworth, whose intelligent and moving performance in *The Quatermass Experiment* did so much to spark off the Hammer fantasy-cycle, told John Brosnan an anecdote which seems to me to characterize better than anything else what Pirie calls the 'universe' of Terence Fisher.

Just before shooting [*The Curse of the Werewolf*] I had to come down to London to get fitted for fangs. When I got to the studio nobody seemed to know anything about it. Anyway, I found someone who knew and said, 'Oh, no fangs. The censor says no fangs. You can either have fangs, or relations with the girl, but not both.' Well, Oliver Reed had to be born, so we had to choose relations with the girl. Terence Fisher was directing that one. We were just about to start the scene where I rape the girl and he turned to the property man and said, 'Have you got the white of egg?' I didn't know what he was talking about and I asked 'er, what's this white of egg for?' 'Oh, this is something we always do', he said. 'You have a mouthful of egg white and when you see the girl you slobber a little of it. But keep it tasteful.' (Brosnan, 1976, pp. 115–16)

'Keeping it tasteful' included, in Fisher's day, permitting the overt sexuality exhibited by Hammer's male and female vampires, but none of the blood-stained nakedness of Jimmy Sangster's *Lust for a Vampire* or the full frontal expositions of Jean Rollin. In a Fisher film, the audience constantly imagines more than it is shown: Ivan Butler tells us that he saw 'a stomach slit open with a knife' in *Dracula—Prince of Darkness*, and so, apparently, did the authors of *The House of Horror. The Story of Hammer Films*. The author of the present book saw nothing of the kind, and believes the assurance Terence Fisher gave to John Brosnan that no version of his film had ever included this particular image. That delight was to be reserved for patrons of *Superbeast* (1972) and *The Godfather, Part Two* (1974).

Sociologists have often pointed out that films, like other mass media, influence the public as much through what is *not* said as through what is. One may well think, therefore, that by absorbing their audiences' attention in the problems of vampires and vampire-hunters in nineteenth-century Transylvania, Hammer Films were performing a political function; that they provided the circuses while the government's social legislation provided the bread. Erik Barnouw, who has applied this argument to American television, adds that telefilms have been 'political' in other ways than through

evasion. 'Public acceptance of a foreign policy based on good guy/
bad guy premises', he writes in *Tube of Plenty*, 'may have been
reinforced by a telefilm mythology of similar obsessions. When
Eisenhower described the world as "forces of good and evil arrayed
as never before", he was offering a picture viewers could recognize'
(Barnouw, 1975, p. 367). Fisher also operates, as we have seen,
with a dichotomy of this kind, proffering a measure of reassurance
in a world of shifting values, of social and economic uneasiness
characteristic of a time in which rising income and consumer
spending combined with low growth and recurrent financial crises;
a time in which Britain—Liverpool as well as London—was a social
trend-setter for the whole Western world, but in which its inhabitants were becoming all too conscious of its decline as a world
power. In an age of social mobility and shifting class-frontiers
Hammer Films offered their patrons the spectacle of a world in
which all the classes knew their place, whether they be the
muttering rustics in the village inn, or the comfortably off professional and *rentier* classes to which the mostly colourless heroes
and heroines of the various tales belong, or the arrogant squires,
or the chief of the vampires (who is invariably a member of the
aristocracy). In view of the rigidity of this scheme it is particularly
interesting to find Fisher, consciously or unconsciously, subverting
his good guy/bad guy model in ways already analysed. The
staking-scene described at the beginning of this chapter functions,
in the plot of *Dracula—Prince of Darkness*, as a restoration of law
and order (and the 'law and order' question, it will be remembered,
came more and more into the foreground in the swinging sixties);
but it whispers to us that if this is what law and order look like,
we had better rethink our values. Regarded in this light the scene
may be viewed as an act of liberation, the shattering of a harmful
cliché at the very moment of its apparent reiteration.

Fisher's film may thus claim a certain interest and significance—
but it is the interest and significance of a symptom rather than that
of a successful work of art. The wide screen is unimaginatively
used in *Dracula—Prince of Darkness*; the language is flat and
without period flavour; even within the story's own logic the
reconstitution through blood of a being whose ashes we have seen
blown away on the wind, and the presentation of a monastery in
which lightly clad young women are allowed to roam the cells and
corridors, are highly improbable. Fisher has given a good deal of

thought to colour-effects; in July 1964 he analysed, in *Films and Filming*, the difference between cameramen like Arthur Grant, who prefer 'natural, neutral colour', and Jack Asher, who 'likes to go for strong colour-effects', and went on to explain:

You really have to stylize and discipline the colour; and the closer you move your camera in, the more you have to bunch your colour. One blob of red in the wrong place and the audience isn't looking at the hero, they're looking at a patch of curtain (or something similar) and your whole effect is lost. (Leyda, 1977, p. 137)

In the event, however, colour-photography never achieves, in *Dracula—Prince of Darkness*, anything to match the uncanny effect of the low-key dramatic lighting characteristic of so many black-and-white horror-movies. The film's over-all construction is unimaginative ('relentlessly linear' Roy Armes rightly calls it in his *Critical History of the British Cinema*); visual poetry is absent, though the production-designer, Bernard Robinson, once again does wonders with a limited budget and even more limited locale; and the formula according to which the whole film is being constructed—the formula that brought Hammer Films ringing box-office success—shows through again and again.

What is meant when one complains about the absence of visual poetry from Fisher's film may best be appreciated if one compares it with a more recent Dracula movie which also uses colour and a wide screen: Werner Herzog's *Nosferatu* of 1979. Again and again Herzog uses the language of European painting: the language of seventeenth-century Dutch painters at the council-meeting, that of nineteenth-century still-life and genre-painting in some ravishing views from a flower-silled window, that of Caspar David Friedrich in some of the mountain-scenes—but these allusions are only part of a highly personal idiom. The German and Dutch landscapes traversed by the solitary figure of Bruno Ganz's Jonathan Harker conjure up the memory of similar landscapes and figures in *The Enigma of Kasper Hauser*, while scenes showing Harker crossing mountains and streams, and Dracula's ship drifting towards its ultimate destination, remind one of similar images in *Aguirre, Wrath of God*. The thematically so important slow-motion shots of a bat in flight recall marvellous scenes of motion through the air in *The Great Ecstasy of Woodcarver Steiner* (1974). Such resemblances are anything but fortuitous—they are part of Herzog's way of seeing the world. In the *Observer* of 20 May 1979 Tom Milne has well described one particularly powerful Herzogian moment in the new *Nosferatu*: that in which Jonathan Harker makes his way on foot, over dusky wild mountains, towards Dracula's castle. 'A low-angled shot', Milne writes, 'discovers him sitting silhouetted on a cliff with his back to the camera, then follows his gaze up to a tiny patch of sky visible between the crags. As though mystified, the camera cuts back to the motionless Jonathan, then back again to the patch of sky he is watching just as one realises that dark clouds are slowly but inexorably rolling forward to obliterate that last little haven of light.' It should perhaps be added that a familiar passage from Wagner's *Rhinegold* is imaginatively used, at this point, to reinforce aurally the sense of doom visually conveyed by the cloudscape.

Fisher's film has nothing to compare with moments like this—or with that in which the skull-like head of Kinski's vampire-count suddenly appears huge in the foreground of an architecturally beautiful, deserted, nocturnal town-square, or that in which (to quote Tom Milne yet again) 'the placid still-life of a canal lined with elegant homes is suddenly disrupted as the bowsprit of the plague-ship noses menacingly into the frame'. *Nosferatu* reveals Herzog as a master of depth-of-field composition who has harnessed the wide screen to the needs of terror-fantasy in a way that has never been surpassed.

Herzog's variation on Murnau has been accused of failing to unify its actors' styles of performance: Klaus Kinski and Isabelle Adjani, it has been said, recall the silent cinema in a manner that sorts ill with the more naturalistic acting of some of the minor characters. The *outré* performance of the cartoonist Roland Topor as a giggling Renfield has particularly jarred on English critics unaccustomed to Topor's brand of 'sick' grotesqueness. It does not jar on me—I marvel, rather, at the way Herzog's style has imposed itself throughout, blending the faces and voices of genuine gipsies with those of the director's German stock-company, making the figures inhabit their nineteenth-century clothes and the landscapes into which they are placed as though they had never known anything else. In unity of style Herzog's company, with its disparate national origin and mingling of amateurs and professionals, seems to me to have little to learn from the much more homogeneous team of *Dracula—Prince of Darkness* at which we must now cast a parting glance.

Christopher Lee has often analysed the elements that went to the making of his celebrated performance of the vampire-count. In the essay 'Dracula and I' which originally appeared in *Midi-minuit fantastique* (January 1973) and was then reprinted in Peter Haining's *The Dracula Scrapbook*, Lee attests first of all his sense of the metaphysical significance of the Dracula tales and of their sad poetry of death:

I have always tried to emphasise the solitude of Evil and particularly to make it clear that however terrible the actions of Count Dracula might be, he was possessed by an occult power which was completely beyond his control. It was the Devil, holding him in his power, who drove him to commit those horrible crimes, for he had taken possession of his body from time immemorial. Yet his soul, surviving inside its carnal wrapping, was immortal and could not be destroyed by any means. All this is to explain the great sadness which I have tried to put into my interpretation.

The second element Lee emphasizes, not surprisingly, is the sexual one. Our post-Freudian age, he feels, can no longer take Stoker's conception quite at its face value—we translate the thirst for blood into something more overtly libidinous:

Blood, the symbol of virility, and the sexual attraction attached to it, has always been closely linked in the universal theme of Vampirism. I had to try to suggest this without destroying the part by clumsy over-emphasis.

The last element, one to which Lee attaches particular importance, will also be unlikely to surprise us, in view of the already analysed class-consciousness of these Hammer epics:

Above all, I have never forgotten that Count Dracula was a gentleman, a member of the upper aristocracy, and in his early life a great soldier and leader of men. (Haining, 1976, p. 97)

Director and script-writer of *Dracula—Prince of Darkness* have not, alas, been able to make much of all this: Lee is given nothing to say at all and does little more than snarl and bare his fangs or his chest.

The film is also distinguished by the presence of Philip Latham, who achieved fame in a television serial of the seventies in which he embodied, to perfection, the Victorian nobleman and politician at the centre of Trollope's Palliser novels. In *Dracula—Prince of Darkness*, however, Latham gives what must surely rank as one of the most ludicrous performances in the history of the terror-film. As Dracula's sinister servant he seems to have stepped straight out of Ben Travers's farcical comedy *Thark*, and the name he is given, Klove, might suggest that some joker had recalled the association of Clov with Ham(m) in Beckett's *Endgame* and winked at the viewer over the head of an actor giving the 'hammiest' performance of his career. Such intellectual winks and nudges, however, are not part of the style of Hammer Films in their heyday. It is interesting to find that when the part of Klove was revived for a later instalment of Hammer's Dracula saga, it was entrusted to Patrick Troughton, whose long apprenticeship in playing Dickens grotesques for the BBC—he was an unforgettable Quilp, for instance—enabled him to enter with much more gusto, and correspondingly greater success, into this role.

The Father Sandor of Andrew Keir, a stolid, hard-working actor, has none of the nervous energy, or the charisma, of Peter Cushing, whose Van Helsing is shown in the brief opening sequence and sadly missed ever after. Thorley Walters's bumbling dottiness is more at home in *The Pure Hell of St. Trinian's* (1960— one of the great surrealist works of the British cinema!) than in the illumination-room of a Transylvanian monastery. The two young people who weather all their perils and are reunited at the end of the film are pleasant enough but fundamentally dull. Only Barbara Shelley's double performance as sour matron and fang-flashing voluptuary has something of the right incandescence; it suits a time that brought fuller recognition and freer discussion of the sexual needs of women than any previous one, and makes one sympathize with her French admirers' regret that she was never persuaded to act in a female version of *Dr. Jekyll and Mr. Hyde*.

Barbara Shelley and Jacqueline Pearce were Hammer Films' best candidates for the two related female avatars of the terror-film: the predatory inspirer of terror and its helpless victim. If one compares their performances in such parts with those of Barbara Steele, however, one sees at once why Hammer's choice should have lighted on Shelley and Pearce rather than Steele. Even in their most convincing performances, as in those of Peter Cushing, a fundamental niceness comes through, the aura of hard-working actresses who play their part with conviction but never shed their English middle-class gentility. Barbara Steele's performances are much more disturbing and *Sadique*; she brings a secret complicity with the torturers to her 'victim' parts and a sexual glow to her vengeful monster roles which recall Justine and Juliette in a way that is quite beyond the charming and talented Miss Shelley. The

Hammer family team was no more concerned with the exploration of the remoter shores of the human unconscious than with any *serious* probing of Kenneth Anger's contention, in 1962, that after two thousand years of Christian domination it was now the turn of Lucifer to rule the world.

Robin Wood—who has eloquently championed the British-made terror-films of Michael Reeves, Peter Sasdy, and Gary Sherman—once suggested that a history of the genre might be written in which Hammer Films were the villains. Their domination, he told readers of the *Times Educational Supplement* in December 1973, 'has reduced all to baseness and squalor'. He wanted no truck, above all, with the enthronement of Terence Fisher by critics like David Pirie and Jean-Marie Sabatier.

Fisher is certainly consistent—the consistency being mainly a matter of unremitting crudeness of sensibility. The most striking thing about the world he creates is its moral squalor. His characters have no aliveness, no complexity. His conception of evil is scarcely more interesting, or more adult, than his conception of good: all is ugliness. I have never come out of a Fisher film feeling in any way extended or enriched (not to mention entertained); if I submitted to their world I would be diminished.

Oddly enough the history of the genre Wood called for had already been written: for Carlos Clarens's excellent book on the horror-film makes Wood's point unequivocally. Commending Jacques Tourneur's *The Night of the Demon* for its Lewtonesque ability to turn prosaic situations into nightmares while leaving its horrors 'understated, ellipsed and in part suggested', Clarens concludes that 'the best examples of the horror film ever made in Great Britain *represent the diametrical opposite of the Hammer way of doing things*' (1968 edn., p. 144; my italics). I still believe that Wood goes too far in his outright rejection—there is much solid craftsmanship to respect (if not to admire) in Fisher, as well as more human decency than Wood allows; and as a document of its time a film like *Dracula—Prince of Darkness* will retain its interest. Except for such charged, multivalent images as that discussed in this chapter, however, a few sequences like the first and last appearances of the vampire in his *Dracula* of 1958, and some of the long tracking-shots that became his hallmark, Fisher's work is too undistinguished to stand comparison with such British terror-films as *Dead of Night*, *The Queen of Spades*, *Witchfinder General*, or *Peeping Tom*; nor is it likely to exert on the viewers of a later generation anything like the

force that we still find exerted by *The Cabinet of Dr. Caligari* sixty
years after it was first shown.

Conclusion

That thing out there is you!
Forbidden Planet (1956)

THE analyses contained in this book should have confirmed Gérard Lenne's demonstration, in *Le Cinéma fantastique et ses mythes*, that the central question of the terror-film is the complex one of 'normality' and 'monstrosity'. There are 'physical' and 'psychological' monsters, and at the level of signifier and signified these may enter into a number of more or less complex relationships: physical deformity may signify moral ugliness or throw moral beauty and intellectual distinction into greater relief; physical beauty may be an outward sign of goodness, or contrast with horrors of the mind and soul and crudities of intellect. Constantly we are brought up against such problems as: what is normality? What is monstrosity? Where are the true monsters? Who is truly sane? What is insanity? What historical, social, moral, physical realities have to come together to produce what we call a monster or a madman? Sickness, enforced isolation, oppression, deprivation, intellectual curiosity, sexual desires, the innate dualities and complexities of the human mind and soul, may produce what passes for 'normality' as well as what passes for 'monstrosity': as H. G. Wells showed in *The Country of the Blind* and Richard Matheson in the twice-filmed *I am a Legend*, the monster is the exception. Intrusions of the 'monstrous', however apprehended, however defined, into the 'normal', are at the very heart of the films that we have examined, whether they depict such intrusions as coming from within man, or from somewhere 'outside'; and the terror they induce in us, and articulate for us, is not infrequently terror at the order we have created or help to uphold as well as the anarchic desires that oppose such order. We live more intensely through such films, we cross frontiers, we test limits, we enter realms in which fear and delight are not strictly separated, we rejoice in the very act of fantasizing, of visualizing the impossible, as again and again we say to ourselves: 'Ça, c'est du cinéma!'—that is how these man-made photographing, recording, and projecting machines should be used to bring out their full potential.

All this, and more, may be said of *The Cabinet of Dr. Caligari*: a film whose power remains undimmed today, whatever pundits may urge against it, because it not only reflects a historical state of affairs in which artists and audiences felt 'unable to decide whether Dr Caligari was a megalomaniac dictator or a compassionate therapist, and whether they themselves were his zombies, his victims, or simply patients to be healed back into conformity by his benevolence. . .' (Richard Sheppard); not only tells its story by means of fascinating multivalent images; not only plays, as every terror-film must, on deep-seated anxieties, fears, and fantasies; not only explores, as most of the great fantasy-films do, the nature of the cinematic experience—but because it also challenges our critical intelligence and the moral judgement that goes with it. Not all the films mentioned in this book do this to anything like the same extent; but even the cruder products of the commercial pleasure-industry may have their uses. It is good, occasionally, to be made to face one's worst fears in a fictional context and to learn that in such a context we *can* face them; it is liberating to satisfy, vicariously, desires that cannot and must not find an outlet in the social world in which we live. We should always remember, however, that these films are also an expression of that social world; that someone is here playing on our fears and our desires; and we should, on occasions, ask ourselves, as Godard, for example, challenges us to do, whether we are not being manipulated to undesirable ends by men who have the kind of money which it costs to make a film; whether we are not being invaded instead of liberated; whether we are not being offered circus-entertainments in order to distract our attention from abuses we ought to remedy in the social world outside the cinema.

Terror, as many of the examples cited in this book should have served to remind us, enters as an ingredient into many films that resist classification as 'horror-movies' or 'terror-films' in the narrower, genre sense. It is an essential part of the cinema, as of all other art—the tensions and contradictions of our daily lives call out for the kind of release that cinematic terror can bring. But even if there were no violence, or fear of violence, in our lives;

even if the sexual current ran simply and smoothly for us all; even if we did not have fantasies and desires that go counter to the law of the land and to our own moral sense; even if we did not, out of past experience and the depths of our being, produce terrors that we then project on to the world and our fellow-men; even if civilization held no discontents—even then terror would still have a function in our art. That function, at the opposite pole of the 'release' or 'catharsis' mechanism so far implied, has been well described by Don Siegel, who once said of his seminal film *The Invasion of the Body Snatchers*, that it was meant to 'scare [us] out of greyness'. Unlike the pod-people in Siegel's film, men need the challenge of adventure and danger and even sorrow; and when the necessary routine of modern life becomes too monstrous, as it sometimes must, the safe terrors of the movie-house may provide a salutary outlet and relief. Here one can only agree with Buñuel, who has more than once defended his use of fantastic terror-images against critics obsessed with neo-realist criteria by pointing to the public's need for 'poetry, mystery, and everything that enlarges tangible reality'.

Nevertheless, we have now to ask ourselves when we must call a halt; when we must say to ourselves that it is no longer consonant with our dignity and self-respect to seek release or vicarious thrills from what we are being shown on the screen.

Terror in the cinema often involves scenes of violence; and there are, as is well known, at least five conflicting theories about the effects such fictional violence may have on violence perpetrated in the world outside the cinema. The first of these tells us that there is no effect: that anything the cinema shows us is counteracted and modified by our more immediate social experience, our encounters and interactions with real people in non-fictional situations. The second would have us believe that the effect film-violence has on us is inhibiting—we recoil from such violence, and are likely to avoid it in real life. The third operates with the venerable catharsis theory: the sight of violence on film acts as a safety-valve, drains off impulses that might otherwise have taken a socially dangerous form. The fourth theory tells us that the more habituated we become to violence in the media, the less we react to it; it loses, gradually, whatever stimulation value it may originally have had. The fifth, on the contrary, asserts that what we see in films can become a powerful factor in our socialization, can provide models for acts of aggression and encourage their acting out in real life. This last theory can point to a good deal of convincing evidence from the observation of children subjected to filmed spectacles in controlled situations; but there can be no doubt that it is always wrong to look at what films and other media show *in isolation*, without taking into account the structure and the health of the society within which particular works are produced and the social circumstances within which they are viewed.

The conclusion I would draw from the voluminous, conflicting, and in many ways mutually cancelling evidence so far presented is that violence on the screen reflects tendencies towards violence present in our society; that there is no single and uniform way in which such presentations may affect cinema-goers, but that they may act in a variety of ways; that constant stimulation and reinforcement of aggression (and, it should be added, of sexuality) dictated by commercial interests must affect emotional reactions and must, in some cases, disinhibit, and in some cases confirm, behavioural tendencies. Such recognitions ask to be tempered, however, by four further thoughts. The first of these reminds us of what most artists know: that the depiction even of extreme violence may be, in the right context, aesthetically and morally justified. The second tells us that as much harm may be done by the approving presentation of apparently bloodless, 'sanitized' violence, and violence perpetrated by figures of authority, as by any other—it may, in fact, be much more insidiously dangerous to commend, or seem to commend, violence which seems bloodless, easy, and employed for socially justified ends, than that which is shown as bloody, messy, and perpetrated by a rebel or outcast. The third reminds us of a truth enunciated many years ago by H. M. Kallen, when he said in *Indecency and the Seven Arts* (1930) that those who sought for causes of moral and cultural pollution in our society would do well to look in other places than the cinema: 'Crowded slums, machine labor, subway transportation, barren lives, starved emotions, and unreasoning minds are far more dangerous to morals, property and life than . . . any motion picture.' Andrew Tudor, writing forty-four years and many research-reports later, elaborates Kallen's contentions while reaffirming that violence in popular culture and violence in the social world *are* related:

The traditional genre acceptance of the violent solution is an entrenched part of our western cultures. The movies (and the other media) form one

part of socialisation, adult and adolescent, *one* source of attitudes and
beliefs. Their stress on the violent solution is hardly unique. They are
repeating a pattern of culture, in dramatic terms, which an adolescent,
say, will also find elsewhere: in his family, amongst his peers, in the history
texts he reads at school, and in many of the institutions of his society.
Civilised societies are officially conducting much-publicised wars and supporting widely advertised institutions specialising in violence. Blaming
popular culture for the violence of modern societies is pernicious scape-
goating; there is much more wrong here than just the movies. The genres
play only one part in the circle of cause and confirmation. (Tudor, *Image
and Influence*, 1974, pp. 214–15)

The fourth thought tells us that the obviously fantastic setting in
which so much terror-film violence is perpetrated acts as a frame
and as a distancing medium that discourage ideas of emulating the
actions on the screen in our own very different lives. There can be
few recorded cases of spectators sallying out at night to bite their
neighbours after seeing a Lugosi or a Lon Chaney Junior movie.

This does not mean, however, that we should simply sit back
and accept all movie blood-baths with a shrug of acquiescence—any
more than we should uncritically accept any other material film-
makers choose to present to us, material, for instance, that we think
calculated to reinforce racial hatreds and distrust. The health of
our society depends to a considerable degree on our habituating
ourselves to making aesthetic and moral judgements on the arts
and on our response to them. When we are startled by scenes that
seem to go beyond our previous tolerance-level, we must consider
them in their context and ask ourselves whether the movement of
thought and feeling of the whole work requires these scenes for
their natural conclusion, in the way that the logic of *King Lear* needs
the blinding of Gloucester. In many cases we shall, in fact, find
that the principle enunciated at the end of the preceding paragraph applies: that 'shocking' scenes are part of an acting-out, in a
deliberately dream-like, fantastic way, of deep desires that we
would not dream of satisfying in our ordinary lives. The terror-
films of Jean Rollin, for instance, are of this kind: their setting is so
stylized and surreal that the images are deprived of most of the
danger they would have had, even for the unstable, in a more
realistically presented world. When the context *is* realistic, as in
Romero's *The Night of the Living Dead*, the action of which, but for
its one central fantasy (the resurrection brought about by some

unknown radiation effect), takes place in a perfectly recognizable American setting, then we must ask ourselves whether the psychological and social action of the film makes sense, has a serious point, or completes a movement of thought and feeling; or whether it is a mere heaping-up of shock-effects for their own sake. If the latter is the case, we are justified in dismissing the film as aesthetically and morally worthless; though I would hesitate to deny other consenting adults the chance to test for themselves whether a cathartic effect can be attained. John Fraser, in his now classic account of *Violence in the Arts*, has made this last point with particular force:

The question of whether or not filmed violences are cathartic is obviously partly a critical one, and discussion of it seems to have been bedevilled by an unwillingness to get involved in critical questions. The term 'catharsis', where tragedy is concerned, points to a real psychological phenomenon: one leaves the theatre after certain performances feeling emptied out and in some measure relaxed, in a beneficial way. At the same time, not all works that offer themselves as tragedies are capable of producing that feeling and neither are all productions even of distinguished tragedies: one can leave the theatre after a bad production of *Othello* feeling tense and irritable. The same variousness obtains with respect to bloodshed and gruesomeness in movies. Watching certain horror movies, among them Bava's *Sei Donne per l'Assassino* (*Blood and Black Lace*) and some of the Hammer ones that used to upset British reviewers so much, can in my experience be genuinely cathartic. And they are cathartic because the shocking parts provide climaxes to certain movements or phases in them and permit certain actions to reach their logical conclusions and certain formal anticipations to be fully satisfied, just as they are satisfied in non-bloody works, such as slapstick comedies. So too with the bloodbaths in Westerns like Leone's *For a Few Dollars More*, Corbucci's *Django*, and at a higher level, Peckinpah's *The Wild Bunch*. The production of a catharsis is not in itself a mark of distinction in a work or spectacle, of course, and no doubt it would be a better world if nobody enjoyed bloodbaths, or read thrillers, or watched wrestling, and so on. Moreover a number of bloody movies, like a good deal of what goes on in the fight industry no doubt, are morally disgusting (I should perhaps confess here that I could not bring myself to see Russell's *The Devils* at all). But that is not a sufficient reason for preventing consenting adults from seeing them, provided that laws against cruelty itself aren't violated. And if what is at issue is the state of mind in which people come out from movie theatres, I can only suggest that they will sometimes be less tense and aggressive after watching gruesome movies than they were when they went in. (Fraser, 1976, pp. 178–9)

That is admirably put, but it leaves one important question un-answered. 'A number of bloody movies,' Fraser tells us, 'are morally disgusting'. Is there not, then, a degree of moral disgust where we ought to act on our convictions and persuade exhibitors, in one way or another, not to offer us fare of that sort? The last work of an artist I have greatly admired in the past, Pasolini's *Salo* (1975), seems to me to go so far beyond my own present limit of tolerance, to offer so gratuitously nauseating a spectacle of sadism and coprophilia, that instead of diagnosis of, or release from, a social and psychological sickness it becomes merely an expression of such sickness which it is degrading rather than liberating to watch. But one still feels a serious artist at work in this desperately sad film; we should not simply lump it together with horror-quickies whose only excuse for existence is that they provide a framework in which we can watch one sadistic exhibition of blood-letting after another. I would certainly do my best to persuade my friends not to see, and exhibitors in my neighbourhood not to show, films of this last kind. Others may then offer counter-arguments which, even if they do not raise my own level of tolerance, may well carry sufficient force to give *I Eat Your Skin* a chance in the local High Street Odeon.

In a democratic society adults should be free to choose what films they wish to see; but this does not absolve society from the duty of protecting the vulnerable and the easily upset as well as those whose religious and moral principles forbid them to witness spectacles of certain kinds. One way to achieve this has been advocated by Enid Wistrich when she was chairman of the Film Viewing Board of the Greater London Council: not to ban contro-versial films altogether, but to release them with an 'X' certificate and require the cinema to display a prominent notice in its foyer characterizing the film's contents in a non-sensational way, warning patrons that certain scenes may give offence. This would offer adults the choice of watching such scenes or avoiding them. The concept of 'choice', as economists, sociologists, and psycho-logists will hasten to tell us, is not at all straightforward—one has to take into account the compulsions that operate in a market-place in which the attractions of television have to be countered by strong sensations of a kind broadcasting companies either cannot or will not beam into our homes; the cultural atmosphere produced by advertising and commercial exploitation; the pressure of peer-groups; the conditioning effects of habituation and social usage; the desensitization and brutalization produced by a regular diet of mindlessly violent movies. All this is true; but when we consider censorship and its application to terror-films we must also ask ourselves how well we know the nature and composition of the cinema-going public—whether it is not largely composed, in a given time and place, of reasonable men and women whose sense of humour and sense of proportion we underestimate at our peril. Movie-goers can think; they bring a personality and a mind of their own into the cinema; they do not simply respond, in sleep-walking fashion, to whatever stimuli the Caligaris of the film-world choose to subject them.

The 'non-sensational' descriptions which Elaine Wistrich wanted to enjoin on cinema-managers are not, of course, part of the tradition of cinema advertising. Most of us can think of many cases where what might on the face of it appear an unwarrantably violent assault on the public's sensibilities turns out, on closer inspection, to be nothing of the kind. Take the poster advertising a movie called *Frankenstein's Bloody Terror*, adorned by drawings of a hideous humanoid monster with blood dripping from its teeth, attacking an exceptionally well-developed young lady who seems about to burst out of her clothes with fright, while from the back a Dracula-like figure holds out blood-stained claw-like hands. The text accompanying this icon is shown overleaf. If one is lured into the cinema by this text, which would seem to have been composed by a particularly bloodthirsty fairground barker, one finds oneself confronted by a relatively mild and inexplicit Spanish version of the Wolfman tale, *La Marca del Hombre Lobo* (1968), directed by Enrique Aquiluz, with a good deal of stylized distancing, from a script by Jacinto Molina who also plays the main part under his acting-pseudonym Paul Naschy. One's astonishment at learning that the American Board of Control had allowed children to attend the film described on the poster unaccompanied by an adult (it was rated 'PG', 'Parental Guidance Suggested') lessens when one sees the film itself.

Nevertheless it is salutary to reflect, when generalizing about the effect of terror-movies, that what may be cathartic or healthily stimulating or harmless for adults may be psychologically damaging for children. Younger children are simply not ready to assimilate such images of violence and sexual activity as are presented in the

films of Jean Rollin; images that might well have a cathartic effect
on the mature or arouse them sexually in ways that easily find
life-enhancing expression. Responsible parents, of course, will not
allow their children to be over-exposed to sensationalist movies of
any kind at an age when they are learning to cope with the world
outside the cinema and away from the television set; but we must
offer some protection to children whose parents are not able to
shield them in this way. Unbalanced, socially damaged, pathologically inclined adults may also find that filmed violence, instead
of purging aggression, acts as a spur to imitation and emulation
in real life, acts as encouragement rather than release. However
saddening the history of censorship in the arts may be, we shall
always need censorship of some kind to protect children; but can
we ever protect the sick? We can never be sure, in any given
instance, that violence inflicted by a pathologically inclined or
socially damaged individual on others or on himself would not
have found a similar outlet had he not seen a film whose action
includes murder or violation; nor can we ever quantify the
amount of aggression that may have been harmlessly drained off
from the real world by the vicarious satisfactions offered by the

cinema. That is no reason, however, why we should not try, at least, to discourage those who, for the sake of profit, use the conventions of the horror-movie as an occasion for mindlessly piling up incidents of sadistic violence and for equally mindless invasions of the privacy of the sexual act. We must, ultimately, stand by what John Fraser has so well called our 'sense of what gives life dignity, and what boundaries cannot be crossed without an intolerable self-betrayal or betrayal of others'.

It needs also to be said, explicitly, that while artistic intent may very well be urged in defence of films like Pasolini's *Salo* and Nagisa Oshima's *In the Realm of the Senses* (1976), nothing, no artistic intent in the world, can ever justify the infliction of cruelty on a living being for purposes of entertainment. The growing number of films in which animals are deliberately set on fire, maimed, and killed, not in a documentary context like Franju's *Blood of the Beasts*, which justifiably forces us to look at where the meat most of us consume in fact comes from, but in fictional contexts, are an abomination we ought not to tolerate. As for the clandestinely made and clandestinely shown movies in which some derelict human being is hurt or even killed to provide illicit thrills for the jaded and perverse—I would not wish to live in any country that does not search out and bring the full rigour of the law to bear on those who indulge, and cater for, that degree of blood-lust. The exploitation of children for purposes of filmed pornographic fantasy, and the inevitable corruption this entails, falls into the same intolerable category.

A quite different case, however, is presented by the films of Lon Chaney Senior, who needed to make himself suffer under constricting costumes and devices that distorted his face and body in frequently agonizing ways, in order to allow the camera to photograph the pain in his eyes, the pain of the crippled creatures he liked to portray, whose problems his own early history made him understand so well. Here an artist deliberately used pain to stretch his powers to the utmost, just as an athlete will strain his endurance almost to breaking-point in order to achieve to the highest degree what he feels he *can* achieve. Here, as in the case of Boris Karloff under the heavy make-up of Frankenstein's monster, we can watch what we know to be genuine pain without a reduction in our own humanity. We know, in such cases, that it was freely chosen by a responsible human being in order to help that human being to express itself more fully than it could otherwise have done; and that the end result was not damage, but, on the contrary, a feeling of fulfilment and achievement on the part of the artist who used this ultimate device.

There can be no doubt that a great many films that depict and evoke terror are shoddily put together, stupid in their conscious attitudes (when they indulge in facile equations of bodily deformity with deformity of mind and soul, or allow some bone-headed 'hero' an all-too-easy victory over a 'mad' scientist, or habitually associate criminality with a liking for books and *objets d'art*), cliché-ridden in their dialogue, wooden in their acting, and grossly inartistic in their *mise en scène*. As an American critic once said of a film called *Macabre*: 'It plods along from its opening scene in a funeral parlor to its dénouement in a graveyard, unimpeded by the faintest intrusion of good taste, literacy, or sense' (Halliwell, 1978, p. 80). There are vast differences in quality between the routine products of Monogram or AIP and the work of Wiene, Murnau, Lang, Browning, Jean Epstein, Whale, Dreyer, and other masters of the terror-film discussed in the pages of this book. While keeping ourselves aware of such differences in standard we must also, however, remember that we may here find ourselves confronted by problems with which a purely formal, purely aesthetic analysis is not competent to deal. The lesser productions of the film industry help us to appreciate tendencies of thought and feeling that we may well miss if we restrict our attention to acknowledged 'classics'; and, as I have tried to show, we can look to philosophy, psychology, theology, and history for some help in our attempts to answer the insistent queries this book has constantly tried to raise: what is the human need that calls for such works? What aspects of experience do they reflect? What attitudes do they betray? What sort of responses do they provoke? What truths, if any, do they reveal?

In her inaugural lecture at University College, London, Professor E. M. Wilkinson has spoken of Goethe's conviction that it was one of the functions of an artist 'to make us *feel* at home in a world changing so rapidly that our intellect can scarcely keep pace with it'. This is what I like to call a Tolstoy truth, and one cannot study any of the arts for long without feeling its force. But there are Kafka truths too, which lead one to the complementary conviction that we also need works that focus a sense of homelessness, articulate feelings of strangeness and disorientation, keep us alive to the possibility of orders of existence which cannot easily be assimilated in the categories of our waking consciousness. Goethe himself, in works that range from 'The Erl King' to *Elective Affinities*, has shown awareness of this opposing pull. The terror-film, with its puzzling, disturbing, multivalent images, often leads us into regions of that kind, regions that are strange, disorientating, yet somehow familiar; and for all the crude and melodramatic and morally questionable forms in which we so often encounter it, it does speak of something true and important, and offers us encounters with hidden aspects of ourselves and our world which we should not be too ready to reject.

Select Bibliography

Adkinson, R. V. (ed.), *The Cabinet of Dr. Caligari* (Classic Film Scripts), London, 1972.

Adrian, W., *Freaks: Cinema of the Bizarre*, London, 1972.

Agel, H., *Esthétique du cinéma*, Paris, 1962.

—— *Métaphysique du cinéma*, Paris, 1976.

Amelio, R. J., *The Filmic Moment*, Dayton, 1975.

Anderson, R. G., *Faces, Forms, Films. The Artistry of Lon Chaney*, New York, 1971.

Andrevon, J.-P., and Schlockoff, A., *Cent monstres du cinéma fantastique*, Grenoble, 1978.

Andrews, J. D., *The Major Film Theories. An Introduction*, Oxford, 1976.

Annan, D., *Ape. The Kingdom of Kong*, London, 1974.

—— *Cinefantastic. Beyond the Dream Machine*, London, 1974.

—— *Robot. The Mechanical Monster*, London, 1976.

Annobile, R. J. (ed.), *Frankenstein* (Film Classics Library), London, 1974.

—— *Psycho* (Film Classics Library), London, 1974.

—— *Dr. Jekyll and Mr. Hyde* (Film Classics Library), New York, 1975.

Armes, R., *Film and Reality. A Historical Survey*, Harmondsworth, 1975.

—— *The Ambiguous Image. Narrative Style in Modern European Cinema*, London, 1976.

—— *A Critical History of the British Cinema*, London, 1978.

Arnheim, R., *Der Film als Kunst*, Berlin, 1932.

Ash, B. (ed.), *The Visual Encyclopedia of Science Fiction*, London, 1977.

Atkins, T. R. (ed.), *Sexuality in the Movies*, Bloomington, 1975.

—— *Graphic Violence on the Screen*, New York, 1976.

—— *Science Fiction Films*, New York, 1976.

Aylesworth, T. G., *Monsters from the Movies*, New York, 1972.

Bächlin, P., *Der Film als Ware*, Basle, 1945.

Bálazs, B., *Der sichtbare Mensch oder die Kultur des Films*, Vienna, 1924.

—— *Der Geist des Films*, Berlin, 1930.

—— *Theory of the Film. Character and Growth of a New Art*, London, 1952 (Dover edn., 1970).

Barna, Y., *Eisenstein. The Growth of a Cinematic Genius*, trans. L. Hunter, Indiana Univ. Press, 1973 (paperback edn., Boston, 1975).

Barnouw, E., *Tube of Plenty. The Evolution of American Television*, New York, 1975.

Barr, C., *Ealing Studios*, London, 1977.

Barsacq, L., and Stein, E., *Caligari's Cabinet and Other Grand Illusions. A History of Film Design*, Boston, 1976.

Barthes, R., *Image–Music–Text*, trans. S. Heath, London, 1977.

Baumert, H., and others (eds.), 'Beiträge zur deutschen Filmgeschichte', *Filmwissenschaftliche Mitteilungen*, vi, 1965.

Bawden, L. A. (ed.), *The Oxford Companion to Film*, Oxford, 1976.

Baxter, J., *Hollywood in the Thirties*, London, 1968.

—— *Science Fiction in the Cinema*, London, 1970.

—— *Hollywood in the Sixties*, London, 1972.

—— *An Appalling Talent: Ken Russell*, London, 1973.

—— *The Hollywood Exiles*, London, 1976.

Bazin, A., *Qu'est-ce que le cinéma?*, Paris, 1955 ff. (English version, sel. and trans. H. Gray, 2 vols., Berkeley, 1967 and 1971).

Beck, C. T., *Heroes of the Horrors*, New York, 1975.

Bellour, R., and others (eds.), 'Psychanalyse et cinéma', *Communications*, xxiii, 1975.

Belmans, J., *Roman Polanski*, Paris, 1971.

Belton, J., *The Hollywood Professionals: Howard Hawks, Frank Borzage, Edgar G. Ulmer*, London, 1974.

Bergman, A., *We're in the Money. Depression America and its Films*, New York, 1971.

Bluestone, G., *Novels into Film*, Berkeley, 1968.

Bogdanovich, P., *The Cinema of Alfred Hitchcock*, New York, 1963.

—— *Fritz Lang in America*, London, 1967.

Bohrer, K. H., *Die Ästhetik des Schreckens*, Munich, 1978.

Bojarski, R., and Beals, K., *The Films of Boris Karloff*, Secaucus, 1974.

Booker, C., *The Neophiliacs. A Study of the Revolution in English Life in the Fifties and Sixties*, London, 1969 (Fontana edn., 1970).

Braudy, L., *Jean Renoir. The World of his Films*, London, 1977.

—— *The World in a Frame. What We See in Films*, New York, 1977.

—— and Dickstein, L. (eds.), *Great Film Directors. A Critical Anthology*, New York, 1978.

Briggs, J., *Night Visitors. The Rise and Fall of the English Ghost Story*, London, 1977.

Brosnan, J., *Movie Magic. The Story of Special Effects in the Cinema*, London, 1974.

—— *The Horror People*, London, 1976.

—— *Future Tense. The Cinema of Science Fiction*, London, 1978.

Bucher, F., and Gmür, L. H., *Screen Series: Germany*, London, 1970.

Burch, N., *Theory of Film Practice*, London, 1972.

Buscombe, E., *Making 'Legend of the Werewolf'*, London, 1976.

Butler, I., *Religion in the Cinema*, London, 1969.

—— *Horror in the Cinema*, rev. edn., London, 1970.

—— *The Cinema of Roman Polanski*, London, 1970.

Buzzi, A., and Lattuada, B., *Vampyr. L'Étrange aventure de David Gray*, Milan, 1948.

Cameron, I. and E., *The Heavies*, London, 1976.

Cavell, S., *The World Viewed. Reflections on the Ontology of Film*, New York, 1971.

Chevassu, F., *L'Expression cinématographique. Les Éléments du film et leur fonctions*, Paris, 1977.

Clarens, C., *An Illustrated History of the Horror Film*, New York, 1967.

Cooper, C., and Skrade, C. (eds.), *Celluloid and Symbols*, Philadelphia, 1970 (Capricorn edn., 1968).

Corliss, R., *Talking Pictures. Screenwriters in the American Cinema*, New York, 1974 (Penguin edn., 1975).

Coulteray, G. de, *Sadism in the Movies*, New York, 1965.

Coynik, C., *Film—Real to Reel*, rev. edn., Evanston, 1976.

Cremer, R., *Lugosi. The Man Behind the Cape*, New York, 1976.

Daniels, L., *Fear. A History of Horror in the Mass Media*, London, 1977.

Davis, B., *The Thriller*, London, 1973.

Denk, R. (ed.), *Texte zur Poetik des Films*, Stuttgart, 1978.

Derry, C., *Dark Dreams. A Psychological History of the Modern Horror Film*, London, 1977.

Dhavan, R., and Davies, C. (eds.), *Censorship and Obscenity*, London, 1978.

Dickinson, T., *A Discovery of Cinema*, Oxford, 1971.

Dillard, R. H. W., *Horror Films*, New York, 1976.

Douglas, D., *Horrors*, London, 1967.

Dreyer, C. T., *Four Screenplays*, trans. O. Stallybrass, London, 1970.

Durgnat, R., *Eros in the Cinema*, London, 1966.

—— *Films and Feelings*, London, 1967.

—— *Franju*, London, 1967.

—— *Luis Buñuel*, London, 1967.

—— *Sexual Alienation in the Cinema*, London, 1972.

Edelson, E., *Great Monsters of the Movies*, New York, 1973.

—— *Visions of Tomorrow*, New York, 1973.

Eisner, L., *Murnau. Der Klassiker des deutschen Films*, Hanover, 1967.

—— *The Haunted Screen. Expressionism in the German Cinema and the Influence of Max Reinhardt*, London, 1969.

—— *Fritz Lang*, London, 1976.

Ellis, J. C., *A History of Film*, Englewood Cliffs, 1979.

Epstein, J., *Écrits sur le cinéma*, Paris, 1974.

Estève, M. (ed.), *Jerzy Kawalerowicz*, Paris, 1967.

Everson, W. K., *The Bad Guys. A Political History of the Movie Villain*, New York, 1964.

—— *Classics of the Horror Film*, New York, 1974.

Eyles, A., *Horror Film Album*, London, 1971.

—— Adkinson, R., and Fry, N. (eds.), *The House of Horror. The Story of Hammer Films*, London, 1973.

Eysenck, H. J., and Nias, D. K. B., *Sex, Violence and the Media*, London, 1978.

Florescu, R., and others, *In Search of Frankenstein*, New York, 1975.

Frank, A. G., *Horror Movies. Tales of Terror in the Cinema*, London, 1974.

—— *Monsters and Vampires*, London, 1976.

—— *Horror Films*, London, 1977.

Fraser, J., *Violence in the Arts*, illustrated edn., Cambridge, 1976.

Fuzellier, E., *Cinéma et littérature*, Paris, 1964.

Gasca, L., *Fantascienza e cinema*, Milan, 1972.

Geduld, H. M., and Gottesmann, R., *An Illustrated Glossary of Film Terms*, New York, 1973.

Gelmis, J., *The Film Director as Superstar*, Harmondsworth, 1970.

Gessner, R., *The Moving Image: A Guide to Cinematic Literacy*, New York, 1970.

Gianetti, L., *Understanding Movies*, 2nd edn., Englewood Cliffs, 1976.

Gibson, A., *The Silence of God. Creative Response to the Films of Ingmar Bergman*, New York, 1969.

Gifford, D., *Movie Monsters*, New York, 1969.

—— *Science Fiction Film*, London, 1971.

—— *A Pictorial History of Horror Movies*, London, 1973.

—— *Karloff: The Man, the Monster, the Movies*, New York, 1973.

Glut, D. F., *The Frankenstein Legend*, New Jersey, 1973.

—— *The Dracula Book*, New Jersey, 1975.

Goldmann, A., *Cinéma et société moderne*, Paris, 1971.

Goldner, O., and Turner, G., *The Making of 'King Kong'. The Story Behind a Film*, London, 1975.

Gow, G., *Suspense in the Cinema*, London, 1968.

Grafe, F., Patalas, E., Prinzler, H. H., and Syr, P., *Fritz Lang*, Munich, 1976.

Gregor, U., Hohlweg, R., and others, *Herzog/Kluge/Straub*, Munich, 1976.

Greve, L., Pehle, M., and Westhoff, H. (eds.), *Hätte ich das Kino! Die Schriftsteller und der Stummfilm*, Marbach, 1976.

Gunn, J., *Alternate Worlds. The Illustrated History of Science Fiction*, Englewood Cliffs, 1975.

Haining, P. (ed.), *The Dracula Scrapbook*, London, 1976.

—— *The Frankenstein Scrapbook*, London, 1977.

Halliwell, L., *Film Guide. A Survey of 8 000 English Language Movies*, London, 1977.

—— *The Filmgoer's Companion*, 6th edn., London, 1977.

—— *The Filmgoer's Book of Quotes*, augmented edn., London, 1978.

Hammond, P., *Marvellous Méliès*, London, 1974.

—— (ed.), *The Shadow and its Shadow. Surrealist Writing on the Cinema*, London, 1978.

Hempel, R., *Carl Mayer. Ein Autor schreibt mit der Kamera*, Berlin, 1968.

Henry, M., *Le Cinéma expressioniste allemand: un langage métaphorique*, Paris, 1971.

Hochman, S. (ed.), *American Film Directors: A Library of Film Criticism*, New York, 1974.

Huaco, G. A., *The Sociology of Film Art*, New York, 1965.

Hurt, J. (ed.), *Focus on Film and Theatre*, Englewood Cliffs, 1974.

Huss, R., and Ross, T. J. (eds.), *Focus on the Horror Film*, Englewood Cliffs, 1972.

Hutchinson, T., *Horror and Fantasy in the Movies*, London, 1974.

Iden, P., Karsunke, Y., and others, *Rainer Werner Fassbinder*, 2nd edn., Munich, 1975.

Irwin, W. R., *The Game of the Impossible. A Rhetoric of Fantasy*, Urbana, Ill., 1976.

Jacobs, L., *The Rise of the American Film*, New York, 1939.

Jarrie, I. C., *Towards a Sociology of the Cinema. A Comparative Essay on the Structure and Functioning of a Major Entertainment Industry*, London, 1970.

Jensen, P. M., *The Cinema of Fritz Lang*, New York, 1969.

—— *Boris Karloff and his Films*, New York, 1974.

Jinks, W., *The Celluloid Literature*, 2nd edn., Beverley Hills, 1974.

Johnson, W. (ed.), *Focus on the Science Fiction Film*, Englewood Cliffs, 1972.

Jung, F., Weil, C., and Seesslen, G., *Der Horror-Film. Regisseure, Stars, Autoren, Spezialisten, Themen und Filme von A bis Z*, Berlin, 1977.

Kael, P., *I Lost it at the Movies*, New York, 1965.

—— *Kiss Kiss Bang Bang*, New York, 1968.

—— and others, *The Citizen Kane Book*, Boston, 1971 (Paladin edn., 1974).

Kaes, A., *Expressionismus in Amerika. Rezeption und Innovation*, Tübingen, 1975.

—— (ed.), *Kino-Debatte. Literatur und Film 1909–1929*, Tübingen, 1978.

Katz, J. S. (ed.), *Perspectives on the Study of the Film*, Boston, 1971.

Kaul, W. (ed.), *Caligari und Caligarismus*, Berlin, 1970.

Keppler, C. F., *The Literature of the Second Self*, Tucson, 1972.
Knight, A., *The Liveliest Art*, New York, 1959.
Knilli, F. (ed.), *Semiotik des Films*, Munich, 1971.
Koszarski, R. (ed.), *Hollywood Directors 1914–1940*, Oxford, 1976.
Kracauer, S., *From Caligari to Hitler. A Psychological History of the German Film*, London, 1947.
—— *Theory of Film. The Redemption of Physical Reality*, New York, 1960 (paperback edn., Oxford, 1965 and 1971).
Kuhns, W., and Stanley, R., *Exploring the Film*, Dayton, 1968.
Kurz, R., *Expressionismus und Film*, Berlin, 1926.
Kyrou, A., *Le Surréalisme au cinéma*, Paris, 1958.
—— *Luis Buñuel*, New York, 1963.

Laclos, M., *Le Fantastique au cinéma*, Paris, 1958.
La Valley, A. J. (ed.), *Focus on Hitchcock*, Englewood Cliffs, 1972.
Lawson, J. H., *Film: The Creative Process*, New York, 1967.
Leahy, J., *The Cinema of Joseph Losey*, London, 1967.
Lee, W., *Reference Guide to Fantastic Films: Science Fiction, Fantasy and Horror*, 3 vols., Los Angeles, 1972–4.
Lenne, G., *Le Cinéma fantastique et ses mythes*, Paris, 1970.
Lennig, A., *The Count. The Life and Times of Bela 'Dracula' Lugosi*, New York, 1974.
Leyda, J. (ed.), *Voices of Film Experience, 1894 to the Present*, New York and London, 1977.
Licart, A., *Théâtre et cinéma. Psychologie du spectateur*, Brussels, 1938.
London, R., *Cinema of Mystery*, London, 1975.
—— *Zombie. The Living Dead*, London, 1976.
Low, R., *The History of the British Film*, London, 1948 ff.

McAsh, I. F., *The Films of Vincent Price*, 2nd edn., London, 1977.
MacCann, R. D. (ed.), *Film. A Montage of Theories*, New York, 1966.
McConnell, F., *The Spoken Seen. Film and the Romantic Imagination*, London, 1975.
McNally, R. T., and Florescu, R., *In Search of Dracula. A True History of Dracula and Vampire Legends*, New York, 1972.
Malthête-Méliès, M., *Méliès l'enchanteur*, Paris, 1973.
Manchel, F., *Terrors of the Screen*, Englewood Cliffs, 1970.
Manvell, R. (ed.), *The International Encyclopedia of Film*, London, 1972.
—— *Masterworks of the German Cinema*, London, 1973.
Manvell, R., and Fraenkel, H., *The German Cinema*, London, 1971.
Manvell, R., and Huntley, J., *The Technique of Film Music*, rev. edn., London, 1975.
Marwick, A., *The Explosion of British Society*, rev. edn., London, 1971.

Mast, G., and Cohen, M. (eds.), *Film Theory and Criticism. Introductory Readings*, New York, 1974.

Masters, A., *The Natural History of the Vampire*, New York, 1972.

Matthews, J. H., *Surrealism and Film*, Ann Arbor, 1971.

Mellen, J., *Voices from the Japanese Cinema*, New York, 1975.

Metz, C., *Film Language. A Semiotics of the Cinema*, New York, 1974.

—— *Le Signifiant imaginaire. Psychanalyse et cinéma*, Paris, 1977.

Milne, T., *Mamoulian*, London, 1969.

—— *The Cinema of Carl Dreyer*, London, 1971.

—— (ed.), *Losey on Losey*, London, 1967.

Mitry, J., *Esthétique et psychologie du cinéma*, Paris, 1963–5.

—— *Histoire du cinéma: art et industrie*, Paris, 1967.

Monaco, J., *How to Read a Film. The Art, Technology, Language, History and Theory of Film and Media*, New York, 1977.

Monaco, P., *Cinema and Society. France and Germany during the Twenties*, New York, 1976.

Montague, I., *Film World. A Guide to Cinema*, Harmondsworth, 1964.

Morin, E., *Le Cinéma ou l'homme imaginaire*, Paris, 1956.

Moss, R. F., *Karloff and Company. The Horror Film*, New York, 1974.

Murray, E., *The Cinematic Imagination. Writers and the Motion Pictures*, New York, 1972.

Naha, E., *Horrors from Screen to Scream*, New York, 1975.

Nash, M., *Dreyer*, London, 1977.

Nichols, B. (ed.), *Movies and Methods. An Anthology*, Berkeley, 1976.

O'Dell, P., *Griffith and the Rise of Hollywood*, New York, 1970.

Pattison, B., *The Seal of Dracula*, New York, 1975.

Perkins, V. F., *Film as Film. Understanding and Judging Movies*, Harmondsworth, 1972.

Perry, G., *The Films of Alfred Hitchcock*, London, 1965.

Peterson, T., Jensen, T. W., and Rivers, W. L., *The Mass Media and Modern Society*, New York, 1966.

Pirie, D., *A Heritage of Horror. The English Gothic Cinema 1946–1972*, London, 1973.

—— *The Vampire Cinema*, London, 1977.

Pornon, C., *L'Écran merveilleux*, Paris, 1959.

Prédal, R., *Le Cinéma fantastique*, Paris, 1970.

Rabkin, E. S., *The Fantastic in Literature*, rev. edn., Princeton, 1977.

Rhode, E., *Tower of Babel. Speculations on the Cinema*, London, 1966.

—— *A History of the Cinema. From its Origins to 1970*, London, 1976.

Robinson, D., *World Cinema: A Short History*, London, 1973.

Rohmer, E., and Chabrol, C., *Hitchcock*, Paris, 1957.

Rosenberg, B., and White, D. M., (eds.), *Mass Culture. The Popular Arts in America*, New York, 1957.

Rosenthal, S., and Kass, J. M., *The Hollywood Professionals: Tod Browning, Don Siegel*, London, 1975.

Rotha, P., and Griffith, R., *The Film till Now*, rev. edn., London, 1960.

Rovin, J., *The Fabulous Fantasy Films*, South Brunswick and New York, 1977.

Russo, J., *Night of the Living Dead*, New York, 1974.

Sabatier, J.-M., *Les Classiques du cinéma fantastique*, Paris, 1973.

Sadoul, G., *Histoire générale du cinéma*, Paris, 1946–52.

—— *Dictionnaire des films*, Paris, 1965.

—— *Dictionnaire des cinéastes*, Paris, 1965.

Sandford, J., *The New German Cinema*, London, 1979.

Sarris, A., *American Cinema: Directors and Directions 1929–1968*, New York, 1968.

Schlockoff, A. (ed.), *L'Écran fantastique*, Paris, 1975.

Siegel, J. E., *Val Lewton. The Reality of Terror*, London, 1972.

Silver, A., and Ursini, J., *The Vampire Film*, New Jersey, 1975.

Simon, J., *Ingmar Bergman Directs*, New York, 1972.

Sitney, P. A., *Visionary Film. The American Avant-Garde*, New York, 1974.

—— *Film Culture. An Anthology*, London, 1971.

Sklar, R., *Movie-Made America: A Cultural History of American Movies*, New York, 1975 (London, 1978).

Skoller, D. (ed.), *Dreyer in Double Reflection*, New York, 1973.

Solomon, S. J., *Beyond Formula: American Film Genres*, New York, 1977.

Sontag, S., *Against Interpretation*, New York, 1966.

—— *Styles of Radical Will*, New York, 1970.

Spiegel, A., *Fiction and the Camera Eye. Visual Consciousness in Film and the Modern Novel*, Charlottesville, 1976.

Stallybrass, O. (trans.), *Carl Theodor Dreyer: Four Screenplays*, London, 1970.

Steene, B. (ed.), *Focus on 'The Seventh Seal'*, Englewood Cliffs, 1972.

Steiger, B., *Monsters, Maidens and Mayhem. A Pictorial History of Horror Film Monsters*, New York, 1965.

Steinbrunner, C., and Goldblatt, B., *Cinema of the Fantastic*, New York, 1972.

Stepun, F., *Theater und Film*, Munich, 1953.

Stevenson, R., and Debrix, J. R., *The Cinema as Art*, Harmondsworth, 1965.

Strick, P., *Science Fiction Movies*, London, 1976.

Taylor, J. R., *Directors and Directions. Cinema for the Seventies*, London, 1975.

—— Hitch. The Life and Work of Alfred Hitchcock, London, 1978.

Taylor, R., Film Propaganda. Soviet Russia and Nazi Germany, London, 1979.

Thomas, T., Music for the Movies, London, 1973.

Thomson, D., A Biographical Dictionary of the Cinema, London, 1975.

—— America in the Dark. Hollywood and the Gift of Unreality, London, 1978.

Todorov, T., Introduction à la littérature fantastique, Paris, 1970.

Toeplitz, J., Hollywood and After. The Changing Face of American Cinema, London, 1974.

Truffaut, F., Hitchcock, rev. edn., London, 1978.

Tudor, A., Image and Influence. Studies in the Sociology of Film, London, 1974.

—— Theories of Film, London, 1974.

Underwood, P., Horror Man. The Life of Boris Karloff, London, 1972.

Vardac, N., Stage to Screen: Theatrical Method from Garrick to Griffith, Cambridge, Mass., 1949.

Verdone, M. (ed.), Carl Mayer e l'espressionismo. Atti del Convergno Internazionale di Studi su Carl Mayer, Rome, 1969.

Wagenknecht, E., Movies in the Age of Innocence, Norman, Okla., 1962.

Wagner, G., The Novel and the Cinema, London, 1975.

Walker, A., The Celluloid Sacrifice, London, 1966.

—— Stardom. The Hollywood Phenomenon, London, 1970.

—— Stanley Kubrick Directs, London, 1972.

Weergaard, E., Carl Dreyer, London, 1950.

Weil, C., and Seesslen, G., Kino des Phantastischen. Eine Einführung in die Mythologie und die Geschichte des Horror-Films, Munich, 1976.

Wetzel, K., and Hagemann, P., Liebe, Tod und Technik. Kino des Phantastischen 1933–1945, Berlin, 1977.

Will, D., and Willemen, P. (eds.), Roger Corman. The Millennic Vision, Edinburgh and Cambridge, 1970.

Willemen, P., and Johnston, C., Jacques Tourneur, Edinburgh, 1975.

Willis, D. C., Horror and Science Fiction Films. A Check List, Metuchen, 1972.

Winston, D. G., The Screenplay as Literature, London, 1973.

Wollen, P., Signs and Meaning in the Cinema, 2nd edn., London, 1970.

—— (ed.), Working Papers on the Cinema: Sociology and Semiology, London, 1971.

Wood, R., Hitchcock's Films, 2nd edn., New York, 1969.

—— Ingmar Bergman, New York, 1969.

—— Personal Views. Explorations in Film, London, 1976.

—— and Walker, M., Claude Chabrol, London, 1970.

Wright, B., The Long View. An International History of the Cinema, London, 1974 (Paladin edn., 1976).

Yacowar, M., *Hitchcock's British Films*, Hampden, Conn., 1977.

Young, V., *Cinema Borealis. Ingmar Bergman and the Swedish Ethos*, New York, 1971.

Ziolkowski, T., *Disenchanted Images. A Literary Iconology*, Princeton, 1977.

Index of Names

Index of Film Titles

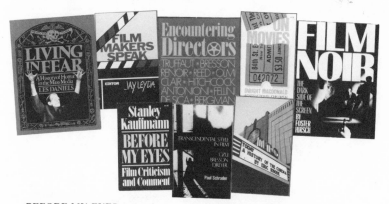